Major General J. E. B. Stuart C.S.A.
Comdg. Cav. Corps. A. N. Va.

April 28, 2000

JEB STUART

by John W. Thomason, Jr.

CAPTAIN, U. S. MARINE CORPS

WITH ILLUSTRATIONS AND MAPS BY THE AUTHOR

Introduction to the Bison Book Edition by
Gary W. Gallagher

Colonel 1st Virginia Cavalry 1861

University of Nebraska Press
Lincoln and London

First Bison Book printing: 1994
Most recent printing indicated by the last digit below:
10   9   8   7   6   5   4   3

Library of Congress Cataloging-in-Publication Data
Thomason, John W. (John William), 1893–1944.
Jeb Stuart / by John W. Thomason, Jr.; with illustrations and maps by
the author.
p.   cm.
Originally published: London: C. Scribner's Sons, 1929.
Includes index.
ISBN 0-8032-9424-7 (pa.)
1. Stuart, Jeb, 1833–1864.   2. Generals—United States—Biogra-
phy.   3. Generals—Confederate States of America—Biography.   4.
United States. Army—Biography.   5. Confederate States of America.
Army—Biography.   I. Title.
E467.1.S9T46   1994
973.7′3′092—dc20
[B]
94-14747   CIP

Reprinted by arrangement with Dr. Thomas C. Cole

∞

INTRODUCTION

by Gary W. Gallagher

Few Confederate generals achieved wider renown during the Civil War than Major General James Ewell Brown Stuart. His memorable appearance, bold actions, and participation in virtually all the campaigns of the Army of Northern Virginia invited the adulation of thousands of Confederate citizens and a grudging admiration from Federal opponents. Further blessed with a famous nickname inspired by his initials, "Jeb" Stuart immediately ascended to an honored place in the Confederate pantheon upon his death after the battle of Yellow Tavern in mid-May 1864. In the century and a third since Appomattox, only a handful of Stuart's peers have received as much attention in the literature devoted to Civil War military operations. He has been the subject of numerous biographies, dominates reminiscences by men who served with him, and figures prominently in many broader studies.[1]

An aura of romanticism continues to surround Stuart and his exploits as chief of Lee's cavalry. One of the great flamboyant figures in either army, he affected a scarlet-lined cape, boots that reached his thighs, a pair of golden spurs, a bright yellow sash, gauntlets of white buckskin, and a hat crowned with a long plume. His retinue, surely one of the noisiest and most picturesque of any general's, included among others banjoist Samuel Sweeney, the immense and convivial Prussian officer Heros Von Borcke, who served as an aide, and John Pelham, whose youthful good looks and hard fighting as chief of the cavalry's artillery won devoted admirers. Daring raids around the Federal army, elaborately staged reviews of his horsemen, and impromptu parties in the midst of campaigning contributed to Stuart's reputation as a knightly character. A few lines from Stephen Vincent Benét's epic poem *John Brown's Body* deftly capture Stuart's cavalier persona:

> His long black beard is combed like a beauty's hair,
> His slouch hat plumed with a curled black ostrich-feather,
> He wears gold spurs and sits his horse with the seat
> Of a horseman born.
> It is Stuart of Laurel Hill,
> "Beauty" Stuart, the genius of cavalry,
> Reckless, merry, religious, theatrical,
> Lover of gesture, lover of panache,
> With all the actor's grace and the quick, light charm
> That makes the women adore him—a wild cavalier
> Who worships as sober a God as Stonewall Jackson,
> A Rupert who seldom drinks, very often prays,
> Loves his children, singing, fighting, spurs, and his wife.[2]

Stuart's position in the front rank of Lost Cause icons is nowhere more apparent than in Charles Hoffbauer's mural titled "Autumn." Part of a quartet of heroic works depicting the seasons of the Confederacy, "Autumn" dominates one wall in a wing of the Virginia Historical Society in Richmond, Virginia. In it Stuart leads his galloping troopers, their sabers unsheathed, up a hill against an unseen foe. Trees ablaze with autumnal yellows and oranges help frame Stuart, who with plumed hat held aloft and flowing red-lined cape sits his horse in a strikingly gallant pose. Apparently fearless in urging his men forward, Hoffbauer's Stuart distills the Lost Cause vision of purposeful Confederate struggle against long odds into one vivid image.[3]

Jeb Stuart by John W. Thomason Jr. offers readers the printed counterpart of Hoffbauer's mural. A career military officer who possessed impressive artistic and literary gifts, Thomason was well suited to evoke Stuart's life and times. Born on February 28, 1893, into a family with a rich Confederate tradition, Thomason spent his youth in Huntsville, Texas, where he listened to stories about the personalities and campaigns of the Army of Northern Virginia. His parents were Dr. John William Thomason, a prominent physician, and Sue Hayes Goree Thomason, whose father, Major Thomas Jewett Goree, had served on James Longstreet's staff during the Civil War. Between 1909 and 1913, a restless Thomason attended Southwestern University in Georgetown, Texas; Sam Houston State Normal Institute in Huntsville (where he earned a teacher's certificate); and the University of Texas at Austin. He left Texas in 1914 to enroll at the Art Student's League in New York City, studying there for a year before returning to Texas to teach in a Houston junior high school. Brief training at the Citizens' Military Training Camp at Fort Sam Houston in 1916 and a subsequent stint as a reporter for the *Houston Chronicle* preceded his decision in 1917 to join the United States Marine Corps.[4]

Thomason sailed for Europe with the American Expeditionary Force of World War I. He fought as a lieutenant in charge of a platoon with the Marine Brigade of the Second Division at Belleau Wood, Chateau-Thierry, and in the Meusse-Argonne offensive, winning the Silver Star and the Navy Cross for his courage and initiative at Soissons in July 1918. He wrote his mother in September 1918 that he was "well and quite cheerful, considering, and making out fairly well, I think, in the profession of arms." The absence of drawing materials had vexed him for much of the summer's fighting, but "a Boche notebook and some drawing pencils" taken from a German command post at Soissons had permitted him to make "some rather interesting sketches under fire. . . . [S]ome of them are rather crude and brutal."[5] Promoted to captain while in Europe, Thomason decided to make the military his career. His later duty reflected the tasks assigned to marines during that era—time at sea, postings to Central America, the Caribbean, China, and the Pacific, and service as chief of the Navy Department's Latin American Section and as a member of Admiral Chester Nimitz's staff. He died in San Diego, California, on March 13, 1944, while a colonel assigned to the Amphibious Training Command of the Pacific Fleet.

During his time with the marines, Thomason published a number of books and articles, most of them illustrated with his sketches. *Fix Bayonets!*, which drew on his experiences in World War I and appeared in 1926, impressed the *London Times* writer as unequaled on "the actual fighting man in the Great War." The reviewer in the *New York World* called the book the "finest monument of the American Expeditionary Force, and a notable volume of prose with drawings that are of permanent interest to American History."[6] In *Red Pants and Other Stories* (1927), *Marines and Others* (1929), *Salt Winds and Gobi Dust* (1934), and *—And a Few Marines* (1943), Thomason offered collections of short stories that drew on his military experiences, and in doing so, one scholar has noted, "almost singlehandedly cast the image of the Marine Corps between the wars." Critics generally praised both Thomason's writing style and artistic skill, as did a reviewer of *Red Pants* in the *Philadelphia Enquirer:* "The war episodes have all the dash and feeling of authenticity that one found in Captain Thomason's earlier book. . . . And the Thomason drawings, as in *Fix Bayonets!*, would be worth the price of the book without a word of writing."[7] In addition to the works based on his marine experiences, Thomason edited and illustrated *The Adventures of Davy Crockett, Told Mostly by Himself* (1934); *The Adventures of General Marbot, by Himself* (1935); *Gone to Texas* (1937), his first novel; and *Lone Star Preacher* (1941), a second novel that brilliantly caught the spirit of the Texas soldiers who fought in Lee's army.[8]

Maxwell Perkins first broached the idea of Thomason's writing a biography of a Confederate general. Editor-in-Chief at Scribner's and one of the most influential literary figures of his time, Perkins believed that Thomason's southern roots, ties to the Confederacy through Thomas Jewett Goree, and interest in the Civil War and military affairs equipped him well to undertake such a project. Douglas Southall Freeman, then at work on his massive life of R. E. Lee for Scribner's, informed Thomason that Jeb Stuart awaited a definitive life. Thomason liked the idea of trying his hand at the biographical genre, and, after flirting with James Longstreet as a subject, settled on Stuart.[9]

This decision brought Thomason to a topic close to his heart. The recollections of his Grandfather Goree and other Confederate veterans had impressed him as a youth. In the foreword to *Lone Star Preacher,* he recalled viewing the old men as "a band of knights, riding most valiant in a golden tale of chivalry." Maturity and experience as a soldier eventually allowed him to "examine critically this legend . . . [to] discover what manner of men they were." He believed that the "core of the thing had more gold in it than most legends," and one of the brightest elements of the saga was Jeb Stuart, whose career had brought a dancing light to the eyes of the aged men in Huntsville summoning memories from their Confederate past. Careful to acknowledge that the Army of Northern Virginia had its share of scoundrels and cowards, Thomason nonetheless expressed an open admiration: "The point is," he concluded, "they all believed in something. No amount of critical fact-finding detracts from that. Their effectiveness in war is attested in official records by their enemies. The heritage they left, of valor and devotion, is treasured by a united country."[10]

Although not a trained scholar, Thomason consulted an array of materials about Stuart. He mined published sources such as the *Official Records*, the *Southern Historical Society Papers*, the principal Confederate memoirs, newspapers, and public documents. He visited archives and libraries in Virginia and Washington and spoke with the general's descendants, who allowed him to read Stuart's private correspondence. He retraced Stuart's campaigns across Virginia, Maryland, and Pennsylvania, and used Francis Trevelyan Miller's ten-volume *Photographic History of the Civil War* for inspiration in preparing his drawings for the book. Although he conducted research for more than a year, Thomason chose not to include footnotes in his book, explaining that they would give the "specious appearance of a scholarship which I may not, with justice, claim." Anyone who had specific questions about any point, he added, should write to him for the reference.[11]

Charles Scribner's Sons published *Jeb Stuart* in November 1930 to a chorus of praise leavened with some criticism of Thomason's emphasis on narrative over analysis.[12] The *New York Times Book Review* averred that "Captain Thomason's Stuart is not merely competent or excellent, it is literature. . . . [E]verything he tells about starts out vividly from the pages and, once told, is there to stay with the reader forever." The *Times Literary Supplement* told its largely British audience that Thomason's text was "based upon the best authorities, and the accuracy of [its] facts cannot be impeached"; moreover, the author "absorbed the atmosphere of Virginia, and describes scenes as vividly as if he had been actually present." In the *Saturday Review of Literature,* Ulrich B. Phillips, a prominent academic historian, sounded a more muted note. "Given a professional soldier of Confederate lineage and loyalty," he observed, "wielding a sprightly, romantic pen on the career of the most alert and high-hearted of cavalry commanders, Captain Thomason's *Jeb Stuart* results." Conceding that he found the work engaging, Phillips detected "no pretense of profundity, and the achievement is rather to exhilarate than to inform." In the *American Historical Review*, Thomas Robson Hay labeled the book "one of the most interesting military biographies of the Confederacy" but lamented Thomason's decision to forego detailed discussion of "the tactical use of cavalry," logistical questions, or the influence of improved weaponry on the mounted arm.[13]

Later assessments emphasized Thomason's ability to bring Stuart to life. In a historiographical study published in 1939, Douglas Southall Freeman called Thomason "brilliant" and praised "his dazzling *Jeb Stuart*, already a classic of Confederate literature." Richard B. Harwell's *In Tall Cotton: The 200 Most Important Confederate Books for the Reader, Researcher and Collector* echoes Freeman's language: "Biography written with the verve that makes his subject exciting and the reading of history exciting and this the most readable biography of the Confederates' beau sabreur." Thomason's biographer, noting that it went through four printings in less than a year and sold steadily thereafter, thought *Jeb Stuart* insured Thomason "permanent recognition among the ranks of prominent authors."[14]

How does the book stand up today? Readers should keep in mind Thomason's purpose. His foreword reveals that he sought to create "not a history of a war, but a portrait of a splendid human soul, expressed through the profession of arms." He frankly admits, "I have tried to be as unprejudiced as is possible to a grandson and nephew of Confederate officers and soldiers, but I learned fairly late in life that Damyank was a compound word." Thomason clearly embraces Stuart's romantic example as well as admiring his military skills: "Jeb Stuart was a symbol, a gonfalon that went before the swift, lean columns of the Confederacy. He served as the eyes and ears of Lee: his hands touched the springs of vast events. . . . His kind of war has given over to a drab affair of chemistry, propaganda, and mathematics. Never, anywhere, will there be his like again."[15]

Thomason's handling of different episodes in Stuart's career betrays a strong identification with his subject. Most interested in the first two years of the conflict, when Stuart and his troopers faced indifferent Federal opponents and moved from triumph to triumph, he lavishes attention on the rides around McClellan, First and Second Manassas, Sharpsburg, and Chancellorsville. In contrast, just one-fifth of the narrative treats the period after June 1863, which witnessed Stuart's near-defeat at Brandy Station, his problematic performance during the Gettysburg campaign, and his inability to achieve dramatic successes while contending with increasing logistical problems and strong Federal cavalry. The battle of Brandy Station, by far the largest mounted action of the war and an event of great consequence in Stuart's military career, receives less than two-thirds the attention given the Chambersburg Raid of October 1862. Similarly, Thomason's discussion of Gettysburg plays down the serious consequences of Stuart's decision to take his best brigades away from the Army of Northern Virginia at the moment Lee marched into Pennsylvania. This imbalance of coverage and tendency to avoid criticizing Stuart results in a skewed sense of the general's role in the war.

On balance, however, the strengths of *Jeb Stuart* easily overcome these flaws. Thomason's compelling narrative carries the reader alongside Stuart through the war in the Eastern Theater, and no other author has managed to convey as effectively the atmosphere and attitudes at cavalry headquarters in Lee's army. Although readers will not find the whole story of Stuart's life and campaigns in these pages, they will gain a sense of the exuberance and sheer energy that made him one of the remarkable characters of the Civil War.[16]

March 4, 1994

NOTES

1. The best scholarly biography, which combines a graceful literary style and interesting analysis, is Emory M. Thomas, *Bold Dragoon: The Life of J. E. B. Stuart* (New York: Harper & Row, 1986). Important accounts by staff officers include Henry B. McClellan's detailed *Life and Campaigns of Major-General J. E. B. Stuart* (Boston: Houghton, Mifflin and Company, 1885), William Willis Blackford's *War Years with Jeb Stuart* (New York: Charles Scribner's Sons, 1945), and Heros von Borcke's colorful but sometimes untrustworthy *Memoirs of the Confed-*

erate War for Independence (2 vols., Edinburgh and London: W. Blackwood and Sons, 1866). Douglas Southall Freeman's *Lee's Lieutenants: A Study in Command* (3 vols., New York: Charles Scribner's Sons, 1942–44) places Stuart within the context of the officer corps of the Army of Northern Virginia.

2. Stephen Vincent Benét, *John Brown's Body* (1927; reprint, New York: The American Past series of the Book-of-the-Month Club, 1980), pp. 182–83. For a treatment that helped to fix Stuart's romantic image, see John Esten Cooke's sketch of Stuart in *Wearing of the Gray: Being Personal Portraits, Scenes, and Adventures of the War* (1867; reprint, Bloomington: Indiana University Press, 1959).

3. For a discussion of Hoffbauer and his murals, see William M. S. Rasmussen, "Making the Confederate Murals: Studies by Charles Hoffbauer," *Virginia Magazine of History and Biography* 101:3 (July 1993): 433–56.

4. The biographical details of Thomason's life presented in this introduction are taken from his March 13, 1944, obituary in the *New York Times* and from Roger Willock, *Lone Star Marine: A Biography of the Late Colonel John W. Thomason, Jr., U.S.M.C.* (Princeton, N.J.: Privately printed by the author, 1961).

5. Letter quoted in Willock, *Lone Star Marine,* p. 60.

6. Arnold Rosenfeld, ed., *A Thomason Sketchbook: Drawings by John W. Thomason Jr.* (Austin: University of Texas Press, 1969), p. 9 (first quotation); Willock, *Lone Star Marine,* p. 90 (second quotation).

7. Rosenfeld, ed., *Thomason Sketchbook,* p. 9 (first quotation); Willock, *Lone Star Marine,* p. 98 (second quotation).

8. Charles Scribner's Sons of New York published the first editions of all Thomason's works. Many of the short stories gathered in his books first appeared in magazines such as the *American Mercury, Scribner's Magazine, Saturday Evening Post,* and *New Yorker.* Thomason also contributed a number of other articles to these and other magazines.

9. For a discussion of Perkins's role, see Willock, *Lone Star Marine,* pp. 107–8.

10. John W. Thomason Jr., *Lone Star Preacher: Being a Chronicle of the Acts of Praxiteles Swan, M.E. Church South sometime Captain, 5th Texas Regiment Confederate States Provisional Army* (New York: Charles Scribner's Sons, 1941), pp. vii, xi.

11. The quotation is on page xviii below.

12. Between May and October 1930, Thomason had published parts of *Jeb Stuart* in *Scribner's Magazine* 87: 485–91, 621–29; and 88: 79–90, 179–94, 297–309, 368–80.

13. *New York Times Book Review,* November 16, 1930, p. 12; *Times Literary Supplement* (London), January 1, 1931; *Saturday Review of*

Literature (December 6, 1930): 418; *American Historical Review* 36:3 (April 1931): 653–54.

14. Douglas Southall Freeman, *The South to Posterity: An Introduction to the Writing of Confederate History* (New York: Charles Scribner's Sons, 1939), p. 88; Richard Barksdale Harwell, *In Tall Cotton: The 200 Most Important Confederate Books for the Reader, Researcher and Collector* (Austin, Tex.: Jenkins Publishing Company, 1978), p. 63; Willock, *Lone Star Marine,* p. 131.

15. The quotations are on pages xx, 14, and 15.

16. For insights into Stuart's personality from his own correspondence, see J. E. B. Stuart, *The Letters of General J. E. B. Stuart,* ed. Adele H. Mitchell (Richmond, Va.: Stuart-Mosby Historical Society, 1990).

FOREWORD

I NEEDED help on this work, and I have been fortunate in the help that I received.

The Honorable Henry Carter Stuart of Elk Garden, Virginia, head of the Stuart family, allowed me to examine letters and papers never before laid open, and he gave me, from his own memory and rich experience, inimitable pictures of the period and of the society with which I had to deal. He remembers Major-General J. E. B. Stuart, Confederate States Army, as Uncle James, the kindest, gentlest uncle a boy ever had. Mrs. Marrow Stuart Smith, and Mrs. Flora Stuart Old, of Norfolk, granddaughters of the General, permitted me the use of Stuart letters and papers which they possess, and which are an integral part of this story as I have written it. Material of the same nature was generously offered me by another granddaughter, Mrs. Virginia Stuart Waller Davis, of Norfolk.

Through the courtesy of the Honorable Andrew J. Montague, of Virginia, I met, and received much information and encouragement from scholarly gentlemen of Richmond, among whom are Mr. St. George Cooke, Mr. Pelham Blackford, and Dr. Douglas Southall Freeman. I have to thank Mr. Kermit Roosevelt, of New York, for an introduction to Mr. Thomas B. Love, of Washington, and to Judge James M. Love, his father, who was a trooper of the Black Horse, in the 4th Virginia Cavalry, and who lost an arm following Jeb Stuart's plume; from them I secured the copy of the commission issued to Miss Antonia Ford, of Fairfax, which I have reproduced.

Miss Susan B. Harrison, of Richmond, gave me the privileges of the Confederal Memorial Museum; she is the keeper of the pantheon of Southern glories.

Dr. John N. Ware, of Rome, Georgia, sent me the Stuart letter, written by the General to the mother of a fourteen-year-old soldier of his command in the February before they killed him.

Mr. William J. Parrish, Jr., of Richmond, was my guide and collaborator on the battlefields in the area of the Confederate citadel; he was an old *compañero* in the Marines, and his local knowledge and good judgment threw light on many points obscure to me. I had a great advantage from Major Robert L. Denig of the Marines, studying with him the field of Chancellorsville.

I am indebted also, more than I can say, to Mr. James Boyd, M. F. H. of the Moore Country Hunt in North Carolina, who has adventured deeply into the Old Time, and who knows the hearts of men, as well as dogs and horses. Nor can I refrain, with or without his consent, from making, as they used to say, my manners, to Mr. Maxwell Perkins, of New York, whose patience, friendly counsel, and, I would add, kindly firmness, has actually put this book between its covers.

For myself, I have had great pleasure and profit in meeting, and talking to, very many Virginia people, who live now along the roads that saw the riding of Stuart's squadrons in the war zone. Of them, and of Virginia, which I have come in some measure to know through the pilgrimages incident to the gathering of my material, I desire to say that, if I were not a Texan, I would like to be a Virginian.

As to sources, I have not wanted to clutter my pages with footnotes and reference numbers, thereby giving the specious appearance of a scholarship which I may not, with justice, claim. I will be happy to furnish specific sources to any person who is sufficiently interested to write me about any given point.

Generally, my military data comes from the compilation of the official records of the Union and Confederate armies. My collateral reading has extended over a term of years, and it has been guided, in the last decade, by my professional training and experience. It may be well to mention a few of the most valuable sources of material, outside the official records.

Many of the conspicuous war chiefs, on either side, wrote of operations. Perhaps the sanest and best Southern document is Alexander's *Military Memoirs of a Confederate*. Then there is Longstreet's book, Joseph E. Johnston's, and Hood's—very controversial, the last two—and the writings of Fitz Lee, Jubal Early, and John B. Gordon; while Grant, Sherman, and Sheridan, have left memoirs, not to mention Badeau, and General Horace Porter. Among the younger men who served, there is Heros von Borcke's *Memoir of the Confederate War*, and the several biographies by John Esten Cooke, and the works of Major John S. Mosby, and the *Personal Recollections of a Cavalryman*, by Colonel J. H. Kidd, who rode with Custer. There is also a very careful and sound chronicle, *The Campaigns of Stuart's Cavalry*, by Major H. B. McClellan, which is the best Stuart biography, although a little heavy. And the memoirs of Long, Dabney, and Taylor, staff officers, are important. The list of regimental histories, and compilations of soldier stories, is too large to mention. The collection of narratives by participants called *Battles and Leaders of the Civil War* is indispensable, and there is a mine of undeveloped material in the current periodicals, published during and soon after the war, such as the *Confederate Veteran*, the *Southern Fireside*, and the *Bivouac*, and in the files of the Southern Historical Society, and of the several state historical societies.

To these you can add innumerable and little-known manuscripts, letters, and documents, reposing in private and public libraries, and in the Library of Congress, and the files of the daily newspapers, which preserve the human flavor of the time. And many of the high civil officials, Davis, Stephens, and their colleagues, have written.

The works of military students and commentators and biographers are also numerous. In this order is Henderson's *Stonewall Jackson*, and the recent studies of General Sir Frederic Maurice dealing with General Lee: the English are well informed on our war.

In *The Photographic History of the Civil War*, I found abundant material for the drawings I have made, the purpose of which is not so much illustration, as the definition of types, so that you can visualize the actors in these scenes.

But controversy and chronicle are confusing, and depend much upon which flag you followed, or what you are trying to prove. For the most part, I have gone to the reports and the messages, and I have drawn my own conclusions from what I considered the best evidence. It is a saying of our General Preston Brown's, whom the 2d Division of the A. E. F. remembers, that the records tell the story. So, if you would verify or disprove anything that I have set down, take the official records, and your maps, and go and look at the ground.

I have tried to be accurate without being tiresome and technical, and I have tried to be as unprejudiced as is possible to a grandson and nephew of Confederate officers and soldiers, but I learned fairly late in life that Damyank was a compound word. What I have attempted is not a history of a war, but a portrait of a splendid human soul, expressed through the profession of arms.

Washington,   JOHN W. THOMASON, JR.
District of Columbia,
1930.

CONTENTS

CONTENTS

JEB STUART

I

PORTRAIT OF A CAVALRYMAN

I SAT at the feet of our old men who fought in our War of the Southern Confederacy and asked them the questions that boys ask: "What did Stonewall Jackson look like? What sort of a man was Longstreet?—A. P. Hill? . . ."

"Well, son"—after deep thought—"Old Stonewall looked —he looked like his pictures. You've seen his pictures. Longstreet, he was a thick-set sort of fellow, with a bushy beard. A. P. Hill was red-headed. . . ." But when you ask about Jeb Stuart, their eyes light up and their faces quicken, and they describe details of his dress, his fighting jacket and his plume—and they hum you songs he loved and tell you how his voice sounded.

Jeb Stuart filled the eye. He was strong and ruddy, and in late 1862, commissioned major-general, with a year and a few months left to live, he was just under thirty. He had a dark brown flaring beard and wide mustaches that showed bronze lights in the sun. He was five feet, eleven inches tall, and he rode at a hundred and seventy-five pounds. He was large boned, long in the arms and the legs and short in the body, and he looked best on a horse. He had a blue and merry eye, which turned dark and piercing when battle warmed him or his temper flamed. His nose was chiselled and adventurous, the kind of nose Napoleon admired in generals. There is a West Point portrait taken when he graduated, which shows him clean shaven—a face not handsome. The jaw is too long and hard in its angle, and the chin too short, and his classmates called him "Beauty Stuart," "in inverse ratio," says Fitz Lee, "to the compliment implied." When he went to duty with the Mounted Rifles out in Texas, he let his whiskers grow, and they wrote back East that "Beauty" was the first man a beard ever improved. Certainly, as a beard, it was impressive, and the face that looked over it was fine and bold.

Also, there was an elegance about him. He wore gauntlets of white buckskin, and rode in a gray shell jacket, double-breasted, buttoned back to show a close gray vest. His sword, a light French sabre—for he never carried, in the Confederate War, the United States Officers' sword of the Old Service—was belted over a cavalry sash of golden silk with tasselled ends. His gray horseman's cloak was lined with scarlet: his wife made it. General Lee, he wrote her, admired it; and he deplored to her the bullet which whipped away its fur collar at Fredericksburg. His horse furniture and equipment were polished leather and bright metal, and he liked to wear a red rose in his jacket when the roses bloomed, and a love-knot of red ribbon when flowers were out of season. His soft, fawn-colored hat was looped up on the right with a gold star, and adorned with a curling ostrich feather. His boots sported little knightly spurs of gold—admiring ladies, even those who never saw him in their lives, sent him such things. He went conspicuous, all gold and glitter, in the front of great battles and in a hundred little cavalry fights, which killed men just as dead as Gettysburg.

This was the Stuart of the cavalry reviews which he loved to hold—the military dandy Richmond saw on his infrequent visits from the front, and his turnout for such battles as Fredericksburg, where he had a fixed headquarters, and time to preen himself. But in the field there was nothing of the parade soldier about him except his bearing; his finery was continually plastered with Virginia mud and weathered with the dust and rain. His wife, who was charged with the replacement of his uniforms, had endless commissions to execute in Richmond, and the military tailors, as long as there was fine gray cloth and gold braid in the Confederacy, must have esteemed his business above other trade. He was seldom at headquarters anywhere. He lived in contact with the enemy; it was his idea of a cavalryman's proper place. He rewards a squadron for smart service by keeping it in its advanced position until the officers represent that it is their turn to go back for rest and refreshment; they are tired. "Oh, you don't want to go back to camp," he tells them. "There's nothing back there. It isn't interesting back there. . . ." For he was never tired himself. He was immensely strong and he died before he found the limits to his endurance.

He wore out his horses and he wore out his men. He rode big animals of the hunter type, blood bays with black points, for choice, and his brother, William Alexander, was kept on the lookout for such mounts. Admirers gave him horses, splendid blooded creatures like Star of the East from Farquier, and Skylark from Maryland; none of them lasted long under the service he exacted. He rides for fifty hours— as in the Gettysburg campaign, holding, toward the last, the wretched troopers behind him in their saddles by sheer force of personality; the column halts while a detail is dismounted to pull down a rail fence, and the detail falls asleep across the rails it is moving, and the rest fall asleep in their saddles, and the horses stumble and roll against each other in ranks—and only then does he grant an hour's rest, very much disgusted because he has to grant it.

Lee's judgment on officers is of attested soundness; he says of Stuart, talking to Wade Hampton in the after years at Lexington:

"General Stuart was my ideal of a soldier. He was always cheerful under all circumstances, and always ready for any work, and always reliable. When he stopped for a night's rest, he could throw himself on the ground, and, with his saddle or a log for a pillow, he would fall asleep almost immediately and sleep as if in a bed. Then, if I sent an officer with an order, he was awake at the first call or touch. When his eyes opened, his mind became fully awake. He did not have to yawn or stretch to get himself awake but his mind and body seemed to awake at the same time and to become active and alert. Before any other officer that I ever had could get himself and his men awake, Stuart would be in the saddle, have his men in line and be ready to move."

It was said of him, also, that he never made a tactical error—a statement, in the light of military history, hardly to be accepted as the literal truth; but it was what they believed of him in Lee's army. There was, however, civilian opinion, such as that of Pollard, the editor, to the effect that he was a fine soldier but too reckless, gay, and irresponsible, to be trusted with important operations. Certainly he took the longest, most fantastic chances, seemed to love danger for its own sake, delighted much in practical jokes, even chaffed the solemn Jackson, made endless fun of Prussian von Borcke's broken English. And yet, the contemporary editors were a little prejudiced; Stuart treated them with scant consideration and refused reporters access to his camps with no courtesy whatever; he believed in secrecy where military operations were concerned. As a consequence, the Richmond papers dealt meanly with the cavalry through most of the war, and Stuart's private letters show that he was highly sensitive to the slights they put upon him. But he might have known that reporters are human; they had to write something.

He was a social type, loving people, laughing much, and leading out in song; for he had a rich and golden voice. He was fond of charades and wrote execrable poetry, and affected anagrams. There was never any sadness where he was.

"Yessir, Ah'll tell you one t'ing," says General Lee's old camp servant, after the war. "It mek no diff'ence how quiet our headquartehs wuz—" and I think General Lee's headquarters were usually quiet—"wid'in ten minutes uv de time Ginerul Stua't ride up to visit us, everybody would be a-laffin! And Ah'll tell you another thing, sah, Ginerul Stua't wuz de only one uv dem *big gineruls* whut neveh did tech a drap!" And Lee says, coming out of his tent to the camp fire, where the young officers of his staff, and some of the old ones too, sat singing with Stuart, and a large stone jug, such as applejack comes in, sat on a stone, "Gentlemen, am I to thank General Stuart, or the jug, for this fine music?" The remark is close to the point, like everything Lee says; Stuart was a strong stimulant to all who tasted of his quality, and not a stimulus that died out and let you down. "Keep him away—keep him away from my camp!" protests A. P. Hill. "Every time Jeb Stuart comes around, with Sweeny and his banjo, he makes all my division want to 'jine' the cavalry!" The headquarters of the Cavalry Corps are dry—utterly so. Stout Major von Borcke, his gallant Prussian aide, who loves his glass, taken in quantity by the camp fire, must ride over to Longstreet's headquarters, to foregather with Longstreet's jolly medical officers, for his evening dram. Himself, Stuart never needed any stimulant; life intoxicated him. He drank deep of it and had a gusto for it all—fine horses, and the beauty of women and the gallantry of men, the rich splendor of the seasons in Virginia, the crash and excitement of battle, and the bright face of danger.

He gathered to himself a train of oddities. When the cavalry commands were forming into regiments at the opening of the war, he came upon Joseph Sweeny, a fellow apt upon the banjo, furnished with all the tunes, who sprang to arms from a minstrel troupe, electing to serve mounted.

Sweeny was at once detailed to the Escort, and where Stuart went, he went, with his banjo and his ditties. The by-ways of Virginia heard old joyous snatches ringing above the thudding of the horses' hoofs. Small country towns awoke at night, and the girls turned out in their stored finery for impromptu dances, where Sweeny's banjo pitched the measure and Jeb Stuart led the rout. But if it chanced to be Saturday night, everything stopped at twelve o'clock; Jeb Stuart had serious ideas about Sunday.

There was also Hagan, an enormous man, smothered to the eyes in hair, and of corpulent habit, a forager of rare parts, with a nose for a Virginia ham, and for Yankee delicacies in an overtaken wagon train, which emergencies only sharpened. This Hagan was a corporal of the Escort in the Peninsula fighting in 1862, and Stuart mentions him in his reports as having been valiant above others in cavalry combat. Approbation exalted the fellow's horn remarkably; his dignity grew with his advancement, and it is related that Stuart made him a lieutenant "just to see him swell." But you also infer that Lieutenant Hagan was an able quartermaster and commissary for the Escort of the Commanding General, Cavalry Corps. Stuart never wasted anything; not even his freaks and ornaments.

Most engaging of all was Major Heros von Borcke, sometime lieutenant of the 3d Regiment of Dragoon Guards, of Brandenburg, in Prussia. He was also a big man, six feet four inches, as tall as Rooney Lee, and heavier in the body. He had great trouble in finding horses that could carry him, and his sword, which you may see this day in the State Library in Virginia, was a straight Damascus blade of archaic pattern, with an iron hilt, large enough for a Crusader.

He ran the blockade to join the Confederate army as a gentleman volunteer, just before the battle of Seven Pines,

Heros von Borcke
Adjutant & Inspector Calvary Corps
A. N. Va. 1862 ?
from   Ambrotype

Major John Pelham
Stuart Horse Artillery
A. N. Va. 1862
from Ambrotype

in May of 1862; and Stuart saw him and took him along, and he served with headquarters of the Cavalry Corps as adjutant and inspector, until a minie ball cut him down at Brandy Station in June of 1863. He was brave: Stuart reports him in the front of furious assaults, charging with deep Teutonic roars and the longest sword in the army; and he was gallant and courteous with an old-world courtesy: Virginia ladies remembered him long afterward; and it was he who took Stuart's present, the new uniform frock of a lieutenant-general, to Jackson, on the Opequon; and he was loyal: he held with the Confederacy to the end, receiving the thanks of the Confederate Congress in 1864, and going, when it was definitely established that he could do no more field service because of his wounds, on a diplomatic mission to England in the last months of the war. He lived to write a book, *My Memoir of the Confederate War*, wherein he makes good stories of the least events and perhaps sins a little against accuracy, but always preserves the authentic flavor of the gallant ways of that Service.

So much for Jeb Stuart as the army saw him. There was another side, perhaps the true one. A letter to his brother, early in the war, gives the key: "I realize that if we oppose force to force we cannot win, for their resources are greater than ours. We must make up in quality what we lack in numbers. We must substitute *esprit* for numbers. Therefore, I strive to inculcate in my men the spirit of the chase. . . ." Here is the answer to Pollard's complaint about his lightness. His military problems were too serious to treat seriously. The weight against him, of men and horses and arms, was too great for his people to be allowed to contemplate. Therefore, he showed a happy face and led them to battle as to a fox hunt, held them joyously to hopeless odds, and fought light cavalry as nobody has fought it since Napoleon's time.

Do not forget that he was Scotch-Irish, that there is a strain of gloom in that blood. His letters to his brother, William Alexander, reveal that the thought of death was never out of his mind. In early 1862 he had his life insured for $10,000, enough to provide something for his wife and children; the thought of them, exposed to want after his death, was always with him. "For I may be killed or captured tomorrow or any day," he says, "and they must look to you for support. . . ."

He believes passionately in the cause of Southern independence: if anything happens to him, he urges his brother to see to it that his wife and children never go north of Mason's and Dixon's line. He thinks blackly on occasions, and reveals it to intimates; does not wish to survive his country's liberties; hopes, if he is to die, that he will be killed in a cavalry charge. And to his brother again, at the opening of the 1864 campaign, "We will have a battle here, probably in ten days. May God give us the victory and cover our heads in the day of battle." This, the man who stands up before the army to be shot at, and risks himself in affairs of videttes like any common trooper, and has a name for flaming courage in an army which refused to respect any officer who was not courageous.

His religion and his God were part of his daily life: "Pray for me in the coming struggle," he writes his brother in 1863; "with me, no moment of the battle has ever been too momentous for prayer." When he was twelve years old he was swept, on the tide of a revival meeting, into the Methodist church. Posted to the Regiment of Mounted Rifles, on the frontier, he found that the only chaplain out there was Episcopalian, and the only active congregation, Church of England. After long thoughts, and correspondence with his parents back in Virginia, he has himself confirmed, because that was the only way in which he could participate in worship. I do not think he was bound by creed, but he had an instinct to take part in things.

In the Confederacy he was active in his support of chaplains, encouraging them to ride with the cavalry, and giving them aid in the distribution of tracts and the holding of meetings among the men. His letters, his remembered conversations, and even his official papers make it plain that his religion was an active force in everything he did, and he had a very simple earnest faith in the wisdom and the goodness of God. Sweeny's banjo was attuned also to hymns: on Sundays, Cavalry Headquarters had its music, but it was sacred music—"Rock of Ages" for "Alabama Gals, Won't You Come Out Tonight?" and "I Would Not Live Alway" for "Old Joe Hooker, Won't You Come Out o' the Wilderness."

On questions of duty, as on questions of faith, he never made any compromise: "I have the reputation of being very fond of saying 'no,'" he writes his wife, "but I have had but one rule of action from the first and that was duty." He writes her again, "I have had to relieve —— from duty with the cavalry corps. He may do well elsewhere but he is not sufficiently fearless for me . . .," this of an officer who bears an honored name and who had served on his staff through four campaigns and served with credit afterward. But the people around Jeb Stuart had to measure up to Jeb Stuart's standards. I do not find that he ever made allowances. Colonel Rosser misunderstands an order—in view of the Confederate habit of sending important orders verbally, no hard thing to do—and goes to the wrong place, Stuart is furious. Though other troops, not tired, are nearer, an aide rides fifteen miles with a peremptory message, and Rosser, just bivouacked after a day's march in freezing weather, must rouse his squadrons and come back through the sleety night to his proper station. And Rosser, a good fighting colonel, does not think so much of Stuart, writing after the war. It followed that Stuart exacted a very high quality of obedience; and men loved him, or hated, or envied, and no doubt some feared him: but they were never indifferent.

When the Cavalry Corps rode north on the Gettysburg campaign, Jeb Stuart had a shopping list, small things his wife needed. Most married officers carried such a list, since the Virginia merchants were experiencing difficulty in restocking, and there were many articles of women's gear that could not be bought at home. On the 16th of July, back in Virginia, he forwarded the list with most of the articles— needles, shoe buttons, hooks and eyes, shoe strings, kid gloves—checked off. One item he could not get—fifteen yards of black silk for a dress. He explained that he had shopped around in Maryland and Pennsylvania and found one store with ten yards of suitable material, but he knew ten yards was not enough.

Active as his service was, he found time to write Flora Stuart nearly every day. Some of these letters are short notes, written on a knee thrown across his saddle-bow. And I attest that they are very lovely letters for any woman to receive. She was the daughter of Colonel Philip St. George Cooke, commanding the 2d U. S. Dragoons when Stuart was a lieutenant in his first year's service. He met her and married her at Leavenworth, all within fourteen days, in November, 1855. They had nine years of married life, broken from first to last by the exigencies of the Service. In Virginia she visited the army as often as she could, and was a charming presence, people relate, in his infrequent periods of repose. But their meetings were never enough for either of them, and he seldom felt free to ask for leave, nor will he absent himself from the lines, while Fredericksburg fight is brewing, to visit the little daughter who is deathly sick. He shows his wife, with much tenderness, how duty and the country's need transcend all personal desires. "I must leave my daughter in the hands of God: my duty to the country requires me here." The little daughter dies, and only two aides know how terrible is his grief and how he yields to it in private: the army sees him ride, splendid and debonair as ever. But when he lies dying, he says: "Soon I'll be with my little Flora." The day before Yellow Tavern, he snatched an hour at dawn with his wife at Doctor Fountaine's house at Beaver Dam, while his brigades were assembling to strike Sheridan: he will be shot presently, and seems to know it beforehand, his aide thinks. And next day, in Richmond, he clung very hard to life, so that he might see her again: but he died before she came.

She was a superior woman, and though all the fine women, young and old, in the counties where he campaigned, lavished admiration upon him with notable unrestraint, she was the only woman in his life.

In the winter of 1862 the Army of Northern Virginia lay behind the Rappahannock, Longstreet's First Corps above Fredericksburg, Jackson's Second Corps below the town, toward Port Conway, and the brigades of the Cavalry Division in extended observation on either flank. The great battles of that year were behind the Army of Northern Virginia: it had defeated three invasions: McClellan on the Peninsula in June, Pope at Second Manassas in August, Burnside at Fredericksburg in December. It had fought the Sharpsburg action in Maryland, in September. From these fights there had emerged enduring military reputations: brigade and battery and division commanders were pointed out to you if you rode through the encampments. There was Wade Hampton, with his curly beard, his air of a great gentleman of an elder time, and his mania for personal combat. There were Fitz Lee and Rooney Lee, the other two cavalry brigadiers. There was Lafayette McLaws, florid, crisp-bearded, of Roman aspect; and peppery D. H. Hill, who is, about now, disapproving an infantryman's application for transfer to the regimental band, with his indorsement: "Shooters, not tooters, are needed in this service." You would see Hood, long-haired and blond and unsubtle; and Gordon of Georgia, and old implacable Jubal Early, and R. H. Anderson, and Ambrose Powell Hill, red-headed and able. And Pendleton and Poague and Pegram, and the gallant Pelham, artilleryists. Riding through the First Corps, you were likely to meet Lieutenant-General James Longstreet, burly and combative as a bull in a field. Toward Moss's Neck, in the Second Corps, was Lieutenant-General Jackson, observing with sour, sharp attention the least activity of his command—a silent, ungraceful officer with a great breath of fame about him, these days. And you might meet, riding thoughtfully on the gray gelding Traveller, General Lee. But when you came upon the long-legged horse soldier, Lee's "young Major-General," James Ewell Brown Stuart, who led the Cavalry Corps, jingling on the frozen road with his red-lined cloak blown free, his smart young aides at heel, all singing as they rode, to Sweeny's music, you saw a man you would remember as long as you lived.

The Confederate service did not lack for picturesque individuals, flaming gentlemen-at-arms, who brought to this war sound military aptitude, and the color, also, of the age of chivalry. But Stuart was something more than any of them. I think each foot-sore infantryman, each gunner pounding by, every hard-riding trooper, saw in Jeb Stuart the man he would like to be himself.

Jeb Stuart was a symbol, a gonfalon that went before the swift, lean columns of the Confederacy. He served as the eyes and ears of Lee: his hands touched the springs of vast events. His Commanding General said of him, at the last, the finest thing history records of any cavalry officer: "He never sent me a piece of false information."

Hereafter I have endeavored to reconstruct some of the works of this man. His type, the general, charging with his sword out, in the front of battle, is gone from the world. His kind of war has given over to a drab affair of chemistry, propaganda, and mathematics. Never, anywhere, will there be his like again.

II

THE STUARTS IN VIRGINIA: YOUTH
OF THE CENTAUR

THE youngest son, and the seventh, of the ten children of Archibald Stuart and Elizabeth Letcher Stuart, was born in Patrick County, Virginia, on 6 February, 1833. That sturdy, restless baby was christened James Ewell Brown Stuart; and some thirty years later his name was entered on the rolls of fame as Jeb.

The family had been in North America for more than a hundred years. The first of them, one Archibald Stuart, a man of substance and a Presbyterian, of the great clan in the Low of Scotland, landed in Pennsylvania in 1726, the mercurial and stubborn Stuart blood having involved him with the troubles of the period. Avoiding Scotland, he had refugeed briefly at Londonderry, in Ireland, and thence come, with many others, to Penn's Colony, where he lived obscurely for seven years. After that, things were calmer, and he was able to send back for his family. But the Stuarts, in common with numerous families of Scotch-Irishry, found neither Pennsylvania nor its placid citizens congenial, for the Scotch-Irish are a clannish lot, and live by preference in the shadow of the hills, with a line of retreat always open. There was a steady drift of them from Pennsylvania south across the Potomac and up the valley of the Shenandoah, and in 1738 Archibald Stuart established his family in what is now Augusta County, Virginia. He raised four children, and acquired large lands.

His second son was Alexander Stuart, who came to manhood with the Revolution, and was Major in Colonel Samuel McDowell's regiment. At the battle of Guilford Courthouse, he commanded the regiment, had two horses killed under him, and took a heavy wound. He was captured, and admired of his enemies, for when he was exchanged, the British returned his sword to him, and it is treasured in the family to this day, with certain other blades that are bright with honor. Major Stuart was an able man. He advanced the fortunes of his family, and took a leading part in the affairs of his generation. He was one of the founders of Washington College in Lexington, now Washington and Lee. He lived ninety years.

The youngest son of Major Stuart, called Alexander after him, was the first Stuart to see the West, and to serve the Federal Government. United States Judge in Illinois and in Missouri, Speaker of the Missouri Legislature, member of the Executive Council in Virginia, he died in 1832, full of honors.

Archibald Stuart, his oldest son, served in the army through the War of 1812, and followed the profession of law. He went to the Virginia Legislature from Campbell County, and later from Patrick, was heard in the Constitutional Conventions of 1829 and 1850, and represented the Patrick District in the Federal Congress. It is said that there was never a man in Virginia public life who was so much beloved. His portrait shows a handsome face, high bred, genial, and ruddy, with a bright eye and certain weakness about the mouth. He was a notable orator, famous on the hustings, admired in legislative halls, and exceedingly convivial. Old men relate that no gathering of gentlefolk in his section was complete without Arch Stuart, to tell the liveliest tales, and troll out songs in his golden voice, when the cloth was drawn and the bottle passed with the sunwise turn. But under him the family affairs did not prosper. Young James was born on the farm called Laurel Hill, which Elizabeth Letcher Stuart inherited from the Letchers. And it is further related that, when Archibald Stuart was defeated for Congress by the Honorable H. T. Averett, the victor's first official act was to give Arch Stuart's son James an appointment to the United States Military Academy.

Young James, it seems, was as much his mother's son as his father's. Elizabeth Letcher Pannill was of the Letchers, who were restless and able, great Welsh gentry in the old country, and folk of important affairs in the new, and of the Pannill's: there was a Pannill shield hung up in Battle Abbey, after the Great Duke broke the Saxons. She herself is remembered as a notable gentlewoman, and her face is that of a shrewd, composed lady, of no special patience with nonsense. Young James had of his father his fine, large-boned body, with the bright, kindling eye, the clear, ringing voice, and the warm, indefinable qualities which go to make up what we call magnetism: people always felt ardently about him, one way or the other; and from his mother came a fixity of purpose and a hard moral texture that grew stronger as his turbulent life unrolled.

It was an age when religion colored every activity, but there was little of the narrow sectarian about Archibald Stuart's family. The Stuarts were for the most part Presbyterian, which was the prevailing creed throughout the Valley of Virginia. Elizabeth Letcher Stuart was, like most of the great Virginia families, Episcopalian. Every surviving letter of James Stuart's, and all the relations of him, indicate that religion was important to him all his life, and we know that the training he had at his mother's knee was simple and sincere and pious, and ineffaceable. He told them, in 1864, as they carried him off the field with his death wound, and offered him brandy to deaden the pain of the ball through his liver, that he had, at the age of twelve, promised his mother never to take liquor, and that he had kept his word and saw no reason to depart from it in extremity. In 1848, being then in his fifteenth year, they sent him up to Wytheville, and he worked for a while in the county clerk's office, forming some youthful ideas on the legal profession, and entering, the same fall, Emory and Henry College. In this year an evangelist held a revival meeting at the college, and with many other students, young James was swept into the fold of the Methodist Church. There exists a letter of this period, written to an old tutor who had grounded him in Latin, "which you instilled into me partly by the mouth and partly by the rod:"—At Emory and Henry they required the first six books of the Ænead, which Stuart had already read, under his tutor, and he applied for a certificate to that effect, in order to enter the advanced courses in Latin. He was, he added, reading Ovid, and he found it a great treat to "launch from the dry facts of Livy into the beauties of Ovid." Latin, Stuart considered, would be useful to him, since at the moment he expected to take up school teaching as soon as he could.

But he was not destined to teach school. When he was seventeen he was appointed to the United States Military Academy, and he became a cadet at West Point, 1 July, 1850.

Little of what we know of James Stuart's early life sets him apart from the run of young Virginians, or young Southerners, of substantial family, in the days before the War. Generally, home instruction was in the hands of the mother. Then there were tutors, and later the small sectional colleges which flourished in the South, little institutions of authentic if narrow culture, firmly based on the classics. Some stories of young James are handed down, but it is hard to distinguish what stories came before, and what stories grew up after the events which made the stories of Jeb Stuart valuable. I have selected one, which his brother, William Alexander Stuart, told when James adopted the profession of arms.

Hornets are much at home in the hills of southwest Virginia, and one day, William Alexander being about fifteen years old, and James about nine, the two boys, roving at venture, came upon an impressive hornets' nest, the size of a football, in the lower branches of a great tree. Hornets and boys are natural enemies, and the brothers took counsel to destroy the insects. It was so situated that they couldn't chunk it down with thrown sticks, and, very valiantly, they climbed the tree to get at it. When they were almost close enough to dislodge it, the hornets swarmed out in defence, and stung mightily, and William Alexander, a practical fellow, dropped to the ground and ran. But the younger brother narrowed his eyes and took the stings, and climbed close enough to ply his stick, and got the nest. From that event, William Alexander deduced that young James might make a fine soldier, for he had great natural courage.

At West Point the annals fall likewise into routine. His class standing improved from year to year, and in 1854 he graduated 13th in the class of 46. Brevet Lieutenant-Colonel R. E. Lee was commandant during these years, George Washington Custis Lee was standing at the head of each successive class, like his father, the Commandant, before him, and Pleasanton and Averell and Fitz Lee were in Stuart's classes or below him. At West Point they remember of him that he was an average student, that he was smart in person, of a high color, and strong, and that he showed marked aptitude for drill and tactics; he was successively cadet, orderly, sergeant, and second captain, which were high attainments. He took numerous demerits, but most of them were for fighting. It was plain that he loved to fight, and some of his colleagues thought that he fought without any particular judgment, since he was frequently whipped, and invariably turned up again, just as eager, for more.

The Stuart men, generation on generation, run to two

clear types: either they are long-legged and long-armed, with short, compact bodies; or they are long-bodied, with short limbs. The trait can be observed in the present generation. James Stuart was of the former classification, and except when he sat a horse, his structure did not make for grace. A story goes in the family that he learned, some months prior to graduation, that his marks were such that he would finish high, certain for a detail to the engineers, who are notoriously the brains of the army. He didn't feel attracted to the engineers, the story adds, preferring the cavalry service. So he relaxed his endeavors, and made certain of finishing far enough down the line to be eligible for his choosen arm. However that may be, he graduated on 1 July, 1854, and was gazetted to the Mounted Rifles, Major Solomonson's regiment on the Western frontier. No vacancy existed at the time: he was brevetted a Second Lieutenant, and his first commission is dated 31 October, 1854.

The Mounted Rifles were serving in Texas, and Stuart, going out through New Orleans, was held up by a yellow fever epidemic, and did not join his regiment until December. It was then at Fort Clark, in the western part of the state, from which base it operated against the Apaches and Comanches. Lieutenant Stuart accomplished his military apprenticeship in the Panhandle and the Trans-Pecos country, over one of the most difficult terrains in the world, then in a condition of nature. Small patrols operated, miles and days out of communication, under junior officers, on duty that called for the highest degree of resourcefulness, courage, and prudence. The infrequent contacts with the Indians were brief and savage, and between them, there was unending struggle with a pitiless climate, not inexactly described by the plaint of an early Panhandle farmer: "I wuz doin' a piece uv plowin', with a pair uv Oxen, an' one uv my critters, Ole Bright, falls down daid with sunstroke. Sez I, no use losin' the hide an' the tallow, an' I squats to skin th' carcass. But befo' I kin git the hide offen it, along comes a Norther, an' t'other critter, Ole Boley, friz to death!" And General Sherman, who saw the region, and judged the whole State thereby, has recorded that if he owned Hell and Texas, and could find a customer who was a big enough fool, he would rent Texas and live in the other place. But the Western frontier was the school of the great soldiers of the Civil War. The Mounted Rifles co-operated in manœuvre with the 8th Infantry in Texas: the records speak of a rendezvous in the Guadalupe mountains, with a column of the 8th from El Paso under Major James Longstreet. And a Captain Ewell was riding with the 2d Dragoons. But Stuart was presently to be detailed to a duty which threw him into intimate contact with most of the officers who afterwards rose to high command in the Civil War.

The reports from the Mounted Rifle regiment in these years are exceedingly rare. I have found one, which tells of how Lieutenant Stuart—because, you imagine, he was junior second lieutenant and therefore entitled to all the dirty work—was put in charge of the cannon that the regiment dragged along on its expeditions. No roads, broken country, and a bored company of Rangers in escort, with the main column airily riding ahead. Falling further and further behind, the cannon followed laboriously to the crest of a ridge, and opened a rocky slope of fifteen hundred feet, at the foot of which the regiment was camped. It was the opinion of experience, there present, that no gun could go down the hill; there would have to be an extensive detour, and they would catch up with the regiment when they could! But the Lieutenant thought not. He rode down the slope, and considered it too much to ask of any horse to take him to the top again. He dismounted and hitched, and climbed back, dismounted the disgusted Rangers, bent lariats to the

Regiment of
Mounted Rifles
Texas · 1854

First Lieutenant
of Mounted Rifles
1855

cannon and the caisson, and got down to the valley by hand, with all his equipment. The work was adjudged by his commanding officer to be remarkable, and his report attested to the fact. I think this gun important, in subsequent matters of wider interest, for the Major-General Commanding the Cavalry Corps, Army of Northern Virginia, in all his extended operations, remembered the Lieutenant, and never abandoned gun, wagon train, or prisoners when he had once set his hand upon them. Lieutenant Stuart did well in the Mounted Rifles. In 1855 he was one of the hand-picked lot of officers detailed to the two new cavalry regiments organized by Mr. Jefferson Davis, Secretary of War.

Under the old order of things, the various arms of the service were specialized and individual in function and in equipment. The mounted branch consisted of Dragoons and Mounted Rifles. The Dragoons were large, heavy men on big horses, equipped with musket and sabre, to fight either on foot or on horseback. Their double function rendered them a little clumsy in application. The Mounted Rifles were simply infantrymen on horses; their animals were for transportation only, and their equipment was otherwise of the infantry line. Mr. Jefferson Davis, himself a West Pointer, considered that the service would benefit from a new organization, designated exclusively for mounted combat. He secured authorization for, and formed, the 1st and 2d Regiments of U. S. Cavalry, to be armed with sabres, and pistols or carbines, horse-soldiers, trained for scouting and outpost duty, and trained also for mounted shock tactics. The law which authorized these regiments was unusually liberal, from the Service viewpoint, providing that the colonels and the majors were to be regulars, and that one-half of the company officers might be regulars, while only the other half of the company commissions were to be filled by those appointments from civil life, whereby, from time immemorial, Congressmen have settled their political debts. The organization of the regiments was attended with interest by the army, Mr. Davis creating the impression that he was forming a *corps d'élite*—as, indeed, he was, and Stuart, writing to a friend, from Texas, after it was known that Albert Sidney Johnston was to command one, and Colonel Sumner the other, is certain that "no regiment was ever marshalled into the field with such brilliant luminaries at its head as each of these has. How delighted I would be to belong to a regiment with Sumner, Lee, Hardee, & Emory for field officers: Expectation is on tiptoe to see the correct list of Captains and Subalterns."

This letter, written to a girl at West Point in April, '55, is bright and gossipy. McLaws, Elliott, Ransom, Howland, McRae, and Edson were among the officers serving with him, and he gives news of all of them, and garrison talk regarding Fitz-John Porter, Howard, Pegram, and others whose names were presently to become known. And he enclosed a pressed cactus flower "for Miss Minnie," whose gentle hands he remembers, and he despairs of ever getting east from Texas, unless he resigns. He mentions, also, writing for the magazines, since he had a fluent pen, admirable to his friends. And so on, for four large, closely-written pages.

Meantime, his name had been before Mr. Jefferson Davis, and all the reports on him were favorable. He was transferred as second lieutenant to the 1st Cavalry as of 3 March, 1855, and proceeded to Jefferson Barracks at St. Louis, where the new commands were being whipped into shape.

In later years, when Mr. Jefferson Davis was the harassed President of the Southern Confederacy, his appointments were much attacked; friendship and other influences, said his critics, blinded him to obvious faults and to obvious merits. But the officer-personnel, selected by him for these regiments, was remarkable. It is not too much to say that it comprised most of the brains and the leadership on both sides in the Civil War.

Colonel Sumner commanded the 1st Regiment. He was later conspicuous on the Peninsula and at Sharpsburg, commanding a Federal Corps. Joseph E. Johnston was Lieutenant-Colonel: he was to be a General and an Army Commander in the Confederacy. The Majors were Emory and John Sedgwick, both subsequent Major-Generals and corps commanders for the Union. Among the Captains, Sackett, Wood, McClellan, Sturgis, Walker, Anderson, and Garnett, and among the Lieutenants, Beale, George H. Steuart, McIntosh, Ransom, Carr, Iverson, Wheaton, Stanley, J. E. B. Stuart, Otis, McIntyre, Vinton, Bayard, and Lomax, all became Major-Generals or Brigadier-Generals, and G. B. McClellan was an Army Commander. In the 2d Regiment, the Colonel was Albert Sidney Johnston, who died at Shiloh, and the Lieutenant-Colonel, Robert E. Lee. Hardee, later Lieutenant-General, C. S. A., and George Thomas, to be called the Rock of Chickamauga, were the field officers. Among the Captains, who rose to General rank, were Van Dorn and Kirby Smith, Oakes, Palmer, and Stoneman, and among the Lieutenants, Evans, Edward Johnson, Field, Gerard, Crosby, Lowe, Hood, Major, and Fitzhugh Lee. Five full Generals of the Confederacy, two Union Army Commanders, and thirty-odd Corps, Division, and Brigade Commanders, served in the 1st and 2d Cavalry. It will be noted that the majority of these officers were of Southern birth, which is hardly material for the critics of Mr. Davis. Most of the large reputations in the army of that day were those of Southern men. The South, more than the North, cherished the military tradition, and the great Southern families delighted to send their sons to Annapolis and to West Point.

In August, '55, the 1st Cavalry marched from Jefferson

Barracks to stations in the Kansas territory. Second Lieutenant Stuart was Regimental Quartermaster, and continued in those duties for two years. The detail was important: again, he was learning in the hardest of schools the business of feed and equipment, and the importance of standing by the stuff.

The regiment went on a brief campaign against the Indians, a sort of shake-down cruise, not marked by any fighting, and returned in November to Fort Leavenworth. While he was on the trail, Lieutenant Stuart had news from Virginia of the death of his father, and his letters are heart-broken that deal with this bereavement, for the family ties are strong in the Stuart clan. But his was a life in which joy and sorrow, sunlight and shadow, were to be closely mingled, love and death not waiting on small niceties.

At Fort Leavenworth was Colonel Philip St. George Cooke, commanding the 2d U. S. Dragoons, and Colonel Cooke had three fine daughters, Flora, Maria, and Julia. James Stuart met, and besieged Miss Flora with all the ardent spirit of light cavalry, and two weeks, according to tradition, was all the time he needed to make good his suit. The word was out for the wedding, and on 14 November they were married.

The Cookes were of substantial Virginia family, and Maria and Julia, after Flora, married also into the service— Maria, the officer who became Surgeon-General Brewer of the Confederate States Army, and Julia, Major Sharpe, who would later wear a general's stars on a blue uniform, with the Union. There was a son, also, John R. Cooke, graduated in this year from Harvard. He followed his brother-in-law out of the Union, to become an able and respected Brigadier of North Carolina Infantry, and to fight well in the great battles of the Army of Northern Virginia.

Three children were to be born to James Stuart and his wife. The oldest was Flora, *la petite* of the General's war letters, who died in 1863. James Ewell Brown Stuart, Junior, was the second child, "Little Jemmie." The story goes that he was named at birth for his grandfather, Colonel Cooke, but they changed his name in 1861. The third was Virginia Pelham Stuart, whose name holds the memory of the war years, and who came in the last winter of her father's life. Frontier marriage was excellent training for the vicissitudes of the approaching conflict, and of James and Flora Stuart's the annals may be brief. They loved each other until he died, and she survived him nearly sixty years, holding always in her heart the memory of the plumed cavalier, who kissed her at Beaver Dam Station in the dawn of the 10th of May, 1864, and rode down to his death wound at Yellow Tavern.

The Stuarts had two slaves, one who came to the young officer with the settlement of his estate, and one who served Flora Stuart. Both were disposed of before the outbreak of the Civil War.

On 20 December, 1855, Stuart was promoted First Lieutenant, and in the year following, Colonel Sumner's regiment was engaged in keeping the peace through Kansas territory, where the Free-Soilers and the slavery people engaged in fierce arguments, frequently attended by bloodshed, as to whether Kansas should enter the Union, Slave or Free. Out there, an enthusiast named John Brown, an abolitionist who held and applied the doctrine that the End Justifies the Means, was in repeated conflict with the authorities, and young James Stuart was with the column which rode to restrain him after certain massacres.

In the next year, 1857, the 1st Cavalry took the trail against the Indians, who were plundering and burning where they found it convenient to do so, by way of asserting the belief that their native prairies belonged to them and not to the white people who were pushing out of the East and killing off the buffalo. In July, seventeen marches from its base, six companies of the regiment, under Colonel Sumner in person, being then in the country drained by the north fork of the Solomon River, rode over a fold in the rolling plain and came upon a band of hostiles, three hundred Cheyenne warriors, advancing toward the column in irregular mass. The six companies went front into line immediately, and it was expected, as they came in gunshot, that they would halt, fire an aimed volley, and then attack with pistols. But Colonel Sumner's first order was: Draw Sabres! and his next was: Charge! Stuart gives the story in a letter to his wife, with far more detail than he afterward devoted to battles which shook the world.

The troopers spurred their horses, yelling, and the Cheyennes wheeled about and fled, very sensibly, and the fight streamed off across the grassland; the cavalry companies losing formation as the stronger horses drew ahead of the weaker ones, and checking and swirling, in smoke and dust, where single Indians and little groups were overtaken and turned to shoot. Stuart says his horse, Dan, kept well forward in the chase for some miles and then began to give out, so that he was forced to rank a trooper out of an animal with more bottom. Catching up again, he came to where a dismounted brave, with a huge Allen's revolver, was standing off three officers, Lomax, Stanley, and McIntyre. Stuart thought the savage might kill Lomax, and he dashed at him with his sabre, slashing him in the thigh. The Indian shot at him and missed, as his horse carried him by. Stanley, riding close, dismounted and wasted his last shot, and the Indian walked coolly at Stanley, to make sure of him when he fired. Stuart, turning about, rode at the brave again, and cut him over the head, whereat the Cheyenne, at about three feet, shot him in the chest. The slug almost unseated him— but not quite, for he was a superlative horseman—and while he recovered himself, McIntyre came up and killed the Indian. They got Stuart off his horse and found that the ball had glanced across his upper ribs and lodged deep in the left pectoral muscle, painful but not dangerous. Thereafter, he suffered the rough mercies of frontier hospital arrangements, convalesced lying on the ground, under the shade of a blanket upheld by four sabres stuck in the sod, and improved the slow hours, he writes, by reading the Book of Common Prayer and the U. S. Army regulations, favorite works of his, and the only literature available. This was the first wound James Stuart took. The next was from the bullet that killed him.

Now we can pass over two more years of soldiering in the West, a time of no little hardship, of some adventure and excitement, and of occasional danger. The winters were spent in garrison, and the summers on the marches. An officer's family could not be with him much, except in winter quarters. You had abundant time on your hands, between expeditions to enforce the peace upon savage Indians and scarcely less savage settlers. You could hunt—which Stuart liked to do; you could study your profession, which he also did; or you could play poker and drink too much whiskey, which pastimes attracted Stuart not at all. Always, in places where the families could live, the army ladies kept up the social round, and you found the finest manners in the land, and some of the finest people, in two-room log cabins, with the skins of animals spread and hung around, not for ornament, but to keep out the weather. But you cannot pity these people in the isolation and wide emptiness of the new West. They carried their resources for entertainment within themselves. You read, in their letters, of debating societies, of temperance societies, of amateur theatricals, and of a great deal of singing and good fun. Where the Stuarts were, there was always a plenty of both music and laughter. Flora Cooke had a deft touch on the guitar, and sung the sentimental ballads of the time most pleasingly, and the Lieutenant owned a ringing baritone and loved to use it.

Always, whether following garrison routine in the posts, or riding the long prairies at the head of his command, an officer had time to think, and the days were coming when a man must say where he could stand. Back East, vast events were shaping. In the autumn of 1859, Lieutenant Stuart had his part in an opening scene. . . .

Shuffle the pages now, and see what came to pass, and how——

III

SECESSION AND JOHN BROWN

ACROSS Charleston Harbor, the morning of 14 April, 1861, the guns opened on Fort Sumter, where the United States flag blew out in the lazy sea-wind over Major Robert Anderson and seventy-odd coast artillerymen. On the pleasant battery walks, the ladies and gentlemen, gathered to see the show, were saying the first shot was fired by the venerable Edmund Ruffin, eminent fire-eating secessionist; and others said it was, on the contrary, young Captain James of the Confederate States Army, who pulled that lanyard.

There was a tremendous and bloodless bombardment, to the confusion of the gulls and the sleepy harbor fowl, until the Gridiron Flag came down. The telegraph ran with the word through all the South, the land of friendly tree-shaded cities, far apart, and tranquil villages, and wide plantations. The word went more slowly by courier and gazette and stage-coach, along the poor dirt roads and the broad, winding rivers, to the little farms by clearings in the woods and in the cane brakes, and to the remote settlements in the lonely hills. But the last corner of the South heard it. *The Ball is Opened!* chanted the passionate Southern Press and the furious Southern orators. . . . And the word rolled through the North.

When the news came to Richmond, in Virginia, it was night, and there followed extravagant rejoicing. The iron cannon of the Fayette Artillery Company, in battery on Shockoe Hill, fired a salute of one hundred guns, and they rang all the bells. The windows rattled in the Capitol, and in the Exchange Hotel, and in the Ballard House across the

33

street from Capitol Square, and the thick powder smoke
welled in slow clouds around the statue of Washington and
the great bronze men who keep him company there, and the
gun flashes illuminated statues and buildings, and rolling
smoke and the animated faces of the people, with play of red
light, continually renewed as the salute crashed on. A parade
formed itself, a torchlight procession a mile long, men and
women bearing transparencies and banners and flambeaux,
waving varieties of a strange new flag. Militia companies,
the Fayette Artillery, the Richmond Howitzers, the Richmond Light Infantry Blues, the Henrico Light Dragoons,
in ranks and under arms, and out of ranks but uniformed,
with fife and drum and brass music, gave a martial touch
to the crowd, and enthusiasts dragged along a cannon from
the State Armory. The saloons, sumptuous bars and corner
groggeries alike, dealt mightily in toddies and cobblers and
straight drams, and a few citizens took time for the imported
lager beer, and Pizzinni's Palace of Sweets served ice cream
and sherberts to gentlemen and their ladies. Marshals, appointed extemporaneously, dashed about on skittish horses,
and the crowd shook itself into a noisy column and passed
along Marshall Street to Main, and so to Broad, and to
Church Hills, and by Franklin Street to Capitol Square and
the State Court House. There were as many women in the
throng as men. The air of April was soft and quickened
to the spring, with an electric thrill that lifted up the
heart. In its course the procession passed the mansion of
Governor Letcher, and paused to invite an expression from
the Chief Executive of the Commonwealth. Honest John, the
Sage of Rockbridge, was annoyed, for Virginia was still of
the United States. He spoke briefly and with a dryness. He
was honored, he said, by such a gathering of citizens, though
why they thus ran together and appeared to celebrate he did
not know, nor could he recognize the emblems they carried,

nor account for that brass cannon, the property of the Military. He advised them to disperse and seek their homes; he thanked them for their courtesy, and he wished them a kind good night. They cheered him, as they would have cheered anything, since only the jostled fringe of the mass could hear what he said, and they proceeded to the front of the Ballard House, around which they milled a little and solidified, and General Ransom of the South Carolina State Forces, and a gentleman from Secession Circles in Baltimore, addressed them eloquently and at length.

Next day, the new flag was displayed from many windows, and it shone on the bosoms of ladies, and adorned the lapels of gentlemen. It was the secession flag. A flag with a blue union, on which were seven stars, of the seven seceded states, and for the rest it was three broad equal stripes, red, white, and red. The flag of the Confederate States of America, South Carolina, Mississippi, Florida, Alabama, Georgia, Louisiana, and Texas, which formed at Montgomery in February, 1861.

That day, interest in Richmond centered upon the Convention, and people were much exercised by a small incident. Two ladies had sent a wreath of flowers to a prominent unionist delegate in the Convention, whose stand was notoriously against the secession of Virginia. Much relief was expressed when the word got around that the regrettable tribute to a mistaken obstinacy had not come from Virginia ladies, but from two females of Boston, transients at the Ballard House. The Virginia ladies were all loyal to their state, and spoke with asperity of the Yankee nation. And people were extremely impatient with the Convention. It had assembled in February, to consider the course of Virginia in the troubled times, and it had been sitting for more than fifty days, talking and talking and talking. One of the first things it did was to call a peace conference, of delegations from every state, to meet in Washington and discuss means for averting conflict. Eight of the Southern states had responded, and a majority of the Northern states, but nothing came of it. As late as the 12th April, when the Provisional Government of the Confederacy was functioning at Montgomery, and the guns bearing on Sumter were shotted but not yet fired, the Convention had sent a commission to wait on the President at Washington and ascertain his intentions toward the seceded states. The Commission was non-partisan and entirely distinguished, consisting of the Honorable Alexander H. H. Stuart of Staunton, a unionist, of Ballard Preston, one of the majority who hoped to find, between union and disunion, expedients for peaceful settlements of sectional differences, and of George Randolph, an ultra-secessionist. The commission had come back, as the world knew, from an interview in which Mr. Lincoln was non-committal and evasive, but with the impression that he would not go to the insane length of coercing a sovereign state. Now, the Convention professed itself amazed at the sending of the U. S. Transport *Star of the West* with reinforcements and provisions to Sumter; distressed at the precipitancy and unwisdom of the Confederacy in opening fire; but still hopeful that Mr. Lincoln would leave some path open to peace. There were old wise men in the Convention, and men who had seen the face of war, and they read the signs aright, and wanted no war in Virginia. They believed in the constitutional right of secession, but they doubted its wisdom and dreaded its necessity. If Virginia could stay, with honor and safety, in the Union, the Convention would keep her there, and they were not to be hurried by the impulses of their constituents. So, on the 15th and the 16th of April the Convention continued its deliberations, while the people ran together in crowds and listened to inflaming speeches, wherein the voice of reason was not conspicuous, and on 17 April, President Lincoln called for

75,000 volunteers, to force the seceded states back into the Union. Virginia was advised that her quota was 8,000 men. Said the *Richmond Examiner*, editorially, in the moment of brief, astonished silence which followed: "Lincoln declares war against the South and his Secretary demands from Virginia a quota of cutthroats to desolate Southern firesides." Governor Letcher at once advised Washington, in language the most emphatic, that Virginia would furnish no troops for such a purpose. The governors of the states still hesitating, replied in similar strain—North Carolina, Arkansas, Tennessee, Kentucky: the governor of Missouri was perhaps the most outspoken. He wired: "The requisition is illegal, unconstitutional, revolutionary, inhuman, diabolical, and cannot be complied with."

In the Convention, the three parties merged into one. Judge Stuart, Jubal Early, all the staunch unionists faced the issue. Lincoln's call to arms drove Virginia out of the Federal Union. Late at night, on 17 April, the Convention in secret session passed the Ordinance:

"The people of Virginia recognize the American principle, that government is founded on the consent of the governed, and the right of the people of the several states of this union for just cause to withdraw from their association under the Federal Government, with the people of other states, and to erect new governments for their better security; and they will never consent that the Federal Power, which is in part their power, shall be exerted for the purpose of subjecting such states to the Federal Authority."

It is a long sentence and involved, but the words have a lapidary ring, and the meaning is perfectly plain. In it focus all the grievances of all the years, all the conflict between two conceptions of government, which had been growing since Bill of Rights Day. All the vexed questions, tariff, slavery, free soil, down to John Brown and the Abolitionists and the elections of 1860. It was made public in the morning papers of 18 April. The new flag, the Confederate flag, was hoisted first from the Tredegar Iron Works across the James, and presently went up all over the city. Business was suspended. The contemporary records describe a day that recalls to this generation the Armistice Day of 1918. There was kissing and embracing in the streets. There was universal congratulation. Orators declaimed from every vantage point, freely alluding to Virginia's mighty past, predicting greater glories in the future. The military companies, rushing about under arms for no apparent reason, were cheered, and veterans of Mexico, and retired officers of the army, appearing in old regimentals, were cheered, and plans got under way for a formal and elaborate celebration on the 19th. A Richmond lady, writing in that time, says: "A Stranger, suddenly transplanted to the city, without a knowledge of preceding facts, would have imagined the people in a state of intoxication or insanity."

The people of Virginia, and of the South, were a rural people, highly local, and not widely travelled. The great families, the rich planters, went abroad, junketted to Northern watering places, imported accomplished tutors for their children, and patronized the Northern colleges, and sent their sons to the service schools. They lived in leisure and magnificence, and knew the world. But they were, in point of numbers, small. The body of the population continued remote, and had its personal ideas of the Northern states from the itinerant peddlers and drummers who came among them, and from occasional uplifters, tainted with the abolition heresy and smacking of the sharp usages of trade. The same people took their political conceptions from their orators and from the shrill Southern newspapers. Politics was at once a diversion and an occupation which old and young followed with enthusiasm, and everybody loved to talk. Information was always colored and adroitly turned. North and South were alike in lack of understanding and sympathy for each other. People held to their beliefs with a single-mindedness, and a fixity, and a passion.

The South believed that the state had the constitutional right to leave the Union for just cause, as freely as it had entered, and they were convinced that just cause now existed. The elections of 1860 held out, to the South, no hope of improvement in relations with the Northern states, and the Abolitionists appeared to dominate the Republican party. There was hardly a conception, among the people, of the superiority of the North in resources and potential power. Very few Southerners—although among these few were Mr. Jefferson Davis and some thoughtful men who had seen the North and gauged its temper and measured its strength— believed that war would follow secession. Of course, when you examined the census returns, there were more people up there; but—quality—not quantity, is what counts in a horse race, said the local wise men. It was widely considered that those Yankees, with their amusing president, were men of business and would not fight beyond the marts of trade. And if they did, the very niggers in the field knew that Europe couldn't get along without cotton. In the unlikely event that help was needed, England and France, hindered in their vital commerce, would be right over, with ships and men. This last was a fatal illusion, obscuring vision in the high places of the South to the very end of the war. And the states went out, joyously.

The South, seceding, felt that she was well quit of terri- torial controversies, and vexatious court decisions, and pro- tective tariff acts, and of the part that characterized the

Federal Constitution as a Covenant with Death and an Agreement with Hell, and of the people who rang church bells and offered prayers for the homicidal maniac, John Brown. The reasonable and cultured representatives of the several states would now, in the light of considered experience, take counsel together and erect a new government, fit for gentlefolk and sovereign commonwealths. Virginia's Secession Ordinance was passed by the Convention subject to popular vote, to be held on 23 May, 1861. Later the *Richmond Examiner* would say (ignoring a not inconsiderate Unionist minority): "The people of Virginia ratified the Ordinance before the Convention passed it: the State seceded long before the Convention found it out. The ratification of the 23rd May is a mere formality."

There was much genuine sorrow for the passing of the Union which Virginians had labored so powerfully to create and to maintain, but, declared the editors from New Orleans to Alexandria, the severance is perpetual. Only John M. Daniel, in Richmond, uttered words that fell like the strokes of a mighty bell, tolled heavily:

"The great event of all our lives has at last come to pass. A war of gigantic proportions, infinite consequences, and infinite duration is upon us, and will affect the interests and happiness of every man, woman and child, lofty or humble, in this country called Virginia. We cannot shun it. We cannot alleviate it. We cannot stop it. We have nothing left but to fight our way through these troubles. . . ."

And he sounded another note, this Daniel. What, he wanted to know, are our means of resistance? "We believe that we inform the public with considerable accuracy on this point, when we declare that the State's public means of resistance are simply nil. Virginia has a few serviceable arms and scarcely any powder. The whole amount on hand is 200 kegs and 240 more ordered."

II

But not many people listened to such croaking. The temper of the day was exultant. President Davis had sent his Major Huse from Montgomery to Europe to arrange for the purchase of arms, and the best arms of the South, asserted the orators, citing classical precedent, were the strong hearts of her stalwart manhood and the valiant hearts of her women. President Davis had induced the Confederate Congress to pass an act providing for a Provisional Army, the men to enlist for twelve months. He had wanted the term to be for three years, but Congress felt that three months was long enough, and the country rather thought so, too. The twelve months' enlistment was absurd, but Congress conceded it. There was a rush to arms that swamped the recruiting offices, and forehanded gentlemen and state governments ordered weapons from arms companies in New York and in New England and in Baltimore—all advertising in the Southern papers. Such orders were filled, as late as June, 1861. In Virginia the state girded itself to act as an independent nation, pending its admission to the Confederacy of the South. On Sunday, 21 April, Richmond was thrown into a panic by a report that U. S. Sloop-of-war *Pawnee* was sailing up the James, with ten thousand Federal troops aboard, bent on murder, rapine, and pillage. The military, most of them in church when the alarm bells sounded, rushed to the armories for uniforms and to the squares for assembly, and the city was in dismay until late afternoon, when some literal-minded horsemen, who had ridden out the Charles City road to meet the *Pawnee*, came back with the word that there was no such ship in the river; and a few days later the 1st South Carolina Regiment, Colonel Maxcy Gregg, and the 2d South Carolina Regiment, Colonel Kershaw, arrived in Richmond with the laurels of

Sumter on their flags. They had a great reception and were much admired, but they were firmly corrected when they announced that they had come to fight the battles of Virginia: Virginia felt that those battles belonged to everybody. And these were the gala days of the war in Richmond and in the South, a little space granted in the spring of 1861, when a new nation was born and hopes ran young and high. Then the war was upon them and the destruction, and it is to their honor that they rose up to meet the war and did not shrink when they passed, at the end, under the yoke.

In the Richmond newspapers there is perpetuated the sharp essence of the time. The advertising columns shone with warlike ardor. The Southern Arms Company, manufacturers of military and sporting rifles, did, in large type, "respectfully call the attention of Southerners wanting such articles" to its unexcelled line of rifles, bayonets, carbines, and revolvers. It could also furnish swords. All orders to Major T. Sparks, Baltimore. West & Johnston, book and music store, advised that *The Skirmishers' Drill and Bayonet Exercise*, translated from the French language by Capt. R. Milton Cary of the 1st Va. Vols., was on sale to such as desired to instruct themselves in the profession of arms. Also, Hardee's *Infantry Tactics;* and the *Volunteer's Handbook*, by Jas. K. Lee, 1st Va. Vols. Kent, Penick & Co. had military goods: a full supply of fine gray cassemeres, military hats and caps. At J. W. Randolph's, 112 Main Street, there were for purchase field glasses for officers, and a superior military spy glass for measuring distances. All book stores carried a new and revised edition of the *Trooper's Manual*, by Capt. J. Lucius Davis, formerly instructor in cavalry tactics at West Point (the United States Military Academy). With it were announced *Flowers of Hope and Memory*, a beautiful book, from the pen of a gifted Virginia lady, Cornelia J. M. Jordan; and

Gilham's *Military Tactics*, by the well-known Major Gilham of Virginia Military Institute; and a work called *Instruction in Field Artillery*, translated from the French language, by a Board of Field Artillery Officers. And the latest novel by Mr. John Esten Cooke, an elevated and improving narrative.

There were other advertisements. Between a pæan in praise of Cephalic Pills, which cure sick headaches, nervous headaches, all kinds of headaches; and a notice of the Royal Havana Lottery, grand prize $432,000.00, was inserted a card from the Louisiana State Military Academy: the office of Superintendent of the Louisiana State Military Academy had fallen vacant, and the authorities would entertain applications from suitable persons. The late incumbent was a retired officer of the United States Army, one William Tecumseh Sherman, lately resigned and gone North. And Hector Davis-Pulliam & Co.; and Davis, Deupree & Co., auctioneers and dealers of established reputation, were holding daily sales of likely slaves. (House servants, washers and ironers, sold privately.) And John H. Reagan, Postmaster-General of the Confederate States of America, called in due form for bids and proposals on government mail bags, envelopes, and stationery, the specifications herein set forth. . . .

Then there were notices purely military: Major Gilham of V. M. I. called upon all graduates of V. M. I. not yet in service to communicate with him in Richmond at the State Camp of Instruction; drill-masters were needed. Men mustering with the 4th Cavalry Regiment of Virginia Volunteers would report to such an address. The McRae Mounted Rangers would receive a few more men, carefully selected; and so on.

The news columns bristled with military episodes; all over the South the Federal arsenals and stations were being annexed with more or less ease. Only in Pensacola a Lieutenant Slemmer of the U. S. Navy was unreasonable: Sumter ought to have been a lesson to him. General Winfield Scott had resigned: General Winfield Scott, on the contrary, turned his back to his mother, Virginia, and had not resigned. But Colonel Robert E. Lee, of Arlington, had resigned, and his appointment to command the Virginia State Forces was acclaimed. And Quartermaster-General Joseph E. Johnston had resigned, and Colonel Magruder of the Flying Artillery, and Captains Magruder, Barron, and S. S. Lee of the U. S. Navy, and Surgeon John Ward, and Lieutenant Stephen D. Ramseur. In Farquier County they were raising the Black Horse Troop of Cavalry, and the Ashby Troop of Upper Farquier, and the Warrenton Rifles. "Virginians, to Arms!" bawled the *Richmond Enquirer*. "For the 3rd time in 241 years you are called on to take up arms in defence of your homes against the invasion of the foe!" Thus, to the 24th of April. On the 23rd, Governor Letcher had named his Advisory Council: Judge Allen, Colonel Smith (of V. M. I.), Captain Matthew Fontaine Maury, late U. S. N.

III

In the State Library at Richmond there is file on file of correspondence for the last days of April and the month of May, handled by Governor Letcher and this council. The tough rag paper is yellowed, and the ink a little dim, but the clear longhand script is perfectly legible. Every sort of person wrote. People sent in petitions, testimonials, appreciations, complaints, addresses, and declarations of patriotism, and canny commercial propositions. On each document is endorsed the date of receipt and the action taken, or action deferred. Selecting at random, one finds a petition from the Southern Guards, a military organization formed within the graduating class of the University of Virginia. At length, and in a clerkly hand, the young gentlemen represented that it was urged against their organization that such a company, "composed, as ours is, of the young men to whom the State will look in the future for counsellors and leaders" might be exterminated in a single action, to the great loss of the Commonwealth. They petitioned, therefore, that they be instructed by superior officers in the profession of arms, so that they themselves might be distributed among the several camps in the state, for duty as drill-masters and instructors, and thus "inspire the rougher material in the Service with some of the Spirit and Fire of the young men who have had better opportunities for Education." One of the names signed is Robert E. Lee, Jr. The idea was entirely sound, for those youngsters were officer material, but it was not adopted. Young Lee enlisted in the Rockbridge Artillery with most of his classmates, and served a gun, and to the end of the Confederacy the company officers in the Provisional Army were chosen by the vicious election system of the militia.

There is another petition, on elegant note paper that must have been scented, once. It is signed "The Ladies of Engleside," that being a place in Farquier County. The Ladies of Engleside, in fine copperplate script, advised His Excellency "that their men had gone to the War, leaving their homes undefended." But they did not desire to add to the heavy burdens of His Excellency by requesting a detachment of Troops to guard them from the rapacity of the Foe. They earnestly besought His Excellency to send them, with the utmost despatch, "a half a dozen of Colt's Revolvers," with which they, the Ladies of Engleside, would capably protect themselves.

A man of business wrote to the effect that he had a salpetre cave on his property, useful in the manufacture of gunpowder; another, that he would like the contract for the construction of a strategic railroad between Strasburg and Winchester, to improve communications in the valley; and a mariner: how about the navigation lights on the water frontier of Virginia, the Potomac River, now that relations with the Yankee nation were broken off? These things the Council referred to Major-General Robert E. Lee, commanding the Military and Naval Forces of the State.

A joint Board of Army and Navy Officers, headed by Major-General Joseph E. Johnston, Virginia Regular Army, met and prepared two lists of officers, compiled from the latest registers of the United States Army and Navy. One was of officers native to Virginia, officers of proved efficiency, who had already resigned; and the other of U. S. officers of merit who, by reason of birth and antecedents, might be expected to resign that service: the Board recommended that commissions be offered them. At once it was decreed that officers accepting Virginia commissions would receive rank and pay from the date of their resigning the Federal service.

And there was a letter from Mrs. Elizabeth Pannill Stuart, born a Pannill of Pittsylvania, widow of the late Archibald Stuart of Augusta, and kin to the Letchers of Rockbridge, to solicit an appointment in the Virginia State Forces for her son, Lieutenant James Ewell Brown Stuart, formerly of the 1st U. S. Cavalry Regiment, who had resigned from the Federal Army and was now hastening to Virginia from his late station in the Territory of Kansas.

In due time Lieutenant Stuart reported in Richmond, having resigned his United States commission, and he was named Major of Infantry in the Virginia State Forces on 6 May. Virginians are never so occupied that they cannot take time to recall the past, and men remembered the young cavalry officer who took part in the suppression of the John

Brown Raid, a year and a half before. Indeed, there was a report that it had been Stuart's sword which cut down old Ossawattomie at Harper's Ferry. This detail was not true, as Stuart himself declared, then and afterward, but it was his first appearance on the Virginia scene, and the story is worth telling.

IV

J. E. B. Stuart, in 1859, still a lieutenant in the 1st U. S. Cavalry Regiment, was stationed in Kansas Territory. That year he obtained a six months' leave of absence, and took his family back to Virginia, visiting his people around Abingdon and Saltville and Laurel Hill. On 5 October of that year the General Convention of the Protestant Episcopal Church met in Richmond, and Lieutenant Stuart, to whom church matters were always of first interest, attended the Convention as a lay delegate. At the end of the second week in October he went up to Washington to call on the Secretary of War. He had invented and patented an improved device for attaching the cavalryman's sabre to the belt, and he was attempting to sell the patent to the War Department. On Monday, 17 October, he was waiting for an interview in the anteroom of the Secretary.

In the late summer of this year a gimlet-eyed old party who gave his name as Smith had leased a farm in western Maryland, a few miles from the Potomac River at Harper's Ferry, where the important United States Arsenal was located. The fact had occasioned no comment. Mr. Smith, or Captain Smith, as people called him, had given out that he was going to make a crop, after the habit of the region. Sunday night, 16 October, 1859, this Smith, with some twenty men, whites and negroes, a number of Sharpe's rifles, and a selection of cutlasses and pikes, had appeared in Harper's Ferry about the time that the citizens were proceeding home from church, and going to bed. They had also cut the telegraph wires. There were no soldiers attached to the Arsenal, and Harper's Ferry was a small town, and the raiders quickly had possession of it. Details of the force went out into the country and dragged citizens from their sleep, bringing them in as hostages. Among these hostages was Colonel Lewis Washington, a grandnephew of the late George Washington. When Monday morning came, the local militia began to assemble, and there was some shooting. The raiders, who had first established themselves in the Armory, were driven out of it and took refuge in the stout, windowless stone house on the arsenal grounds, in which the fire engines and hose carts were stored. Some of them were killed, and some citizens.

In the afternoon the news, relayed through Frederick and Baltimore by officials of the railroad, reached Richmond. The first bulletin was "There is trouble of some sort at Harper's Ferry. A party of workmen have seized the Government Armory." This was amplified by the next: "The men at Harper's Ferry are not workmen. They are Kansas Border Ruffians, who have attacked and captured the place, fired upon and killed several unarmed citizens, and captured Colonel Washington and other prominent citizens of the neighborhood. We cannot understand their plans or ascertain their numbers." Governor Wise of Virginia was roused from his siesta to read these messages, and he at once telegraphed orders to Colonel John Thomas Gibson, of Charlestown, which is a few miles west of Harper's Ferry, to raise the militia infantry in the region, and sent similar orders to Colonel Robert W. Baylor, commanding the 3d Regiment of Militia Cavalry. He himself called out the Richmond regiment, and prepared to accompany it to the scene by special train. Incidentally, the local troops were already swapping shots with the raiders—at long range—and

Maryland militiamen were crowding down to the river from the north.

The news reached Washington a little earlier than it came to Richmond. During the forenoon, while Lieutenant Stuart waited for his interview, one came out of the Secretary's office, and asked him if he would take an important note over to Lieutenant-Colonel Robert E. Lee, who was then at his home, Arlington, on leave from his command in Texas. A forward-looking youngster would be eager for any contact with the admired staff captain of General Scott, the officer who was regarded as the coming man in the army, and Stuart took the envelope and rode out with it through Georgetown and across the Potomac. What he carried was the order for Lieutenant-Colonel Lee to proceed by special train to Harper's Ferry, and to suppress the disorder reported at that place. Stuart, who heard of it for the first time, since it was not made public in Washington until afternoon—asked and obtained permission to go along with the Lieutenant-Colonel as aide. They left Washington by special train at five o'clock in the afternoon.

In the meantime, there being no soldiers available, Chief Clerk Walsh of the Navy Department had gone at noon to the Marine Barracks and ascertained from the Officer of the Day that there were ninety Marines at hand. These were ordered out by the Secretary of the Navy, "furnished with a proper number of ball-cartridges, ammunition, and rations, and . . . two howitzers and schrapnel" and placed aboard the 3:30 B. & O. train, under the command of Lieutenant Israel Green, U.S.M.C. Green's orders were to report to the senior army officer present at Harper's Ferry, if there was an army officer there, and otherwise to "take such measures as in his judgment may be necessary to protect the Arsenal and other property of the United States." At Frederick the Marines were ordered to wait at Sandy Hook—a mile short of the Ferry—for Lieutenant-Colonel Lee, and at 10 o'clock in the evening Lee and Stuart came up, and the force marched across the bridge and entered the Armory grounds. It had grown dark, and the Virginia militia had the engine house closely surrounded. They were relieved by the Marines, and drew off to a distance. At daylight, Lieutenant-Colonel Lee directed Green to form a storming party, with a second party to support it. The howitzers had been left on the cars. Orders were given to the Marines not to fire, for the safety of the hostages penned up with the raiders. There is a story that Lee, as a courtesy to Virginia, offered the militia the honor of going in after them, but that the militia declined, on the ground that some of their friends, the hostages, might be hurt by them, and they couldn't bear the idea. Governor Wise was scathing in his remarks about his militia, afterward.

At 6:30 o'clock, in the misty October morning, Lee sent his aide forward with a note to the men in the engine house. If they came out and surrendered, wrote Lee, their lives would be protected, and they would be held in safety for such disposition as the proper legal authorities saw fit to make of them. Otherwise, the Marines would come in and get them. Stuart was directed to present this note, and to take the answer—yes or no. He was not to parley. The Marines covered the approaches to the engine house, and the storming parties, twelve leathernecks to each, Green's biggest men—stood in readiness at the front, forty yards' distance. Lee sat on a horse under a tree, near by, and Green walked a little way forward with Stuart: they arranged that, if the men inside refused to give themselves up, Stuart was to jump aside and wave his hat, and the Marines would come at the double.

The engine house was perhaps thirty by thirty-five feet, longer than deep. Large double doors opened from the front of it, with stone abutment between them. The doors were of massive oak construction, iron-bound and studded with metal. Inside, a fire engine habitually stood behind each door, with the hose-cart in the centre, behind the abutment. Stuart approached the door on the right. It opened a little, and a gimlet-eyed old fellow, whom Stuart recognized perfectly as Ossawattomie Brown of Kansas, held a cocked carbine on him and received the note. He read it deliberately. No: he would not surrender, but he had a counter proposition, and he proceeded at length to set it forth. He and his men were to be allowed to come out; to be given a specified start on the pursuit—Stuart jumped away from the door and waved his hat. Green says it was a feathered hat, of a type afterward famous.

The Marines, in dark blue frocks, with sky-blue trousers and white belts, and armed with sledges from the Armory, came on the run, and thundered mightly against the door, without effect. Inside, they fired with carbines through the door, and the powder smoke seeped out around the edges of the timbers. A long, heavy ladder lay on the ground in front of the engine house, and Green cried to his men to take that ladder, and batter with it. They caught it up, ran back, dashed it against the door; ran back, and assaulted the door again. At the second shock the righthand section broke in, low down, and the timbers splintered upward. Green, who stood with Stuart between the doors, dived through the opening, his sword in front of him. Inside, the place was full of smoke. Green thinks that old Brown had just emptied his carbine, and was reloading, and so he passed safely. No other of Brown's party seems to have fired. Green ran to the right of the engine at the door, passed behind it, and came to the centre of the enclosure, by the hose-cart, where Colonel Lewis Washington was standing. Colonel Washington was a man of serene habit. He gave Lieutenant Green a clasp of the hand, for they were acquaintances, and he said, "Hello, Green!" And he added, "This is Ossawattomie—" indicating a kneeling figure, dim in the smoke, a pace to the left. In those quick seconds while Green doubled around the engine, old Brown had been in action: the first two Marines who followed their officer through the hole were down, one shot through the belly, and the other, through the face. Green saw "an old man kneeling with a carbine in his hand, with a long gray beard falling away from his face, looking quickly and keenly toward the danger that he was aware had come upon him"—and he slashed powerfully at that old man's head. He missed the head, for old Brown dodged, but the blade bit deeply into the neck at the base of the skull, and as old Brown, stunned, rolled sideways, Green thrust, and a leather strap on old Brown's chest took the point, and the light dress sword bent almost double. Now the Marines were through the smoke and over the fallen men, and they bayoneted one fellow skulking under the engine, and pinned another against the rear wall, so that they died. And Lieutenant Green ordered them "to spill no more blood."

Presently old Brown lay on the grass, outside, and the men with him were all dead, or prisoners, and the hostages were liberated. Colonel Lewis Washington was a fastidious man, and he had been without toilet facilities in the engine house, and he delayed to draw his kid gloves over his unwashed hands, before he would come to pay his respects to Lieutenant-Colonel Lee. They moved old Brown on a mattress to the jail at Charlestown, and Governor Wise, arriving that day, saw him in prison, and has recorded his admiration of his courage, quite aside from his reaction to old Brown's politics and ambitions. "He was the gamest man I ever saw." And the Governor likened his attitude to a "broken-winged hawk, lying on his back, with a fearless

the Engine House
Harper's Ferry 1859

1st Lieutenant
US Marines
1859

Sergeant US Marines
1859

Old John Brown
1859

eye, and his talons set for further fight, if need be—"
There was no exultation over him, when he was received
from the Federal Forces by Virginia, or at his trial, or at his
hanging. . . .

The next day old Brown, recovered from the shocks of
his wounds, talked freely to the Governor, and to the military officers, and to the newspaper persons who had rushed
more lately to the scene. He came, he said, on a Christian
mission; he was a man of good will. He desired, not to harm
anybody, but to free an oppressed people. He dwelt at
length on the purity of his motives, and on his high inspiration, and said that he was justified in all his acts. Lieutenant
Stuart listened, and he was the only man present who could
identify old Brown as the Ossawattomie Brown of Bleeding
Kansas, for out there he had ridden, with Colonel Sumner's
cavalry, to liberate certain victims of Ossawattomie on the
troubled Kansas marches, and had met him in the section
where mayhems, arsons, and murders, with attendant horse-
theft and nigger-stealing, had marked him in abolition
circles as a rising man. He said now, "But, Captain Brown,
don't you believe the Bible?"

To this old Brown returned no answer. . . . He remarked,
looking at Stuart, "I believe that the Major, here, would
not have been alive but for me. I might have killed him, just
as easy as I could kill a mosquito, when he came in, but I
supposed that he came in only to receive our surrender. . . ."
And he added that he called surrender, as loud as he could,
before the Marines attacked him, and that they killed his
people and wounded him after they had given up. This Lieutenant Green denied in all its details. . . . Colonel Washington left no written evidence. But Green reported, and Stuart
wrote immediately to his mother. All other testimony must
be hearsay.

And old Brown spoke to them again, looking up from his mattress with his hard, pale, killer's eye, to the Governor of Virginia, and the Marine, and the bearded cavalryman, and the militia officers, and the craning reporters: "I claim to be here in carrying out a measure I believe to be perfectly justifiable, and not to act the part of an incendiary or a ruffian—but, on the contrary, to aid those suffering of a great wrong. I wish to say, further, that you had better, all you people of the South, prepare yourselves for a settlement of this question. It must come up for settlement sooner than you are prepared for it, and the sooner you commence that preparation the better for you. You may dispose of me very easily: I am nearly disposed of now; but this question is still to be settled—this negro question, I mean. The end is not yet."

v

So, in material effect, the assault on Virginia by old Brown, old Ossawattomie, old John Brown, Captain Smith, was a moderately bloody failure. He freed no slaves at all. Colonel Washington's negroes, a batch of whom he seized when he took the Colonel, refused to participate in the defence of the engine house. Others fled from him: none rose to join him. He accomplished the death of a few citizens, of a free negro employed by the railroad, and of a United States Marine. He died, himself, at the end of a rope, and his followers suffered with him. The dead were buried, and remembered as the dead are, with appropriate emotions, and the glaziers of the Armory replaced the broken glass in the windows of the government buildings, and artificers repaired the shattered door of the engine house at Harper's Ferry, and Governor Wise told them at Richmond that something drastic would have to be done about the militia: they were too inefficient, and in Colonel John Thomas Gibson's whole regiment there were not more than one hundred serviceable muskets. But the echoes of the affair reverberated monstrously.

Virginia, and the South after her, took the riot, and the ensuing trials at Charlestown, with surprising calm. There was a vast excitement in the North. The Southerners presently learned, with shocked incredulity which turned to anger, that old Brown was rather widely regarded, up there, as a man of consecrated life: in effect, a martyr. From New Hampshire came the voice of a minister of the Gospel, at a meeting for prayer on the day of the hanging at Charlestown: old Brown "died for righteousness' sake!" A New York paper declared, on the exchange desks of Southern editors, "That gallows as glorious as a cross!" The South became very angry indeed. Old Brown, to them, meant servile insurrection, and men remembered Nat Turner in Southampton County. It appeared that these Northern people, furiously vociferous, at the extreme applauded, and at the mean did not condemn, the fomenting of a slave uprising in a peaceful, unoffending sister state. They were out to free the slaves at any cost in blood and tears. And slaves were property, like horses and land cattle, and whether a man owned any or not—most Southerners owned no slaves and never expected to—what Virginia did about it was not the affair of Massachusetts. The South began to regard the ties which bound it to such people as undesirable and actively dangerous. Old Brown, being well dead at Charlestown, became a national issue: who is not with us is against us! The part he played in the elections of 1860 would have gratified him immensely. He worked powerfully in the minds of men, North and South, and he was more effective, dead, than he had ever been in all his stammering and futile life.

IV

LIEUTENANT STUART JOINS THE CONFEDERACY

YOU can conceive that Lieutenant Stuart had fine tales to tell when he went back to duty at Fort Riley, and he told a story well. The officers in those far places had their news from home infrequently, and there was time to examine from every angle, to discuss and digest, each budget of letters and papers before the next one came. Yet it does not appear that political talk had much part in the life of the army posts. A man's politics, if he had any, were those of his section. Rawle's Constitutional Law, the text-book studied by this generation at West Point, enunciated clearly the doctrine of State Sovereignty, and no reasonable person questioned it. When disunion began to be mentioned, increasingly in 1860, the impression prevailed throughout the army and navy that an officer's course of action would properly be guided by the action of his state. In the meantime, the superior man attended to his regimental duties, formulated measures for his own conduct, and carefully refrained from critical utterances against the honest convictions of his brother officers.

During the year 1860, the 1st Cavalry built Fort Wise, near the site of the old Bent's Fort, on the Arkansas River, and First Lieutenant Stuart served there through the winter. His family was not with him, because Wise was not yet a suitable location for the families of officers, even by the Spartan standards of that generation of army wives. Flora Cooke Stuart and the two children lived at Fort Riley in comparative civilization, where Colonel Philip St. George Cooke commanded the 2d Regiment of Dragoons. But Fort Wise was sufficiently in touch with the world to know that something was going on, and the South Carolina officers had already departed, resigning their commissions. Stuart, observing the trend of the times, had made up his own mind. On 11 January, he requested leave, "for the purpose of removing my family to this station"—Fort Wise—such leave to become effective on 1 April, 1861.

During the first two weeks of January, things had happened in the East: South Carolina had seceded in December, and by 11 January, Georgia had seized the Federal Arsenal at Pulaski, Alabama had taken over all the arsenals within her borders, Florida had hoisted her state flag over the posts at Apalachicola and San Augustine. These events were quickly followed by the actual withdrawal, from the Federal Union, of Alabama, Florida, and Mississippi; and other states were preparing to follow. But the news went slowly out to the far frontiers, and on 15 January, Stuart had not yet heard that Mississippi was no longer requiring representation at Washington, for on that date he addressed a letter to: The Hon. Jeffn. Davis, U. S. Senator from Mississippi, Washington, D. C. He wrote:

"SIR: In view of the impending condition of affairs in our country, no sane man can fail to calculate on a rupture of our national bonds as a thing strongly probable. In view, therefore, of the consequent dismemberment of the Army, and of your prominence as one likely to exercise a large control in the organization of the Army of the South, I beg leave respectfully to ask you to secure for me a position in that army. I have the honor to refer you to Gen. J. E. Johnston, Cols. Cooke, Lee, and Emory, and the Captains of my

Regiment, for whatever of merit I may possess. Please file this application.

"With sentiments of high regard, your obedient servant,

"J. E. B. STUART, 1st Lt., 1st Cav."

Jefferson Davis, it will be remembered, had been Secretary of War in the Buchanan cabinet, when the 1st and 2d Cavalry regiments were formed; Colonel Cooke was Stuart's father-in-law; General J. E. Johnston was the first Lieutenant-Colonel of Stuart's regiment; Colonel Lee had been his commandant at West Point, and Emory was his Major, later his Lieutenant-Colonel, in the 1st Cavalry. On 15 January, Virginia was still in the Union; but Stuart did not believe that she would stay there. Further, he had been in the military service for eleven years, and he had no other profession. Consider these things if the letter seems to be launched before the event.

Three days later, on the 18th, he wrote a long letter, full of personal items, to his brother, William Alexander Stuart in Virginia. Of larger matters, he said: "Events are transpiring rapidly that furnish us so little hope of perpetuating the Union, that I feel it incumbent upon me to tell you my course of conduct in such a contingency. Of course I go with Virginia, whether she be alone or otherwise, but I am sure that a large military force will be required for a time by the State, and I am anxious to secure from Wythe (county) a legion of cavalry—200 men—myself as commander, or a battery of light artillery, 100 men or less. With Gov. Letcher as Governor, and you on the spot, I ought to be able to get such a command. . . ."

He mentioned the resignation of Floyd, Secretary of War, and his friend, and he was inclined to think that Floyd, before he left office, might have seen to it that the experienced first lieutenant of the 1st Cavalry regiment receive one of lately vacated captaincies. And he went on to tell his brother of the Christmas observances in the Fort Wise garrison: "I made a temperance speech here Christmas, which gained me great *éclat* among the officers and soldiers— there are ¼ of the command Sons of Temperance; they had a grand procession and ovation. I had only a few days' notice, and spoke 20 minutes. . . ."

It appears that Stuart not only practised abstinence from alcohol, but preached it.

Meantime, his request for leave of absence went down to Department Headquarters at St. Louis, and was approved on 12 February. Back east, Louisiana and Texas had seceded, U. S. S. *Star of the West*, with reinforcements and supplies for Major Robert Anderson's Coast Artillerymen in Charleston harbor, was fired on, off the bar, by South Carolina State troops, and the Virginia Legislature had issued a call for a peace conference to meet in Washington. On 4 February, seven seceded states, in convention, assembled, at Montgomery, Alabama, adopted a provisional constitution; elected Mr. Jefferson Davis provisional president, and announced to the world the existence of the Confederate States of America. On 4 March Stuart wrote again to his brother: he was taking two months leave of absence: he would go to Fort Riley and join his family, and there, "quietly and calmly await the march of events." His leave became effective, and he went down to Riley. Again, he wrote his brother: "The moment she (Va.) passes the ordinance of secession, I will set out immediately for Richmond, and report in person to Governor Letcher, unless I am certain that my service would be more needed at some other point in the State—(here he wrote 'South,' scratched it out, and substituted 'State'). . . . If no war ensues upon Virginia's secession, I will quit the army, and if I can obtain no desirable position in her (Virginia's) regu-

lar army, I will resign and practise law in Memphis, Tenn.
... I am a captain, now, by the vacancies which have already
occurred in the Army, but I had rather be a private in Va.'s
army than a general in any army to coerce her. . . . Col.
Cooke will, I think, become a Missourian in the event of dis-
ruption, as he is perhaps more identified with that State
than any other. . . ."

In April, Stuart was at Riley, and on the 18th he wrote
from Leavenworth to Headquarters, Department of the
West, at St. Louis, requesting that his mail be held there for
him "until his return." On the back of this letter, there is
a departmental note: "Lt. Stuart passed through St. Louis
3 May." Among the letters held for him was one from the
War Department, dated 25 April, advising James E. B.
Stuart, Headquarters, Department of the West, that he was
promoted to the rank of Captain, First Regiment of Cavalry,
to take effect 22 April, 1861, vice-Captain George H.
Stewart, Resigned. (George H. Stewart was a Marylander,
West Point, a grade senior to him in the regiment.) But
there is no record of his acceptance of this commission, no
commission was issued to him, nor did his name go to the
Senate for confirmation.

There are two letters of his, dated 3 May, in Cairo,
Illinois, where he went from St. Louis with his family. One
is to Colonel L. Thomas, then Adjutant-General of the
United States Army. It is:

"COLONEL: From a sense of duty to my native state (Va.),
I hereby resign my position as an officer in the Army of the
United States.

"Most respectfully,
"Sir,
"Your obt. servt.,
"J. E. B. STUART."

The records show that his resignation was accepted 14 May, and announced to the Service by Special Orders 134, War Department, Adjutant-General's Office, Washington, on 16 May. These orders refer to him as Captain J. E. B. Stuart, First Regiment of Cavalry.

The second letter was to General Samuel Cooper, Adjutant-General of the Army of the Confederate States of America. General Cooper was a native of New Jersey, and a warm friend of Jefferson Davis, and he had been for some years Adjutant-General of the United States Army. He resigned early in 1861, and was immediately appointed to the same office in the new Confederacy. The letter follows:

"GENERAL: Having resigned my position (Capt. 1st Cavalry) in the U. S. Army, and being now on my way to unite my destinies to Virginia, my native State, I write to apprize you of the fact in order that you may assign me such a position in the Army of the South as will accord with that lately held by me in the Federal Army. My preference is Cavalry—Light Artillery—Light Infantry in the order named, but I would prefer a position as Assist. Adjt. Gen. or Topographical Engineer if such a position would give me greater rank. My address will be: Care Gov. Letcher, Richmond. . . ."

Four days later, with his wife and family, he was in Richmond. Governor Letcher had ready for him a commission as Major of Infantry in the State Forces of Virginia.

In the February just passed, he had reached his twenty-eighth birthday, and he had worn the uniform since he was seventeen, with no ambitions outside of the profession of arms. His service reputation was already that of a valuable and accomplished officer, and if he had elected to hold with the Union, his future was assured. He had a family, and he was dependent on his pay.

Travelling down the Missouri to St. Louis, the Stuarts found the city in an uproar, with Union sentiment distinctly on top. The Federal Government was accepting the resignations of Southern officers and allowing them to proceed at will, but in St. Louis and elsewhere through the border states unpleasant and effective restraints were being laid upon secessionists. Lieutenant Alexander, returning from San Francisco to Georgia, by way of steamer to New York, was obliged to take the cars to Kentucky, and cross that frontier. Cadet John Pelham, West Point, 1861, started for Alabama by the western route, and was obliged, in New Albany, Indiana, to give out that he was a courier of General Scott's: that relieved him of immediate arrest, but did not get him out of danger, and a pretty Union girl, who melted at his blond elegance, rowed him across the river from Jeffersonville to Kentucky under pretense of a boat ride. Otherwise, he thinks he would have been confined. Stuart spent several anxious days in St. Louis before he could get off, by boat and stage and rail, to the East. He had investments in St. Louis amounting to $6,000, no small sum in that day, which he was forced to leave behind. It was a trouble to him, for there was always a certain Scotch thrift in his anxiety for the support of those dependent on him.

The Cooke family was broken up. Two of the girls went south, one north. John R. Cooke went with his brother-in-law. He fought through all the great Virginia battles, and took five heavy wounds, and lived after Appomattox to raise a family in Richmond; and he would, at the end of twenty years, become reconciled to his father in a meeting at the Willard Hotel in Washington. But Colonel Philip St. George Cooke, although he was born a Virginian, did not become a Missourian. He held with his Dragoons, and was very soon a Brigadier-General of United States Cavalry. A little more than a year later Stuart's horsemen were snatching at his father-in-law's outposts, behind Fitz-John Porter's flanks, on the Peninsula.

Commissioned Major of Infantry by Governor Letcher on 6 May, 1861, Stuart was ordered to Winchester, where General Joseph E. Johnston was whipping into shape the Confederate Army of the Shenandoah.

V

THE MUSTERING OF THE SABRES—SOMETHING ABOUT THE SOUTHERN ARMIES AND THE SOUTHERN SOLDIERS

THROUGH all the South a bugle blew, and in that spring of 1861, 650,000 men offered themselves to the recruiting officers in the seceded states. This, out of a population of 11,000,000, 4,000,000 of whom were slaves, indicates a very general approval of the war. The difficulty lay in the attitude of the Confederate Government, and in the attitude of the state governments. The Richmond authorities did not believe that so many men would be needed, and had no intention, then or afterward, of waging offensive war, nor did they ever subscribe to the view expressed forcibly by * Jackson and by other distinguished soldiers; that the best defensive was one pursued in the territory of the enemy. * And the governments of the states were disinclined to submit to centralization, especially in the matter of pooling the military material then existing in the South.

Contrary to the general impression, there was a great deal of this military material in the seceded states. There were, in the Federal arsenals and depots seized by the several states on the act of secession, a total of 190,000 small arms and 8,000 cannon. In the state arsenals, under the control of the governors, there were 350,000 stand of rifles and muskets. These pieces were not all modern: they ranged from flint-lock muskets, of Mexican war stocks, to the latest model of percussion-cap rifle. A great many of them were rifled muskets, modified recently from flint-lock to percussion-cap. Among them were some cavalry carbines, and some of the old artillery carbines, ante-dating the war with Mexico, described as being about as useful as crossbows. But they were at least weapons, and could have been used as effectively as the shotguns and sporting pieces, with which whole regiments of the first volunteers were armed. A year later, Confederate regiments were still going into battle armed with shotguns, while excellent rifles reposed in state armories.

It was the announced policy, theory, and law, that all former Federal property was to be turned over to the Confederate Government; but this was done by the states in a very limited number of instances. The governors held such stocks for the state troops, or, if pressed, turned in an equal number of out-moded militia weapons, retaining the modern ordinance for the state guards. It followed that, out of 650,000 volunteers who came forward in 1861, only 400,000 were accepted, the others being told to go home and wait until they were sent for. Later, they were not so willing to come.

There did exist a very real shortage in the matter of equipments: most of the cannon were old smooth bores, without carriages, caissons, or harness; and the infantry stocks on hand did not include the leather belts, cartridge boxes, knapsacks, canteens, or haversacks. Also, there was very little powder, very few sabres or revolvers, and, except the Federal armory at Harper's Ferry, no plant in the entire South where arms could immediately be manufactured or repaired. The foreign importations, contracted for by the Confederate Government before the ports were closed by blockade, were absurdly small and inadequate. But in the matter of ordnance, the Confederacy was better served than in any other department. Under General Gorgas authentic miracles were accomplished. Colonel Rains of the Ordnance was presently making for the Southern armies the best powder in the world. Leather was scarce, but belts, harness, and military equipments were devised from heavy cotton cloth. The Tredegar works in Richmond began to turn out cannon. Strong, serviceable rolling stock was manufactured. The Southern people applied their talents to the machinery of war with an infinite ingenuity and resource. The Ordnance Department was able, after it got under way, to meet admirably the calls upon it; and the shortages of armies in the field, which always existed, were due to faulty distribution and to an inadequate system of supply: the stuff was there for them.

The actual basis of the Confederate armies was the old militia structure. The state militia were organized into companies: so many companies, drawn loosely from the same region, were called a regiment. They were about as effective as militia usually is: remember Governor Wise's scathing comments on the militia regiments that went to Harper's Ferry in 1859.

Nothing had been allowed to trammel the militiaman's individuality. Reading the records of the early musters, you find Fencibles, Highlanders, Ancient and Honorable Artillery Companies, Rifles of various gallant names, Raccoon Roughs, Hornets, Wildcats, Tigers, Light Infantry, Heavy Infantry of the Line, Zouaves, Sharpshooters, Grenadiers, and Tirailleurs, surrendering with reluctance their identities to become lettered companies in numbered volunteer regiments. The mounted organizations were Hussars, Lancers, Dragoons, Mounted Chasseurs, or Light Horse—the name Cavalry hardly occurs. Uniforms were just as various. The footmen were turned out as local fancy and tradition dictated: you see, in the old photographs, white cross-belts, plastrons, leather shakos, *kepis*, zouave jackets and trousers, gaiters, coatees, coonskin hats, and hunting shirts; while the gentlemen on horseback rejoiced in jackboots, hussar boots, frogged jackets, braided jackets, and elegant coats with choker collars and silken facings. Colors were as diversified as patterns. There were dark blues, sky-blues, rifle-greens, cadet grays, and the gay zouave plumage. An Alabama regiment marched to First Manassas all in red; a Virginia Artillery company was there in black broadcloth trousers and Garibaldi shirts. Most elegant of all were the mounted companies, gentlemen of substance, who, in the years before the war, had uniforms and sabres from Horstmann, pistols from Colt's, and carbines from Belgium. Troopers paraded with shabrak, sabre-tasche, and dolman, like Austrian Hussars. It is noted that the saddle furniture alone, of such an 1861 soldier, would have paid the entire cost of one of Stuart's cavalrymen, horse and all, in 1864. These were holiday braves, who played at bearing arms in the spacious days of the South. And, as the Southern foot regiments of militia became, under the hammer blows of war, incomparable infantry (that phrasing is from a Yankee historian—not from me), so the genteel associations of riders developed into fine and useful cavalry.

The Confederate Government never found itself able to furnish mounts for its cavalry regiments: providing horses for the artillery taxed to the utmost its resources. Consequently, in the beginning, the cavalry was limited to those people who could bring their own horses into the service with them. In those days the entire South was a horse country; the roads were few and bad—other than country tracks—and men went mounted everywhere. The horse was the preoccupation of whole sections, and in every state there were splendid animals, evolved by use and breeding to meet the exactions of the climate and the country. Parts of Virginia, Kentucky, and of the Carolinas had been, from the days of the earliest settlements, noted for excellent horseflesh. The names of famous sires, Sir Archy, Boston, Eclipse, Timoleon, Diomede, Exchequer, Red Eye, persist unto this day. It followed that the mounted arms, the cavalry and the field artillery, were considered *corps d'élite*, and enjoyed the highest patronage among the spirited youngsters who came forward to serve. Most Southerners owned horses of some kind, either good or indifferent, and nobody wanted to walk, even to a battle.

With these men the Confederate Government, reluctant to be burdened, in those innocent first days, by any large amount of cavalry, made a contract. You enlisted, with your personal mount, usually your own property, bred and trained for your riding. The Government took over your horse, credited him to you at a fair valuation on the lists of public property, and contracted to furnish forage, shoes, and the services of a smith, and to pay you for the use of him at the rate of forty cents per day. If the horse were killed in action, the Government reimbursed you, in cash, the assessed value of the animal, and it was cavalry usage to furlough a man, so dismounted, long enough for him to go home and get another horse. If, however, the horse was captured, worn out or broken down in service, or fallen sick, it was the owner's loss. The Government would neither issue a remount to him, nor pay him for the incapacitated animal.

No other plan for remounts was ever devised by the Confederacy. It was applied from the beginning of the war, and although its results were increasingly unsatisfactory, and under it the constant trend of the cavalry strength was downward, it was continued to the end. The Confederate cavalrymen, officers and troopers, were better horsemasters than the Federals, and got far more use out of their animals, and the horseflesh, also, was superior. The most sincere evidence of the excellence of the Southern horses is, indeed, from the Federal Cavalry Generals, Pleasanton, Gregg, Kilpatrick, and Stoneman.

There accumulated behind each cavalry command a growing number of dismounted men, "Company Q" of deplorable mention. Company Q contained many excellent soldiers, unhorsed through no deficiency on their part, but by the chance of war, and victims of a vicious system. And there were also the invariable fringe of riffraff, malingerers, and inefficients, who found Company Q preferable to the uncertainties of straight cavalry duty. A Virginia cavalryman stood some chance of taking furlough to his home, and returning, remounted, in the course of the same campaign. But for a South Carolinian, a Georgian, a Mississippian, to travel to his native pastures, find a horse and bring him back, was a serious matter. As the war went on, as supply failed on the front, and as the original material wore down, horses grew very hard to procure, and honest men had of necessity to absent themselves for longer periods, while the by-paths out of the service were made easier for the rascals. The consequence was over-padded muster rolls and under-manned regiments in the cavalry. At the time of the Kelly's Ford fight, in March, 1863, Fitz Lee's brigade, guarding Lee's up-river flank around Culpeper, had 2,100 men on its rolls. But when Averell crossed and attacked him, General Fitz could only mount 800 sabres. The others were lying in Company Q, or on furlough, trying to remount themselves.

A worthless man stayed in Company Q as long as he could, and a good man ate his heart out—there is nothing so sad as a cavalryman without a horse. And when, all efforts to procure a remount having failed, an honest trooper was transferred to artillery or infantry, he went with a broken spirit.

As the war developed, the mounted arm was greatly expanded, and by the autumn of 1863 Jeb Stuart's original cavalry command had grown, from the single regiment he led at First Manassas, to a corps of two divisions and six batteries. But the muster roll strength of a Confederate regiment became less and less the figure of its effectiveness in the field, and the wastage, under hard service conditions, unreplaced, reduced the cavalry efficiency more than battles did.

The Federal cavalry had remount difficulties, but their trouble lay in the quality of horses supplied rather than the quantity, and in the fact that the Northern troopers had to learn, in the field, how to care for their animals. Mounts were provided on the most lavish scale. Reading the reports of Quartermaster-General Meigs, you wonder what, under heaven, the army did with them; it is improbable that they ate them, but their horses could not have lasted much longer at the front than did beef cattle. And the combination of bad horsemanship and inferior stock was not equal to the fierce exactions of duty in front of Jeb Stuart and his light-heeled riders. By dint of hard and merciless instruction at his hands, swingingly administered, from the James up to the Susquehanna, and from the Chesapeake to the Blue Ridge, the blue coats learned at last to shoot and ride. By that time, Stuart's material was running down, and theirs was mounting, and they had their best man to lead them: Sheridan. But while Stuart lived, the gray cavalry, man for man and horse for horse, was more effective than anything ever thrown against them.

The gray cavalry was drawn from all classes of Southern society. They had one thing in common: the love and the knowledge of horses. And physically they were very fit: they had to be.

From Farquier County came the Black Horse Troop, Captain William Payne. "Black Horse Troop" was a name promptly seized and played upon by the press on both sides of the Potomac, destined to endure terribly through the war. The Black Horse, in 1861, was mustered into the Confederate service as a company in the 4th Virginia Cavalry. The record also runs of a company raised in Abington, called the Washington Mounted Rifles, and commanded by Captain

W. E. Jones, of whom there will be more hereafter. This Jones was a West Point graduate, about whom stories cluster. He was eccentric and irrascible and profane, and of great ability. There is some legend about the death of his young wife, soon after he married; he resigned from the army and lived the life of a hermit in the Virginia mountains, morose and peculiar, until the war broke. Then he emerged from his retirement and offered his sword, but it was his conceit that patriot soldiers, fighting for the sacred principles of liberty, should be above the gauds and vanities of military pomp. Consistent, he appeared in blue jeans, and a hickory shirt, and sewed shoulder straps on an old homespun coat. For his company, who came in with their horses only, and personal weapons, and no uniforms, he procured clothing from the state penitentiary, made cheap and coarse, for convicts. His spirited young men would on no account receive such garments, and piled them in a heap in front of his tent, with scorn—except two privates, one of whom was a young Abington lawyer named John Singleton Mosby, a small, sandy man, very quiet. He and his comrade donned the stuff and wore it. A year later, comments Mosby, such of the company as then survived would have been very glad to have those suits, or any others. This company was the nucleus of the 7th Virginia Cavalry, which Jones commanded with distinction until he rose to Brigadier.

His nickname in the old army had been Grumble Jones, and it followed him in the Southern service. He could not get along with anybody, could not get along with himself. Stuart, who knew him, and appreciated his capability, put up with him for a long time, in spite of continued personal friction, and Jones reciprocated Stuart's feelings with interest. A final breach, in late 1863, made it impossible for them to serve together any longer, and Jones went off to southwest Virginia, to independent command, where, in the fall of 1864, he was killed in battle. His remark, on hearing of Stuart's death, is recorded: "By God, you know I had little love for Stuart, and he had just as little for me, but that is the greatest loss the army has ever sustained except the death of Jackson!"

The story also tells of a body of countrymen who marched into Harper's Ferry in the spring of '61, with neither arms nor equipment. This lack was pointed out by one who met them. Oh, yes, they said. We ain't got no guns. But we can throw rocks like the devil. And at the other end of the scale, were such organizations as the Goochland Troop, rich young planters and sportsmen, to every man his body servant and spare mount, not ten horses in the hundred less than three-quarters thoroughbred. Formed in line, they represented enough cash to equip a regiment of regulars. And they became, too, a lettered company in a Virginia regiment.

Arms and equipment presented a great difficulty to the Richmond Government. The state governments, generally, sent organizations to the Provisional Army of the Confederacy without arming them: let Jeff Davis see to that! An early inspection report of Stuart's regiment notes that the troopers have a few swords, a few small pistols, and otherwise, shotguns and sporting pieces, mostly without ammunition. There was a Colonel Angus MacDonald, in the Virginia mountains, who raised a regiment of mounted men and requisitioned on Richmond for a chaplain—the souls of the men being of the first importance—and for hatchets, about two and one-half pounds in the head, which were, he thought, superior to sabres for combat. At first there was nowhere any uniformity, except that shotguns, firing buck and ball— one round lead bullet and three buckshot—were the most common; and very many of the swords were heirlooms which had done duty in the Mexican War, and the War of the Revolution. The majority of the men used the round tree

English saddle. Later, the Confederate depots turned out a saddle which was easy on the horse but very hard on the rider; and eventually the Confederate cavalry was pretty well equipped with United States regulation saddles, provided by the enemy. Firearms were a harder problem. Colt's revolvers were plentiful in time, from the same unfailing source. Rifled muskets were issued to the cavalry regiments as they became available, and very early Stuart was managing to arm at least one squadron in each regiment with weapons of precision. Carbines were always hard to get, and by the time that they could be generally distributed, the Federals were using breech-loading carbines to great advantage. The indefatigable Gorgas reconditioned, and even manufactured, some supply of these—and by that time the blue troopers were carrying a repeating carbine—a terrible gun, said the gray people, mournfully, which a Yank could load on Monday and shoot all the rest of the week. From time to time large captures of Federal breechloaders were made in Virginia, but the Confederates were never able to manufacture ammunition for them, having no brass for cartridges.

Through the entire war the Confederate ordnance equipment was inferior to that of their enemy. Their cavalry advantages may be briefly summarized: they were a nation of horsemen, accustomed to living and caring for themselves in the open. They operated in their own country. They had, to begin with, better horseflesh. And they had better leaders. Finally, the mounted arm was better understood, and more usefully applied, in the Army of Northern Virginia than in the Army of the Potomac. Immediately after the Seven Days' Battle, in 1862, the cavalry of the army was put under one officer, and functioned thereafter, through all its expansions, as an independent corps. Stuart was an active commander, handling his own organization as a distinct unit of the main army, and able, therefore, to employ the cavalry in such a way that its full strength was felt where he wanted it. The Northern generals, with more sabres at their disposal, invariably dispersed the strength on various scattered missions. Even after a cavalry corps was formed the corps commander was more of a staff officer than a combat officer. Not until Sheridan came East with Grant was their superiority in numbers and material exploited to its full possibilities.

The Confederate Military Law, passed in 1862, gave the Provisional Army its final form. It provided for universal service—a full year ahead of the North—but the Conscription Act had so many exemption clauses, and was so tactlessly applied, and so repellent to the governors of the several states, that it never functioned adequately. The prosecution of the war depended at all times on the will of the people to fight. It perpetuated the evil elective system for commissioned officers in the regimental grades. It was an ideal law for an army, as the President submitted it to his Congress; but when the Confederate Conscript Fathers had trimmed it to meet their joyous ideas of a Military Bill, it was just a little better than no law at all. It had, however, one magnificent virtue: it provided for the maintenance, by a flow of replacements rather than by new formations, of the existing Confederate regiments of 1862. Thus, a gray organization always had in it a saving leaven of veterans. The Southern generals did not have to dry-nurse, after every campaign—or in the heat of a campaign—a mob of raw civilians, all inexperienced, from the colonel down to the drummer-boys.

Virginia raised forty regiments of cavalry, first and last, and the Virginia regiments were the backbone of the mounted arm in Lee's army. There were, also, some very fine formations from farther south: The Jeff. Davis Legion of Mississippi, the Cobb Legion of Georgia, the North Carolina regiments raised and commanded by Beverly Robertson, and the South Carolina troopers brought north by Wade Hampton. The enlisted personnel was superlatively good, representing the best fighting blood in the country. And the senior officers attracted to the cavalry service were worthy of the men they handled. Stuart, Fitz Lee, Rosser, J. Lucius Davis, Robertson, and Jones, were West Pointers. But some of the most able and daring were men from civil life: Hampton, Rooney Lee, Young, Chambliss, Flournoy, Munford, Butler, and Wickham. Pelham and Beckham of the Horse Artillery were West Pointers; Chew was V. M. I. Staff, and the company officers, generally, were from the ranks.

The matter of junior officer personnel was always a weak point in the Southern armies.

In the first years of the war there was a pervading feeling, among the best educated and most intelligent youngsters, the university boys, and the young professional men, that it was undemocratic, unsocial, even to try for commissions. A gentleman shrank from giving orders to another gentleman. He preferred to remain in the ranks, avoid responsibility, and share the rude gusts of war on equal footing with his fellows. No attempt was made in that war to select out the men who, by birth and training were fitted to be leaders. It follows that much of the finest material was thrown away. Some very able men emerged—John B. Gordon in the East, and Forrest in the West, are examples—and by 1863 the armies were veteran, and appointments were generally better. But many potential Pelhams and Stuarts died humbly, serving a gun, or carrying a musket.

Nor was there ever anything like the present-day schools of the staff and line. Perhàps they were too busy fighting to study the matter.

Up to and including regimental commanders, officers were

elected by vote of the enlisted men, who naturally inclined toward the most genial—seldom toward the most able— gentlemen. Once a regiment had its complement of officers, promotions to fill vacancies was by seniority, the lowest grade, when vacated, being supplied by further election. Worst of all, the noncommissioned officers were elected: an outfit can stagger along with poor officers, but poor noncoms are fatal. Commissions of general officers were issued by the President, the Provisional Army of the Confederacy accepting from the States no officers above the rank of colonel. This was the system, and a wretched one, in the first year of the war. A military bill was passed and made a law, in the winter of 1861-2, which modified a little this feature of the establishment. On a given date, a final election was to be held, up to and including the grade of colonel; after that, promotion was to be by seniority in all grades, and, under certain special cases, by appointment. All general officers were selected, and passed upon by Congress. Grotesquely, this election was held while the army of General Joe Johnston was in the Yorktown trenches. Men came back from the skirmish line to cast their ballots—to determine whether the officer who had put them in action that morning should continue in command over them. In many cases, command passed——

Where meritorious officers failed of reelection, a brigadier could provide for them on his staff. Thus, at Yorktown, in the Cavalry Brigade, Major Patrick and Captain Blackford, both able men, were not chosen, and Stuart retained them as aides. Grumble Jones was thrown out by his regiment in favor of Fitz Lee, but as Jones was a West Pointer, the President took care of him. As the war progressed, capable men trended to come forward and to hold their jobs. By 1863, Stuart's colonels were all good, and their regiments were so small that their personal influence could be felt in action. But the company officers remained, in every branch of the service, the point of weakness, and to their inefficiency is largely attributed the poor interior discipline, the straggling, and the laxity of camp and guard duty which detracted from the Confederate strength. The most effective counter to the election situation, that I have found, was Mosby's. He came to command, under the President's commission, a body of partisan rangers, irregular horse, who operated mostly in the enemy's rear, and attracted restless spirits, brave enough, but unwilling to submit themselves to the discipline of the regular service. At election time, Mosby submitted to the rangers a list of officers he wanted chosen. Balloting, he directed, would be public, and every man who did not vote for his candidates would be immediately transferred to the cavalry of the army. Whereat, all hands voted loudly for the straight ticket.

The tactics of the Confederate Cavalry in the East were set forth in the *Trooper's Manual*, adapted by Colonel J. Lucius Davis from the *Poinsett Tactics*, used in the United States Mounted Arm from 1841 to 1861. A regiment consisted of five squadrons, a squadron of two troops or companies. A company consisted of 80 men and three officers, a captain and two lieutenants. The senior company commander led each squadron. There was a colonel, a lieutenant-colonel, and a major to each regiment. According to law, in 1861, 78 men was the minimum for a company: thus, a regiment would be about 800 strong. But this was paper strength. I have not found a gray cavalry regiment that had more than 650 effectives. The regiments of 1862 would average about 500; in 1863, from 350 to 500, and after that, never above 350. Some ran as low as 100 troopers by the end of a campaign. Two or more regiments made a brigade, unusually four or five. Horse Artillery batteries, of from three- to six guns—usually four—were handled as brigade units.

Tactics provided for squadrons formed in double or single rank, double for ceremonies, single for the field. In routine combat formation, the regiment was formed with two squadrons in line, say—if it was a large regiment, 200 men abreast. At squadron distance—150 to 200 paces in the rear, were two squadrons in line of companies in column of fours or twos. Behind the flanks of this line was the 5th squadron, in line of companies, also in column of fours or twos, according to the nature of the terrain. Stuart managed to provide at least two squadrons in a regiment with rifles or carbines, and these were held in readiness to act upon the flanks or to cover the front dismounted, when a fire fight was indicated. He fought dismounted when he had to— notably and stubbornly in rear guard actions, or when he had to fight for ground. But all his feeling was for the white weapon, and his favorite formation was a brigade in column of squadrons. That was, regiments formed on squadron front, with successive squadrons following at close distance— twelve paces or so. A yelling, furious block of men, standing in their stirrups, with the bright glitter of steel above them, and the horses at a pounding gallop, two hundred yards across the front and half a mile deep. Such a charge was Hampton's, when he swept Gregg away from Fleetwood Heights, and so Wade Hampton and Fitz Lee led down, at Gettysburg. Where the ground was cut up by fences or ditches, cavalry might have to come on in column of fours, or dismounted files might have to hold the front, while the mounted columns felt around the flanks for an opening. And, mounted or dismounted, Stuart always provided a storm of horse artillery to soften the enemy before the charge hit him.

Federal tactics and formations were similar: Poinsett's,

adapted in 1861 by Stuart's versatile father-in-law, Colonel Cooke. But the blue people had a preference for dismounted actions—dragoon fighting—and you conclude that they distrusted themselves on horseback. And dragoon tactics were better suited to the broken terrain of Virginia than mounted tactics.

You can read, if you care to, the regulations and principles laid down for the Southern trooper in the solemn pages of J. Lucius Davis. He opens with the statement that volunteers are expert horsemen, but reluctant to master the minutiæ of training, so he submits only the essentials. Much space is devoted to what the cavalryman will wear: a conical forage cap with a waterproof cover extending to the shoulders when unrolled, a waterproof cape extending from neck to hips, a close-bodied coat or round jacket, overcoat, pants, short top boots. "Fancy hats," he says—perhaps with an eye on a certain young colonel, who had been a cadet when he, Davis, was a captain—"and plumes of ostrich and other feathers are only suitable on parades and reviews, but on compaign, they are a useless encumbrance."

Very soon the bright plumage disappeared in the ruck of war and weather, and the Confederate Government was never able adequately to clothe its soldiers. Most of the mills for uniforms and shoes were in the states of North Carolina and Georgia, and the Richmond authorities were never able to control them. The state governors insisted on their rights, and profiteered shamelessly in the sale of uniforms and boots. North Carolina troops were usually well found, but the soldiers of states which had no mills were not. Stuart's troopers were wearing, by 1862, anything they could get. Even Federal uniforms, looted from Yankee stores; their officers had to choose between that practice and nakedness. Many a rebel trooper was shot by his own friends, because he rode up in Yankee blue. But the arms were bright, and the formations were smart and soldierly in motion. Jeb Stuart could at least see to that.

I have tried to sketch in, now, something of the material with which young Major James Stuart had to work, when he went up from Richmond to report to his old friend General Joe Johnston at Winchester in the spring of 1861.

It is related by Major McClellan, Stuart's biographer, that Stuart accepted his cavalry detail with reluctance. He was properly ambitious, and it did not seem to him that cavalry offered much in the way of opportunity and advancement. In the American Revolution, cavalry had been used with force and effect: Colonel Tarleton and Richard Henry Lee had done notable things with their light regiments. But in the years between, cavalry had languished. General Scott, who had shaped all the thought and policy in the army for a generation, did not rate cavalry important in the field of large operations. Although there had been some use of it in Mexico, no important cavalry reputations had emerged from the fighting south of the Rio Grande. Since the Mexican War, the mounted regiments had been dispersed along the frontier in small detachments, a troop here and a troop there, and seldom a concentration so large as a squadron. A single regiment might be scattered from the Republican in Kansas Territory to the Pecos in Texas, and a colonel would command for years, and never see his organization completely assembled. Nor was there, in the opening months of the Civil War, any assurance that the rôle of the cavalry would assume importance. Major McClellan relates further, that Stuart told him of a conference, held by General Johnston and his officers, in the late spring of 1861. The matter in hand was the organization and training of the volunteer masses which were coming forward; and it was necessary to find somebody who would take charge of

the horsemen. Nobody wanted the job. The road to glory
was considered to lie with the infantry, or with the artillery:
not with the mercurial units of mounted men. But somebody
had to take charge of them, because they insisted on fighting,
if at all on horseback. And Stuart, as reluctant as the others,
felt that it was a time for personal sacrifice: that an officer
owed something, after all, to the public welfare, and that,
while he might forego immediate promotion and enlarged
reputation by such a course, he would still be serving his
country. Furthermore, he was fresh from a cavalry command, and thought himself perhaps better fitted for such
duty than were the older officers.

He looked the recruits over and chuckled, and somebody
heard him say—regarding the untidy camps, the squabbling,
grinning black body servants, the beautiful, high-bred
horses, and the beautiful, high-bred young men, in fine linen
and high stocks, going to call on the girls after drill—
"They're pretty good officers now. They'll be pretty good
soldiers after a while. All they need is reducing to the
ranks." And he set about reducing them.

Under his hand, inspection reports show, the 1st Virginia
Cavalry regiment took shape: Colonel Deas, in June, 1861,
finds their arms clean and serviceable, although various, their
drill excellent, and their discipline admirable. Besides his
regiment, there existed, with Johnston's Army of the Shenandoah, an irregular force called the Ashby Rangers—a
number of independent companies, without regimental organization. The inspectors from Richmond do not seem to
have known what to do with them. Their Colonel was Turner
Ashby, of a conspicuous Valley family, a notable rider and
sportsman. He had no military training, but he revealed
an aptitude for war. Old memoirs indicate that he was
much disturbed at the idea of formal service under Colonel
Stuart, having, like most young Southerners, a passionate

distaste for discipline. He won wide applause, about this time, by a daring adventure into the Yankee lines north of the Potomac: he assumed citizen's clothes, and the character of a horse doctor, and took a wagon load of approved remedies, and drove though the camps of General Patterson, up the Cumberland Valley, and around to Frederick, treating U. S. horses for ring bone and spavin, and taking minute data on strengths and dispositions. So recommended, he put his case before Jackson, the immediate superior in command, and was granted latitude to retain his Ranger companies. To Ashby belongs the distinction of employing the first battery of Horse Artillery in the war: it was young Chew's, authorized in September, 1861. The second was Pelham's battery, formed by Stuart in November.

Ashby was killed in May, 1862, a general officer, very famous, having served Jackson well in the Valley Campaign of that year. At that time his command consisted of more than twenty independent companies, some 2,000 men, of whom less than 400 were ever assembled together. After his death, they were regimented, and served in the brigade of old Grumble Jones.

You can picture the 1st Regiment of Virginia Cavalry on a June morning, in the soft Valley sunlight, drawn up in a green field below Winchester, with the Blue Ridge ramparted in the background. There are perhaps five hundred men, divided into companies of fifty or so, each company paying casual allegiance to such captains and lieutenants as they had chosen from among themselves. The field officers are exalted fellows, commissioned by the Jeff Davis Government, suspected of snobbery; but just now the matter in hand is regimental drill, and the majors are silent, the regiment being formed in line. Every trooper is watching the broad, erect soldier on the big bay hunter, who sits easy in his saddle, front and centre, and gives each man the impres-

Colonel 1st Virginia Cavalry
1861

sion that he, personally, is being examined in detail, from cap to boots.

The Colonel has a dancing eye: they like that. There is more than a touch of the dandy about him, and they approve that, too. Gauntlets of snow-white buckskin hide half the golden *galons* on his sleeves, and his buttons—Gentlemen, hush! the Colonel's nigger must have a time with his buttons! He runs his eye along the line, and strokes his beard—a fine, flaring beard, dark, with bronze lights in the sun. . . . In the first squadron, a gentleman-at-arms thinks of something he wants to mention to his captain, and he spurs his mare out of ranks, to dispose the thing before it leaves his mind. At once there is a blast, in a bronze, ringing voice, that blows him back, crimson-faced, into ranks, amazed and furious. Never in his life has he been so spoken to! He sits and quivers, conscious of sympathetic glances from the adjacent files. No way to talk to a gentleman, by God! By God, these West Pointers!

Now the West Pointer is talking, simply and reasonably, of the School of the Cavalryman; the position of the soldier— First: Stand to Horse. The tall fellow—now that he is dismounted, you notice how long-legged he looks, in his short cavalry jacket—is on the ground: so: heels together: left hand hanging naturally at the side, body erect without stiffness: right hand grasping the reins, so many fingers' breadth from the bits: head and eyes to the front— Like this: everything starts from this. Now. Prepare to Mount— half face to the right, pivoting on the heel. . . . Now— Mount— There is a beautiful smooth precision about his every movement, a sureness, and a control. Forgetful of his deplorable manner with gentlemen, the regiment, horse lovers and sportsmen to the last file, desire to be like him. A moment later, they are trying it themselves. . . . Draw Sabres! How much need a chap practise, do you think, to be able to whip out his blade in that lovely flashing arc, like the Colonel does? . . . In brief, he takes them through every movement in the drill; an officer, he says, must not only be an officer—he must be a better trooper than any man he has, which is embarrassing to some of the officers. Presently, company drill, and the command, broken up into its elements, is wheeling and evoluting all over the green meadow, with the Colonel everywhere at once. The men observe that now it is the company officers who are catching it, hot and heavy. Captains sweat and strive, under the West Pointer's fussy eye, wishing that they had stayed in camp to study J. Lucius Davis' *Trooper's Manual* last evening, instead of calling on the girls at Fisher's Hill. . . .

But the drill period in the Virginia armies is not prolonged. In May, the Yankee nation begins its invasion. Alexandria is occupied: Joe Johnston falls back from Harper's Ferry, which the Yankees immediately enter; and by every ford, between Charlestown and Washington, they thrust across the Potomac. For the most part they stay within galloping distance of the river; but the border country is full of armed men, scampering about. Joe Johnston's Army of the Shenandoah falls back on Winchester, with advanced posts at Bunker Hill, and Martinsburg, and Darksville—regiments of infantry relieving each other in the outpost line. But for the small bodies of cavalry—Turner Ashby's Rangers, and Colonel Stuart's regiment—there are no alternates. Stuart, with 350 men, watches a front of fifty miles, from Leesburg to Shepherdstown: pickets on every road leading in from the river—contact with the Yankees all the time. Little clashes and affairs at arms, that keep you interested, and occasionally kill a man, and are very hard on men and horses.

Even so, the regimental training goes on, in the presence

Colonel · 1st Virginia Cavalry · 1861

of the enemy. A trooper of the 1st Virginia, George Cary Eggleston, describes one episode: the enemy are drafted by Colonel Stuart to point his lessons. The Colonel rides out, one morning, in the lower valley, with a squadron. A scout has come into camp on a lathered horse, and talked to him. He leads the troop off in fours, singing to himself at the head of the column, like a man well pleased. In a wood, behind a hill, he halts them, and rides off at a gallop with his orderly; presently he returns, his eye dancing in his bronzed face. "Come on, you fellows: we're going to have some fun!" They move in fours over the hill, and advance through the edge of a thin woods. They hear bugles in the distance, and over the ridge in front comes a long line of blue skirmishers, infantry, with the sun on their rifles. Stuart throws the squadron into line; the skirmishers stop: a field officer, by his sash, comes to the front and looks with his glasses, and puff-balls of smoke blossom along the skirmish line. It is long range, and the balls whine harmlessly. The squadron watches the Colonel, and the Colonel still looks pleased. Now the heads of two infantry columns come upon the ridge: my stars! what a lot of Yankees! Two regimental flags—the old gridiron flag—flap on the ridge. They are deploying. And the next thing is a gun, that gallops handsomely over the crest, whirls into battery, and inclines its bright muzzle toward them. A little quiver runs through the squadron. The men look at each other: the Colonel faces about, his back to the enemy, and his face serene. They are busy around the gun: a great burst of smoke comes from it: there is a bumping crash, and a round shot howls overhead and bursts in the wood behind. "There," says the Colonel! "I wanted you to learn what a cannon's like, and hear it. They fired high; they always do. You see, there's no harm in them. Now: fours about—Trot! Remember, cavalry gallops at the enemy, and trots away

from him. No other gait is worthy of a cavalryman. . . .
A good man on a good horse need never get into
trouble——"

I know one old gentleman, who was in 1861 just out of
the university. He says he was thinking about enlisting for
the war, and a friend said, "Will Payne is raising a Black
Horse Troop, over in Farquier. Take your horse and go in
with him." But, he pointed out, he didn't have any horse.
"Well, buy one," says his friend. "Can't do that—I haven't
any money," he admitted. "Oh, shucks!" says his friend,
"I'll loan you the money." . . . So he joined the Black Horse,
and lost an arm at Brandy Station. He is reticent about it,
except when you bring up personalities. . . .

Then, there is a commissary sergeant's tale, which I heard
once——

"It war about this time uv the yeah, come nex' week, when
they war a meetin' down t' th' settlement, an' I rode my mar'
down to see whut th' confabulation was about. At the gath-
erin', thar war Thad Thomas an' Otious Jones an' Whitfield
Ballingeh, an' they infohm's us that them thar Yankees war
comin' south, an' buhn up ouah houses an' run off ouhaw
stock an' take ouhaw wimmen, an' it war ouhaw bounden
juty ter spring ter ahms an' molest th' pizon varmints. Right
much uv the boys war enrollin' ter jine th' wah, but I sez to
m'self, I sez, I'll jes' go home and stay a'w'ile longer wit' my
wife. Then, one day, Ise crossin' the turnpike, nigh untoe
Buttermilk Spring, an' a feller in a uniform comes along, an'
w'en he sees me, he puts his hoss toe a trot, an' hails me,
right thar on th' turnpike. 'You,' he says, 'do you belong to
this wah?' 'Naw, suh,' I tells him, 'Ah don't.' 'Well,' he says,
'is you got a hoss?' 'Naw, suh,' I tells him, 'I got a mar'.'
'That's all right,' he says, 'you take yo' mar' an' repoht to
the camp in the grove over yonder.' Wall, I does. They en-
rolls me on th' muster, an' they tells the kit an' boodle uv us

to saddle up, an' a peart, loud-voiced feller takes us up on the ridge, an' uv all th' wheelin', an' tuhnin' an' dang-fool goin's-on you ever seed er hyard tell uv, thet feller made us go through wit'. An' nuthin' we did pleased the little cuss. My mar' got hot an' vexed, an' I neveh war so tired uv a man in my life. Toe cap it all, they piles up seve'l panels uv rail fences, an' makes us jump ouhaw hosses over in squads uv five. An' eveh time we jump, they puts on anotheh rail. Finally, I rid my mar' up to the jump—an' Gentlemun, hush! I goes over, but she don't. She put her fo' feet against the bottom rail, an' stops. But I goes right on over. . . .

"An' w'en I gits time toe look aroun' th' camp, I don't see Thad Thomas, an' I don't see Otious Jones, an' I don't see Whitfield Ballangeh. Whar wuz they? Right at home wit' they wives, thet's whar they war, an' that's whar they stayed. An' w'en I gits home to talk to the boys an' fin' out whut th' ruckus is all about, I fin's its over nuthin' but a passel uv niggers!"

Thus the commissary sergeant of a company in a regiment of Southwest Virginia Cavalry. And he served through the war to the end of it.

There is story of this period, when the Potomac counties of Virginia were a sort of No-man's land, the exercise field of both armies. One morning, Stuart, riding ahead of his outpost line, with an orderly, as was his custom, came upon a fine United States Captain, trotting alone. The morning was sharp, and Stuart's gray jacket was covered by an old army overcoat, sky-blue, as was the Northern officer's Yankee blouse. The two knew each other: they had been in the same class at West Point: the Yankee was Captain Perkinson, of the United States Artillery. As they drew together, Stuart hailed, joyously: "Why, howdy, Perk! when did you come over? It's good to see you—what's your command?"

At that moment, a smart battery of United States Artillery came into view, half a mile behind: it was trotting, and its flag blew out. "Hello, Beauty! How are you? That's my command, right yonder—" Captain Perkinson pointed. "Oh, the deuce!" said Stuart. "I didn't know you'd stayed with the Union—*Good*-bye—" and he put spurs to his horse and galloped off.

VI

THE FIRST MANASSAS

IN the last week of May, 1861, the Federals began the invasion of Virginia. On the 24th, forces gathered at Washington, crossed by Chain Bridge and Highway Bridge, drove off the Confederate pickets whose fires you had seen, at night, blazing on the hills across the Potomac from Washington, and entrenched a line from Alexandria to Arlington. The Confederates, advanced details from Beauregard's Army at Manassas Junction, fell back on Annandale, Vienna, and Falls Church. McDowell commanded in Washington.

Another Federal Army was formed, basing on Frederick City in Maryland, under the aged General Patterson, a veteran of 1812, and Mexico, for the forcing of the upper Potomac, held for the South by General Joseph E. Johnston with 11,000 men, at Harpers Ferry. Elsewhere, in West Virginia, two small armies faced each other, George B. McClellan for the North, and Floyd, late secretary of war under Buchanan, for the South. The Federal armies were under the direction of old Lieutenant-General Scott. No Confederate officer was appointed to supreme command. Mr. Jefferson Davis, then and afterwards exercised his constitutional function as commander-in-chief of the Confederate States Army and Navy.

About June 1st, McDowell was directed to make a study of an offensive movement, southwestward from Washington, in co-operation with a thrust into the Shenandoah Valley by Patterson: McDowell's part was to be the engaging of Beauregard, so that he would not detach forces to the assistance of Johnston when Patterson attacked Harper's Ferry. But before McDowell completed his plans, Johnston had solved the problem by evacuating his posts on the Potomac and falling back to Winchester. Patterson crossed into the Shenandoah Valley and lapsed into inaction.

June was marked by small military episodes, which served chiefly to increase the war fervor on both sides. Lieutenant Tompkins, with B Company of the 2d U. S. Cavalry, dashed into Fairfax Court House at daybreak one morning, captured a sleepy picket, and galloped a mile and a half, out to Germantown. Returning, he found his way blocked by Captain Marr's company of Warrenton Rifles, fifty light infantrymen, while two companies of horse, Powell's and Ball's, who had few pistols and no ammunition at all, hovered in the outskirts; the whole under command of Lieutenant-Colonel Richard Ewell, late Captain, 2d U. S. Dragoons. There was a running fight, in which Tompkins lost a few men and a few horses, and Captain Marr was killed and Lieutenant-Colonel Ewell shot through the shoulder: both sides reported a victory against vastly superior forces; Lieutenant Tompkins was complimented for personal gallantry and reprimanded for indiscretion, and Lieutenant-Colonel Ewell was advanced to the rank of colonel; and Brigadier-General Bonham, the senior Confederate officer present, urged officially that the cavalry companies be issued, immediately, some sort of fire arms—shotguns, if nothing else.

On the 17th of June, Colonel Schenck, commanding an Ohio brigade, was ordered out on reconnaissance along the Loundoun and Hampshire Railroad, toward Vienna, with an Ohio regiment, on a train of platform cars. He proceeded slowly, dropping off detachments to examine the country on both sides of the track, and as he approached Vienna, with 271 men, riding comfortably, he had the ill fortune to come upon Colonel Maxcy Gregg, who, with his South Carolina regiment, a troop of cavalry, and two smooth-bore six-pounders of Captain Kemper's battery, was operating in the vicinity. Kemper opened on the train at four hundred yards, with round shot and canister; the Ohio Infantry made an extremely rapid movement from the cars, to left and right, into cover, and the engineer, whose locomotive was in the rear, pushing, uncoupled hastily and returned to Alexandria. Colonel Gregg did not press the enemy, who rallied at some distance, and retired in good order along the railroad, having lost twelve men. The Confederates looted a quantity of arms and equipment from the cars and burned the rolling stock. Elsewhere, U. S. Sloop-of-war *Pawnee*, engaged Confederate shore batteries along the Potomac; and the killing of a mule and some chickens at Matthias Point, by her shells, is recorded: afterwards, U. S. Sloop-of-war *Pawnee* is described as lying "coiled along the shore like a wounded viper."

Early in July, the Valley armies were heard from: Colonel T. J. Jackson, with his Virginia brigade, and the cavalry regiment of Lieutenant-Colonel J. E. B. Stuart attached, fought a small action with Patterson's advance at Falling Waters, up-river from Harper's Ferry. Stuart, riding alone in the woods on the edge of the fight, came unexpectedly upon a company of Pennsylvania volunteers, ordered them to surrender before they could decide what to do about it, and brought them in, prisoners. Jackson's conduct of his brigade was admired, and General Johnston recommended both for promotion, Jackson to Brigadier, Stuart to Colonel. They had their new commissions promptly.

By the end of June, the situation in Virginia had assumed some coherence. The Confederates held what was called the Alexandria Line. J. E. Johnston was at one end of it, before Winchester, with some 10,000 men, the Army of the Shenandoah. Sixty miles southeast, based on Manassas Junction, Beauregard stood with 18,000, the Army of the

Potomac, his advanced posts pushed forward to Falls Church, Vienna and Annandale. Thirty miles east of Manassas, at the mouth of Aquia Creek, was Holmes with 3,000 men; and Magruder watched the lower Potomac, and the York and James rivers, facing Butler's landing force at Newport News. The key point to Richmond was Manassas Junction, a railroad and highway centre, accessible from all directions. There were now in Virginia about 65,000 Confederates under arms.

The Confederates showed no offensive intentions: only their cavalry and outposts were active. Patterson and Johnston confronted each other and did nothing, and both gave cogent reasons for inaction, powerfully submitted to their respective governments. Beauregard drilled at Manassas, issued remarkable proclamations, and did, nothing. But pressure upon McDowell, in Washington, developed overwhelming force. The Administration needed a victory. Congress insisted upon it. Furthermore, the Federal troops assembled at Washington were three-month volunteers, enlisted in the spring and now approaching the expiration of their contracts. They lacked organization and discipline, but there was nothing better available, and by August they would be going home. Sound military opinion urged that they be allowed to go: that the campaign wait until the three-year men, for whom Lincoln was now calling, be assembled and trained. But the politicians were in the saddle, and in the first weeks of July, McDowell pulled together an army of five divisions, about 35,000 men, to move out from Arlington on the 16th of July, against Beauregard's army at Centreville. It was called The Army of Northeastern Virginia. Its regiments, loosely brigaded, were strange to their commanders and to each other.

The march of the Federal Army from the Arlington lines to Centreville, twenty-two miles in two days, had the bright aspect of holiday excursion. A host of civilians, ladies and gentlemen of quality, with picnic hampers of food and drink, congressmen, governors of loyal states, sutlers with vans of refreshment for the weary soldiers, a theatrical troupe or two, for the diversion of the warriors at evening, gamblers, ladies of pleasure; all these followed the marching columns and got in the way of the military trains. The troops straggled in the hot sun, wandering off the road at will, for water, or to pick berries, or to rest in the shade. Some barns were light-heartedly burned, and some chickens stolen, disorders in the way of pillaging which McDowell sincerely condemned, but found himself powerless to punish or prevent. Tyler's division, moving in advance, drove off Confederate outposts at Falls Church and Fairfax Court House, eight and twelve miles from Washington. This was the 16th of July. The only enemy seen were far, scampering gray horsemen.

On the 17th, Tyler pushed on to Centreville, which the Confederates evacuated as his division came up, going into position behind Bull Run, four miles farther on. Here Tyler took the sole trophy of the campaign, "a Secession Flag," alleged to be the property of an Alabama regiment, and found cased in a storehouse. On the 18th, the blue army closed on Centreville, its camps congesting the approaches from the east. That day, at noon, Tyler was ordered to make a reconnaissance in force, toward Blackburn's Ford on Bull Run, thought to be about the Confederate centre. Tyler sent forward Richardson's brigade—the same Richardson who was to die gallantly, next year at Sharpsburg, somewhere in front of the Bloody Lane; and Richardson fumbled down at Longstreet's brigade, in line behind the Ford. Reinforced by Early, Longstreet reacted vigorously: Richardsons' infantry broke and ran back, and Longstreet's people, going out later, picked up sixty-four dead, a few wounded, twenty prisoners, one hundred and seventy-five rifles, and one hundred and fifty hats, on the ground where Richardson came under fire. Longstreet had his own troubles: one of his regiments, in low ground behind Bull Run, took flight out of its rifle pits and Longstreet had to ride in personally and rally them, with his threatening presence and his blunt, compelling voice. The affair then passed into the hands of Richardson's and Longstreet's artillery, which shelled each other most of the afternoon. The only conspicuous damage was done by one Federal shell; that exploded in the dining room of the McLean house and ruined Beauregard's dinner, set and ready for him on the table. The Confederate loss was sixty-eight, killed and wounded.

The rumor of the affair ran large through both armies, and decreased the Northern morale. It so depressed one regiment and one battery of three-month enlistment, whose contracts were due to expire on the 21st of July, that they withdrew from service the minute their time was up: "marching to the rear to the sound of the enemy's guns"—in McDowell's acid language.

The discouraging results of Tyler's reconnaissance in force confirmed McDowell in the opinion that subsequent reconnaissance had better be by stealth. For the two following days, the 19th and 20th of July, he and his engineers examined the terrain so discreetly as to occasion the Confederates no alarm. Beauregard made energetic use of the time given him. On the 17th, he had wired President Davis that McDowell was moving against him. He had, on the field, or coming up, 21,833 men and 27 guns: he was outnumbered three to two, or a little more.

His information came, not only from his scouts, but, he asserts, from a patriotic lady in the first circles of the Federal capitol, who learned of McDowell's orders at the White House when they were issued, and had advised Beauregard of their content by trusty messenger almost as soon as Mc-Dowell received them.

Late on the 17th, President Davis wired Johnston at Winchester: "General Beauregard is attacked. To strike the enemy a decisive blow, a junction of all your effective force will be needed. If practicable, make the movement, sending your sick and baggage to Culpeper Court House either by railroad or by Warrenton. In all the arrangements exercise your discretion."

This message became the basis of fierce controversy between Johnston and the President, Johnston contending that it allowed him discretion, to move or not to move: Davis, that it was mandatory. But note the fatal phrase: "if practicable."

At 1:00 A.M. on the 18th of July, Johnston was issuing orders. He sent Colonel J. E. B. Stuart, his cavalry commander, to draw a screen across the valley, as near to Patterson's lines as he could go, and to assume threatening attitudes, where the Federals would be sure to see him. Stuart rode out under the stars with the 1st Virginia Cavalry, and at the same hour the infantry began to move, Brigadier-General T. J. Jackson's Virginia brigade leading. Through the 18th, Stuart's horse harassed Patterson's outposts, chased in pickets on every road, conducted themselves with such ardor and impudence that Patterson wired Washington: Johnson, with 35,000 men, was about to attack him, his own force was outnumbered, but Washington could be assured that he would hold out to the last. Patterson remained firm in his resolution—and in defensive postures—for the next four days.

This day Jackson marched seventeen miles, forded the Shenandoah at Front Royal, passed Ashby's Gap, and bivouaced at Paris, east of the Blue Ridge. Bartow, with half of his brigade, then Bee with half of his, then Kirby

Smith's brigade, got in motion behind Jackson. Elsewhere, President Davis' orders started Holmes, with 1,200 men, from Aquia Creek, and Hampton's Legion, less its cavalry, about 700, was entrained at Richmond. After dark, on the 18th, Stuart assembled his regiment and marched on Front Royal, with the artillery of Johnston's army, five batteries, twenty pieces, under Pendleton. Colonel Angus MacDonald, old militia cavalryman, who preferred hatchets to sabres as cavalry arms, was left to raise a dust in front of Patterson.

By 8 o'clock on the morning of the 19th, Jackson had marched six miles to Piedmont Station and entrained his brigade. He was set down at Manassas Junction, thirty-seven miles away, at 1:00 P.M. Beauregard's 21,000 were now 23,000. The trains went back and moved Bartow with two regiments: they were in before dark. No trains ran that night: the Manassas Gap Railroad personnel refused to work overtime and had to have their sleep. The day passed fair and warm along Bull Run: McDowell's engineers proceeded, unmolested, with their reconnaissance by stealth.

On the 20th, Stuart's cavalry and Pendleton's guns arrived, having marched sixty miles in two days. Holmes came in from Aquia Creek; Hampton was enroute from Richmond. The railroad brought down the rest of Bee's Brigade, and Johnston in person. Beauregard now had nearly 30,000 men, with only Hampton and Kirby Smith to come. That day McDowell's reconnoitering was finished: he drew up his plans.

*　　*　　*　　*　　*

You drive out from Washington, between the Arlington Heights and the Potomac, on the Lee Highway. The fine concrete road passes Falls Church and Fairfax Court House, and at twenty-two miles from the capitol you flash through a cross roads where a few houses stand. This is

Centreville: about the size now that it was in 1861, and you have come in less than an hour as far as McDowell came in two days. At Centreville, a ridge runs northwest and southeast, the highest ground in the region. It was the position of Beauregard's Army of the Potomac, given up when McDowell approached. On ahead, the ground falls and rises in parallel ridges: beyond the first is Cub Run, two and a half miles west of Centreville; beyond the second, Bull Run, four miles from Centreville. In 1861, the road, called then the Warrenton Turnpike, ran straight west, and our new concrete road follows in its trace. Cub Run was crossed by a long wooden bridge: Bull Run by a stone bridge, the original abutments, with a restored arch, standing now on the right of the road. A mile and a quarter west of the stone bridge, a square stone house is on the right, a little stream called Young's Branch, loops across the road; there are service stations and a tea house—gasoline and Virginia ham sandwiches—and a country road crosses the highway at right angles. If you stop here, you are in the place where the First Battle of Manassas was won and lost: where the vortex of the fight whirled on that July Sunday, sixty-nine years ago. The intersecting road ahead is the Sudley-Brentville road, from Sudley Ford on upper Bull Run down toward Manassas. The high ground to the north is Matthews Hill, where the battle opened. The small flat-topped hill, a plateau, rather—to the south, with Young's Branch curving around its foot, and the Sudley road skirting its western edge, is Henry Hill, where stood the house of Judith Henry, and the house of the free negro Robinson. Both are gone, but the old stone house on the turnpike was full of wounded that day. From the highway, here running between high banks, you can see the tops of some pines on the south side of Henry Hill: under those pines Brigadier-General T. J. Jackson stood like a stone wall. Through the oak woods, farther west, came Kirby Smith's Brigade, uttering for the first time in battle the strident angry cry which history calls the Rebel Yell. On the little ridges farther west, Jubal Early, with Stuart's cavalry and Beckham's guns thundering on his flank, delivered the knock-out blow of the battle.

* * * * *

Go back those sixty-nine years. When Sunday morning came, the 21st of July, 1861, Beauregard's Army of the Potomac lay behind Bull Run, from Union Mills Ford, near Manassas Junction, up to the Stone Bridge, a distance of six miles. His line was not continuous: his brigades held the several fords that crossed the Run, in more or less mutually supporting positions. Ewell's brigade was at Union Mills, Jubal Early's brigade, and Holmes, behind Ewell, support and reserve. D. R. Jones' brigade was next, at Mitchell's Ford: then James Longstreet, at Blackburn's Ford, nearest to Centreville—four miles. Bonham and Cocke were at Ball's and Island fords, respectively. To Cocke's left, astride the Turnpike at Stone Bridge, the extreme Confederate left, was Colonel Nathan G. Evans, with the 4th South Carolina Infantry, Wheat's Louisiana Battalion, and two six-pounder guns. Jackson, Bee and Bartow, of Johnston's Army of the Shenandoah, and Stuart's 1st Virginia Cavalry Regiment, were stationed behind the Confederate right and centre, in reserve. Hampton's Legion, and Kirby Smith, were not yet arrived. Beauregard had a plan: to attack with his right, Ewell leading from Union Mills, against McDowell's left at Centreville, and get between McDowell and Washington. This plan the cautious Johnston approved in theory, when he arrived and took command, but he ordered that its execution be delayed until McDowell's intention was more fully developed, so, the night of the 20th, Beauregard's brigadiers are directed to place themselves in readiness to attack. Early Sunday morning, orders are issued for the attack to open, Ewell leading. All the brigadiers except Ewell receive the order and stand by: Ewell never gets it, and before the lost order is traced, there are new developments and it is all abandoned.

This same Saturday, the 20th, McDowell sets out his orders. He regards the Confederate centre too strong, the right too difficult, to attack. His engineers have found a road running north from the Turnpike just beyond Cub Run, and circling west to Sudley Ford on Bull Run, connecting with the Sudley-Brentville road. Tyler's 1st Division, 12,000, he will send forward to pin the Confederate left at Stone Bridge on Bull Run, Hunter's 2d Division and Heintzleman's 3d, about 12,000 together, will march by the Sudley road and come down behind the Confederate left. When they are in position, Tyler will attack in front and they in rear, and the Confederate left will be destroyed, and the Bull Run line rolled up. Hunter and Heintzelman are camped east of Centreville, and McDowell thinks they should move up to Cub Run that afternoon, but his officers urge against it: better make it all one movement, with an early start, next day. Miles' and Runyon's divisions, 10,000 or so, remain at Centreville and eastward, in reserve.

In the calculations of McDowell, of Johnston and Beauregard, there is for each another army: McDowell hopes that Patterson is holding Johnston before Winchester, sixty miles away, and will continue to hold him. He does not know that Johnston is on his front, although one of his generals, a railroad man, has heard the laboring Confederate engines on the 19th and the 20th and thinks they were bringing troops from the Valley. But McDowell has Patterson's assurance, through Washington, and does not agree. Across Bull Run, the Confederate officers are not so sure about Patterson: Patterson may follow and fall upon their rear: there is nothing to keep him from doing so if he gets the dust out of his eyes.

At 2:00 o'clock Sunday morning Tyler, Hunter, Heintzelman are alerted, without bugles, have coffee and hardtack, and get in ranks on the roads east of Centreville. They move off slowly in the dark, Tyler leading; the columns of Hunter and Heintzelman must wait, shuffling, for hours, until he gets clear, for they use the same road as far as Cub Run. This is bad for green troops: they get to thinking— At 4:00 o'clock, Longstreet's scouts report the masses on the Turnpike, moving forward. This goes to Beauregard, and his attack orders are issued—not to be received by Ewell. All the other Confederate brigades stand to arms, ready to move—drink coffee—peer and listen in the growing light. Between 5:30 and 6:00, Tyler's brigades begin to deploy on the ridge east of Bull Run, 1500 yards from Evans at Stone Bridge, and Evans' outposts are driven across the stream— Evans mans his line. He has about 1500 muskets. Behind Tyler, Hunter and Heintzelman are fairly started; the sun is up, and immediately it is hot; the sky clear, but the air close and still; going to rain tomorrow, say the weather-wise farmers and sportsmen standing to horse in Stuart's regiment, in all the Virginia regiments, who know the country.

Then for two hours, nothing happens. Tyler's skirmishers bicker at long range with Evans, and Tyler brings up two great rifled cannon and fires some desultory rounds at the far side of Bull Run. The shells do no damage, but Evans' men regard them with concern—enormous projectiles— thirty-pounders, no less! The flanking column marches, be-ginning to sweat. The engineers said they had six miles to go: they find it nearer twelve. Beauregard and John-ston are wondering, at Headquarters, why Ewell doesn't

start. Eventually, they might have sent somebody to find out.

On Van Ness Hill, near the Confederate Headquarters, young Captain Alexander, with his new and improved system of flag signals, is perched disconsolate since dawn, Beauregard's signal officer. He wants to ride up and join the fighting, and he sits morosely at his spy-glass. The ridge west of Cub Run hides the Yankee area from him, but he can see the green course of Bull Run, running off small to the northwest. At 8:45, he picks up a glint and a sparkle about where Sudley Ford would be: looks closer, sees the brass jacket of a howitzer, the hard flicker of bayonets and musket barrels in the sun. He sees batteries, counts battle flags—a sizable column. He wigwags to Evans at Stone Bridge: "Look out for your left: you are turned." He writes a message to Beauregard.

At Stone Bridge, Evans has about decided that Tyler means nothing serious: while he is considering Alexander's signal, a galloper, from an outpost he had at Sudley Ford, dashes in on a lathered horse. "Colonel, they're crossing up at Sudley—a whole mess of them—infantry and guns—" Evans, called "Shanks" Evans, a small, alert man, with a thin square beard and a pale, hard eye, thinks fast. Sudley Ford is two miles from the Turnpike, by the road that intersects, a mile behind him. The Federals, then, were nearer than Cocke, his nearest support. He sends a note to Cocke, detaches four companies of South Carolina Infantry to keep Stone Bridge, and with the rest of South Carolina and Wheat's Louisiana Tigers and his little guns, he draws off and moves west on the Turnpike at the double. It is the quickest and coolest bit of military thinking done in this battle; Evans will have another opportunity at Ball's Bluff in December, and do supremely well with it. Thereafter, he goes into obscurity: the records don't show why. He hurries to Sudley Road and forms line some hundreds of yards north of the Turnpike, across Matthews Hill, his left on Sudley road and his right in the air. He is here by 9:30. Beauregard, after some indecision—still waiting to hear Ewell's battle open—sends Bee and Bartow, Hampton, just off the cars, and later Jackson, to support the left.

The Federal turning column rested half an hour at Sudley Ford. Then it marched a mile, Burnside of Hunter's Division, leading, with his New Englanders. The woods covered them, almost to the foot of Matthews Hill: there the country opened, and Burnside saw Evans standing in the path. He attacked, met a sustained fury of musketry, fell back and tried again. Evans even counter-attacked, his Carolinians and Louisianians running down, whooping, to snatch prisoners, to capture a stand of colors. The fight opened at 10:30, and Burnside was finished by 11:00 o'clock. He withdrew into the woods and sat pensively until afternoon, with a variety of reasons for doing nothing. His loss was nominal. Hunter, the division commander, was shot as Burnside deployed, and Colonel Porter took command.

Porter followed Burnside, New York Volunteers, Major Sykes' battalion of regulars, and Reynold's battalion of marines. They got closer to Evans: two fine regular batteries, Ricketts and Griffin, came into action, and the Confederate line, 1,000 men or so—begun to suffer. Bee and Bartow reached Henry Hill and took up position, well-chosen: they sent word to Evans: retire on them. Evans, still holding his ground, replied that they had better come out to him. They came into line on his right, in time to sustain the full shock of Porter's brigade, now beginning to be reinforced by Heintzleman. Also, Tyler was at last in motion: his batteries were firing from across the stream, and Sherman was crossing Bull Run above the Stone Bridge. Evans, Bee and Bartow gave way. Porter pressed them: Sherman's brigade approached their right, and they broke, streaming back across the Turnpike. Wade Hampton arrived in time to hold Sherman for a little, along Young's Branch. But very soon all the Confederates were south of the Turnpike, and Sherman, Porter, and Heintzelman were upon it.

This ended the first phase of the battle. Advised by the great crash of sound, by the blue-white powder smoke rolling up in the still air, Johnston and Beauregard put Ewell out of their minds and rode to the left, to find a sorry rout at Henry Hill. Both forgot the army commander in the combat officer: Johnston rides with the flag of an Alabama regiment, to form some kind of line. Beauregard stands in his stirrups and addresses fugitives on *la gloire*, on *la patrie*: some of them stop to listen and remain to fight. Ricketts and Griffin, ardent cannoneers, fire now from Matthews Hill: Judith Henry's house burns, and the old bedridden lady is carried out, to be killed by a shell. The Northern troops swarm, in dust and smoke, on the Turnpike, and lap across it. McDowell, present there, also forgets the general, and rides in, ordering regiments and fragments of regiments to seize Henry Hill: victory is in his hand.

On the hill, Confederate batteries, Imboden, Pendleton, Stanard, Alburtis (there is a lieutenant with Alburtis named John Pelham) fight Rickett and Griffin with outmoded smooth-bore guns, and are being smashed up. The Federal infantry begins to get forward—chases the guns away, meet blasts of musketry that blow them down into the Turnpike again.

For, in the pines at the south edge of Henry Hill, is Jackson's Virginia Brigade, some 2,000 men. Jackson has had them there, lying down, since 11:00 o'clock. Now it is past noon. He has observed the breaking of Evans, Bee and Bartow. He has reproved Captain Imboden for swearing. He has told an anxious officer that, if he thinks they are losing, he had better say nothing about it. He has been shot in the hand. Bee, just before he was killed, has observed that Jackson is Standing like a Stone Wall—an observation that will endure—and some Confederate elements are re-forming behind him. Lying down, Jackson's men are hidden: as the Northern infantry mounts the sky line in front, they are simply shot off of it. They run back, reload, and try again: McDowell cannot make them stay. So McDowell orders his fine artillery forward, to go where his infantry cannot go, and, plying whip and spur, Ricketts and Griffin cross the Turnpike and come into battery on Henry Hill, flinging canister into the faces of the Confederate at five hundred yards. Jackson is pinned to the ground: loses men. Imboden and Stannard are swept off. The infantry support for Ricketts advances through the smoke, and Jackson sends to Stuart; behind him, to protect his flank: that infantry is overlapping it.

There is a great drift of smoke across Henry Hill, and Stuart, riding out of the oak woods to Jackson's left, sees a regiment, all in red, running toward him. An Alabama regiment is red-uniformed, and Stuart, three hundred men in column of twos, trots to meet them. "Don't run, boys," he calls in his golden voice, "we are here!" Then their flag blows out: the gridiron flag: they are the Fire Zouaves of Heintzelman's, and he rides over them. They deliver fire: he loses nine men and eighteen horses, but they scatter and are not again rallied.

More infantry comes—too much. Stuart takes position in the edge of the oak woods, near the Sudley-Brentville road, and gets up Beckham's light battery.

Now, something decisive happens—Jackson's left regiment, Colonel Cummings' 33d Virginia, moves out of the pines, on its own initiative, toward Ricketts' guns. Ricketts sees them, thinks he had better traverse a section and give them canister—but McDowell's chief of artillery, who has ridden up, thinks not; says they are some of Heintzelman's Wisconsin troops, who also wore gray. At seventy paces, the 33d Virginia halts and fires, wounding Ricketts, killing and wounding his gun crews, killing his horses. Griffin, farther out, also suffers. Jackson's people run, yelling, and lay hands on the guns. But they cannot stay there. The Federal infantry comes again: the guns are three times taken and retaken: some Maine troops try to drag them off by hand—get two pieces as far as Sudley road. Heintzelman and his brigadiers decide to turn the Confederate left, and begin to throw out a line, across the Sudley road. Only Stuart's little horse battery and handful of cavalry hamper them: they build up a mass, hurl it forward, astride the Sudley road, and meet Kirby Smith, who has marched up, six miles from the train. Kirby Smith falls wounded; Colonel Elzey leads in his place. The brigade, Virginia, Tennessee, Maryland, goes forward with a loud, high scream—a sort of pack-cry, dangerous-sounding. One brigadier of Heintzelman's, Wilcox, is captured—the infantry breaks. Stuart moves swiftly to Elzey's outer flank and puts his guns in action again.

Heintzelman is stubborn: he still has Howard, his last brigade: it is 3:00 o'clock and he puts Howard in, again extending, to flank the Confederate left. Stuart volleys with his battery, sends a courier to hurry Jubal Early's brigade, marching from Union Mills, the last reserve. Early, with Virginia and Louisiana troops, forms quickly, Stuart shifting across to his left. He sweeps back Howard, rolls him across the Turnpike: Beckham's guns fire down the Turnpike on the press at Henry Hill. With that, the Federals have enough. A retreat begins, a falling away of individuals, a streaming back of regiments—a disintegration of all units. The officers can do nothing: the men are through:

they throw down their pieces and leave that place. The Confederate infantry does not press them hard, but the cavalry rides out, in unco-ordinated bands, Stuart's and Radford's, and independent companies, perhaps 800, and the rout begins. A shell—claimed to have been fired from Captain Kemper's Alexandria Light Battery, by that same venerable fire-eater, Edmund Ruffin of Charleston, here present as gentleman volunteer—burst on Cub Run bridge and overturned a wagon. There was panic. Infantry cut artillery horses from their traces, horses from the carriages of civilian spectators, and rode them off. The Confederate cavalry gobbled up prisoners while the light lasted—officers and men: the governor of Connecticut was flushed and taken in the thicket by Cub Run. Stuart followed as far as Sudley Ford, where he camped for the night, having detached men as prisoner-escort until he had a scant squad left with him. In all McDowell's army, only Major Sykes' battalion of regulars held firm and covered the retreat: Major Sykes was mortified, in his report, that he could not bring off the blankets of his men—dumped somewhere and not found again.

The Federal army did not stop in Centreville. It kept on, by individuals, to Washington, and many soldiers proceeded farther without halt, to their armories in Philadelphia, New York and Boston.

Mr. Jefferson Davis, riding up from Manassas, in the afternoon, through a drift of stragglers, wounded, and malingerers, thinks the battle lost until he reaches the front. Jackson, having his hand dressed, says he can be in Washington, given 5,000 fresh troops, by morning, but nobody pays any attention to him. In the last hours of the day, dubious orders for pursuit are sent to Longstreet and to Bonham: they move from Blackburn's Ford, fall immediately into argument as to which brigade has the right of way—Bonham being senior but Longstreet having moved first—and while they debate, a strange column is reported toward Union Mills, thought to be Yankees. They halt: it turns out to be Ewell, or D. R. Jones, or somebody, counter-marching on the chow wagons. Then it is night, and Mr. Davis, with Johnston and Beauregard, deliberate endlessly as to pursuit or non-pursuit, and McDowell gets away.

It is a grotesque battle, fought bewilderedly by armed civilians, who had no idea what a war they were getting into. Each side engaged about half of its effectives on the field. McDowell's plan was sound, and failed largely because he attacked by driblets. Also, he was poorly served by Tyler, who engaged seriously only one of his three available bri-gades, that one Sherman's. McDowell's army of Northeast-ern Virginia lost, killed, wounded and missing, 2,700 officers and men, of whom 40 officers and 1,176 were prisoners. The weight of the loss was on Sherman and Porter.

The Southern armies lost 1,982 officers and men, of whom 13 were captured. The Confederates had the gleaning of the field. They took a thirty-pounder Parrott gun, twenty-seven other cannon, thirty-seven caissons, sixty-four horses, four thousand stand of small arms, ammunition, and stores of lesser equipment—all very valuable to the harassed ord-nance officers.

The next day, in the rain, they buried the bedraggled dead, while the Confederate cavalry looked again at Wash-ington from the hills on the Virginia side.

VII

FROM FIRST MANASSAS TO THE PENINSULA

AFTER First Manassas, Colonel Stuart did not return to the Valley of Virginia. General Beauregard went to duty elsewhere in the South. The Valley district was turned over to General Jackson, who, as the tales of the battle spread, was beginning to be called Stonewall. General Joe Johnston remained with the Army of the Potomac in the vicinity of Centreville, and he held Colonel Stuart with him, since he had the highest opinion of the young cavalryman's abilities as an outpost officer, and considered him a person upon whom you could depend to furnish early and accurate information of the enemy's movements. Stuart, with his 1st Virginia Regiment, and additions from the mounted companies coming in, pushed his pickets forward until he looked across the river at the spires of Washington, from Mason's and Munson's Hills, and kept up such an activity that every night the careful wardens of the Federal City removed the planks from two or three sections of the bridges, on the Virginia end, so that the rebel troopers might not come rampaging in and murder important officials in their beds.

Down in the South, there was some amazement that the Yankee nation still persisted under arms. People were slow to realize that Manassas had not won the war. Numerous patriot soldiers, in the honest impression that there could be no more fighting, had gone home from the field without the formality of applying for leave of absence, and were incredulous when ordered sternly back. The North drilled, organized, and postured furiously, and both sides came to the reso-

116

Jeonoto Cotorel
lot Manassas

so Manassas · 186

Lieutenant Chesterfield Dragoons · 1861

Louisiana
Tiger
1861

skirmish line en place

lution of seeing the thing through. But it was plain that nothing more would be done in the East this year.

In the way of expansion and reorganization, Joe Johnston thought that he might have more cavalry, and on 10 August, he sent to the President a recommendation that Colonel Stuart be promoted: "He is a rare man, wonderfully endowed by nature with the qualities necessary for an officer of light cavalry. Calm, firm, acute, active, and enterprising, I know no one more competent than he to estimate the occurrences before him at their true value. If you add a real brigade of cavalry to this army, you cannot find a better brigadier-general to command it."

This letter bears an approving endorsement from General Longstreet, through whom it was forwarded, since Longstreet commanded the advanced zone of the army. You find, also, supporting letters from Governor Letcher—whom Stuart is importuning, at this time, for a couple of light guns out of the state arsenal—and from some other worthies, and Mr. Davis takes pleasure, on the 24th of September, 1861, in sending up a commission: James Ewell Brown Stuart, to be Brigadier-General of Cavalry in the Provisional Army of the Confederate States. You can see, if you care to, his first pay voucher as Brigadier-General. He made it out in his own hand, and went all adrift in his calculations for his forage allowance—23 days' pay as a Colonel, with 3 horses, and 7 days' pay as Brigadier, with 5 horses. An irreverent clerk has red-inked it to correctness.

There are no records for the cavalry brigade as first organized, but the nearest return, December, 1861, shows the 1st, 2d, 4th, and 6th Virginia Cavalry, the 1st North Carolina, and the Jeff. Davis Legion. The officers were W. E. Jones, Radford, Beverly Robertson, C. W. Field, Ramson, and Major William Martin. Jones we know; he followed Stuart as Colonel of the 1st Virginia. Robertson we will hear of. Field, who eventually transferred to the infantry, had been a company commander of Lieutenant Stuart's, in the old army.

The reports are filed of many little fights, through the fall months, and into winter. Cavalry headquarters were near Fairfax, and the camp was named by Stuart, Camp Qui Vive. To this period belongs the tale of the Lewinsberg notes. Lewinsberg was a hamlet by a cross roads, frequented of the outposts. Orlando M. Poe, a classmate of Stuart, now a cavalry officer of the Union, was around the place; he sent Stuart a message: "Dear Beauty—come and see me some time. I invite you to dine with me at Willard's Hotel in Washington, next Saturday night. Meantime, keep the Black Horse off of me, will you?—" That was Wednesday, and on Thursday Stuart rode into Poe's camp, surprised it, and scattered Poe's Horse to at least three-quarters of the compass. He forwarded Poe's note with his report, and wrote on the back of it—"From the manner in which Captain Poe left here, he was going in to get that dinner without waiting for Saturday night!"

Stuart regarding this a splendid joke, Poe's reaction is not on record.

As he trains and shapes his command, he has his eye out for the kind of officers he needs. Fitz Lee is tolled away from General Ewell's Brigade of Infantry, and given a cavalry staff job, and presently gets a command. From Albutis' battery Stuart draws John Pelham, gets him commissioned captain, and forms the Stuart Horse Artillery—a light three-gun battery. In the Washington Artillery there is a Lieutenant Rosser, just out of West Point, apt with guns, and a good horseman. Stuart takes him. He is slow about forming his staff—writes his brother that picking an aide is like taking a wife: it should be for better or for worse, and he will not be hurried in the selection. But he sends away, unceremoniously, a young cousin who applies for something soft at headquarters—tells him that, if he has real grit and sand, he will enlist, and learn from the ground up how to be soldier, and take his rewards as he earns them.

"The man who, when his country is invaded, & his home threatened, waits for position or office instead of shouldering his musket, is totally unworthy of consideration at my hands," he writes his brother, in comment on the incident.

Already he is beginning to come into the public eye; a lady in Maryland—for how many gifts were the gray gentlemen indebted, to those anonymous ladies of Maryland—sends him a fine spy-glass, which he will carry through the war. A volunteer aide presents him with a charger—Star of the East—and he writes, "I am now better mounted than any general in the Army." His brigade fills him with pride: he tells his brother, "It is considered the handsomest command in the Service . . ." which is the way every good officer ought to feel. Enough of memoir is preserved to assure us that his brigade heartily returned his esteem and pride. On duty, they remember, his aspect was firm and high: off duty, or relaxed upon the road, he was fond of calling around him such of the files as had good voices, and singing. And one day in the glamorous Indian Summer of that year, when the leaves were turning and the air was clear and keen, a courier rides to the headquarters in Camp Qui Vive on some message or other. The young brigadier is outside his tent when the soldier dismounts, and he receives the communication, his eyes going thoughtfully over the points of the fellow's horse. Then he says: Come on: you ride my horse, and I'll ride yours—I want to try him. They mount, and Stuart heads toward the outpost line: trot, walk, canter. They pass the gray picket, fartherest out on the road toward the enemy, and keep going. Stuart turns off into the fields, to try the animal over broken ground, and cuts into another road, leading homeward through the woods. The courier, who knows the lie of the land, is worried. General, he says, there's a Yankee picket on this road, just a little way, yonder. Oh, that's all right, says the general. They won't be expecting us from this direction—we're behind them. Come on— He gathers his horse and drives home the spur. The horses extend themselves, and they rush like the wind past the gaping blue jackets, and are a hundred yards away before the soldiers can collect their wits and fire; the balls whine harmlessly past. No more conversation until they reach Stuart's camp. Then he says: Did you ever time him over the half-mile?

This same courier was waiting for a train at the station one day, in a great crowd of soldiers and officers and civilians. Many children were in the place, with their parents, and the youngsters were being agitated and delighted by a tall, bearded officer, all sabre and spurs and feathered hat, who, with a squealing child under each arm, was delivering cavalry charges at the rest of them, shouting commands, and uttering golden laughter. That was Jeb Stuart, enjoying himself.

The name Jeb dates from this time, because, I suppose, he signed all communications—even the letters to his wife— J. E. B. Stuart. And also the conviction of the Southern troopers—Jeb, he never says, 'Go on'—what he says, is 'Come on, boys!' He leads us—he don't send us— Wherefrom, a whole brigade of cavalry soldiers, swanking in feathered hats—chicken feathers, if they couldn't obtain ostrich —and hopefully cultivating whiskers, for which most of them are a little young, and trying to be like the General. And such a cavalry scurrying and thrusting through the debated counties, that—if you read the Washington papers—you assume Fairfax and Alexandria to be fairly teeming with

Black Horse troopers, patrolling every road, lurking in every thicket, with terror in their hands.

The war had not yet pinched the pleasant homes of this Northern strip, and the social side was much enjoyed. His men remember Jeb Stuart riding his area with lovely girls: the General appears on the picket line is such company, details somebody to entertain the lady, goes aside himself, and becomes all soldier, putting the outpost commander through a searching inquisition as to his station, and delivering instructions. Serenades were the order of the nights, especially the fine ones lighted by the autumn moon. Now appears the minstrel-fellow Sweeny, who came out of a black-face company which stranded in Richmond, enlisting in the 9th Virginia, the regiment which also received the oldest son of General Robert E. Lee—W. H. F. Lee, late stroke oar at Harvard, a gentleman said to be too big for a man and not big enough for a horse, called Rooney. Stuart hears Sweeny in the camp, and forthwith transfers him to headquarters, over the protests of his regiment, and from this time on has his personal gleeman, to discourse, at his whim, with ready banjo and agreeable voice, melodies grave or gay.

The seekers after romance should delve into the old letters of the time, when the war was still an exciting adventure, and the gray horsemen—well acquainted with *Ivanhoe*, most of them, and the other works of Sir Walter Scott—saw themselves as knights riding to slay dragons, and the Virginia girls had the air of ladies overlooking from bright pavilions the lists of chivalry. In the country between the armies, a local belle received the addresses of gray gentlemen one day, and Yankee officers the next, and many a gentle person sent, or rode herself, from an interview with some smitten Northern officer, to detail such things as this: Averell will be on the Warrenton Pike tomorrow with a squadron. Most of the ladies were rebels, and deep with guile, and fatally charming to their foes. To such an one, Jeb Stuart, in gallant mood, issued this commission:

(Copy)

To all whom it may concern

　Know ye

That reposing special confidence in the patriotism, fidelity and ability of Antonia J. Ford, I, James E. B. Stuart, by virtue of the power vested in me as Brigadier-General in the Provisional Army of the Confederate States of America, do hereby appoint and commission her my *Honorary aide-de-camp*, to rank as such from this date.

She will be obeyed, respected and admired by all true lovers of a ——* nature.

Given under my hand and seal at the headquarters of the Cavalry Brigade at Camp Beverly, the 7th October A.D. 1861 and the first year of our independence.

(Signed) J. E. B. STUART

= Impression of his signet ring.

A true copy

　(Signed) L. L. LOMAX

It is sad for me to give her latter end. At the close of the war, she married a Yankee.

The season's large adventure at arms is the affair called the battle of Dranesville. In the official records, you learn that, on the 20th of December, General Stuart was placed in command of a detachment of four regiments of infantry, 1600 muskets, and 150 cavalry—say, two squadrons, and a battery. His mission was to cover a wagon train, sent up from Centreville to collect forage, reported to be abundantly gathered on the farms west of Dranesville, which is a village on the Leesburg-Washington pike, 20 miles west of the Cap-

---

* Obliterated in the original.

itol, and five miles south of the Potomac at Rowser's Ford. That same morning, it happened that there marched from the Federal lines west of Arlington a blue column, Ord's brigade of McCall's division, and a Pennsylvania rifle regiment, 3950 strong, with two more of McCall's brigades in support. Their mission was to drive off Confederate patrols, who had been reported around Dranesville, and to gather in that same forage.

The Federals, their advance not burdened with a wagon train, reached Dranesville first, and chased off the Confederate pickets found in the place. These gentlemen-at-arms retired only as far as they had to, and hung around the skirts of the blue columns, not thinking to send back any message to Stuart, who came on serenely. Short of the town, he directed his wagons to the west, and kept on to Dranesville, intending to take position there to cover the foragers from the side of the enemy. Later in the war, he would have examined the region carefully before he passed his wagons from the rear; now he was learning. His cavalry found Dranesville full of Yankees, provoked by the stubborn gray pickets into battle formation, and already stretching out an arm toward the wagons, which had been seen west of the town. Stuart had to attack at once, to save his foragers. His cavalry detachment rode to the left, to round up and draw off the wagons, and his four regiments were deployed and sent forward, into a zone of effective fire from the United States regular battery with Ord. There followed two hours of fighting, in which the raw Confederate regiments became intermingled, fired into each other, and otherwise did most of the things that green troops do in their first action. Ord stood fast in the village and volleyed mightily. The wagons were collected and escorted back to safety and Stuart drew off his infantry in fair order, the artillery covering its retirement. One regiment left its knapsacks and blankets on the field where it had deployed for action, and these were the Federal trophies of the fight, for they remained in position until the Confederates were gone. An infantry captain wrote a letter about the affair, in which he described Stuart, the last man in the retirement, riding out alone, his saddle draped with harness cut by him from the fallen horses of his battery, for harness was scarce in the Confederacy. He retired five miles, halted, and sent for reinforcements. That night, Johnston ordered up to him two infantry regiments and some more cavalry, and he marched angrily back to Dranesville in the morning. The enemy had departed, leaving the Confederate dead on the field, and some of the wounded. Stuart's loss was 194 killed, wounded, and missing, and Ord's, 68.

Here follows his letter to his wife, written on his return to camp. From it you learn that the best evidence in any fight is the official reports, and that estimates of the enemy's casualties are always unsafe.

"Camp Qui Vive, December 23d, 1861.

"My Dear Darling,

"I have been so intensely occupied in the saddle & on my report since the battle that it has been literally impossible for me to write to you until now. I rec'd the bank acct's last night & enclose one set signed, have them cashed, the money placed in your dear little pocket; as you are my better half, I send you the better half of a month's pay (20 days).

"On the 20th I was placed in command of 4 Inf'y Regt's, 1 Battery & some Cavalry to protect an expedition after forage over next to Dranesville. I marched over & found the enemy had that day advanced a large force to that point and in order to prevent our wagons falling in his hands, I had to attack him vigorously attracting his attention to me

until the wagons could escape. This I did, saving all the
wagons, & came very near whipping the enemy, so near that
they left the place soon after I did, & left several of our
wounded having so many of their own that they couldn't
carry them off. I found after a fight of two hours that, I
could not force the position, on account of their great superiority of numbers—& being myself beyond the reach of
reinforcements, I determined to withdraw my troops from
the field, which was done in perfect order, the men marching
leisurely & without confusion, and the enemy being too much
crippled to pursue us. The loss on our side was severe 43
killed or since dead, 143 wounded and 8 missing. But
strange to say the citizens of the place declare that the
enemy's loss was heavier than ours, that 20 wagon loads of
killed & wounded were carried off by them, it seems almost
incredible yet it is vouched for by the people of Dranesville,
of which I took peaceable possession next day, bringing off
our wounded and killed, to Centreville. The people declared
that we engaged 15 Regt's several batteries & 7 Co's of
Cavalry. Whether this force was so large or not, we can't
tell, but that it was 4 times larger than mine (1600) there
could be no doubt. Our side therefore came out first best—
I am perfectly satisfied that my conduct was right, and I
have the satisfaction to know that it meets the approval of
General Johnston, & all others who know the facts, and my
reputation has no doubt been the gainer. I was never in
greater personal danger & men & horses fell around me like
ten-pins, but thanks to God to whom I looked for protection, neither myself nor my horse was touched.

"There is a good deal of envy in this army among such
as Ransom, Robertson & al—but I assure you I let it trouble
me precious little. I have had several Brigade drills to show
them how I could handle a Brigade of Cavalry, & it went off
splendidly, all hands seemed delighted. All the Generals were

out to witness them, & expressed themselves highly gratified. If you telegraph me the morning you start, I will have the conveyance for you. All hands are preparing for winter quarters.

"Kisses to the dear ones and kind regards to all hands— write me often—write me long——

"Tell all our friends the correct version of the battle as they will get it mixed up in the paper.

"Kisses, Dear ones. Ever yours

"J. E. B. STUART."

As to Dranesville, Stuart declared afterwards that the newspapers botched it terribly. But he writes his brother: "I notice that Congress (January, '62) voted thanks to all who have been engaged with the enemy except the brave men who were with me at Dranesville. . . . Have I no friends in Congress?" I do not think, in the whole war, he ever received as much credit as he thought his command deserved. But let it be recorded that he kept his disappointments private, and that he never sulked.

Flora Stuart and the children spent Christmas with him, and for a while she lived, after Christmas, in Warrenton— no great distance, but in the wrong direction for his visits. Being fond and foolish, after the habit of women who love greatly, it would appear that she suggested that he try to secure some appointment less active, that would allow him to see something of his family: undoubtedly, a great many gentlemen of the first consideration, were doing so, and were respected none the less for it. He mentions it to his brother. . . . "I have told her that if I neglect the higher duties of the patriot to be a daily companion to her, I would make a husband to be ashamed of hereafter." Again and again the thing turns up; she loved him, and persisted. "How much better to have your husband in his grave after a career true

2nd. U.S. Cavalry 1861

Confederate Gentleman at arms . 1861

to every duty and every responsibility, to you, his country, and his god, than inglorious existence—a living shame to you and to his children——" Well. she would have liked to have her husband. . . .

All the letters of this period are interesting. Take a few passages, quoted at large, for by his letters you know a man——

About Joe Johnston—"Johnston is in capacity head and shoulders above every other general in the Southern Confederacy. . . ." "General Johnston is the dearest friend I have on earth. . . ." Concerning Lee, after the Kanawa reports were published—"with profound personal regard for General Lee, he has disappointed me as a General. . . ." He came to change this last opinion. "General Lee . . . to his wisdom, patriotism, and self-abnegation we owe much and will owe more before this war is over." And he thinks, "Gen'l Lee's manœuvring the Yankees out of Virginia the grandest military achievement ever heard of—(1862)." Finally, Lee had no more blindly devoted officer than Stuart; after Gettysburg, when Lee's preliminary report blamed him for the disappointments of the campaign, he does not seem to have uttered or written a word in his own behalf; his report of the cavalry operations in the Gettysburg movement is in no respect controversial.

And he mentions the Military Bill as Congress passed it, in January, '62— "Congress has thoroughly disgraced itself by passing the most outrageous abortion of a bill ever heard of for the reorganization of our forces. . . . But" (this to his wife) "tell it not where —— and other of my pets will use this speech against me." He had his unfriends, and the Confederacy dearly loved gossip—as who does not? Yet he advises his wife—who occasionally thinks he is slighted, and is indignant over it—"Never join in abuse of the Govt. and its agents. The salvation of the country, under Provi-

dence, in with the Govt. Sustain them all with stout hearts
and strong arms—" He does.

The winter ended. The year 1862 opened to the tramp
of armies. McClellan is going to Richmond by the water
road, and already Federals have made lodgement on the sea-
coast, down from Norfolk, so that Stuart writes, "the news
from Roanoke is sad but not disheartening. The reflecting
mind will rather take courage at such wholesome reverses,
for such only can arouse our people from the criminal
apathy into which they have fallen." Joe Johnston will give
up the northern strip and go to cover Richmond, and Stuart
tells his wife, "I am enduring the saddest, sorest trials of the
soldier, to see this beautiful country abandoned to the
enemy. . . ."

Here is a letter, written just before the opening of the
spring campaign. I give it in full because it is the declara-
tion of a faith which hardened under stress and never
wavered, and because it shows the heart of a brave and tender
gentleman, who loved his wife, his country, and his God:

> "Hdqu's Cav. Brigade
> "Centreville, March 2d, 1862.
>
> "My Dear Wife:
>
> "As I apprehended it is now impracticable for you to join
> me. I wrote some time since that if your visit was postponed
> till after 1st March you could not then come. I had set my
> heart on seeing you, but must be disappointed. When or
> where we will meet again the future must determine. I am
> and have been very busy. I must therefore be brief—Many
> thanks for the tasteful & pretty & becoming hat—it is the
> admiration of every one, & speaks well for your good taste.
> I wish you would get one like it for J. E. J. no. 7 1-2 in
> Size—& crown higher. The next summer will probably be
> the most eventful in a century. We must nerve our hearts for

the trial with a firm reliance on God. We must plant our feet firmly upon the platform of our inextinguishable hatred to the Northern Confederacy, with a determination to die rather than submit—What a mockery would such liberty be with submission—I for *one*—though I stood alone in the Confederacy, without countenance or aid, would uphold the banner of southern Independence as long as I had a hand left to grasp the staff—& then die before submitting. I want my wifey to feel that sort of enthusiasm, think it over & let me hear her noble words of encouragement & faith.

"Tell my boy when I am gone how I felt & wrote. Tell him never to do anything which his father would be ashamed of —never to forget the principles for which his father struggled. We are *sure* to *win*, what the sacrifices are to be, we cannot tell, but if the enemy held every town & hill top— southern subjugation would be no nearer its consummation than now. The mail is waiting for me. So I must bid you good night. Tell Powers I wrote to the Qu M'r Gen'l about his appointment, & to see him about it.

"Much love to all friends. Kisses to our Dear ones & keep them in mind of Pa. Ransom's Regt will not I presume leave here till another relieves it. The candy was very nice. I did not see Geo H. Jno Dabney S. has resigned.

"In haste your devoted hubbie——

"STUART."

VIII

THE RIDE AROUND McCLELLAN

IT is related, in George Cary Eggleston's "Rebel Recollections," that, at Stuart's headquarters, "Camp Qui Vive," in the winter of 1861-62, Staff talked of what the Yankees might do next. Would they try again through Manassas, now that General McClellan, the "Little Napoleon," was in command? Or would they thrust at Fredericksburg, or what? Stuart laid his hand on that portion of the map where the James and the York rivers wind down to Chesapeake Bay, and said:

". . . I think he knows the shortest road to Richmond. If I am not greatly mistaken, we shall hear of him presently on his way up the James River. . . ."

In March, when the winter began to loosen its hold, the newspapers and the busy Confederate agents reported vast activity in Washington, troops embarking there and at Annapolis. Confederate cavalry patrols on the Potomac, at Matthias Point, sent word of a continuous procession of transports, store-ships, ships of war, passing down the river. In the middle of the month General Johnston fell back from the Manassas Junction position to Richmond, and hurried down the Peninsula between the James and the York rivers to man the lines Magruder had laid out at Yorktown the year before. The last two weeks in March McClellan's army was landing at Fort Monroe; on the 4th of April he advanced on Yorktown, and for a month Johnston and McClellan confronted each other, inactive except for small affairs of outposts and patrols, in which Stuart's cavalry brigade was constantly engaged. Meantime, C. S. ram *Virginia* —the ex-U. S. steam-frigate *Merrimac*, burned by the Federals at Gosport Yard—raised by the Confederates and housed in the first armor-plate ever rolled in America— appeared in Hampton Roads. She sank U. S. S. *Cumberland* and U. S. S. *Congress*, fought Ericsson's *Monitor*, and outmoded in a day the wooden navies of the world. But there was only one of her: she drew too much water to ascend the James, and the army had to evacuate Norfolk, her sea base. They scuttled her behind Craney Island in the Elizabeth River; United States gunboats entered the York and the James, and McClellan ponderously advanced on Yorktown, now untenable because the rivers on either hand were lost. So Johnston did not wait to fight; on the 3d of May he left his lines, with Stuart's cavalry covering the rear of the army. So languid was McClellan's movement that it was the 4th before he found Johnston was gone and midday of the 4th before a pursuit began. That afternoon there was hard cavalry fighting between Yorktown and Williamsburg: Colonel Wickham, with the 4th Virginia Cavalry, was broken up on the Telegraph Road in the centre and himself wounded by a sabre thrust; and Emory, with the Pennsylvania cavalry, got through on the right and blocked Stuart's rear. Stuart abandoned this road and slipped by on the river beach, under the broadsides of the Federal gunboats on the York. Next day the Federal Army came up to Williamsburg, where Longstreet, with the rear guard, turned so savagely upon McClellan's advance that the Confederate brigades were not again molested; Johnston gathered his army behind the Richmond defenses.

Here follows Stuart's letter to his wife, written when the situation stabilized and a cavalryman had time to get his boots off and rest a little:

"Hd. Qu's in the Saddle,

"May 9th, 1862.

"My Darling Wife—

"Blessed be God that giveth *us* the victory. The battle of Wmsburg * was fought and won on the 5th. A glorious affair, brilliantly achieved by the rear portion (Longstreet's) of our army. On the 4th my Brigade distinguished itself, and on the 5th by its attitude and manœuvering under constant fire prevented the enemy's leaving the woods for the open ground—thus narrowing his artillery scope of fire. *I* consider the most brilliant feat of the 5th to have been a dash of the *Stuart* Horse Artillery to the front. Coming suddenly under a galling fire from the woods, from a reinforcement of the enemy, they wheeled into action sustaining in the most brilliant manner the fortunes of the day till the Inf'y could come to their support, and all the time under a continuous Inf'y fire of 200 yards or less distance. For *myself* I have only to say that if you had seen your husband you would have been proud of him. I was not out of fire the whole day. The day before (4th) the Cavalry made several charges—and Lawrence Williams told the bearer of a flag of truce that I came within an ace of capturing my father-in-law. Our Cavalry charged their Cavalry handsomely and, even they were entirely routed—their artillery captured, the Cav flag of the enemy was captured—but the 4th Va Cavalry lost its standard bearer and flag. Col Wickham was wounded on the 4th and Major Paine, severely wounded on the 5th. Robertson is sick in Richmond. The Floyd County Militia in Pelham's battery behaved in the most handsome style astounding every one beyond measure— I only got them as I passed through Richmond. The 3d Va Cavalry (Col Goode) is now in my Brigade and made a handsome charge. We were without rations & therefore had to with-

* Williamsburg.

draw that night from the field, leaving our wounded with the ladies at Wmsburg—the enemy was driven from the field entirely.

"God bless you——

"Yours,

"J. E. B. STUART."

You can identify most of these incidents in the official reports—but the reports are not so animated in tone as this letter. Notice, also, the assurance: "For *myself* I have only to say that if you had seen your husband you would have been proud of him. I was not out of fire the whole day. . . ." You find something to the same effect, in heavy formal phrase, in Longstreet's report of the action. Stuart wanted to be admired, and himself saw to it that he was always admirable.

Now, basing on the York River, White House on the Pamunkey, at the head of the York, serving as his depot, McClellan approached Richmond with 100,000 men and a siege-train, but so cautiously that nothing happened for the rest of May. Said the Richmond *Examiner*, impatient, "With 120,000 men under his hand, he [McClellan] proposes to attack Magruder's fortifications by regular approaches. As the Confederate generals never attack anybody, it is presumed that he will be met with regular defenses."

But Johnston does attack, at last. About the end of May, McClellan lies astride the Chickahominy, with his left, the corps of Sumner, Heintzelman, at Seven Pines, within five miles of Richmond, from where his camp fires can be seen at night. On the 31st of May, Johnston throws Longstreet, with D. H. Hill, Huger, and G. W. Smith, upon Casey's division, which holds the front lines. Casey, in a confused, bitter fight where the infantry wallows hip-deep in mud, and engages in flooded swamps where the wounded drown, is thrown back two miles. Next day the Confederates, having lost nearly a third of their assaulting troops, and salvaged 6,400 good Northern rifles and ten cannon, retired from the field, and the Federal troops reoccupied their old lines. Stuart was all day with Johnston and with Longstreet: cavalry was not engaged. He appears to have enjoyed it immensely, and writes sparkling letters to his wife and to his brother.

The most important result of Seven Pines was the wounding of General Joseph E. Johnston, and the appointment to command, in his place, of General Robert E. Lee, then military adviser to the President.

The appointment of Lee was not acclaimed. He had been unsuccessful on the Kanawa in West Virginia, against this same McClellan: "Evacuating Lee," the sharp-penned Southern editors named him. The editors had approved of his subsequent detail to construct harbor defenses in Southern waters, and hoped, editorially, that he would be more effective with the spade than he had been with the sword. Now they were extremely critical; nobody very sanguine. Only Mr. Davis stood, imperturbable, behind Lee, regarding criticism not at all. Davis was like that: he sustained Lee and Jackson when they were obscure and distrusted; he dismissed Johnston, who was popular; and he favored Hood, against advice, and championed Gorgas and Rains, ordnance officers of enormous ability; and protected the Chief Commissary Northrupp, who never, at any time, succeeded in feeding or clothing the men in the field.

Stuart himself writes: "Johnston is in capacity head and shoulders above every general in the Southern Confederacy"; and—in January, 1862—"with profound personal regard for Gen'l Lee, he has disappointed me as a general." Meantime, Lee takes hold of the army without ostentation, makes a few changes in command; sets it working steadily upon intrenchments, as if preparing for a siege, has all the division and brigade commanders at headquarters for one conference—the only formal conference he ever held, I believe—more to get acquainted, some of them think afterward, than to ascertain their views.

There are a number of threads that must be picked up and woven together, to reconstruct the pattern of the Peninsula Campaign. Lee's idea for the defense of Richmond—a place by nature indefensible, but become at once the moral citadel of the Confederacy—was to hold the Northern forces as far away as possible. He did not think Richmond would ever stand a siege: closely beset, it must fall. And so, eventually, it fell. In 1862 three Federal forces converged upon it: one, of several small armies—Banks, Frémont, and Shields—would come by the Shenandoah Valley; one, McDowell, by Fredericksburg. The third, the main army, was McClellan's, to which all the others would accrue when the Valley and mid-Virginia were cleared. Therefore Mr. Davis —Lee being his military adviser—maintained Jackson in the Valley, and Jackson not only neutralized Banks, Frémont, and Shields, but alarmed Washington. Washington held McDowell immobile, and even drew troops from McClellan before Richmond, to cover the capital against the threat of Stonewall Jackson's clanging victories. Therefore McClellan, with 100,000 men, stayed in his lines, where he could see the spires of Richmond, through May and into June, calling for more troops—convinced that there were 200,000 Confederates on his front—quite unwilling to do anything until, at least, McDowell joined him from Fredericksburg, and he was free of importunities for drafts to guard the capital. He was a great organizer, and a capable drill-master, but his idea of a safety factor was seven to one.

Actually, Johnston had faced him with 60,000 men from April to the end of May, and Lee, in the ultimate, attacked him with 80,000.

Early in June Lee's offensive plan, of which he said nothing to anybody, was matured. McClellan's right, composed of Fitz-John Porter's corps, 25,000 men, with the cavalry reserve of the army under Brigadier-General Philip St. George Cooke, was north of the Chickahominy, like an arm extended toward McDowell at Fredericksburg. McClellan's line of communication ran back across the Peninsula to White House on the Pamunkey, at the head of the York River.

It seemed to Lee that he might bring Jackson down secretly and swiftly from the Valley of Virginia, behind Fitz-John Porter, and then fall on him front and flank. The possibilities of the manœuvre were vast, and included the utter ruin of the North's largest and most threatening force in the field. To this end Lee's first requirement was exact information as to Fitz-John Porter's flank, its situation as to intrenchment and natural defenses. About the 10th of June he sent for Stuart and talked to him, perhaps showed him all his mind. On the 11th of June he issued a written order: Stuart would "make a scout movement to the rear of the enemy on the Chickahominy, with a view to gaining intelligence of his operations—communications, etc. . . . Another object is to destroy his wagon trains, said to be daily passing from the Piping Tree road to his camp on the Chickahominy . . . you will return as soon as the object of your expedition is accomplished; and you must bear constantly in mind, while endeavoring to execute the general purpose of your mission, not to hazard unnecessarily your command. . . ." Thus, in part, Lee's order. It contained details as to the organization of the raiding column, particulars such as Lee never troubled to bring up again. It was the first large operation in which the two were associated, and all Lee's instructions to his cavalry chief hereafter are loose and general. Too much so, it will be seen.

On the 11th of June Stuart made up a force of selected officers and men and horses from the 1st, 4th, and 9th Virginia Cavalry, and the Jeff Davis Legion, 1,200 sabres in all. Colonel Fitz Lee, the 1st, and Colonel Rooney Lee, the 9th, divided between themselves the 4th Regiment, whose field-officer, Wickham, was still down from his sabre wound at Williamsburg. Lieutenant-Colonel William Martin led the Jeff Davis Legion—Mississippians. There were two light guns of the Stuart Horse Artillery under Lieutenant James Breathed. Stuart did not mention what he was going to do. In the escort rode, among others, the volunteer John S. Mosby, a quiet little man, formerly a trooper of "Grumble" Jones's, but now without rank; and Corporal Hagen; and the giant Heros Von Borcke, late 3d Dragoon Guards of the Royal Prussian Army. This Von Borcke, to whom we are indebted for the most vivid pictures of Stuart and his men, had taken leave of absence from his king and run the blockade to join the Confederacy. A Yankee frigate chased his vessel, off Charleston, and he threw his letters of introduction overboard. He landed at Charleston, and made his way to Richmond in May, 1862, where he observed with a guardsman's amusement the highly individualistic soldiers of the Confederacy, but admired the fine blood-horses he saw, and the way their riders sat them. After some hanging around the War Department he is advised to go out and inquire for a job with Brigadier-General J. E. B. Stuart—since he seems to be a horse soldier himself—and he turns out in hunt kit—pink coat, white breeches, top-boots, and his long dragoon sword, making sure of notice. So Stuart met him a few days before Seven Pines, and was delighted: he took him in at once. Von Borcke rode with him the day of the battle at Seven Pines, endured shelling with gratifying equanimity, and carried messages ably under fire. Stuart includes him on this enterprise and comes to love him and to make good use of him.

The column was formed, says Stuart, without flag or bugle: no glitter or show about it. On the Brook road, a fine wide turnpike, it could ride in fours, taking up, in close order, with the artillery section, about half a mile. After it turned eastward from Hanover Court House, threading along the country roads that traverse the low river lands between the Pamunkey, the Chickahominy, and the James, it would have to ride in twos, and, with advance guard, main body, and rear guard, it would fill well over a mile of road space. And that mile would progressively lengthen, for the rear of a column is always losing distance.

It was assembled on the Brook turnpike, north of Richmond, and rode out through the infantry camps the morning of the 12th of June. Infantry assumed that Jeb Stuart was riding up to join old Stonewall, in the Valley—the Brook road led that way—and Infantry called, "Why don't you stay where the fightin' is?" An Old Army friend passed: "How long you goin' to be gone, Beauty?" Stuart turned in his saddle and laughed joyously.

> "Oh, it may be for years,
> And it may be forever . . ."

he sang, and Sweeny's gleemen, with no delay at all, can raise——

> "Kathleen, Mavourneen, the grey dawn is breaking,
> The horn of the hunter is heard on the hill . . ."

So the column jingled off, singing in the dew-spangled June morning, Breathed's horse-guns clanking behind, northwest, toward Louisa Court House. Not a bad idea for Richmond and for McClellan that Lee feels able to send reinforcements to Stonewall Jackson, in the Valley: the papers mention it next day. The column passed a place called Yellow Tavern, inclined west to cross the Richmond, Fredericksburg & Potomac Railroad, passed west of Ashland station, and, just short of the South Anna River, turned sharply east down the stream. It bivouacked without camp fires, scouts well forward: and the troopers remark that this ain't the way to the Valley. Twenty-two miles it covered that day. Stuart had some information, from previous examination of the front: Fitz-John Porter lies at Mechanicsville, and his outposts operate along the Virginia Central Railroad, northward.

On the morning of the 13th the column got quietly to horse, and the scouts went eastward, toward Hanover Court House, five miles away. Stuart assembled his field officers and told them his mission, "so as to secure an intelligent action and co-operation in whatever might occur." Now he will move on Old Church: directly in Fitz-John Porter's rear. They ride through the quiet morning, and close to Hanover Court House the enemy is reported, in and around the place—cavalry. Stuart hears his scouts and sends Fitz Lee with the 1st Virginia to detour and get behind whatever it is, over there. Himself, he follows gently with the main body, his points keeping in sight of the bluecoats.

They are about 100 troopers of the 5th U. S. Cavalry, Fitz Lee's old regiment, under a Lieutenant Leib. Their main body, Captain Royall, is camped at Old Church, ten miles east, and they are on patrol. Leib sees the first of the graybacks about the time they see him, estimates them at two squadrons, and falls back slowly, showing no alarm. A sergeant of Leib's falls out and is captured. At Cash Corners, where a road branches off to Mechanicsville, the Yankees turn south and Stuart does not wish to follow; his mission takes him east. Fitz Lee rejoins the column, much disap-

pointed, having been detained in crossing a marsh; and
Stuart proceeds on the Old Church road, by Taliaferro's
Mill and Enan Church, meeting nobody. But Leib has sent
messengers to Captain Royall, who rides keenly up from Old
Church, with another 100 men of the 5th. About noon,
Royall hears firing ahead; Stuart's advance guard, Rooney
Lee and the 9th Virginia, have collided with a 5th Cavalry
picket and ridden it down. There was a running fight for a
mile or two, past Hawes Shop, where Von Borcke got among
the Yankees with his long sword, to the admiration of all:
then across the Totopotomoy Creek, where Stuart slows up
and throws out flank guards as well as he can in the thick
country (it is such a fine defensive position that he thinks
there should be Yankees in it, but there are not); and on
toward Gibson's Mill, where the woods are heavy to right and
left, and flankers ineffective. Here they collide with Captain
Royall, and Captain Latané's squadron of the 9th Virginia
rides at him—both forces in column of fours on the road.
"Cut and thrust!" yells Royall, his pistol out; "On to them,
boys!" yells Latané, leading with his sword. The columns
shock together: Latané is shot and killed, and Royall falls
with a bad sabre wound.

When two cavalry forces ride into each other there is a
screaming confusion and a dusty tumult, wherein nothing is
very clear, then or afterward; and where, after the fewest
frantic minutes, one party or the other runs. The horses,
already brought to the highest excitement, plunge and rear,
trying to get free of the press, and their men hack and slash,
each trooper just as likely to shear an ear from his own
mount, or to rake a comrade's ribs, as to get home on the
enemy. All things being equal, the men and horses will break
first who are least hardened by discipline against their
natural aversion to getting hurt. Latané's squadron forced
Royall's back to where the ground opened a little, on the

sides of the road, and the blue cavalry drew clear and tried to reform—true, the Confederate officers noted, to the steady tradition of the Old Army. But the Confederate column had its elements exactly spaced for combat, and before the Federals could recover from the first charge Rooney Lee's second squadron was flung against them and they were swept away, scattered irretrievably. Fitz Lee's regiment passed rapidly to the front and led the pursuit, following the fugitives through their camp under the pleasant shade trees at Old Church, where the pious folk of the region were wont to hitch their animals on Sundays. The camp was looted and burned, and numerous prisoners gathered, but more escaped in the woods to the south and east. Among these last was Lieutenant Byrnes, a junior of Royall's, who took with him the remarkable impression that the Confederate cavalry was supported by from three to five regiments of infantry. He may have seen a few dismounted troopers, thrown out by Stuart to the flanks where the going was thick, before the skirmish; more likely he was a young officer in his first fight, who thought he saw things which were not there.

By 3 P.M. Fitz-John Porter's cavalry commander, Brigadier-General Philip St. George Cooke, had heard the news: a report from Leib, a report from Royall before the fight at Gibson's Mill, a report from Lieutenant Byrnes afterward. Fugitives arrive at headquarters. The last report affirms that three to five regiments of rebel infantry, as well as several thousand cavalry, are on the Old Church road, and the mention of infantry causes Philip St. George Cooke— who is also Stuart's father-in-law—to stop and think. Cooke sends cavalry, Rush's Pennsylvania Lancers, and some of the 1st Regulars, and six squadrons of the 5th and 6th. These go a little way, discover that they have no forage with them, and halt and send back for it. Cooke also wants some infantry and guns, and they must wait until the infantry and guns arrive. By 10 P.M. the Federal pursuit force, all arms, is on the Old Church road near where the fight occurred, and makes for itself no easy problem. In the first place, its pace must be set by the infantry; General Cooke and General Emory did not care to risk a cavalry contact with those reported Confederate regiments of foot. Then, in an obscure country of woods and swamps, where all the roads were crooked and narrow and looked exactly alike, especially in the dark, and where there were no prominent natural features to guide one, there was no telling which way the rebels had gone: the pursuit seems to have halted and pondered at every cross roads and searched for tracks, and examined all the natives, white or negro, that they came across. The Federals lacked friendly guides. They had no Private Frayser or Lieutenant Christian, resident in the locality, to direct them, as Stuart was directed. Their unwieldy column—horse, foot, and guns—was nearly eight miles long when it had shaken itself out, and it moved very slowly; the infantry, it is reported, suffering much from the heat. All of Fitz-John Porter's corps was thoroughly aroused and entirely mystified.

Stuart, meantime, reassembled east of the Old Church camp, had two courses open to him—go back the way he came, or go ahead. His scouts, working to the south during the day, had brought in reports on Fitz-John Porter's dispositions, and that was what Lee wanted to know. The Federals were gathering—or ought to be gathering, across the road back: Stuart was now well in the rear of the infantry lines. Considering the matter, he decided to return by making a circuit of McClellan's army, riding right across his lines of communication. Certainly nobody would expect him to do such a thing, and that was in his favor. This decision he characterized, in his report, as "the quintessence of prudence." He had scouts from the New Kent company of the

3d Virginia Cavalry, local people who knew the country which he would have to traverse, and he told his officers what he proposed to do. "While none accorded a full assent"—it did look risky—"all assured me a hearty support in whatever I did," he reports. So—"with an abiding trust in God, and with such guarantees of success as the two Lees and Martin and their devoted followers"—he turned his horse's head eastward—toward Tunstall's station. It was afternoon. He had marched and fought for fourteen miles.

The column moved, and Stuart reported: "There was something sublime in the implicit confidence and unquestioning trust of the rank and file in a leader guiding them straight, apparently, into the very jaws of the enemy, every step appearing to them to diminish the faintest hope of extrication." Stuart could always find time to savor, happily, moments like this. But he never let them take his mind from the matter in hand.

The rear was now of as much importance as the front; in fact, there was no rear, with the enemy all around. Rooney Lee leads: Lieutenant-Colonel William Martin and Breathed's guns pound behind. About dark Martin thinks he will be attacked, and faces about, but it is a party of Federal soldiers who want to surrender; meeting rebel cavalry back here, it seems to be the sensible thing to do. The day declines and the column makes good progress, snatching amazed prisoners, and upsetting supply-trains along the road that fed the Yankee army. At Garlic's Landing, ten or twelve miles from Old Church, where the Pamunkey loops within a mile of the road, Stuart sent a squadron to burn whatever was there: prisoners had mentioned supplies at Garlic's. They found, and fired, two laden schooners and a park of wagons, and the supply trains of the 17th and 44th New York Volunteers.

A few miles ahead was Tunstall's station, on the York

River Railroad, and the aides, Burke, Farley, and Von Borcke, with Mosby and a detail, were sent galloping ahead to capture it and cut the wires. They seized two bewildered squads of infantry, station guards, and learned that a train was expected. Before they could tear up the road, the train appeared, took alarm at the obstruction they had begun to build, put on speed, and dashed through toward White House. Von Borcke thinks he killed the engineer, "firing my blunderbuss into the cab," and a few soldiers in the cars were hit by the ragged fire of the troopers. Stuart and the main body came up: they found at Tunstall's a loaded wagon-train, and freighted cars, and numerous sutlers' stores and provision dumps. The rolling-stock and stores were fired, and the Black Creek railroad bridge destroyed, and the men allowed to ration themselves as they pleased on the Yankee abundance. It was getting dark, and a body of blue cavalry came out of the woods from the east, observed the scene, and retired discreetly. Five miles in that direction lay White House Landing, McClellan's main supply base. It was guarded by gunboats on the river, and soldiers ashore. Stuart weighed the chances of an attack, but thought that the country was getting too warm to hold him. He assembled and rode on, seven miles, to Talleysville. White House plantation was the home of Rooney Lee, and you imagine him looking that way in the dark.

Over at White House there was much alarm: stout Colonel Ingals, McClellan's quartermaster, was mustering the sick, the wounded, the teamsters, the commissary clerks, the roustabouts—every man able to lift a weapon—these in addition to his guard, 600 strong. He expected to be attacked, but he sent no appeals for aid. "I have not been pressing for troops, because I hoped we could defend the depot with the force provided, and because I knew the General Commanding wishes every good soldier with him in front of Richmond," he writes McClellan, reporting the affair. A very sturdy, able officer, who deserves to be remembered for the way he stood by his stuff.

At Talleysville, or Baltimore Store, there is a hospital—army surgeons, nurses, and several hundred sick and wounded. Stuart, riding now by moonlight, arrives about nine o'clock, and allows his column to halt and close up. They rest for three and one-half hours, after some thirty-five miles, no little fighting, and a long day in the saddle. On the hospital, the Federal officers handsomely concede, Stuart commits no depredations.

During the halt the tired horses draw breath: troopers remount themselves, here and there, on captured animals, the plunder is stowed—such as a man can carry on his saddle—and the prisoners are sorted out and put astride their fellow captives, the horses and mules, with the U. S. brand. At midnight Stuart leads straight south, having eight miles to go to the Chickahominy, which he must ford. Behind him, two hours later, the first of the pursuit arrives—some of Rush's Lancers, very tired. They stop and rest until dawn. Stuart is making poor time, over heavy roads, his guns now double-teamed, and Rush halted just four miles in his rear.

The Chickahominy, astride which McClellan lay, is a little winding stream of black, sluggish water. In dry weather it is fordable at many places, but it rises quickly and its current becomes treacherous and swift. It meanders through a wide, swampy bottom-land, impenetrable except by the narrow country roads. Stuart expected to ford it at Sycamore Springs, by a private ford on the property of Lieutenant Jones Christian, who was now guiding the column. They rode down to the river after daylight and found it risen, so that the ford was gone. Rooney Lee swam his horse across to try it, and had such a time that swimming was at once abandoned. The main body arrived, closed up, and waited, and every man looked at Jeb Stuart, who sat his horse and gave the river his bright regard, and stroked his beard reflectively as was his custom, his aides say, in times of crisis. He sent off a corporal with a despatch to Lee, giving his situ-

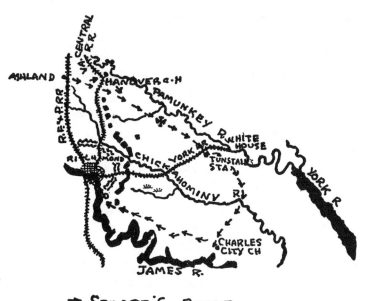

→ STUART'S ROUTE

✠ OLD CHURCH

🪖 CONFEDERATE LINES

🪖 FEDERAL LINES

(FROM RICHMOND TO TUNSTALL'S STATION ABOUT 20 MILES

ation and asking that the infantry make a diversion on the Charles City road, to engage the attention of McClellan's left wing, behind which he had yet to pass. Then, no bridge being possible here, he cast about, and they set upon the ruins of the old bridge on the road from Providence Forge to Charles City Court House, a mile below Sycamore Springs. It had been burned during earlier operations, but the piling stood, and there was an empty warehouse near by. He set the whole command—energetic aid being gotten from the prisoners also—to tearing down the warehouse and constructing a passageway. Very soon there were foot-planks, and they began to swim the horses over, leading them from the planking. By the time the warehouse was down a sort of structure was up, and the remainder of the command, with Breathed's guns, crossed dry-shod. Fitz Lee was the last man over: at 2 P.M., as he climbed the southern bank, the first of Rush's Lancers rode out and shot at him from the other side. Lee's men put fire to their bridge and rejoined the column; they had to ford another branch of the Chickahominy, muddy and shallow, and lost there a limber, the only piece of equipment not brought back. There was no pursuit south of the Chickahominy.

Richmond was now thirty-five miles away: it was late afternoon of the 14th, but the worst danger was over. Stuart had to ride twenty miles, with the James and its gunboats on his left, and Hooker's infantry line on his right, before he was entirely safe, but he made it without incident. By Christian's, down to Charles City Court House, and thence to Buckland, he came by dark. Here he allowed the command to bivouac, giving orders to Fitz Lee to follow with it at eleven o'clock. Himself, he took an orderly and rode on to Richmond, reporting to Lee's headquarters before sunrise on the 15th. His column had with it 165 prisoners and 260 animals, and had burned and destroyed notably, and suffered just one battle casualty, Captain Latané. The regiments reported four enlisted men missing, straggled, or lost in the woods.

Latané was a man well-born and much beloved, an officer of promise. They left his body at the house of Doctor

Brockenborough, where the women were alone, all their men serving with the Confederate Army. Next day the Brockenborough ladies, and the Newton ladies, neighbors, buried the body, slaves digging the grave for it. They asked the Northern cavalry, in the vicinity, for a chaplain, but no chaplain was detailed, and the service was read by some person there present. This is one of the romantic and tender stories of the Peninsula Campaign: from it came a poem of Thompson's, and a painting, "The Burial of Latané," copied much in steel engravings, which hang now in old Virginia homes.

On the morning of the 15th of June the column rides through Richmond, behind Jeb Stuart, who galloped ahead to report to Lee, and galloped back to lead his people into camp—which adds at least thirty miles to his personal distance, but he will not rest until they are bedded down. The colonels are at the heads of their regiments—brisk, compact Fitz Lee, with the jolly gleam of white teeth in his dark beard; big Rooney Lee, with his heavy, dependable air, tall on his tall horse; Lieutenant-Colonel William Martin—hard and competent. Then the troopers—the smart soldiers, their gray jackets buttoned, sitting up in their saddles—the dull, tired soldiers, slouching on their weary horses—the gay soldiers, with keen, roving eyes for the pretty Richmond girls. And Lieutenant James Breathed and his guns, hoping nobody will notice that he is a limber short; Captain John Pelham of the Stuart Horse Artillery will be displeased about that limber, even though the general said: "Leave it." The column is dirty and unshaven, and red-eyed from lack of sleep. Hanover dust, New Kent sand, and Chickahominy mud are plastered thick from horse's fetlock to rider's cap, and the horses are drawn and gaunt. But the people cheer, and the ladies wave, and a song starts at the head of the column, and rings back to the solemn guns:

"If you want to have a good time—
Jine the Cavalry!"

You can drive today over Stuart's ride, about a hundred miles, following the roads he used. The country is much as it was then, and the roads follow the same trace—little narrow wagon-ways, winding through the densest country, seldom used by any vehicle. A column, following such roads, rides blind and needs great confidence in its leader. But the country favors an enterprise like Stuart's: a compact body of determined men, knowing what they are going to do, can slip readily through an unwieldly host that is of several opinions. The thing made a great noise in the world: cavalry had not been so used since Napoleon loosed Murat and Kellerman and LaSalle upon the Germans. The Southern press was triumphant, and the Confederate Army notably enlarged in spirit. Congratulatory orders were published by everybody concerned: Stuart recommends his regimental commanders for advancement, which they receive; asks a commission for Von Borcke, which he is given; and singles out Redmond Burke, Farley, Mosby, Doctor Fountaine, Robbins, his chaplain the Reverend Mr. Landstreet, and Corporal Hagan, for special praise. All statements give much credit to Almighty God; the Governor of Virginia presents a sabre to Stuart's orderly Farley; and the girls in Richmond throw flowers before Stuart's horse when he rides through the town.

Even the Northern papers admire. McClellan finds it hard to explain; Fitz-John Porter reports: "I have seen no energy or spirit in the pursuit by General Cooke," and Stuart's father-in-law is called upon for a statement in writing as to why he let the rebels get away, and stews for days, explaining it. It was a great and brilliant cavalry deed-at-arms.

But, thinking it over, with the maps and the reports, and

the knowledge of what came afterward, one wonders. Stuart could, as the events turned out, have retreated up the Pamunkey, a little north of the road by which he came. Being a trained officer, he assumed—as he had been taught to assume—that the enemy would use good judgment, and block this line of retreat at once. But Cooke proved incapable, and Stuart could have gotten out. The only advantage in the course Stuart took lay in the fact that it was totally unexpected by the enemy. And McClellan was, of all generals, most sensitive about his communications: after Stuart had thus cut across his lines of supply, he began to take thought, and correspondence with Ingals the quartermaster, and with the navy in the rivers, regarding the practibility of supplying the army from a base on the James, began within two days of Stuart's ride. In consequence, when, in the last week in June, Lee brought Jackson upon Fitz-John Porter's flank and attacked in front with the Richmond army, and swept down the north bank of the Chickahominy, McClellan was able, with no loss of time at all, to shift his base by water around to the James River. McClellan was a slow thinker, but Stuart's ride applied a very powerful stimulus to his careful brain.

It is hard to assess fair judgment upon such an exploit. Its moral value was enormous: the Southern trooper was confirmed in his opinion that he could outride, outfight and outdare anything the Yankee nation might put on four legs, and for a full year the Confederate cavalry superiority was hardly disputed. The Seven Days' battles, which followed at the end of June, were opened on the information brought back by Stuart as to Fitz-John Porter's dispositions; and his examination of the terrain, gained in the raid, was the basis of Lee's orders to his striking flank. But if Stuart had turned back from Old Church after the fight on the 13th, he would have missed his fun among the wagon-trains, yet

he would have had most of the important information—and
I do not believe that McClellan would have been ready for
that change of base which saved his army from complete
disaster. Still military history would be poorer by a fine
and daring thing.

IX

THE SEVEN DAYS' BATTLE

THE Peninsula Campaign, which opened in April, 1862, with the approach of McClellan's Grand Army of the Potomac to Yorktown, and closed with the Seven Days' Battle about 1 July, 1862, was a thing shaped and dominated by the water-ways of the region across which it was fought.

There is the James River. From Richmond, on its north bank, at the head of navigation, it winds down, about seventy miles, to Hampton Roads and the Chesapeake, a crooked meandering of tawny water between flat, wooded banks that are studded, here and there, with bold bluffs of red clay. In its lower reaches it becomes very wide. North of the James, and roughly parallel, from fifteen to twenty-five miles distant, sprawls the York, which enters the Chesapeake on the other side of Old Point Comfort. The York is a wider, quieter stream, with more of marsh and lily-bed along it. The general flow of both rivers is southeast. At White House, twenty-two miles east and a little north of Richmond, the York becomes the Pamunkey, which derives, just above Hanover Court House, from the North Anna and the South Anna. This land between the rivers—the James and the York—is the oldest settled region on the Atlantic Seaboard. The ancient shot-tower still stands at Jamestown, where the first permanent settlement was; and there were stately houses, Shirley and Westover and Brandon, and the like, built graciously, in the 1700's, with bricks and tiles and ornaments that came out from the Old World.

Williamsburg and Yorktown are the villages of the Peninsula: otherwise, small farmers and large planters lived through the region, and the courthouses—Charles City, Hanover, New Kent—were the assembly places of the citizens, the focal points of the country roads.

The Peninsula is divided, in its upper length, by the Chickahominy River, that passes four miles north of Richmond and feeds into the James well below Westover Landing. Where the James and the York are wide and slow and yellow, the Chickahominy is narrow and swift and black— except when the rains raise it out of banks, and it runs red from the clay of the up-country. Chickahominy is swampy, too—not the open marshes of the larger streams, wide expanse of sedge and sky and water, attractive to sea fowl— but with thick growth of pin oak and white oak, mirrored in standing water; and masked with underbrush and trailing vines; so that you may not say where the land gives over to the stream. Along the Chickahominy there are no vistas: the trees, in full leaf at this time of year, cut off all perspectives. Here and there, as east of Boatswains' Creek, where Gaines' Mill stands, you come upon surprising elevations, flat-topped plateaus that rise above the trees. South of the middle Chickahominy is White Oak Swamp.

Low, uncertain watersheds, more sandy than the bottom lands, veer along between the streams: the best roads follow these ridges, and the best roads are narrow, obscure, and very bad. Yet only by them can wheeled transport move, and even men and horses follow them where they may, for the going, off the roads, is choked and nightmarish and impossible. Down there, you ride for miles and never see the sun through the interlacing branches overhead. There are interminable twists and turns—the track of a leisurely horse-drawn time, siting its path with the curves of the high ground, to avoid the drowned lowlands; and there are frequent cross roads, that may lead to the Williamsburg Pike, or blind into a farmer's wood lot—all unmarked. It is silent along these roads, and oppressively remote. The whole country has the air of waiting, sullenly, for something to happen. It was sparsely settled in the '60's: it has no more inhabitants now—perhaps less: for, following the old traces through virgin woods, you find most of the houses deserted—long deserted. It is a land full of mosquitoes; of poor surface wells; and you breathe close, dead air, stagnant between the forest walls.

*   *   *   *   *

Into this watery wilderness, following slowly up from Yorktown to Williamsburg, on toward Richmond as Johnston's brigades retired, McClellan had moved his Army of the Potomac. He says in his later writings that he wanted, originally, to base his force upon the south bank of the James, about where the Appomattox River comes in from Petersburg—and this was the key to Richmond which Grant found, two years after him. But in the vague Northern strategy of 1862, McClellan was one of three spears, driven fumblingly at the heart of the Confederacy. The other two were: those 60,000 men, three little armies, Banks, Frémont, and Shields, that entered Virginia by way of the Shenandoah Valley: and McDowell, who came with a corps down by Manassas, to Fredericksburg, fifty miles north of Richmond, on the Rappahannock. Banks, Frémont, and Shields would sweep the Valley clean of the annoying rebel forces under a General T. J. Jackson, called Stonewall. McDowell would clear the central strip, stretching across as a sort of connecting link, and eventually he would march from the north and join hands with McClellan who came from the east, all converging on the Confederate capital. Therefore (McClellan says), to facilitate his junction with McDowell, he was forced by Washington to establish his base of supplies on the York River, rather than on the James.

Basing on the York, he still had plenty of water for his naval echelon, and he could use the York River Railroad as his axis of supply as he advanced. The great disadvantage was, that his line of communication became increasingly precarious as he lengthened it. The difficulty of defending every part of it in the thick country through which it passed was probably one of the reasons which induced him to abandon it when Lee attacked him. The position on the James was the actual key to Richmond, and McClellan might, in time, have realized it. Grant, at a cost of 100,000 battle casualties, would place his army in McClellan's old camps, two years later, after trying every other route——

* * * * *

The York River Railroad crossed the Chickahominy ten miles east of Richmond. McClellan, pressing on, divided his army at this point: the right wing held along the north bank of the Chickahominy; the center and left moved across, and ascended the south bank; the extreme left feeling toward— but not extending to—the James. In May the left and center encircled Richmond from the east and the northeast, and dug in. The right established itself at Mechanicsville, five miles due north of Richmond, and thrust out feelers to the north and west, as far as Hanover station on the Virginia Central Railroad. The United States North Atlantic Blockading Squadron held the rivers, undisputed on the York, much annoyed by rebel light forces from the south bank of the James. A great depot of stores built up at White House on the Pamunkey, and the trains shuttled back and forth by the York River line, and Federal wagons toiled along the bad roads behind the army.

* * * * *

Such was the situation of the Federals at the end of May: Seven Pines did not change it. So it was when Stuart

rode around the Army of the Potomac, in the middle of
June: only, after that, McClellan, and Quartermaster Colonel
Ingals, and Flag Officer Goldsborough of the Navy, put their
heads together and made plans: it was disturbing to have
rebel cavalry depredating in your intimate rear. Further,
the reports McClellan had from the Shenandoah Valley and
from Washington were not good: Stonewall Jackson, in a
thirty-day campaign with 17,000 men at his strongest, had
beaten in detail Banks, Frémont, and Shields, and expelled
them from the Valley, so that Washington feared an assault:
that fellow, with any number of screeching rebels behind
him, was quite likely to come rampaging down the Potomac
and into the Federal city itself. Therefore—McClellan, who
had in June 105,000 men and believed he faced 200,000,
could look for no reinforcements: therefore, McDowell must
stand at Fredericksburg, within supporting distance of the
uneasy capital: and it followed that McClellan must do the
best he could, by himself. Afterwards, he will accuse his
government of deserting him, most basely. Certainly there
was taken from him the co-operation of the Valley forces,
and of McDowell from central Virginia—two of the three
Yankee spears blunted and turned aside by Stonewall
Jackson.

*   *   *   *   *

So you come to the last ten days of June. The Yankees
sit, immobilized everywhere: on the upper Potomac, at Fredericksburg; and in the lowlands between the rivers, where
malarial mosquitoes are beginning to fight for their Southern
homeland. Stonewall Jackson, reinforced from Richmond,
and with the rumor of him terrible beyond the border, has
drawn a screen across the lower Shenandoah Valley, where
Banks, Frémont, and Shields stand beaten and apprehensive, prepared to sell their lives dearly; and he has moved

east over the Blue Ridge, 18,500 men with him. Lee, commanding in the field since Johnston was wounded at Seven Pines, has gained, through his cavalry chief's enterprise, minute intelligence of McClellan's outflung right wing: Lee's eye has been on that corps for a month. He knows it to be very strong in front, behind Beaver Dam Creek, at Mechanicsville; and he knows that, by fortifying the Chickahominy watershed, from the head of Beaver Dam, a scant mile across to Totopotomoy Creek, which is the nearest affluent of the Pamunkey—McClellan might have made his right wholly secure. But Stuart, who went and looked, has reported that the Federal right is in the air, innocent of field fortifications and natural defenses. Lee has 60,000 men, a few more than Johnston had: and with some new troops from the South, and Jackson, who is in the Valley, he counts nearly 85,000. He thinks it is enough. Where he will fight, the thick country can be depended on to neutralize numbers and to discount the powerful Federal artillery, always superior in metal to the Confederate guns. He makes all things ready.

*   *   *   *   *

The Federal Army had, under McClellan, been organized into corps: there were five of these, the 2d, Sumner, who was Jeb Stuart's colonel at the Solomon River fight; the 3d, Heintzelman; the 4th, Keyes—these officers were at First Manassas—the 5th, Fitz-John Porter, and the 6th, Franklin. Cavalry, artillery, and special services were allotted among the corps, with some cavalry and guns held in army reserve. Each corps was 20,000 men, more or less, about the size of an American World War division.

The Confederate organization was still rudimentary. Johnston's army was made up of brigades and divisions, and there were a few free units, legions, independent battalions, and the like, which are hard to classify. The Confederate service was always highly individualistic. A legion might be 200 men, or 1,000, of all arms. A regiment might vary just as much in numbers: a Confederate order of battle never offered any clue to numerical strength. A regiment, like a legion, was as likely to have 200 rifles as 1,000. From two to six regiments made a brigade, and two or more brigades a division. All the regiments were local in personnel: brigades were generally formed from regiments of the same state, and brigades and divisions were habitually designated by the names of their commanding officers.

On assuming field command, General Lee had taken some steps toward a more compact and effective organization. His divisions were not yet grouped in army corps—that did not come until September, 1862. But a senior or selected division commander might be placed in charge of a group of divisions for a specific mission. Thus, Magruder, with his own, Huger's, Holmes', and D. R. Jones' divisions, had command of the forces south of the Chickahominy in the first of the Seven Days' Battle. Jackson had his own, Ewell's, Whitings', and D. H. Hill's. Longstreet and A. P. Hill led their own divisions, and to Longstreet were assigned some of Magruder's divisions in the later fighting south of the river. These groupments were called wings, or, simply, commands. They were temporary, and no increase of staff personnel was provided to the generals who received them. This looseness of organization caused many of the Confederate tactical failures during the battle. But the Confederate Service drew some benefit from its mistakes, and with the Second Manassas Campaign, the corps arrangements began to function informally. After the Second Manassas, they became permanent.

It is hard to fix the effective strength of either army, at any given date, and it is especially so with the Confederates, since so many of their records disappeared. But McClellan had, from first to last, 120,000 men, and in the Seven Days' Battle, with deductions for sick, line of communication troops, and special services, he had 105,000 effectives. Lee's numbers are nowhere authoritatively given. Johnston had accumulated some 50,000 men on the Peninsula: Lee, after him, received a few brigades from the Department of North Carolina, and some new formations from the South, of which Lawton's strong Georgia Brigade—four 1,000-man regiments—was one. Then, Jackson brought 18,500 from the Valley, not counting his detachments en route. Lee probably had 85,000 men, less some sick, when his battle opened. In the course of the action, Lee engaged practically every unit he had: McClellan, however, fought less than half of his men. Of his 16,000 battle casualties, 7,500 occurred in Porter's Fifth Corps alone.

There was little to choose between the armies in point of personnel. Both were largely volunteer, and the material was splendid. The Northern troops were men enlisted or re-enlisted in late 1861, for three years: some of them had been at First Manassas, and in the winter skirmishes in northern Virginia. Of the Confederates, Jackson's divisions had the most combat experience—more than any troops in either army. The majority of the Southern regiments had been under arms for at least a year—longer by some months than the Federals. The South Carolinians had been mustered in December, 1860. On the whole, the Southern soldiers were more inured to an outdoor life, and perhaps had more drill, and were better shots—circumstances neutralized by their armament and organization, both inferior to the Federal. The battles that followed were the heaviest that had ever taken place in the Western Hemisphere. But tactics and strategy on both sides were characterized by the mistakes of inexperience. A year later, both armies were more capable. In general, there was no great inequality between

them: the deciding factor lay in the command—Lee's calculated audacity against McClellan's fumbling prudences.

*   *   *   *   *

Lee's headquarters were in the Dabb house, two miles
out of Richmond on the Nine Mile road. The 23d of June,
three of his division commanders assembled there to meet a
fourth. It is worth your while to look at them, for their
footsteps will be mighty in this war. All wore the stars and
wreaths of major-generals. The senior was James Longstreet.

* Longstreet was forty-one years old; West Point, 1838,
born in South Carolina. He had a brevet for gallantry in
Mexico: we saw him later, a major, commanding a column
of the 8th Infantry in Texas, when the Mounted Rifle Regiment campaigned against the Comanches, and Jeb Stuart
was Second Lieutenant and Regimental Quartermaster.
After that, Major Longstreet transferred to the Paymas-
ter's Office, and resigned from it in 1861 to become a Confederate colonel. It is remembered of him that he served in
the old 4th Infantry when one U. S. Grant joined the command, and that he was, with Cadmus Wilcox, a groomsman
at young Grant's wedding to Julia Dent. This year he is a
large-boned, burly man, with a ruddy face and a bushy
brown beard, and steady blue-gray eyes. The mud of the
Chickahominy is on his boots, and his uniform—even the net-
ted silk sash Jeb Stuart gave him last month—is weathered
and faded. His aspect is a little fierce: not of the bright
headquarters. He is slightly deaf, has no small conversation, and delivers his opinions deliberately and with a great
finality: all his life he is invincibly stubborn, and prefers
his own views to any others. But the enemy finds him stubborn too: no triumph excites him, and no disaster ever shook
him. He takes the most excellent care of his troops, looks

largely on the dark side of things, and Grant thinks that he was Lee's best general. "Old Pete," they called him in the United States service, and Lee says, here is my Old War Horse. Lee loved him. The after years blow somewhat on his reputation, but you cannot imagine the Army of Northern Virginia without James Longstreet. He sits now, nursing his sword, and thinks gloomily of battles. Lee takes too many risks, he considers. I believe that Longstreet, who was never afraid of any enemy, was always a little afraid of Lee. •

Next senior to him, classmate at West Point, forty-one years old, is Daniel Harvey Hill, another South Carolinian, who served also with distinction in Mexico, but left the army afterwards and taught the military sciences in a North Carolina college, and has the reputation of a pungent, facile writer on almost any subject. He is smaller than Longstreet, a little stooped, and his clipped beard is shot with gray. His eyes are very honest and kindly, and look out, with quizzical regard, through thick spectacles. One knows of him that Stonewall Jackson's first wife was his sister: that Jackson owed his appointment at V.M.I. to Major Hill's interest, and that, like Jackson, he is an ardent Presbyterian, though not fanatic. There is a fiery earnestness about his fighting methods, too, that later in this war reminds men of Stonewall Jackson. He has a division of North Carolina troops, remarkably steady soldiers, whose reputation is going to grow. Outspoken, critical, impolite, he will incur the enmity of Mr. Jefferson Davis and pass, next year, from the field of large operations, one of its finest generals, that the Confederacy neglected.

The third general, and the youngest, not quite thirty-six years old, is Ambrose Powell Hill, of Culpeper, in Virginia. He finished West Point, just in time to go to Mexico, and was lieutenant, with George Thomas, in Captain Bragg's famous battery: "a little more grape, Captain Bragg!" He resigned from the U. S. service to go with Virginia, and Mr. Davis commissioned him colonel of infantry: when his aunt, old Mrs. Powell, a notable lady of Culpeper, heard of it, it is related that she laughed and laughed: This Confederacy, she said, was mighty hard up, if they made Ambrose Hill a colonel! He is slender and tall, not robust, with keen, handsome features, red hair, and a short red beard. He affects the little shell jacket and the flat kepi, all smart and tight, rather than the double-breasted frock coat and broad brimmed hat most general officers wear. His green eyes have a genial twinkle in them that turns readily to anger: his temperament goes with his hair. Yet, an old courier of Longstreet's, who carried messages between the corps headquarters of the Army of Northern Virginia, remembers after sixty years, that, of all the generals, A. P. Hill was the one who never failed to have, in the hottest place, a kindly word and perhaps a little joke, for the couriers who served him.

Lee has picked these three as his hardest-hitting generals, and they will be known hereafter. Now they wait, in the Dabb house, with roses blooming at the windows and mocking birds singing in the garden, and the cannon on the Chickahominy shaking the casements now and then, until two horsemen stop outside and dismount stiffly, as men who have galloped a long way. They hear boots, and the jingle of spurs in the hall, the murmur of Major Long, Lee's aide, and a flat, reedy voice: "Tell General Lee, some one from the Valley." Major Long ushers into them the fourth general: "General Jackson; General Longstreet, General Hill, General Ambrose Powell Hill—" and leaves them together. They stand up, you conceive, with some scraping of chairs: this is Stonewall Jackson. You see a rumpled, uncomely officer, an inch over six feet. The red dust of three Virginia counties lies on his cloak, on his queer black cap, his rusty, ill-fitting frock, and his great horseman's boots. Stars and braid are tarnished: there is no gleam about him anywhere except the light in his hard blue eyes. On his bony face are the etched lines of fatigue, incised under the eye, and down from the thin nostril. His beard does not hide the cold firmness of his mouth. He sits ungracefully, not responsive to the compliments that come pleasantly from the Hills, heavily from Longstreet. He plants his large feet precisely, folds his hands over his sabre hilt, and says he has ridden, since one o'clock that morning, from Frederickshall, where his troops are—sixty miles by country roads—and he will take a glass of milk. Lee joins them, and they spread a large scale map and draw around it.

All of Virginia is Lee's battlefield, but his immediate problem is to free Richmond from the blue army yonder on the Chickahominy, where the city watches the light of the Yankee cooking fires on the sky every night. His plan is to bring Jackson down from the northwest, as swiftly and secretly as may be, upon the flank and rear of the enemy's exposed right wing, Fitz-John Porter's corps, north of the Chickahominy. In the Richmond lines, he will pass his strength from his right to his left, D. H. Hill, Longstreet, and A. P. Hill, three divisions, standing in readiness to combine with Jackson's three divisions from the Valley of Virginia. Meantime, Magruder, with 25,000 men, will guard Richmond. When Jackson is in position to strike, Lee will launch them all—six divisions, 55,000 bayonets—on the 25,000 of Porter's Fifth Corps. Two to one, or very near it, they will crush Porter before McClellan can send help from his main army south of the river. Without pausing, the assault, Jackson leading by the left, will sweep down the north bank of the Chickahominy and cut the York River Railroad, severing McClellan's lines of supply, shutting him off from his naval support. The thick Peninsula country, the swamps, the obscure roads, will hamper the Federal movements. Then, with Magruder attacking in turn from the city, and a sufficient force holding the crossings of the Chickahominy against him, McClellan will have to fight for his life on ground of Lee's choosing, and his destruction is not too much to expect. Every good general keeps the Cannæ battle, the battle of annihilation, in the background of his mind. Lee sets this forth and leaves his officers to discuss the details.

Everything will be timed on Jackson: Jackson says he can be in position the morning of the 25th. His troops are fifty miles away, and they must come by Ashland and along the high ground between the Chickahominy and the Pamunkey rivers, making the last stage of the march against possible resistance. Longstreet suggests that he give himself another day, and Jackson agrees to the 26th. He will cross the Virginia Central Railroad at dawn, the morning of the 26th, between Pole Green and Atlee's Station, eight miles from Mechanicsville and Fitz-John Porter's flank.

Lee returns to the room, and confirms the arrangements by verbal orders. Written orders will follow the next day, the 24th. Longstreet and the two Hills go back to their stations, and Jackson mounts and racks off to join his command. He rides all night, again, and meets his column at Beaver Dam Station in the morning. At Beaver Dam, he remarked to his staff doctor that he was suffering from a fever and a feeling of general debility.

*   *   *   *   *

Lee's plan, embodied in General Orders of the Army of Northern Virginia No. 75, 24 June, 1862, was simple in conception, but the directions were a little vague. Jackson's command would proceed, on the 25th, from Ashland to some convenient point on the Central Railroad. A. P. Hill would send a brigade from an upper crossing of the Chickahominy to make contact with him. Longstreet and the Hills, were, meantime, massed south of the Chickahominy, A. P. Hill at Meadow Bridge, two miles above Mechanicsville, and the other two opposite the town. Jackson would cross the Railroad at three o'clock the morning of the 26th, communicating his advance to Hill's connecting brigade, Branch. "As soon as the movements of these columns are discovered," A. P. Hill would force Meadow Bridge and advance on Mechanicsville. When his advance uncovered the Mechanicsville bridge, Longstreet, then D. H. Hill, would cross, Longstreet supporting A. P. Hill, and D. H. Hill marching on to gain contact with Jackson. All divisions were to keep in communication, Jackson leading on the extreme left. They would then flank the Federal corps behind Beaver Dam Creek, and sweep down the north bank of the Chickahominy, toward the York River Railroad. Magruder and Huger would cover Richmond while this was developing, maintaining themselves in readiness to attack if opportunity offered.

General Stuart, with three designated cavalry regiments and three independent formations (a little more than half his brigade), would move on the 25th to Ashland, where he would meet Jackson and cover his front and flanks as he advanced on the 26th. The remainder of the cavalry was placed at the disposal of Magruder, on the right flank of the army.

Lee's plan was possible. Its weakness lay in the fact that its execution depended upon the most careful and exact cooperation between his striking elements. He proposed to unite the parts of his army for assault in the presence of the enemy, and perfect timing of all movements was necessary to this end. It would be as dangerous for one unit to be ahead of time as for another to lag behind. All movements required good maps, dependable guides, and precise staff work. In the event, it failed in execution. The War Depart-

ment of the Confederacy had not yet, in 1862, come around
to mapping the terrain immediately surrounding Richmond.
The guides—although there were plenty of local men available in the army—performed poorly. The Staff arrangements were all inadequate. As things worked out, there was
no orderly system for liaison. Jackson, on the day of contact, the 26th, neither reported his location to Lee, nor received orders from Lee. There was no communication between A. P. Hill and Jackson. Nobody knew, or seemed to
greatly care, what anybody else was doing.

On the 24th of June, the head of Jackson's column
marched from Beaver Dam station, with forty miles to go.
Beyond Beaver Dam the railroad no longer served: it had
been torn up by Federal raiders operating from the vicinity
of Hanover Court House. It must have been manifest, this
day, that Jackson would hardly be on time. Ashland station was twenty-two miles from Beaver Dam station, and
his troops did not reach Ashland until late on the 25th. They
had been due there the night before. At Ashland, it was
seven miles to the Virginia Central crossing. One wonders
why Jackson did not push on that night, for he had marched
only twelve miles, since morning.

Only one of Jackson's division commanders was new to
him, General Whiting. Of his two brigades, Hood's Texans
had seen some fighting in the retreat from Yorktown, while
the Georgia brigade had not yet been in action or done
much marching. But the soldiers of Jackson's own division,
under young Winder, and of Ewell's division, were fresh
from the Valley campaign and possessed more actual combat experience than any troops in either army. Their combat achievements had been remarkable, and their reputation
for marching was especially high. Twenty-five to thirty
miles a day, even thirty-five miles, under stress, day in and
day out, had won them the name of Foot Cavalry. That

marching had been done on the open roads, in the cool dry air of the Shenandoah Valley. They came now into a country entirely different, and strange to them, where the damp heat of the Virginia lowlands sapped their vitality, and the narrow roads, deep with sand, muddy along the streams, and winding between forest walls that cut off light and air, were heavy under their feet. Also, each element was burdened with its trains, which impeded further the slow pace of the infantry. Jackson had not commanded so large a force before, and his logistics were bad. On the 23d and the 24th and the 25th progress was halting and unsatisfactory. Jackson kept his own council; his bearing toward his staff and his division commanders was, during these days, more austere and forbidding than was usual, even with him. It is related that he rode like a man in a dream, with no word for anybody, his spirit utterly withdrawn.

*   *   *   *   *

On the 25th of June, Stuart's column rode through Richmond and trotted north by the Brook turnpike. He had with him three of his Virginia regiments, the 1st, Colonel Fitzhugh Lee, the 4th, (Wickham's) Captain Chamberlayne, and the 9th, Colonel Rooney Lee. To these were added new formations, the cavalry of the Cobb Georgia Legion, Colonel T. R. R. Cobb; and Lieutenant-Colonel William Martin's Jeff. Davis Legion, and the cavalry of the Hampton Legion, and the Stuart Horse Artillery, under Captain John Pelham. These legions were two squadrons each; in all, his command was about 2000 sabres and a light battery. He left behind him the rest of the cavalry brigade, the 3d Virginia, Colonel Goode, the 5th Virginia, Colonel T. L. Rosser—this Rosser was a Texan, classmate, at West Point, of Custer—the 10th Virginia, Colonel J. Lucius Davis, he of the Trooper's Manual—and three companies of the 1st

North Carolina, Colonel Lawrence Butler, new-arrived from the South. These, under Rosser, the senior colonel, were detailed to Magruder, and were disposed to watch the right flank of the army, down the Charles City and Williamsburg roads, and toward the James River.

This afternoon Stuart's squadrons rode light, with no baggage or trains, three days rations of corn pone and bacon in their haversacks, and their colors uncased. They passed Yellow Tavern, that deserted desolate house set in worn-out fields, and crossed the Chickahominy at Upper Bridge, by the Fredericksburg railroad. Here they passed through Branch's Brigade of A. P. Hill, which waited for something; and bearing always left, they reached the vicinity of Ashland Station about dark, seeing in front of them the low dust-clouds that rise from marching infantry. Jackson's divisions were coming from the Valley: they had been due to march from Ashland that morning: now they were, cavalry found, going into bivouac there at sundown. Stuart swung left, to cut behind Jackson's trains, followed them to Ashland, and disposed his regiments toward Hanover and the Virginia Central Railroad, well out, covering Jackson's halted columns. His orders were to place himself on Jackson's flank and screen his advance, and to receive subsequent orders from Jackson. That night he reported to Jackson and described the ground ahead: he made no comments to any person on his interview. But he knew that Jackson was expected to cross the Virginia Central at daylight, next day, and that he had halted seven miles short, after a moderate march.

* * * * *

Back on the Chickahominy, Lee's officers were anxious. Their uneasiness has been preserved in memoirs and letters, and has crept into official reports: Magruder and Longstreet are both on record. Good, schooled soldiers, they remembered their military reading: they recall how, at Austerlitz, the Russians and Austrians were passing their strength from one wing to the other, and how, after they had completed the movement, Napoleon drove through the weakened centre and destroyed them. Now, they said, if McClellan is watching—but McClellan was not that small sallow, fiery Corsican, or anything like him. The movement of the designated divisions began in the first hours of 26th of June: by dawn, Longstreet and the Hills were in position behind the low ridge south of the Chickahominy: Ambrose Hill at Meadow Bridge, up the river, and the other two at the bridge on the Mechanicsville pike, opposite the village. All day, to cover their change of position, Magruder demonstrated furiously out the Williamsburg and Charles City roads, on McClellan's front. He was a picturesque officer, this John Bankhead Magruder, late of the Flying Artillery in the old Army. Lieutenant T. J. Jackson had served in his battery at Cherubusco and Contreros in 1846. He had entered West Point in 1826, one year behind Lee and Joe Johnston. In person he was magnificent: "Prince John," they called him, for his elegance, and "El Capitan Colorado" for his great florid face and red side-whiskers. With 25,000 men, on the 25th and the 26th and the 27th of June, he held McClellan thoroughly bemused.

*　　*　　*　　*　　*

Cavalry was moving before dawn on the 26th of June, by Wickham's mill on the Hanover road, with advance guards flung fan-wise south along the Virginia Central, covering the Valley Army's front and centre. Jackson's columns got off much later, crossing the railroad between 10:00 and 11:00 o'clock at Peake's Turnout, seven hours behind time. There, Branch's brigade of A. P. Hill's, which had marched

up from the Chickahominy along the railroad, made contact
with Jackson's right, and turned down toward Mechanicsville, Branch's mission being to preserve touch between Jackson on the flank and the demonstration Lee was to make in
front. Neither Branch nor Jackson reported themselves:
Lee, and the divisions crouched south of the Chickahominy,
waited all morning, past noon, into afternoon. Momentar-
ily they expected to hear the crash of battle to the north—
Stonewall Jackson striking Fitz-John Porter's right.

Stuart's orders were: to place himself in position on the
front and left flank of Jackson's columns and to cover their
advance. Eventually his mission would be, to keep contact
with the enemy, to find which way he went, and by what
roads he might be struck again. Before the sun climbed
above the dawn-haze of the river lands to the east, his troopers were in the saddle. The advanced posts heard, faint and
far as the horns of elf-land, bugles, Yankee reveilles behind the pickets on the Virginia Central line. There may
have been coffee: more likely, Stuart's troopers munched
cold corn pone and bacon as they stood to horse, for the mess
kettles were with the wagons, back in Richmond. The regiments trotted out the Ashcake road, to Merry Oaks Church,
five miles. About Merry Oaks Church, where Jackson should
have been at dawn, they took up the business in hand. A
mile east was the Virginia Central, and the zone of Yankee
outposts. Two main roads, with numerous small interesting
ways, branched south from the Ashcake road. By these,
Jackson would advance, and the cavalry must scout them
thoroughly. That means, points, alert troopers alone or in
twos, well ahead, with connecting files to the rear, and small
flank detachments to work down every cross roads, and watch
until the column passes. Behind this rides the advance guard
proper, a force large enough—one or two squadrons—to
beat down light resistance, and to hold heavy opposition

Artillery on the march - august 68

40 miles today

Virginia. Infantry

until the main body gets up. Fitz Lee has the advance guard, Von Borcke and sharp young Mosby riding with him. The main body is Rooney Lee's 9th Virginia and Captain Chamberlayne's 4th Virginia, and close behind is the rear guard, the Jeff. Davis Legion and Pelham's guns, Hampton's Legion, and Cobb's. Messages to the advance guard, where Stuart rides. On the railroad, with the sun just up, they strike the first blue horsemen, scattered cavalry videttes, who peer keenly in the morning mist, fire a few carbines, and gallop off. Gray horsemen pursue. At Tallieferro's Mill, there is a sizable body, a squadron of old U. S. regulars, who wait, dismounted and deployed, and deliver long range fire until Fitz Lee's combat squadrons appear; then follows a running fight, three miles, as far as Shelton's Corners. There are four or five small roads, and Stuart's people scatter, fan-wise, sweeping them clean. The flat crackle of carbines is continuous through the morning. Before noon, they come to the last of the open country, between Dr. Shelton's and the Totopotomoy, and develop a blue force, cavalry and some infantry, in line east of the creek: a blue formation, with a flicker of bayonets, covering engineers, who are busy at the bridge, laying fire. Jackson will need that bridge, and Fitz Lee's files get as close as they can, dismount, and begin to shoot. The Federals answer with ordered volleys. They are Stoneman's regular cavalry and some New York and Massachusetts rifle regiments. Gallopers dash back: Stuart is up, his eyes bright, his horse shying a little at the slugs that rip the dust around his fetlocks. Rooney Lee's 9th Virginia comes on the run— one squadron dismounts, the others ride up stream to find a ford: a brisk little fight begins. Smoke curls from the bridge, now beginning to burn. The Federal infantry withdraws. Pelham's guns arrive, unlimber, and open with canister. That is too much! The blue cavalry gets to horse, falls back, and plunges into the woods beyond the creek. Captain Blackford, Stuart's staff engineer, leads details to put out the fire, and axmen cut timbers to repair the bridge. Jackson's advance-guard infantry, Hood's Texans, come along, accelerated by the firing: Law and Trimble follow— Ewell's division—Jackson's Own—and they pass without much delay. Stuart moves on cautiously, keeping Pelham's guns to the front, feeling through the woods for more Federal infantry, and not finding it. Stoneman has drawn off to the eastward, and Stuart keeps some squadrons out in that direction; but his principal mission now is to cover Jackson's road to the south, down toward Mechanicsville. It was afternoon, perhaps two o'clock, and Jackson was within three miles of Fitz-John Porter's line and a little behind it. And he was nine hours late. He pressed on. Five miles south, across from Mechanicsville, on the Chickahominy, Ambrose Powell Hill, red-headed and impatient, heard faintly Stuart's guns on the Totopotomoy. He had received no word from Branch, his connecting file, nor from Jackson —but he thought those were surely Jackson's guns, and he did not like to wait. At 2:30 o'clock, he gathered his eight brigades, 14,000 men, and flung them across the Meadow Bridge, drove Porter's advanced force, under Reynolds, from the town, and went up against the Federal battle position beyond Beaver Dam Creek. His batteries galloped through Mechanicsville, and unlimbered in the fields to the east: his brigades shook themselves out in line of battle; and, with a great burst of sound, the fight roared up in the still afternoon. Jackson's column, pressing down by Pole Green Church and Hundley's Corners, heard it. Longstreet and Daniel Hill followed promptly, Hill by Meadow Bridge, Longstreet by Mechanicsville Bridge, now uncovered. Hill marched north to join Jackson: Longstreet filed right to support the assault.

The Federal Fifth Corps, Fitz-John Porter, held a position immensely strong. The left was on the Chickahominy. Beaver Dam Creek, a deep, sluggish stream, covered the front. The east bank of the Creek was higher than the west bank, and commanded all the level ground toward Mechanicsville. The Federal engineers had opened slashings in the woods, built entanglements and obstacles of fallen timber, carefully laid out the field of fire. Porter had eighty guns, all that there was room for; his infantry, securely intrenched, included the fine regular division of Sykes, and McCall's steady Pennsylvania reserves. Musketry and guns commanded every part of the ground over which the assault must approach, and Porter was a cool and skillful soldier. His weakness was his right flank, which hung in the air, open to the north and east. No serious frontal assault had been intended by Lee: Hill's mission had been merely to hold Porter while Jackson rolled him up, and Lee sent A. P. Hill an order—which reached him too late—that would have prevented his attacking until Jackson was definitely heard from.

When Ambrose Hill attacked, then and afterwards in this war, he attacked with vigor. Now he sent his brigades across the fire-swept fields and the open slashings, into the tangled abatis, up to the edge of Beaver Dam itself. They lost terribly: casualties lay presently "like flies in a bowl of sugar," Federal officers noted. The lines reeled back, broken: A. P. Hill reformed them and threw them in again. Longstreet became involved: and his batteries entered the fight. Fitz-John Porter's line flamed from the heights east of the creek, and in that fire Hill's brigades melted. His troops were in their first fight, young regiments from Georgia, and the Carolinas, Tennessee, and Mississippi. Given anything possible to do, they would have done it. Now they were simply shot down: 1350 of them fell while the afternoon passed, and men strained their ears for Jackson. Hill persisted: Long-street stood ready: any minute, now. . . .

At 4:30, the head of Jackson's column was between Hund-ley's Corners and Bethesda, on the Cold Harbor Road, two and a half miles from Fitz-John Porter's right, and behind it. He halted his command, and went into bivouac. Himself, he sat apart, withdrawn and brooding, while his officers fumed and his soldiers wondered. No man knows, to this day, what was in his mind. They relate that he sent Stuart off to station on his left, and Stuart rode amazed, his hand wrist-deep in his beard, his back turned to the smoke clouds rolling up in the southern sky. Ambrose Hill's battle died down with the sun: his broken regiments hunted in the dark for their dead. Porter's Fifth Corps had engaged only about a third of its effectives, and had everywhere held its line, at nominal loss—361 men. But Porter knew, by dark, that the Confederates were behind his flank, and that the Beaver Dam line was forthwith untenable. He knew, also, that it was Jackson, for his cavalry outposts had taken prisoners during the day. At dark he began to withdraw his troops from the Beaver Dam lines, and he fell back to his second position, carefully prepared, at Gaines' Mill, between New Cold Harbor and the Chickahominy. McClellan, bemused all day by Magruder, was not quite sure as to what was going on. The Jackson report, forwarded to him, was disturbing, but it was not significant in the mass of misinformation he was receiving from his Pinkertons and from Washington.

*   *   *   *   *

At daylight, Fitz-John Porter's rear guard drew off from the Beaver Dam line, in front of which the Confederate skirmishers were coming on again, over their dead of the day before. A. P. Hill, then Longstreet, followed hard, and five miles down the Chickahominy they came up with the Federal Fifth Corps, standing on the plateau behind Boatswain's Creek, on which is Gaines' Mill, and behind Powhite Swamp, each flank curved back to the river. Jackson, meantime, with D. H. Hill paralleling him, marched by the left, on the Old Cold Harbor road. Stuart's cavalry swept a wide front, as far north as Old Church, toward the Pamunkey, keen after the first signs of the Federal retreat. For Jackson, it was a slow, confused march. About noon, the heads of his column and of D. H. Hill's collided at a cross roads and fired into each other.

Shortly after 2:00 P.M., Jackson, with D. H. Hill's division on the left and his own on the right, approached Old Cold Harbor and heard the battle open on the plateau to the south. It was Ambrose Hill, and Longstreet, again attacking. D. H. Hill, whose division was echeloned ahead of Jackson's, pushed forward and became engaged with Porter's right. Jackson, hearing the guns, sent Hill orders to break off the engagement and retire out of range: Hill, with compressed lips, drew back his brigades a little way and stood, puzzled and angry, through the afternoon. Jackson's report indicates that he expected Porter to be driven, by the assaults of Longstreet and A. P. Hill, into his arms; but Fitz-John Porter was very hard to drive. His position was strong, and A. P. Hill and Longstreet dashed their brigades to pieces against him.

During these hours, while the Valley soldiers and D. H. Hill lay on their arms and waited, Stuart thrust forward by the left, with Captain John Pelham and a section of the Horse Artillery—a Blakely gun and a Napoleon. They saw a movement of Federal artillery; guns coming up, on the road from Grapevine bridge. Pelham wheeled his section into battery and opened fire. At once, four Federal batteries, concealed in the foreground, replied to him, and a vicious artillery fight developed. The Napoleon was smashed up:

Pelham changed position and maintained fire with the
Blakely: they got his range and he moved again, losing
horses and men, but keeping his gun in action. The racket
drew Jackson's attention: an old artilleryman himself, he
loved a well-fought gun. He sent the batteries of Brockenborough, Carrington and Courtney, and forty guns, north
and south, fought each other there, a bloody and inconse-
quential duel, through the afternoon.

Meantime, the brigades of Ambrose Hill and Longstreet
were shattering themselves in desperate rushes against the
triple tiers of musketry, and the steady batteries of Porter's flaming line. They sent couriers, staff officers on sweating horses, to ask Jackson for help. It became apparent to
him that Porter was not going to be driven, and finally, Lee
rode over in person and met him, near the Confederate centre. They talked earnestly—it was their first meeting in
battle—but all the conversation is not reported. At the last,
it is related that Lee said, indicating the great fury of musketry that raged on the plateau: "That firing is very heavy.
Can your men stand it?" "They can stand almost anything!
They can stand that!" replied Jackson, and spurred Little
Sorrel to a pounding gallop. Then he struck, and struck
like Stonewall Jackson.

He sent his orders to his divisions at 5:00 o'clock: a little
after 6:00, the exhausted brigades of A. P. Hill and Longstreet heard on the left a faint yelling, growing louder.
They roused themselves for one more effort. All Lee's line
advanced: Fitz-John Porter's men, now weary too, gathered
themselves to meet it. Whiting's division, the Texans and
the Georgians, came into the fight on the left centre, and
found a narrow strip of solid ground, between Boatswain's
Creek and Powhite Swamp. Through this the Texans
rushed, Hood leading, on foot, his old regiment, the 4th
Texas. They breached Porter's front, and the red battle

flags poured through the widening gap and swarmed to right and left on the plateau, snatching prisoners—one New Jersey regiment entire—and taking guns.

On this part of the field, among the batteries in the support line, stood the 5th U. S. Cavalry, two and a half squadrons, under Captain Whiting. Them, General Philip St. George Cooke now ordered to charge, to hold the enemy while the guns got off. Obediently, Captain Whiting and 240 sabres rode, at a gallop, right into the muskets of the 4th Texas, which still held its formation, with Hood in front of it. The Texans shot the head of the charging squadron away: it was Hood's Old Army regiment, and Captain Chambliss, who fell from his saddle at Hood's very feet, had been Hood's classmate, and tentmate in the West. Captain Whiting was shot; every officer, except one, was shot: the regulars broke and streamed back, stampeding the battery horses of the guns they had charged to save, and riding through some nervous infantry supports that had been gathered. From end to end, Fitz-John Porter's corps was broken. Still fighting stubbornly, it plunged into the forest toward the Chickahominy. By Grapevine bridge, too late to restore the situation, it met the fresh brigades of French and Meagher, sent at the eleventh hour by McClellan. The quick summer darkness fell, and on the plateau above the river, the Confederates, disorganized by victory, halted the pursuit, herded their prisoners together, and bivouacked on the field. All formations were confused and scattered, and Jackson, senior officer on the plateau, did not see fit to continue pressure in the dark woods—which was not like the Jackson known to fame.

Fitz-John Porter, with the Fifth Corps considerably mauled but still a unit, and French and Meagher, fresh brigades, covering his rear, crossed the Chickahominy by Grapevine bridge, after dark. Porter left his wounded, his dead,

twenty-two guns, 10,000 stand of small arms, and 2800 prisoners. For these fruits of victory, 8358 Southerners lay,
killed and wounded, on the two-mile front. Again the weight
of the Confederate loss was with Ambrose Hill.

The Gaines' Mill fight lasted seven hours, and not until
the last hour before sunset had Lee been able to bring his
55,000 bayonets together against 27,000 Federals. It was
a very near thing: if McClellan had sent, in midafternoon,
the tardy reinforcements that came up at dark, Lee's battle
might have broken down. The young Confederate soldiers
had attacked with ardor everywhere, and the failure lay in
the combination of poor staff work and inexperienced
leaders.

*　　*　　*　　*　　*

So, with Mechanicsville the opening skirmish, and Gaines'
Mill the first shock, opened the Seven Days' Battle. In
Richmond all this month of June was a valiant and dreadful
time.

The Southern people stood up and met the war, and
Richmond was the point of contact. It was always a city of
fine women and of gallant ways: now the ladies nursed by
day in the improvised hospitals, and showed themselves
debonair of nights, at balls and receptions. Society was brilliant: all the great families of the South were there, the men
in the army and in the government: the women helping as
they could—to be ornamental and high of heart not the least
of that help.

Life and youth made strong heady music in the shadow
of death: fine gentlemen in gray danced under crystal chan-
deliers, to the music of flutes and violins, and kissed white
hands in the intimate darkness of wide porches, and galloped
off to the Chickahominy lines. Then, quite possibly, they returned feet-first in springless ambulances or country wagons,

and rode slow out to Hollywood Cemetery, behind led chargers, riderless, while the Dead March from Saul beat on the heavy air. There were many weddings. There were partings and greetings and joyful reunions and cruel sadnesses. . . . The family of Colonel Munford sits, of an evening, in cheerful talk on the cool porch, and a caisson drives up, a few walking-wounded escorting it. On it is the body of young Ellis Munford, the son of the house, killed that day in battle.

A lady of quality who, the night before, at the Executive Mansion, stood in line beside Mrs. Davis, and danced with Wade Hampton and Jeb Stuart, kneels in a tobacco warehouse at the pallet of a shattered gaunt soldier of D. H. Hill's, to feed him chicken broth and eggs à la creme from her own table. "Jest as yuh say, young miss," drawls the North Carolinian. "It mought be good fer me, but meh stummick's set agin hit. Ther' ain't but one thing I'm honin' atter, an' thet's a dish o' greens an' bacon-fat, wit' a few mo-lahses poured on ter hit." And delicate folk laughed politely that night, in elegant places, at the naive country hero. . . .

The iron was presently to enter the soul of Richmond, but here, on the threshold of the war, not all the women went in black, and the scene by the James was bright and splendid. There was still old wine in the cellars, and silks and merinos in the shops, and gold braid and stout gray cassimeres: and Jeb Stuart can write his personal letters on delicate monogrammed note paper, run through from London.

Daily the cannon shook the windows in the town, and all night the groaning columns of transport rolled through the streets with the wounded. It was the blooding of the army of Northern Virginia.

This Army of Northern Virginia was not yet a weapon adequate to its general. But, like its Northern adversary, it had in it, rank and file, the cream of the nation's young men—the people who were under arms because they wanted to be; the men with a personal interest in the fight. There were few in either army who had been shot over: they were new to war. Yet never, on any field hereafter, would the South attack more ardently, nor the steady Northern men stand to their ground with a more valiant stubbornness. They rushed together in a country tangled and obscure beyond conception: they fell down from sunstroke in the stagnant heat of the lowlands: they grappled blind in thickets from which fled deer and wild turkeys and amazed Virginia bobcats. They fumbled and floundered in black morasses, disturbing the moccasin snakes and the whippoorwills, and they groped for each other in the hot June nights, through the pale mist that rises in the dark of the moon from the Chickahominy swamps. They were led astray by bewildered guides who forgot in the stress of battle roads by which they had lived all their lives; they were confused and disarrayed by green, unskillful staffs, and mishandled by young generals too eager, and by old generals overcautious. Out of their striving were born two armies of enduring reputation, the Army of Northern Virginia and the Army of the Potomac. They would contend for three years, giving and taking terrible blows, until the one was destroyed by the other. And when their fighting ended, the war would end.

*　　*　　*　　*　　*

On the morning of the 28th of June, the Confederates drew breath. In front of Gaines' Mill the Confederates sought out their wounded and buried their dead. McClellan had his army united, on the south bank of the Chickahominy. Lee was astride the stream—only Magruder's 25,000 stood between the Federals and Richmond. There was still time for the Austerlitz manœuvre, for a drive straight up the Williamsburg road, the Charles City road, to the Confederate capital. The French Princes were with the Federal Army, and it is told that one of them suggested such a move. But McClellan was thinking of something else.

He had been much impressed by the demonstrations of Magruder, during the past three days. That one had so conducted himself on the 26th and 27th that McClellan was sure the main Confederate army was still south of the Chickahominy. And McClellan, with his right wing hustled back upon him, and somewhat forewarned by Stuart's ride two weeks before, and no longer expecting friends from Fredericksburg, decided to get his army back from danger: he was that kind of a general. He sent orders to his base commander, General Casey, and to his quartermaster, Colonel Ingals, at White House on the Pamunkey, and there was furious activity in the naval echelon on the York River and the James. Early on the 28th, he began to withdraw, most discreetly, from the lines in front of Magruder. Here Lee was poorly served by *El Capitan Colorado*. Magruder had never shared Lee's confidence about this battle, and he had been careful, in his exercises, not to provoke McClellan too much, or to seek too close a contact. He failed to discover McClellan's movement until next day, the 29th. Then, when he moved out to develop the Yankee works—Longstreet having been sent across to help him—his skirmishers found the Yankees gone.

This decision, to change his base from the York to the James, and the stubborn skill with which he accomplished it, marks the high point in McClellan's military career. Having accepted—as, he did, after Gaines' Mill, the failure of his campaign, it was the only movement which could save him from the destruction that Lee had prepared. But it was so unlike his character, as Lee read it, that the Confederate staff had not considered it among the possible developments of the battle, and they were not prepared to meet it with a counter move. The 28th was, for Lee, a day lost. His enemy had disappeared from his front, and the cavalry under Stuart was sent off along the abandoned York River line, and rendered no service, other than negative, in discovering McClellan's intention.

*   *   *   *   *

Colonel Kyd Douglas, engineer officer of A. P. Hill's division, and afterwards Hill's corps engineer, relates a story of the night of the 28th. Hill's division had moved south of the Chickahominy that day, and General Lee, having given orders to Jackson regarding dispositions on the north bank, was also across. Colonel Douglas, with a lieutenant, was reconnoitering to the front, dispositions for tomorrow's battle on his mind. Somewhere off the Darbytown road, well forward, Colonel Douglas had dismounted. All at once, his lieutenant saw him throw himself down, his head sideways, and listen. "Don't move," said the Colonel, "and don't let the horses move." Then he said, "Get down: come here: put your ear to the ground . . . now, what do you hear?" The lieutenant thought he heard wagons, many wagons, moving. It came along the earth to them, by some strange freak of ground structure, in that place and nowhere else.

"General Hill—go bring General Hill here—" ordered Douglas. The young officer galloped off, and returned with Ambrose Hill. His colonel asked him to dismount, just here, and listen. . . . Hill put his ear to the ground, and rose quickly. "Wagons!" he said. "That's McClellan's whole wagon train, and it's moving toward the James! General Lee must know this at once!" They sent an aide spurring for Lee, and Lee came presently, a tall shape in the starlight on gray Traveller. He heard them, kneeled sideways, and listened for a time. Then he rose, brushed the leaf-mold from his knees, and struck his hands together, and made a small depreciating sound. "Tch, tch, tch," he said: "I fear McClellan is escaping me."

Next day he had Stuart's note from White House, and observed the resolute Northern stand at Savage Station. He had not prepared himself for anything as daring as McClellan's change of base. He had expected to seize the Chickahominy river line and receive a desperate Northern assault for the crossings, and he was ready for it. McClellan's right wing had saved itself: now the main army might escape. But there was still opportunity to hem it in the swamps, to capture or destroy large elements of it.

By midnight of the 28/29th of June, Lee knew what McClellan was trying to do. The exposed wing, Porter's corps, had escaped him. McClellan's army was united and under control. But it was also cut off from its naval support, in a thick, difficult region. Magruder was directed to pursue rapidly down the Williamsburg road. Huger, on Magruder's right, took the Charles City road. Longstreet and the diminished brigades of A. P. Hill were passed across Magruder's rear, by New Bridge on the Chickahominy, and directed upon the Darbytown road, south of the Charles City road. Jackson was again given the post of honor. With his own, Ewell's, and D. H. Hill's divisions, 25,000 men, he was ordered to move directly south, crossing the Chickahominy by Grapevine bridge, and to fall on McClellan's rear with his whole force. He had the shortest and most direct road to march: also, the most obstructed, and he had a river to cross. These orders were in circulation soon after daylight on the 29th, and Lee himself rode over to join Magruder.

McClellan's problem was, now, to extricate his army, with its enormous trains, from the wooded labyrinth south of the Chickahominy, between that river and White Oak Swamp, and to move it down to some convenient landing, which would afford a defensive position ashore, and sea room for the gun-boats and the transport fleet that served him on the James River.

White Oak Swamp is a strip of wooded, marshy country, with a little creek meandering through it, which rises just south of Seven Pines, and flows eastward for about twelve miles, to join the Chickahominy below Despatch Station and Bottom Bridge. The ground between White Oak Swamp and the Chickahominy, covered on three sides by water and marsh, had seemed a safe place for the advanced base of the army, and in it were concentrated, safe from Confederate raiders, the army trains—one detail was 4500 wagons. On the abandonment of the York base and everything north of the Chickahominy, the lines of supply were broken off: some trains and transport were drawn south of the Chicka-hominy, and others tried to reach White House, and most of the Confederate captures were from these unfortunate ele-ments, caught between one point and the other on the 28th and 29th of June.

McClellan had to hold off the Confederate assault until the train could be moved south of White Oak Swamp, and therefore he stood on the 29th at Savage Station, facing north against the Chickahominy crossings and west against Magruder's people, who pressed along the Williamsburg pike. That day, by incredible exertions, his unwieldy wagon trains got safely across White Oak Swamp, and in the night his infantry, which fought at Savage Station, followed it. Other advanced elements fell back along the Charles City and Darbytown roads, and on the 30th, the blue soldiers turned and stood, where the roads from Richmond and from the Chickahominy intersect, south of White Oak Swamp, at Charles City Cross Roads. There was a day of heavy fight-ing, the battle being called variously Gendale, Charles City Cross Roads, or Frayser's Farm. Longstreet and A. P. Hill

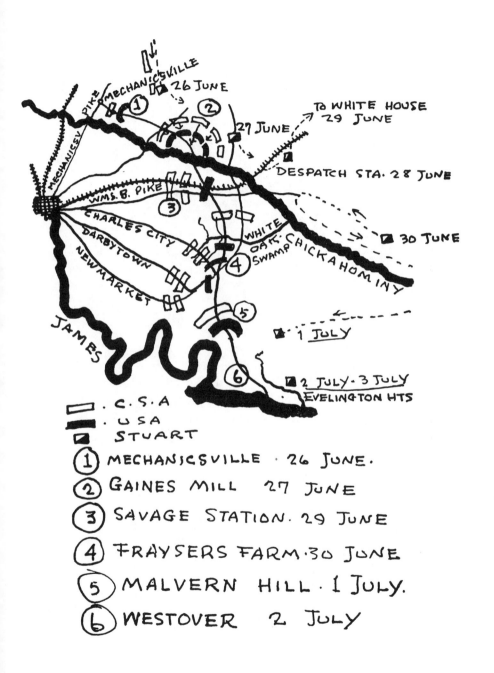

MECHANICSVILLE
MECHANICSV PIKE
26 JUNE
① ②
27 JUNE
TO WHITE HOUSE
29 JUNE
MECHANICSV
DESPATCH STA. 28 JUNE
WMS. B. PIKE
③
30 JUNE
CHARLES CITY
DARBYTOWN
WHITE
OAK
SWAMP CHICKAHOMINY
NEWMARKET
④
⑤
JAMES
1 JULY
⑥
2 JULY - 3 JULY
EVELINGTON HTS

▭ . C · S · A
▬ . U S A
◪ . STUART

① MECHANICSVILLE · 26 JUNE.
② GAINES MILL 27 JUNE
③ SAVAGE STATION. 29 JUNE
④ FRAYSERS FARM · 30 JUNE
⑤ MALVERN HILL · 1 JULY.
⑥ WESTOVER 2 JULY

were up. Magruder had followed more slowly and was not effective. Lee, who now comprehended the situation perfectly, had ordered Jackson to hasten across White Oak Swamp and strike the northern flank of the enemy, but Jackson never got into the fight at all—for reasons known to him and to nobody else on earth. His divisions were assembled, fresh, and rested: Imboden, his divisional cavalry leader, found one good crossing over White Oak Swamp, and Wade Hampton found another, undefended by any Yankees, past their right flank; and Jackson lay, north of the swamp, less than four miles from the battle. But Jackson did not move, and Keyes, Porter, Sumner, and Hooker were able to hold off Hill and Longstreet. The 30th was the critical day, and the Federals won it. At night they retreated by the Quaker road, marching south from Charles City Cross Roads to the Malvern Hill region, from which convenient roads lead on to Harrison's Landing, the point McClellan had selected for his new base. At daylight on the 1st of July, McClellan's trains were south of Malvern Hill and out of danger, and the blue army made its final stand, in overwhelming strength of position and guns, against a gallant, headlong, and unco-ordinated Confederate assault.

The evidence is strong that Lee considered his enemy to be demoralized by his repeated hammering and their prolonged retreat, and he had picked up, in his pursuit, enough prisoners, abandoned guns and stores, and stragglers, to justify this belief. His attack on the 1st of July was simply a reckless lunge, the divisions of Jackson, Longstreet, and Magruder going in without reconnaissance or combination. Brigades, and even regiments, rushed out in detail, across a long, fire-swept approach, and were simply shot to pieces by the excellent and unshaken Federal artillery, the blue infantry not being seriously engaged. In the night, having accomplished their mission—which was to cover the trains—

the Federal forces withdrew to Westover at Harrison's Landing.

Return now to the Confederate cavalry, drawn off to Jackson's left through the afternoon of June 27.

Rumor ran across the Confederate front as night fell and the fires of battle died on the plateau, and one told Jeb Stuart that D. H. Hill, on the extreme left, was pursuing the Federals down the river by the Despatch Station road. Stuart gathered his waiting squadrons and dashed that way, as far as Tyler's, three miles east, but found no Yankee rout. He stationed squadrons across the river road, and the White House road, and returned to Old Cold Harbor with his main body, to get further orders. By morning, the picketing squadrons were so burdened with prisoners—stragglers who had run into their arms in the dark—that they had to be reinforced.

Before dawn, Lee was at New Cold Harbor, on the edge of the Gaines' Mill battlefield—with His Excellency the President, and other important persons: and Lee sent for Stuart and told him to strike for the York River Railroad at the nearest point, and to cut it, since McClellan had to retreat that way. Ewell's division of Jackson's was detailed to follow on the same mission, and by sun-up they were marching, Rooney Lee's 9th Virginia being attached to Ewell as advance guard. Stuart took his main body—Fitz Lee, Wickham's 4th, and the Legions—and rode swiftly ahead, gathering stragglers and picking up two fine rifled guns abandoned by the enemy. It was about eight miles to Despatch Station, and Stuart was there before noon. A blue squadron stood across the approach, disposed to fight, and Cobb's Georgians were flung forward, whooping. The blue people wheeled left, and galloped toward the Chickahominy by the Bottom Bridge road, and the Georgians reported that they equipped themselves with fine new carbines, thrown down by the Yankees as they went away. Despatch Station was occupied without a fight, and cavalry industriously set about tearing up the rails and cutting the wires, while gallopers went back to Ewell and to General Lee with reports. It was very puzzling to Stuart, the ease with which he cut McClellan's vital artery.

Ewell came up, and decided to wait there for further orders. Prisoners related that Generals Stoneman and Emory, with cavalry and infantry, had gone off toward White House, where Casey was said to be in command. Stuart had been fighting Stoneman and Emory for two days, and his orders authorized him to follow. Leaving pickets on the approaches to Despatch Station, he assembled his column and rode for White House Landing. It was fifteen miles away.

Along the road, cavalry overtook and captured wagon trains and sutler's establishments, bewildered and adrift, and drove before it small detachments of blue horse. Tunstall's Station, about halfway, was found deserted, and Stuart was flattered to observe extensive field works, built around the place since he rode through two weeks ago. He took this as a personal tribute. From Tunstall's he could look down the valley of the Pamunkey, and all the sky toward White House had a drift of smoke across it; they were burning things at the Landing. Just this side of White House is Black Creek, a deep stream with high, muddy banks, and Stuart's points found the bridge destroyed, blue cavalry in formation on the heights beyond, and what appeared to be artillery in position supporting them. Rooney Lee was dismounted, the Cobb Legion and Martin's closed up, and Hampton's Legion came with Pelham's guns. A salvo of shell dispersed the Yankee horse on the hill, and canister, flung into the underbrush on the nearer slope,

flushed a dismounted force which lay in ambuscade against
the crossing. The artillery proved to be of the Quaker
variety. Captain Farley, with a troop, found a ford and
got over. But the bridge had to be rebuilt for the guns; the
corn pone and the forage brought from Richmond were exhausted, and it was nearly dark. The Engineer Captain
Blackford went to work on the bridge, and the command
was rationed from the Federal stores salvaged at Tunstall's.

Stuart would have done well to push on to White House
that night, but his information indicated a large force there,
5000 men at least, all arms, and his people had been three
days riding and fighting; nor could he cross his guns over
Black Creek. He rested by Black Creek until dawn, and his
sentries watched, all night, the glow of a great fire over
White House Landing, and listened to the explosions of ammunition dumps. One wonders how much Rooney Lee slept.
White House Plantation——

By the time the sky was gray, Blackford had the bridge
in shape, and Pelham's guns clanked over. Cavalry went
forward, well in hand, prepared to fight, and came, about 8
o'clock in the morning, to the White House plain, where two
miles of Federal depots burned, and except for stragglers
no blue soldiers remained. The advance guard of the gray
troopers rode among the smoldering dumps, and the main
body was held together in case of developments. Stuart sees
that a Yankee gunboat lies off the Landing with blue soldiers on her deck, and he strokes his beard and looks at her
reflectively.

She is U.S.S. *Marblehead,* and she had taken aboard the
last of General Casey's Base Detachment, three companies
of the 17th New York Infantry volunteers, who remained
through the night to see that things were well destroyed—
among them the White House itself "set fire to, though
against my express order," reports Casey. Now U.S.S.

USS Marblehead
White House Landing
29 July 1862

Horse Artillery

USS Monitor
off Harwell's Landing

Pennsylvania
Lancer Regiment

Marblehead observes gray cavalry ashore and opens on them at 1000 yards with her 11-inch naval rifles. The graybacks scuttle into the woods, and the shells burst fearfully among the trees beyond them.

Jeb Stuart orders up seventy-five men, armed with rifled carbines—some of the 1st and the 4th Virginia, and of the Mississippians, dismounted. He sends back for John Pelham and a gun. He is, he writes, determined "to expose this Yankee buggaboo, called gunboat," regarded heretofore as dangerous by simple Southern boys. The troopers run out in a wide skirmish line, and their bullets spatter on the tawny York. U.S.S. *Marblehead* accepts the challenge: her bugles call away the boats, and two cutters full of New York infantry shove off for the shore. The skirmishers fire briskly, wounding a Yankee soldier called Garrett G. Majarey. Then Pelham, with his little horse-howitzer, opens from the woods. His shells burst accurately over U.S.S. *Marblehead's* crowded decks. The cutters turn about and foam back to the ship. U.S.S. *Marblehead* weighs anchor, and churns off down the York, and they enter in her log that all the equipment of the 2d cutter is lost, by reason of the cutter capsizing as it was hoisted in—an indication of extreme haste, for the navy is fussy about small boats. Pelham limbers up and follows down the shore at a gallop, flinging shells until the curve of the shore throws him out of range. Jeb Stuart's joyous laugh rings golden from where he watches, and, immensely cheered, the lean Confederates are authorized to help themselves to what they can find.

Von Borcke, who lost his horse at Gaines' Mill and has had difficulty in finding another, up to his weight, rejoined at noon, and came upon Stuart and his staff at ease on the White House lawn, drinking iced lemonade; and he has to hear at once about the gunboat—when did cavalry ever fight a gunboat—and whip it—before? And von Borcke, of the frugal German service, is amazed at the lavishness with which the North had supplied its army. Champagne, cigars, oranges and lemons by the crate, ice machines, and quantities of ice in store, luxuries of every kind, necessities without stint—all these things lie around, burned or partially burned; and cavalry gorges itself on tinned food and preserves: the ordnance officers salvage, for one item, 10,000 stand of fine new rifles, and there is corn and long forage for the gaunt horses. Stuart assembles his regiments and systematically re-equips them with such of the stores as he can use.

Among the Confederate troopers, merrily looting in the half-burned stores at White House on the 29th, was one who came late and salvaged at personal risk an important-looking box, which proved to contain only some dozen pairs of white kid gloves, such as officers wear on formal occasions. Profoundly disgusted, he made to throw the things back into the fire, but a reflective file caught his arm. "Man, have sense! Don't burn them things up! Don't you know Richmond is full of weddings these days, and all the officers want white gloves to wear? Save 'em, and you can ask your own price in town."

And these gloves served numerous gallant affairs, when Cavalry returned to Richmond, after the Seven Days.

This is the 29th of June. During the morning, a note comes from Lee; what does Stuart think the enemy designs? He replies that there is no evidence of a retreat this side of the Chickahominy, toward White House or Williamsburg— although he has learned that Stoneman's cavalry rode toward the latter place. He tells Lee that he thinks McClellan is planning to retreat upon a new base on the James, giving up the York entirely. He sends Fitz Lee and the 1st Virginia toward the lower Chickahominy, to watch the fords from Bottom Bridge to Forge Bridge. There is a chance that some enemy may return to White House, by water or from Williamsburg. Stuart cannot conceive, himself, of letting go such a lot of stores without a fight—and he remains at White House with his main body all day, until his orders come, riding after midnight—Monday, the 30th— for the lower fords of the Chickahominy. Cobb's Legion is left to guard White House. Monday, Stuart's plume goes up and down the Chickahominy, from Long Bridge to Forge Bridge, a six-mile stretch. There is bickering with enemy detachments on the south bank, and they watch for any move to force the crossings. Pelham is much in action, and the Napoleon gun breaks its trail: that leaves only two 12-pounder howitzers for the Horse Artillery. This day, the 30th, they hear firing upstream: they are fighting at Charles City Cross Roads. At 3:30, Tuesday morning, July 1st, Stuart has Lee's order to cross the Chickahominy and cover the left of the army as it moves south, toward the James. Stuart's information led him to believe that the fight was still upstream, and he rode for Bottom Bridge, to find Jackson's division using the bridge there and filling the roads ahead. He turned back, crossed his command downstream, at Forge Bridge—Munford having joined him with Jackson's divisional cavalry—and then bore right by what roads he could find, to come up with Jackson's advance. The roads, from Forge Bridge down to the James, are crooked and roundabout, and he had to make a wide detour to the east. In the afternoon he heard prolonged cannonading, and drove his jaded people mercilessly under the July sun. It was the Malvern Hill fight, and it died down toward dark, and Stuart, aiming now for Haxall's Landing on the James, came to Turkey Creek and saw beyond it in the woods the camp fires of a great force. He was still out of touch with Jackson, and had met no enemy, but his command had covered forty-two miles that day, and there was nothing more in it. He bivouacked in the oat fields east of Turkey Creek, where his horses could graze, and sent his staff officers to find Jackson. They located the Confederate line—a very sore and battered line, which had given up, at dark, the bitter sanguinary assaults on Malvern Hill, but they did not find Jackson until nearly dawn. At the same time came orders from Lee, a day old, and missent, directing Stuart to the position on Turkey Creek which he had taken up by his own judgment the night before. In his report, he pointed with pride to this circumstance. It was a very dark night, with heavy rain, and he thinks his presence on Turkey Creek greatly stimulated the Federal withdrawal from Malvern after the battle. He describes it as a disorderly retreat, although the Federal generals say it was made in excellent order: but Stuart points to substantial bags of prisoners, and to small arms, some cannon, and the miscellaneous baggage of an army, which he found behind Malvern as he rode out with Jackson after daylight.

He led his column, at Jackson's orders, toward Haxall's Landing, up the James. Near the battlefield of the day before, he met Rosser, Baker, and Goode with the regiments that had stayed with Magruder. This meant that Lee's flanks had joined hands across McClellan's army—but behind it. Stuart galloped hard for Haxall's, hoping to intercept the enemy's line of retirement. There was nothing at Haxall's, however, except U.S.S. *Monitor*, lying off the landing, while some of her people took a run ashore. These, Martin's Mississippians captured—and some mules along with them: Martin's squadrons were wearing new Yankee overcoats from White House, and U.S.S. *Monitor* was not alarmed.

It was clear now that the enemy had turned down stream, and Stuart went back along the river, in the rain.

At Shirley, he found some infantry, entrenched, and took

prisoners who identified it as Sickle's brigade. Here the river bends sharply to the south, and Stuart held across, eastward, still feeling for the enemy. They found the Yankees south of Malvern Hill, obstructing all the roads, retiring sullenly; and small cavalry events took up the day. This country is thickly wooded, with no vistas. The rain continued heavy, and the Confederate infantry, back at Malvern Hill, advanced only two miles, to the Poindexter house. By dark, Stuart had gone as far east as Charles City Court House, and had eliminated all the possibilities except the Westover region, between Haxall's Landing and Charles City itself. Cavalry was dispersed across the country between these places, feeling for the place to hit. Late at night, a message came from Captain John Pelham; he was sure that the enemy was between Shirley and Westover, nearer the latter place. He thought that by getting artillery upon Evelington Heights, a plateau overlooking the Westover Plain, the whole Federal position could be dominated. Stuart forwarded this report to Lee through Jackson, and rode to join Pelham. He had, at the same time, to maintain a cavalry screen to the east and north, for he knew that Stoneman, who rode away toward Williamsburg, was still at large, and Yankee cavalry was exclusively his affair. At dawn, having with him Pelham and one 12-pounder, and Martin's Jeff Davis Legion, he rode under the dripping trees to Evelington Heights.

Evelington Heights has an approach from the north like Malvern Hill. You go across wide, flat fields that slope gently upward toward the south. The Charles City road runs east and west across the highest ground. Beyond that are narrow fields, and then a fringe of forest where old Westover Church is standing to this day. To your right, as you approach, is the low, wooded line of the West Run of Herring Creek, and to the left is the depression that leads down to Buckland Creek. It is about two miles from one stream to the other, and about two miles from the woods on the north to the trees where the church stands. Just beyond the church, the ground falls abruptly to Herring Creek, which winds through a wet marsh across the south face of Evelington Heights. Standing above the slope, you look down into the little flat peninsula between Herring Creek and the James, a strip three miles long by a mile and a half wide, narrowing to a mile at the head, between Herring Creek and the river. Below you, are Harrison's Landing on the James, and the old mansion Westover, that William Byrd built under grant from the English king.

Jeb Stuart found, among the trees by the church on Evelington Heights, a Yankee squadron which fled toward the head of Herring Creek. Then he looked down upon McClellan's camp, a vast blue host, jammed upon the narrow Westover plain, huddled and miserable, over smoky feeble camp fires of wet wood. The energetic Martin, following the blue cavalry, took prisoners and caught up infantry stragglers, and Stuart identified enough Federal corps to make it plain that the Army of the Potomac was before him. He rushed a message to General Lee, a few miles away, and was advised that Longstreet and Jackson were moving then to his support. He ordered Pelham into battery on the River road, and Pelham began to throw 12-pound horse howitzer shells into the Grand Army of the Potomac. William Martin's squadron was deployed, dismounted, and Stuart prepared to hold Evelington Heights until the infantry came. Longstreet and Jackson, he knew, were at the Poindexter house, hardly five miles away. It was reasonable to suppose that they would begin to arrive within three hours.

"Judging from the great commotion and excitement caused below, it must have had considerable effect," wrote Stuart, of Pelham's shelling. It had the effect of bringing home to the Grand Army of the Potomac its dangerous situation. The Commanding General was absent: he was on Commodore John Rodger's flagship, writing curious despatches to his Government: boasting that he had saved his army, and complaining that the Government had abandoned him to disaster. The corps and division commanders appear, from their recorded correspondence, to have been doing the same thing: there are some peculiar letters to congressmen and such in the records. The army was profoundly conscious of misfortune, cramped, and inert. But Pelham's shells applied a stimulus: some cavalry adventured out to see, and was driven back. Then General Franklin, an energetic man, roused his division, and made a slow, methodical advance. He got some guns forward, deployed his infantry brigades, and began to exert pressure on Stuart's right. Stuart fought him, with the little gun and his handful of dismounted troopers, from 9:00 in the morning until 2:00 in the afternoon. He fired his last cartridge and his last shell, and withdrew from the Heights. Riding furiously in search of the infantry, he found that Longstreet, misled by guides, had moved east instead of south, and was toward Nance's Shop, and Jackson was plodding behind him. Their columns reached Evelington Heights about dark. Stuart urged an immediate attack: Jackson thought not: Evelington Heights looked like another Malvern Hill, and he referred decision to Lee. That night Franklin was largely reinforced, formidable defensive lines were laid out by the Federals, and a number of gunboats were brought into position to cover the river flank. Next day, Jackson drove in the enemy's skirmishers and the ground was reconnoitred, but Lee decided against an attack. Malvern Hill was a sore, fresh memory.

On 5 July, Stuart wrote his wife, enclosing a silver wreath, a Yankee hat ornament:

"At last I have leisure to write a note. I have been marching and fighting for one solid week. Generally on my own hook, with the cavalry detached from the main body. I ran a gunboat from the White House and took possession. What do you think of that?

"We have been everywhere victorious and on the 3d I had the infinite satisfaction of slipping around to the enemy's rear and shelling his camp at Westover. If the army had been up with me we could have finished his business. The enemy is now under the protection of his gunboats. McClellan is badly whipped; but the fighting is not yet ended. Gen'ls McCall & J. F. Reynolds were taken, Sumner wounded, I have been mercifully spared this far. I am sorry to hear of Jemmie's spasms but glad to hear he is better. I want to see you and the pets very much and hope to very soon. Love to friends . . . *reverse*: trophy of White House."

During the following week, Stuart's cavalry picketed the flanks of the army, and his Horse Artillery, augmented by some of Stephen D. Lee's batteries, had adventures with Federal gunboats and troop ships, harassing them from the river bank above and below Westover Landing, "demonstrating," says Stuart, "that gunboats are not as dangerous as supposed." On the 6th, 7th, and 8th of July, there were small cavalry affairs on the River road below Westover, for which Colonel Rosser is favorably cited.

It was now apparent that McClellan had no fight left in him. Lee considered him harmless where he was: in fact, it was perfectly certain that, if he stayed at Westover, malaria and typhoid and hot weather would destroy him. On the night 8/9 July, Lee withdrew his army behind a cavalry screen, and marched up to Richmond. Stuart's regiments remained another day, and followed on the 10th, leaving a few pickets on the important roads. D. H. Hill, with two divisions of infantry, was stationed on the James in observation. So ended the Seven Days battle.

The cavalry mission had been: first, to cover Jackson's approach, and to guard his flanks after contact was made with the enemy. This took up the 25th, 26th, and 27th of June, and was fully accomplished. On the 28th, the mission was to cut the York River line, which was done. Observation, to determine the enemy's intention and his movement north of the Chickahominy, was next enjoined, to which reasonably followed the affair at White House Landing on the 29th. The 30th, Stuart watched the lower Chickahominy—to all his task now added measures of security against Stoneman's command, which had been left free to harass the Confederate flank—and although Stoneman took no action at all, he might have done a great deal of damage. The long march of the 1st of July, to the flank of the army, was made necessary by the conformation of the ground and the trace of the roads, all the direct routes being congested with infantry and transport. This day Stuart would have been valuable on the Confederate left: he might have discovered the easy approach to Malvern Hill, and guided the assault around the Federal right, where it was vulnerable: but you can't be in two places at the same time, and he was where his orders sent him.

The loss of contact with the Federal army on the 2d July, after Malvern Hill, is perfectly understandable when you examine the nature of the country, and consider that the commands of Longstreet and Jackson made no effort to keep touch with the retiring enemy. Indeed, Lee's infantry seems to have been so staggered by the repulse it suffered that it was, for twenty-four hours at least, incapable of anything aggressive. Stuart had the enemy correctly located by midnight of the 2d, and I think it entirely reasonable that he should have expected the infantry to come forward early on the 3d. If what he did at Evelington Heights—a thing any active cavalryman would do—was injudicious, you must assume that the Federals would have remained all that day, if unmolested, inactive on the crowded Westover plain; and with such able officers on the ground as Porter, Franklin, Sumner, and Keyes, that ineptitude was unlikely. It was not Stuart who failed, throughout the Seven Days' Battle, in energy, boldness, and judgment.

His regiments were continuously engaged from daylight on the 26th June, until the 10th July. They made one march of forty-two miles, and several others of more than thirty. They rationed and supplied themselves entirely from the enemy. They engaged unbroken infantry, gunboats, and artillery, kept the Federal cavalry away from every important point, and captured prisoners and transport all over the Peninsula. Only one unfortunate incident occurred, and that was on the right flank of the army, where Colonel Baker, with the 1st North Carolina, cavalry, and the 3d Virginia, Colonel Goode, moving impetuously ahead of Magruder down the Quaker road on the night of the 29th, rode into an ambush of infantry and artillery. The casualties were—from one volley—57 officers and men, and a number of horses. The cavalry loss was, otherwise, less than one hundred, all ranks. Nowhere, Stuart regretfully states, did the enemy horse stand to face him.

From Mechanicsville on the 26th of June, to Malvern Hill on the 1st of July, the Confederates had 20,000 men, killed, wounded, and missing. McClellan lost 16,000 men, of whom 9,000 were prisoners, including three generals. He abandoned a very great quantity of stores, and lost, in battle and on the road, fifty-two pieces of artillery: and the Confederate ordnance officers picked up and reconditioned 31,000 stand of small arms. Twenty thousand casualties is not an excessive loss for an army that attacks a larger army

in position, but Confederate soldiers were increasingly hard
to replace. What the North lost was not important, except
for one thing. The men, and the guns, and the stores didn't
matter; because there were plenty more where they came
from, and the Union could supply them as they were needed.
But here began the extraordinary ascendancy of General
Lee. Hereafter, the officers and the armies who proceeded
against him were haunted by the idea of defeat before they
met him, and this state of mind would endure until Grant
came. The thing the blue people lost was morale. Morale
was an item which the Lincoln Government couldn't reissue
to the troops.

After the Seven Days' Battle, the Richmond editors did
not again refer to the commanding general of the Army of
Northern Virginia as Evacuating Lee. Everyone wondered
at Stonewall Jackson: he had been expected to strike like a
thunderbolt, and he had hardly struck at all. But he was
Stonewall Jackson, and few presumed to criticize. The reputations of Longstreet and the two Hills were considered to
have enlarged enormously. But no officer profited more
than Jeb Stuart. He had even fought, and chased away,
with his hard riding people, Yankee gunboats!

Some of Longstreet's infantry, marching through Richmond in the first part of July, had a glimpse of him which
they remember. He was on his horse, backed against a wall
and held close prisoner by a group of pretty girls in crino-
lines and little bonnets. They had thrown a wreath of red
roses around his charger's neck, and bestowed a great cluster of red roses that blazed now in the crook of his arm,
against his new gray jacket. He sat, bareheaded, a willing
captive, beaming down into their flushed, merry faces, and
he was—Infantry observed, as its leading files came around
the corner—reciting poetry to the ladies. Probably that
thing he is said to have composed on "The Ride Around Mc-

Clellan." The delighted gray footsoldiers, who always expressed themselves freely, and who, in ranks, had neither fear nor reverence, broke into full cry.

Jeb Stuart stared in horror. He truncated a nimble verse, and clapped on his plumed hat—"Excuse me, ladies!— Good-bye, all!—" His big, clever horse shouldered free, his golden spurs drove home, and he fled, with red rose petals eddying behind him.

X

THE SECOND MANASSAS—STUART LOSES HIS HAT—POPE LOSES HIS COAT AND PRESENTLY HIS ARMY

RICHMOND, after the Seven Days, breathed in a lessening tension. The place was a hospital, and the green slopes of Hollywood were scarred with new graves, and slow, heart-breaking music throbbed behind flag-draped coffins on caissons, from morning until night. But there was also rejoicing, presentations of colors to distinguished regiments, triumphant blaring of bands, "Dixie," and the "Bonnie Blue Flag." Picnic parties went out to view the battlefields. The Army of the Potomac was only twenty-five miles away, but Richmond considered that its teeth were drawn. The soldiers of Jackson, Longstreet, of the Hills, and Magruder, and the troopers of Jeb Stuart, swanked through the streets, wearing their weathered gray uniforms like garments of honor. Timid folk, who had fled south in May and June, returned, and dwelling places were at a premium. The whole South took heart. It would be long and terrible, this war: but there was also much glory.

The Confederate High Command was not so confident. An hundred thousand men, shoved from the door step to the front yard, so to speak, still needed watching. And there was trouble in the Valley, and in Central Virginia. Washington, on 26 June, had consolidated the little armies of Banks, Frémont, and McDowell—the Mountain Department, the Rappahannock Department, and the Department of the Shenandoah, in one, and so formed the Federal Army of Virginia. General Halleck was brought from the West to be Commander-in-Chief at the Capital—in effect, Chief-of-Staff, and meantime, one Major-General John Pope, an officer who had done well on the Mississippi at Island Number Ten and Port Hudson, was placed in command of the new army. All his corps commanders were senior to him: he was the first of Mr. Lincoln's queer appointments, and he took the detail—he says—reluctantly and with misgivings. Frémont refused to serve under him, and the German, Franz Sigel, was given Frémont's corps. Pope's assignment was: to threaten from the north and west, to the end of drawing Confederate forces from McClellan's front. But the corps of the new army were scattered for a hundred miles, from Fredericksburg to Winchester, and by the time they were concentrated on the upper Rappahannock, McClellan had been thrown back from Richmond. Pope was then ordered so to demonstrate with his army, that McClellan be not further attacked. Early in July he moved southward from the Rappahannock, and thrust toward Gordonsville and Charlottesville, with intent to cut the Virginia Central Railroad by which Richmond communicated with the West.

Up to the coming of Pope, the war in Virginia had been alleviated by humanities, by a general respect for the rights of non-combatants, by a certain pleasant chivalry. Pope brought bitterness. He directed his army to live off the country. He seized unoffending civilians, took hostages, imposed iron restrictions on the unfortunate Virginians within his lines. The immediate effect was to stimulate Confederate recruiting, and to light off the fires of hatred which heretofore had smoldered fitfully. And Lee sent Jackson, with his own, and Ewell's Divisions, about 11,000 men, up to Gordonsville to watch the Army of Virginia. Jackson moved on the 13th of July, by rail. There followed about a month of small activities between Richmond and the Blue Ridge.

Pope used his cavalry with boldness and energy, more than any Federal general before him. He had two brigades,

Buford's and Bayard's. He flung them out, twenty miles in advance of his infantry columns. Daring reconnaissances were pushed into sections which had not yet seen a blue soldier. Bayard and Buford struck at the Virginia Central, and pushed south of Fredericksburg. General Lee sent Stuart, with Fitz Lee's brigade, from Richmond to Hanover Court House, and for some weeks cavalry was occupied in numerous onfalls and bushments. On the 25th of July, Stuart was promoted to Major-General, and placed in command of all the cavalry of the Army of Northern Virginia. This was a long step forward for the Confederate Service. Administratively and tactically it gave a great advantage.

Stuart's Headquarters were then in the vicinity of Hanover, and his family was with him: we have a charming view of the group; Flora Stuart, and the two children, Flora, aged five, and little Jemmie, otherwise James Ewell Brown Stuart, Junior, three. The Prussian's careful journal notes that, in their company, his General would seem to forget the dangers and duties of his exciting life in the enjoyment of his domestic happiness. "The bold rider and dashing swordsman playing with his children, or listening to his wife as she sang him a ballad, was a picture the soft lights of which were in effective and pleasing contrast with the Rembrandt shadows of the dark wood and the rude warriors that lay there." On Sundays religious services were held in the grove near Headquarters, by the Reverend Mr. Landstreet, Chaplain to the Cavalry, with camp stools for the ladies and the officers, and the troopers sprawled on the grass, and the General leading mightily in the singing. As often as the situation permitted, there were brigade drills, with fine music and flaunting of flags and guidons, social occasions, for which the ladies came out from Richmond. But July ran into August, and these pleasant days were ended.

When Jeb Stuart came up from Richmond, with the new jacket of a Major-General—buttons spaced in threes, and an added stripe of gold to the *galons* on his sleeves, he brought commissions for his officers: Captain Von Borcke becomes, to his delight, a Major of the Staff, Adjutant and Inspector; Captain John Pelham becomes a Major of Artillery; to another Captain Stuart gives his old colonel's coat: "See if that fits you!... Good! Pull two of the stars off the collar; go down to Richmond, and tell them I said you're a Major now!—" The cavalry brigade becomes a cavalry division. Wade Hampton, Colonel of his own Legion at Bull Run, and wounded, Brigadier of infantry on the Peninsula, and wounded again, is named senior Brigadier of cavalry and finds his *metier* at last. . . . He was a South Carolinian: before the war, the richest gentleman in the Confederate States. His town house was in Columbia, South Carolina: he had rice lands on the sea, and his cotton plantation in Mississippi; and he had always been a notable sportsman and a horse-lover. His fame as a bear hunter in the cane brakes on his river lands was wide: he had a record of eighty bears, killed, as was his custom, with his hands; with a long knife when his dogs brought the animal to bay. He was a large man, very noble in appearance, with a great flame of leadership in him, and he fought in front with his sword, like a Knight of the Elder Time.

Next senior was Beverly Robertson, an Old Army officer, who had raised and organized the North Carolina cavalry. He was the weakest of Stuart's brigadiers. The junior general was Fitzhugh Lee, who had succeeded Stuart in command of the 1st Virginia Regiment. We saw him at First Manassas as Ewell's Adjutant: he had served in the old 1st U. S. Cavalry and had been instructor at West Point. He was a man much admired and loved, with gallant ways, and a joyous, singing courage. Major John Pelham had now two batteries of Horse Artillery: his own, and Captain Hart's.

Of these three brigades, fourteen regiments, two batteries, which made up the cavalry division, Hampton was down with D. H. Hill, watching McClellan. Robertson's brigade, not yet concentrated, was partially with Jackson at Gordonsville. Fitz Lee was with Stuart. Early in August the Commanding General sent Stuart orders: to ride Fredericksburg-way, where the Yankee cavalry was active, and to do what he could to relieve these suffering counties in that region, until the army came. There followed what Stuart calls *petit guerre*. Yankee cavalry had forayed down to Beaver Dam Station, and captured Captain John Mosby, who was waiting for a train. Houses were burnt, crops destroyed, and stock run off. There was clamor from interested parties for detachments of horse to guard the railroad line, but Stuart refused to countenance the policy of "frittering away the command into little detachments, on any of which the enemy could concentrate and destroy it." He took Fitz Lee and Pelham, on 4 August, and rode north from Hanover to Bowling Green, and on the next day dashed into Port Royal by the lower Rappahannock, catching an enemy detachment in the town. His scouts that night, toward Fredericksburg, brought information of a Yankee column of all arms on Massaponax Creek, on the Telegraph road, pointing toward Richmond; evidently, decided Stuart, another raid at the Virginia Central. Dawn of the 6th, he rode for Massaponax Church, and in the forenoon struck the Telegraph road where a long column of wagons, under an infantry escort, was moving south.

The Yankees were proceeding confidently, without flankers, and the Confederate cavalry, favored by the woods to the east of the Telegraph road, approached them unobserved. Fitz Lee threw his heading squadron from route-column into line, and it burst upon them, says Stuart, "like a thunderbolt." The blue infantry fled without resistance, the weapons were taken, and only one courier, who out-ran his pursuit, got away toward Fredericksburg. Prisoners advised that the trains belonged to the brigades of Hatch and Gibbon, proceeding south, and Fitz Lee sent two regiments and the Horse Artillery down the Telegraph road to overtake them. Some miles to the south, at the Po River, these caught up with the Federal rear guard and pitched into it. The rear guard faced about, communicating its alarm to the main body, and Hatch and Gibbon returned in line of battle, astride the road. This was what Stuart wanted, and he fell back slowly, the Horse Artillery in action from every convenient ridge, until the scene of the first contact was reached. His prisoners—85 men, a number of wagons, and some horses, had been sent to the eastward, and he broke off the action and followed them at leisure, to bivouac at Bowling Green. His loss was two men, mortally wounded. Next day he was back at Hanover Court House, receiving the approval of General Lee. There was no further Federal movement south from Fredericksburg.

During this expedition, in bivouac near Bowling Green, Von Borcke had a shocking experience: he awoke to find a large Virginia rattlesnake sharing his blankets. His roars roused the Headquarters camp, his famous dragoon sword gritted out of its scabbard, and he cut the snake apart, to delighted applause from Stuart and the aides.

After the Massaponax action, Pope's activities centered more upon the headwaters of the Rappahannock, and along its south fork, the Rapidan. Stuart left Fitz Lee in charge at Hanover, and started on an inspection tour of the cavalry of the Army of Northern Virginia. On 4 August, Washington had sent McClellan orders to retire from the James and bring his army around into the Potomac River. He protested the order for ten days, was overruled, and began on the 14th to carry it out. Meantime, Pope was ordered to cover his withdrawal by threatening more sharply the Gordonsville-Charlottesville vicinity, and he flung Bank's corps and some of Sigel's down into Culpeper Court House, preparing to follow with his main army. Stonewall Jackson was ready for him. Immediately on arrival in Gordonsville, back in July, Jackson had asked the reinforcements to deal with Pope, and after two weeks of waiting, Lee sent him A. P. Hill's Light Division, which brought his force to 24,000, including Robertson's brigade of cavalry. Learning that only a part of Pope's army was in Culpeper, it seemed to him that, "through the blessing of God," he might overwhelm this detachment before it could be reinforced. He moved from Gordonsville on the 7th, Robertson covering his advance, and camped that night at Orange, twenty miles south of Culpeper. He proposed on the 8th to march eighteen miles, which would bring him within striking distance of Culpeper, but the 8th was one of his bad days. The head of his column made only six miles, the rear of it two. Hill's and Ewell's divisions, infantry and trains, became entangled near Orange. The weather was brutally hot: this, or the excessive quantity of applejack available on the line of march, or sulkiness on the part of Hill, who was yet unaccustomed to Jackson's habitual reticence, are variously blamed for the day's misadventures. Jackson took the last view, and put Hill under arrest for neglect of duty: the correspondence is acrimonious. Robertson skirmished hotly until dark with details of Buford and Bayard, who showed marked stubbornness. Early on the 9th, the infantry moved again, and moved more like itself. It made ten miles by mid-afternoon, Robertson's cavalry finding it increasingly hard to drive the Northern horse, and eight miles from Culpeper, on Cedar Run, by a hill with the ominous name of Slaughter

Mountain, blue cavalry and gray drew off to left and right, and Jackson's Own Division, under Winder, collided violently with one of Banks' divisions, marching south.

Banks was outnumbered: he had less than 9,000 men on the field, but it is remembered of him that he was always ready to fight—even though, adds Jackson, he usually got whipped. Winder deployed, Banks deployed: artillery galloped into battery: Hill and Ewell followed to form on Winder. Banks attacked with vigor; Winder was killed, and for a little while Jackson's Division fought for its life on the slopes of Slaughter Mountain; the famous Stonewall Brigade was broken and driven, and there, the only time on record, Jackson rode in with his sabre out, to rally his disintegrating battle-line. Ewell and Hill came into action as Banks' impetus was expended, and Banks was overpowered and driven in turn. At dark he fell back. Bayard covered him with great gallantry, his 1st Pennsylvania Cavalry losing 103 out of 164 officers and men engaged. Jackson, at the last, brought 17,000 bayonets to the push, and Banks gave up the field.

It was Jackson's intention to drive straight through to Culpeper that night, by the light of the moon, and he ordered Robertson forward to press the enemy, while Hill and Ewell followed hard. But, after a mile and a half, Robertson developed resistance, felt the front, and came up against solid lines of battle. Pouncing at the blue pickets, Robertson took prisoners, and identified formations in Sigel's corps. This meant that Banks was not alone, and Jackson prudently halted where he was and organized a defensive position. At daylight, Jeb Stuart, on his inspection tour, reported, and Jackson ordered him to take Robertson's brigade and reconnoitre. Stuart rode widely, beat up the Federal outposts, took prisoners, and had identifications. He discovered that most of Pope's army was up, and Pope

in person. Too many Yankees for Jackson's 24,000—
diminished in the fight by 1,300 casualties. On the 10th
there was no fighting: on the 11th, in the night, Jackson
withdrew toward Gordonsville.

This was the Battle of Cedar Mountain, a small *rencontre*,
characterized by very savage fighting in the few hours it
lasted. Winder was one of the Confederacy's most distinguished young officers, and had a splendid future. Banks'
attacking division, and the elements of Sigel which reinforced
him, lost 2,800 men, including a general and 400 prisoners.
Their conduct in the action was wholly admirable, especially
since they were the same troops Jackson had so heavily defeated in the Valley Campaign. But it was considered by
Pope that their fighting edge was burnt away on this 9th of
August, and little further use was made of them in the
campaign.

Pope, moving forward on the 11th, and occupying the
battlefield, claimed a victory—largely based on the numerous abandoned rifles he found in the Confederate positions.
As a matter of fact, Jackson's regiments had thrown these
arms away, re-equipping themselves from the 5,000 stand of
superior small arms they salvaged where Banks had fought
them. Ascertaining—as his cavalry was permitted to learn—
that Jackson had not stopped at Gordonsville, but had retreated through the place, southward, Pope proposed to
follow, but Halleck refused to be drawn: feigned retreats, he
cautioned Pope, were well-known secesh tactics, and he advised that he would reinforce the Army of Virginia as Mc-
Clellan's returning troops became available. In this Halleck
was wise: Jackson had drawn off in the hope that Pope would
rush after him, and give him an opportunity to turn and
cut up exposed Federal elements. Restrained by Halleck,
Pope took up a position on the north bank of the Rapidan,
and waited for the promised divisions from the Army of the

Potomac. Meantime, Lee, in Richmond, learning that the movement of McClellan from the Peninsula was ordered and getting under way, moved Longstreet's command, about 30,000 bayonets, by rail to Gordonsville. He was now free to bring his strength against Pope. Only D. H. Hill, with his own and McLaws' divisions, and Hampton's cavalry brigade, remained near Richmond, to oversee McClellan's embarkation. From the 13th to the 15th of August Longstreet's divisions were coming into Gordonsville. Jackson, on the 14th, had exactly located the Federal Army: it lay, compactly grouped, northeast of Slaughter Mountain, the Rapidan River covering its front from Rapidan Station to Somerville Ford. The Orange and Alexandria Railroad ran through Pope's camps and was his axis of supply. Jackson moved up to Pisgah Church, just south of Clarke's Mountain, and from Clarke's Mountain Pope's whole army area was closely overlooked by Confederate observation posts. Pope had 50,000 men: Lee, when Longstreet was up, about 55,000. But Pope would have, very soon, heavy reinforcements from the Army of the Potomac.

General Lee's problem was, to bring Pope to battle before his numbers were too much increased. On the 15th, at Orange Court House, and on the 16th, he assembled Longstreet, Jackson, and Stuart, in council. It was decided to cross the Rapidan below Pope's army, turning his left flank and placing the Confederates between him and Washington. Lee expected to destroy him. Jackson would force the Rapidan at Somerville Ford, Longstreet, preceded by Stuart, at Raccoon Ford, while Stuart would cut the railroad in the Federal rear, near Culpeper. Longstreet would then swing in upon Pope's left rear, while Jackson assailed his left front. To Jackson, for the screening of his advance, was given Robertson's cavalry brigade. Stuart would employ Fitz Lee in front of Longstreet. The 18th was the day set for the movement. All the troops were on the ground, except Fitz Lee's cavalry brigade, which had moved west from Hanover a few miles to Davenport's Ford, in the vicinity of Beaver Dam Station on the North Anna River, and on the 16th Stuart ordered Fitz Lee to march up and meet him at Raccoon Ford. Also, on the 16th, Jackson approached Somerville Ford, and Longstreet moved to face Raccoon Ford. Stuart, early on the 17th, rode with his personal staff from Orange Court House, to rendezvous with Fitz Lee.

Now the imponderables come into the campaign, the incalculable elements of luck and chance, inseparable from affairs which include the human equation. The orders Stuart sent Fitz Lee have not been preserved, but it is clear that in them the time element, the immediate urgency of the movement, was not made clear to the officer who received them. And it is certain that on the 17th of August the Confederate's officers, looking down from Clarke's Mountain on the tranquil camps of Pope, counted the Yankees already in the bag.

From Davenport's Ford on the North Anna to Raccoon Ford on the Rapidan is nearly thirty miles, northwesterly. Fitz Lee had sent his wagons to Louisa Court House, another thirty miles, about due west from Davenport's, and thirty miles south of Raccoon Ford. When he received Stuart's orders, the haversacks of his men were empty, and no rations were available nearer than Louisa Court House, so instead of riding straight northwest, he marched on the 17th to Louisa, to supply himself from his train.

At Orange Court House, on the 16th, Stuart had from General Lee the final directions for cavalry's part in the rounding up of Pope, and he received a written order which set forth the cavalry mission in detail, as well as the general

plan of the army. This order Stuart intrusted to his adjutant, Major Fitzhugh. Meantime, Fitz Lee, starting for
Louisa, had sent a despatch advising Stuart of his route:
but this despatch did not reach Orange Court House before
Stuart departed for the rendezvous.

On the 17th, Stuart, with his party of five—Lieutenant
Chiswell Dabney, Major Fitzhugh, Major Von Borcke, Captain Mosby, and Lieutenant Gibson—rode east on the Orange
Plank Road to meet Fitz Lee at Raccoon Ford. The army
of General John Pope lay off to the west, beyond Clarke
Mountain and the Rapidan, and Stuart was not seriously
concerned about it. He was, however, annoyed at his failure
during the day to fall in with Fitz Lee's brigade, which
should be marching up from the southeast; and when, about
dark, he reached Verdiersville—a little village on the Orange
Plank Road, ten miles or so from Raccoon Ford, on Fitz
Lee's line of march—and learned there that no gray cavalry
had passed, he sent Major Fitzhugh out to find Fitz Lee's
column and hurry it along. He, with his staff, stopped for
the night at Verdiersville. The weather was fine, and they
settled on an old house, set back a little from the road, with
a wide porch in front of it. The August dark came down;
the party ate from their haversacks, listened a while to the
noises of the night, and rolled up in their cloaks on the
porch to sleep. Their horses were in the yard behind the
house, and Stuart, perfectly accustomed to living between
the lines, was not at all uneasy, especially since the citizens
told him that no Yankees had been seen near Verdiersville
for a month. Only the thorough Von Borcke seems to have
regarded their situation as dangerous, and he turned in
with his sword-belt and equipment, heedless of Dabney's
suggestion that he'd sleep more comfortably with that gear
off. The horses were saddled, but free to graze. Nothing had
been heard from Major Fitzhugh, but he would, most prob-

ably, remain with Fitz Lee. The Confederates slept until dawn.

Major Fitzhugh, plodding on his tired horse, sent no messages for a very good reason. He had been captured. During the night he rode into the arms of a Yankee cavalry column, coming from the direction of Louisa Court House. They gathered him up and took him along, for they were in a hurry. They had halted about dark, intending to bivouac, but soon as their horses were unsaddled some troopers went straying into a corn-field just off their line of march, intent upon supplementing their diet with fresh roasting-ears. Deep in the tall corn, they came upon a Confederate infantryman who was rationing himself on those same roasting-ears. Him they took, having their side-arms with them, and they extracted from him the information that Longstreet's wing—to which this soldier belonged—and probably Stonewall Jackson's wing, and Stuart's cavalry division, and such other details as the grayback's imagination could supply— were just on the other side of the corn-field. These interesting facts were promptly reported to their colonel.

The Yankee regiment was the 1st Michigan Volunteer Cavalry, under Colonel Brodhead, which, with the 5th New York Cavalry, had been out for a week's scouting in the vicinity of Louisa Court House, and was now returning to Pope's army. They did not wish to meet Longstreet, or Jackson, or, least of all, Stuart's cavalry division. They got to horse without bugles, and withdrew swiftly toward the Rapidan, on a road that led through Verdiersville, and they met Major Fitzhugh some miles from that place about midnight. And, going through Major Fitzhugh's papers, they came upon the autograph letter from Lee which gave his full plans for the destruction of Pope. They could hardly have made a more important capture—yet, in a few hours, they came very near doing so.

At dawn they approached a cluster of houses—Verdiers-ville. On a porch of one of the houses Jeb Stuart, who had ears like an Indian, stirred, sat up in his cloak, and listened. . . . cavalry, coming from the southeast—Fitz Lee, certainly! He called to Mosby and Gibson, and told them to ride out and make sure. Himself, bareheaded, leaving his cloak and hat and haversack on the porch, he strolled down to the gate to watch.

Just beyond the house the road curved off, and Mosby and Gibson trotted out of sight around this bend. A minute later a spatter of pistol shots broke the morning quiet; there were yells, and a great noise of hoofs, and Mosby and Gibson came around the curve, low on their horses' necks, shouting, "Yankee cavalry!" The officers ran for their horses. Stuart vaulted into his saddle, jumped the garden fence, and made off, bareheaded, behind the house, toward the nearest woods. Von Borcke, fully accoutred, mounted his big black, received (he says) the pistol fire of numerous Yankees at close range, and rode through a side gate and across a field, with a squadron after him. Dabney caught his horse somehow, and fled after Stuart. The Yankees, led by a major on a strong horse, considered tall Von Borcke the important prize, and chased him, firing from the saddle; but his mount was fresh and theirs were tired, and they did not follow very far. Stuart, safe in the woods, watched with chagrin as they looted the gear on the porch—waved his red-lined cloak about, rifled his black leather haversack. And one of them tried on, and wore away, the famous plumed hat. Then he saw them re-form and pound north, forcing their jaded nags. They did not know what noble game they had started, until Major Fitzhugh, riding gloomily in the rear of their column, saw the captured hat and turned pale. "Where," he said urgently, "is the man who wore that hat?" Oh, they told

him, with good humor, he got away, the dam' spry rebel!
"Thank God for that!" said Fitzhugh, "that's Jeb Stuart's
hat!"

In the woods above Verdiersville Stuart's party assembled—all out of breath, but unwounded—and Von Borcke
asks Dabney, wickedly, if he is quite comfortable now, without his side-arms. Stuart—Stuart is a major-general, and
he is not amused, and they say nothing when he ties a handkerchief around his head against the August sun. They ride
on, and come upon Longstreet's infantry, and find a Georgia
regiment with a well-stocked sutler, who supplies the general
with a plain wool hat such as poor infantry soldiers wear.
The tale runs through the army with the amazing swiftness
of soldiers' grapevine telegraph—and all day Stuart en-
dures the joyous shouts of the irreverent gray columns, who
have little enough to make them merry in this time of forced
marches. "Lookee, boys—Jeb's got a new hat!" "Hi!
Cavalry! whar's yo' hat?"—and acquaintances call out, Old
Army and New Army, delightedly. "I am greeted on all sides
with congratulations and—'Where's your hat?' "—Jeb
Stuart writes his wife. . . . "I just had time to mount my
horse & clear the back fence, having no time to get my hat or
anything else. I lost my haversack, blanket, talma, cloak, &
hat that had that *palmetto star*. Too bad, wasn't it?" And
he adds, "I intend to make the Yankees pay dearly for
that hat——"

There is yet another minor event which hinged on Fitz
Lee's tardiness. Longstreet, directed to Raccoon Ford,
marched on the 16th from Gordonsville, and late on the 17th
was in position facing the lower fords on the Rapidan, while
Jackson, on the left, under similar orders, covered the upper
fords. Longstreet expected to make contact with Fitz Lee
at Raccoon Ford, and when night fell and no cavalry ap-

peared, he considered it necessary to watch the Raccoon Ford
Road, and he ordered two regiments out to picket it until
the cavalry came.

The detail fell upon Toombs' Georgia brigade. General
Toombs himself, when Longstreet's order arrived, was absent
from his headquarters. An old Congressional crony of his
lived in the neighborhood, and Toombs had leave to ride over
and pay a visit. Colonel Benning, second in command, executed the order and posted the two regiments as directed.
Next day General Longstreet heard of Stuart's adventure in
Verdiersville, and heard also that the Yankee cavalry had
gone out by Raccoon Ford, which he had ordered closed. He
sent at once to inquire why his pickets had allowed the
Yankees to escape, and discovered that General Toombs,
riding back to his brigade from some hours in congenial company, had come upon his own regiments across the Raccoon
Ford road, and had been indignant that anyone, even Longstreet, should order out his men without sending the order
through him, personally. General Toombs was not a West
P'inter, as the Confederate Service put it, but he was a
punctilious gentleman, and he took his regiments right back
to camp. It followed that the Raccoon Ford road was open
for Colonel Brodhead when he came along, with Major Fitzhugh, Lee's army order, Jeb Stuart's personal effects, and
the Michigan horsemen.

Longstreet was a West Pointer, and had no patience with
gentlemen when they questioned his authority. He despatched
his adjutant, wearing sword and sash as provided by regulations, to convey General Toombs under arrest and send him
to the rear. But events came too fast for due court-martial
procedure; Toombs offered sweeping apologies and was for-
given. We have a picture of him, catching up with Longstreet, in the heat of the last fighting on Manassas Plain, his
gray horse dark with sweat, and his hat off, asking to be

directed to his brigade, which presently greeted him with joyous yells as it swept forward.

Fitz Lee reached Raccoon Ford the night of the 18/19 August, his horses so tired from their sixty-mile march that General Lee authorized a day's rest for them, and set the 20th for the movement. It is related that Jackson wanted to go ahead without the cavalry, but Lee thought better not. By the 20th the opportunity had passed.

Thus, because Fitz Lee (says Stuart) failed to comply with instructions, or because (Fitz Lee says) he misunderstood them, Lee's first snatch at John Pope went adrift.

Stuart's report of this phase of the cavalry operations is exceedingly severe on Fitz Lee. That officer's brigade reached Raccoon Ford a whole day late—the night of the 18th—and in no shape, because of its Louisa Court House detour, to ride fast with Beverly Robertson's brigade for Culpeper. Late on the 19th, after a necessary day of rest, Stuart shifted his column down to Mitchel's Ford. That night despatches from Lee indicated that Pope had moved beyond immediate danger. Stuart also points out that, by failing to be on time, Fitz Lee also made possible the escape of the considerable body of blue cavalry—the 1st Michigan and the 5th New York—which flushed him at Verdiersville.

The records contain no excuses from Fitz Lee. He took his reprimand in silence. But, says Stuart's biographer, Major McClellan, if Fitz Lee had understood that he was wanted on the 17th, he would have been there, fed or empty; and, as to explanations, Fitz Lee was always fonder of fighting than of writing. Years afterward he touched briefly on the incident in his *Life of General R. E. Lee.*

Jeb Stuart's report does not mention the loss of the important papers which Major Fitzhugh carried. But from them Pope drew an urgent warning. Further, his reiterated instructions from Halleck enjoined the necessity of maintaining intact his rail communications with Alexandria, and it was always considered his first duty to keep his army between the enemy and Washington. With Stuart headed for his rear and Longstreet preparing to work around his left flank—his home flank—the Culpeper country was becoming dangerous. Therefore, on the 18th, immediately after Pope received Colonel Brodhead's report, the Confederate signal stations on Clarke Mountain wigwagged that there was motion in his camps. On the 19th General Lee himself, with Longstreet, climbed the hill and looked at the great prospect spread below: the wide Yankee camp was visibly diminishing, and long lines of dust, crawling northeastward, indicated that Pope was fully awake to his danger and was prudently withdrawing from it. Lee had to spin new schemes. Perhaps he could catch Pope on the Rappahannock. He issued orders when he came down from Clarke Mountain.

On the 20th Lee sent Longstreet and Jackson forward. They marched at moonrise—about 4 A.M. Longstreet, Fitz Lee's brigade his advance guard, crossed the Rapidan at Raccoon Ford and reached Kelly's Ford on the Rappahannock the same afternoon, Fitz Lee effectively screening him, and skirmishing hotly with Buford's blue cavalry near Kelly's.

Jackson, farther west, with Robertson's cavalry brigade, and Jeb Stuart, in person, going before, and Munford, and a battery of the Horse Artillery on his left, crossed the Rapidan at Somerville Ford and marched on Brandy Station. That day Bayard's cavalry had been covering the retreat of General Sigel's corps from Culpeper, and in the afternoon Bayard was near Brandy Station, where he was ordered to halt for the night, south of the Rappahannock and its small tributary, Hazel Run. He had seen, all day, dust clouds over the roads to the southeast, and his scouts brought in reports of an enemy advance. He had five regiments of volunteer cavalry—the 1st Pennsylvania, 1st Rhode Island, 1st New Jersey, 1st Maine, and 2d New York—and they had covered the ten-mile stretch between Raccoon Ford and Brandy Station—a Maine squadron having encountered, early in the day, some of Fitz Lee's people in front of Longstreet. Now they assembled to their right, on Brandy Station, where, between Stevensburg and Hazel Run, there is open country. In the late afternoon Stuart approached them with Robertson's brigade. Bayard's regiments were drawn up in a deep echelon, the New York (Harris Light) regiment, Lieutenant-Colonel Judson Kilpatrick, standing the most advanced. As soon as the enemy came into clear, reports Bayard, they formed line and charged him, "with loud shouts and wild yelling."

They fell first upon Kilpatrick's Harris Light, and scattered the New Yorkers. The New Jersey regiment was next, and its colonel, with his adjutant, rode alone to meet the rebels—his Jerseymen rode off toward the river.

This Confederate regiment was the 7th Virginia, Colonel Grumble Jones, the remainder of Robertson's brigade having been sent by Stuart, after a hasty reconnaissance, to sweep by the left, toward Barboursville, and turn the Federals. The fugitives streamed before the gray horse, toward the river, and between Brandy Station and the Rappahannock, the other three regiments of Bayard's brigade were formed in column of squadrons and disposed to fight. The 7th Virginia recoiled from their fire. It was soon apparent that Robertson had missed his road to the flank, and there was some delay while Stuart's staff officers galloped to find him. He was brought back, and the impatient Stuart threw his regiments, as they arrived, against the enemy in columns of fours—the 6th and 12th regiments, and the 17th Virginia Battalion, Ashby's old troopers. Bayard's men did not wait to cross sabres. They broke again and reformed on the bank of Hazel Run, under the cover of Sigel's artillery beyond the stream. Stuart estimated their numbers and their supporting guns in position to be too formidable for him, and he sent after Fitz Lee, now down toward Kelly's Ford, and for the Horse Artillery. Two regiments and Pelham's battery came in response, but by the time they arrived Bayard had crossed Hazel Run to safety. Robertson's brigade lost three killed and thirteen wounded, and took, Robertson reports, sixty-four prisoners; Bayard admits a loss of sixty-one, all ranks. Stuart's report is generous, citing equally General Robertson and Colonel Jones—neither of whom he liked— and Major von Borcke and Captain Redmond Burke, who were dear to him.

This little action, in which four Confederate regiments were engaged against five Federal regiments, on the plain of Brandy Station, was the first considerable cavalry engagement in Virginia. Stuart fought his men altogether mounted, while Bayard, in the second stage of the action, had some squadrons on foot. There was no actual contact between blue and gray. Stuart's people advanced at the gallop, and Bayard's, standing in ranks to receive them, turned away before the shock. Afterward there would be many fights at Brandy Station. The place was a cross roads: all the routes south, over the headwaters of the Rappahannock, as you go to Culpeper, led through it. It would become one of the commonest of the war names.

Stuart, with both Fitz Lee and Robertson in hand, picketed the line of the Rappahannock River for the night from Kelly's Ford to Beverly's. Jackson's infantry reached the vicinity of Brandy Station after dark. The gray cavalry, thrusting everywhere, took numerous prisoners—stragglers and enemy outpost detachments, and identified among them men of Burnside's corps, just joined from the Army of the Potomac. They also learned that Pope's main army, substantially reinforced, had crossed at Kelly's Ford and Rappahannock Station, and that his trains had been sent well ahead. The information went to General Lee.

Elsewhere that day, the 20th, on all the roads leading up to the Rappahannock, from Freeman's Ford below Rappahannock Station to Beverly's Ford above, were fought a whole rosary of cavalry skirmishes. These were prolonged through the 21st and the 22d of August, for Lee at first held his infantry out of sight, south of the river, and sent the cavalry to test the fords and feel out the dispositions of the blue people on the other side. Buford and Bayard met these sallies vigorously, but their brigades were widely dispersed, and Stuart was usually able to bring superior strength against the points he wanted to investigate. Rosser, near Beverly's Ford, made a dash and scattered a battalion of infantry on picket, falling so suddenly upon them that he took their muskets, all smartly stacked. Major John Pelham, with the Horse Artillery, seems to have been everywhere at once. By these researches it was made plain that Pope was drawn up in excellent order to defend the river line, and in great strength. He was uneasy, because he continually shifted his strength from one flank to the other, as his estimate of Lee's intention varied, but Lee failed to find anywhere an opening. Light rains fell during these days, but there was heavy rain in the Blue Ridge, and the Rappahannock began to rise between the armies.

On the 22d of August Stuart proposed to the Commanding General that he be allowed to ride around Pope's upper flank and interrupt his rail communications with Alexandria. The proposition was attractive. It was evident that no advantageous battle could be delivered against Pope where he stood, while a demonstration in his rear might start him into some hasty move that could be turned into an opportunity, and meantime Lee could not lie idle and let his enemy accumulate strength. Also, the armies were stabilized on the river, and cavalry could be briefly spared. Lee gave his consent, and Stuart immediately assembled the brigades of Fitz Lee and Beverly Robertson—less the 7th and 3d Virginia regiments, left with the Army—took two of Pelham's guns, and rode up-stream, past the flanks of the infantry, to Waterloo Bridge. Here, in the forenoon of the 22d, he crossed his column and went twelve miles east, to Warrenton. To his professional zeal was added a personal urge: there is the letter—"I intend to make the Yankees pay dearly for that hat——"

At Warrenton, there was a great reception from the sympathetic civilian population. The column rested an hour: Stuart gathered as much information as he could on Yankee habits in the locality; Von Borcke became acquainted with a number of charming girls; and the regimental officers amused themselves by registering formally at the Warrenton Hotel. Stuart then took the road eastward, seven miles to Auburn, on Cedar Run, and, being well behind Pope's army and north of the Orange and Alexandria Railroad, he turned, about dark, down toward Catlett's Station. The weather had been threatening all day, and with nightfall it began to rain, and Stuart says it was the darkest night he had ever seen. Fitz Lee with the advance guard rode into Catlett's, captured the place, and scattered its defense, for the Yankees were all bewildered in the dark and the driving rain—and then the Confederate troopers, still held compactly together, halted; they were where Stuart wanted them, but in the night and the storm it was impossible to tell which way to strike next— or even to distinguish friend from foe. Cavalry cannot wait long in such a situation: it must hit hard and quickly, or go away.

Then Stuart had the thing called a break: Napoleon

placed luck high among the essential qualifications of a successful general. A negro teamster, taken, among other Yankee prisoners, from an overrun wagon park, recognized Jeb Stuart: he was a Berkeley County negro, a slave with an otherwise unrecorded odyssey—and he was glad to see his white folks. He told the general that Pope's headquarters were camped right near to Catlett's Station, by the railroad, between the Station and Cedar Run: there were his headquarters' tents, his personal horses and wagon park, and all his staff. He volunteered to show the way. Stuart consulted briefly with Fitz Lee, and accepted the negro's proposition: whatever was to be done had to be done quickly. Fitz Lee designated Rooney Lee and the 9th Virginia to rush the headquarters' camp, while the 1st Virginia and the 5th Virginia, Colonels Brien and Rosser, went to make diversion at the next camp to headquarters; and he told off Engineer Captain Blackford and a detail, with Wickham's 4th Virginia, to destroy the railroad bridge over Cedar Run.

They moved swiftly and in close order, the rain covering all small sounds. Rooney Lee led quietly up to the tents "occupied by the convivial members of General Pope's Staff," and charged, shooting and yelling. Sleepy sentries, sheltering against the wet, lay discreetly low, or ran out to be ridden down. The camp guards fled or surrendered. The soaked gray troopers ravaged about, cutting tent-guys and upsetting wagons, rounding up prisoners and horses, and putting fire to everything that would burn. Pope was, unfortunately, from home, but they caught Pope's field-quartermaster and other staff officers, and secured the general's letter-books and correspondence files, and his tent furniture, horses, and baggage, as well as the headquarters strong-box.

Rosser and Brien, guided by lightning flashes, crossed and

recrossed the cuts and fills of the railroad and turned out more camps. An active youngster swarmed up a telegraph pole and hacked down the wire with his sabre. Captain Blackford got at the bridge, a double-decked trestle, very strong, and tried to fire it: but the sodden timbers would not take fire. Colonel Wickham sent a detail through the camps for axes, and a few were found, and with these Blackford attacked the trestles. Fitz Lee himself came to hurry the work. The storm continued with increasing violence, and a Federal command came up and opened fire from the far side of Cedar Run on the axemen, who were pecking away at the bridge. Fugitives from the alarmed camps rallied on this formation and their firing grew heavier. Worst of all, Blackford was making no useful progress at the bridge. Stuart comes, strokes his wet beard, and decides, most reluctantly, that the difficulties are insuperable. Cedar Run was rising: a message came from Robertson's brigade, in reserve with the artillery, that it was already swimming-deep where the column would have to cross. And the Rappahannock was getting the same rain. And the cavalry had to get back to the army. "The Commanding General," writes Stuart, "will, I am sure, appreciate how hard it was to desist from the undertaking, but to any one on the spot there could be but one opinion—its impossibility. I gave it up."

Cavalry bugles sounded recall, and assembly. Rooney Lee and Rosser and Brien formed in the gutted camps, with 300 prisoners—including high-ranking staff gentlemen—a number of horses and mules, and as many wagons as the column could escort. Stuart drew off in the dark by the Auburn road.

Soon after daylight they were at Warrenton, receiving the compliments of the citizens. Some inventory was made of the loot, and Stuart was delighted to find Pope's best uniform coat, a major-general's frock, very elegant, with the buttons spaced in threes. A black-eyed Warrenton lady, one of the staff writes, ran out with a bottle of wine to pay a forfeit to Major Goulding, the captured Yankee staff quartermaster: she had wagered him this champagne that he would not, as he had predicted recently, be in Richmond within thirty days. Now he was Richmond-bound, and she felt that she should settle up. It is related that the major took his winnings handsomely, and pledged the lady when he drank.

A courier went galloping ahead with Pope's correspondence for General Lee: it contained the most intimate details of Pope's plans, and, most interesting of all, the schedule of expected arrivals from the Army of the Potomac, now landing or landed along the river, from Aquia Creek to Alexandria.

The column marched, unpursued, and crossed again at Waterloo Bridge, rejoining the army by noon of the 23d. John Pope's uniform coat was mounted on a frame and carried conspicuously through the Confederate camps, to the delight of all ranks, and later it was displayed in a Broad Street show-window in Richmond.

"My Dearest Wife," Stuart wrote, on the 25th, "I have had my revenge out of Pope, I captured part of his staff, all his baggage and baggage train, horse equipments, by a rapid dash upon his rear near Warrenton Junction. . . ."

The cavalry loss was four killed, one wounded, and seven missing. Stuart feels bound "to accord to the officers and men, collectively, engaged in this expedition, unqualified praise, for their good conduct under circumstances where their discipline, fortitude, endurance, and bravery stood such an extraordinary test. The horseman who, at his officer's bidding, without questioning, leaps into unexplored darkness, knowing nothing except that there is certain danger ahead, possesses the highest attribute of the patriot soldier.

It is a great source of pride to me to command such men."

General John Pope's comments on the Catlett's Station affair are not good-humored. He estimated the enemy which dashed into his camp at 300 sabres—almost the only underestimate of an opponent's strength that I have found in the official records—and adds that the camp was guarded by 1,500 blue infantry and five companies of cavalry, and that the success of the rebel raiders was disgraceful to the guard in charge of his trains. Pope had opened his campaign with trenchant remarks to his troops about lines of retreat and bases of supplies—"certain phrases which I am sorry to find much in vogue amongst you. . . . Let us study the probable lines of retreat of our opponents, and leave our own to take care of themselves. Let us look before and not behind!" "Old Headquarters-in-the-Saddle! The Man Without a Rear—" gibed the sardonic Southern troopers. Seldom in history have a man's words come so humiliatingly back upon him. Here was Stuart, running off with his personal baggage, and there was much worse being prepared for his army.

The important item in Stuart's booty was the headquarters' correspondence. From it Lee learned what his enemy intended, what his strength was, and what he proposed to do with it. Most important of all was the movement of troops from McClellan's army: Porter and Burnside, the Fifth and the Ninth Corps, were up, and others were in supporting distance, and Lee saw that in a very few days Pope would be too strong for him. Already he had 80,000 men on the Rapidan, and he would soon have, in hand and within call, 150,000 men. Lee's possible reinforcements, now starting from Richmond, were D. H. Hill's two divisions and Hampton's cavalry brigade. On the field he had now all the troops he was going to have. Pope must be attacked before the rest of the Army of the Potomac reached him, and, considering Pope, Lee thought his 55,000 were enough.

He could not be attacked on his river line: the rains had swollen the waters, rendered the fords impassable, and even swept out bridges. From the 20th to the 23d of August Lee had failed to find an opening for a thrust. Now, on the 24th, at Jefferson, he went with Jackson through Pope's correspondence, and the results of the conference were exciting.

On the Rappahannock Pope's 80,000 were too strongly posted, and 20,000 more stood under his orders at Aquia Creek; and more would come. Lee decided to divide his army, draw Pope from his river line, and bring him to battle on ground of the Confederates' choosing. Things began to happen. On the 23d and 24th Stuart skirmished hotly at every ford on Pope's front and had hard fighting to save Waterloo Bridge. Longstreet's infantry displayed itself in force to Pope's observers across the river. Behind this show of activity Jackson's command was withdrawn and assembled at Jefferson, Longstreet extending to occupy his old front, facing Sulphur Springs.

Under the morning stars, before the dawn of the 25th of August, Stonewall Jackson took the road northwest from Jefferson. He had his own division, A. P. Hill's Light Division, and Ewell's, about 21,000 men. Stuart's cavalry, he knew, would presently follow, but nobody in his column knew where Jackson was leading, or why. This day and the next he did the most notable marching of his career.

The column passed Waterloo Bridge, where some of Longstreet's infantry and Stuart's Horse Artillery were bickering with Pope's extreme right flank, and held on up-stream. Five miles above, at Hinson's Mill, it turned and forded the Rappahannock, the flood stage having passed. By Amissville, thence north to Orleans, and thence to Salem, through the hot, clear August weather, it marched. About midnight Jackson halted at Salem, on the Manassas Gap Railroad, and his men fell down in ranks and slept like the dead. They had come twenty-six miles. Where they bivouacked, the long rampart of the Blue Ridge rose to the west, and the undulating mass of Bull Run Mountain lifted itself on the other hand. The regiments had marched with colors uncased, to stimulate the files, and Pope's observers on the hills west of Warrenton had seen, and by counting flags and batteries made a close estimate of, the column's strength, and deduced that it was Jackson's. This was the first intelligence Pope had of enemy movements since the 22d. He rather thought it must be a flank column, covering a movement toward the Valley—Winchester, possibly. Amazingly enough, he sent no cavalry to investigate. Bayard and Buford were engaged that day, the 25th, along the river, and, their reports say, very much exhausted from the hard service they had already undergone.

Jackson moved from Salem before dawn and headed eastward—the first hint his people had as to his intention. This day, as on the day before, his march was unopposed: Munford, with the 2d Virginia Cavalry, riding in advance, had nothing to do but ride. During the forenoon the column passed Thoroughfare Gap in Bull Run Mountain, and opened the tranquil plateau of Manassas, all empty of blue soldiers. In the afternoon they came to Gainesville, and met Stuart's brigades, riding from the southwest.

Stuart, at 1 A.M. the night of the 25/26th, had received orders to follow Jackson. He marched at two o'clock in the morning of the 26th—he mentions in his report that he had no sleep that night, himself—and trailed the infantry as far as Salem, where he came upon Jackson's trains, filling the roads at his rear. Detaching his own light wagons to join those of the infantry, he turned right and passed Bull Run Mountain south of Thoroughfare Gap, and caught up with Jackson at Gainesville. With him he had Fitz Lee and Beverly Robertson, and Pelham's Horse Artillery, which always kept up.

Gainesville is on the Warrenton turnpike, a few miles west of the 1st Manassas battlefield. Jackson ordered Stuart to take the front and flanks and move on to Bristoe Station, by the country road leading southeast from the Warrenton turnpike. Stuart detached squadrons to watch east and west on the Turnpike—toward Warrenton and toward Centreville—and the long dusty column—Fitz Lee, Robertson, and Ewell's infantry in close support—marched southeast, and before sunset the leading squadrons dashed into Bristoe station and captured it.

Bristoe Station, on the Orange and Alexandria Railroad, lay five miles southwest of Manassas Junction, and fourteen miles east of Warrenton, and was squarely on Pope's line of communication. Immediately to the east, centring on the Junction, was Pope's great army depot. Fourteen to twenty miles westward were the masses of the Federal Army, still echeloned upon the Rappahannock, engaged in watchful waiting. As Stuart occupied the place, and before he could tear up the rails or destroy the bridge over Broad Run at Bristoe, an empty train drawn by the engine "Secretary" came through from Warrenton, and got away to Alexandria. We learn that "Engine 'Secretary' is completely riddled with bullets." Behind it were two more trains, which were derailed and taken. A fourth approached cautiously from the west, smelt danger, and retired, which meant that both Alexandria and Washington would be warned of trouble at Manassas; and they were. Both places decided that it was just another cavalry raid.

Soon after dark Jackson's divisions closed on Bristoe,

having made a twenty-five-mile march from Salem. But
Jackson's objective was still seven miles away, the depot at
Manassas Junction. Brigadier-General Trimble, with a
North Carolina and a Georgia regiment, volunteered to go
ahead, and Jackson sent Stuart and the cavalry brigades.
Cavalry rode wide to get behind the Junction; infantry
plodded up the track. Stuart was in charge of the operation.
At midnight the depot was surrounded, and there was some
spasmodic, ineffective firing in the dark. At the gray of
dawn, on the 27th, Wickham's 4th Virginia, from the north,
and Trimble's infantry, from the west, closed in and took
the depot without difficulty, capturing most of the small
guard. Jackson arrived with daylight, bringing his own and
Hill's divisions. Ewell remained in line at Bristoe, watching to the west for Pope's reaction.

The sunlight of a lifetime ago falls golden, across the
years, on Stonewall Jackson and Jeb Stuart, the foot cavalry
and the gray horsemen, in the Manassas Plain, this August
morning, the 27th of the month. It was one of the joyous
days of the Army of Northern Virginia. The infantry had
marched, in midsummer heat and dust, nearly sixty miles in
two days. Cavalry had covered the same distance in twenty-
two hours. This marching had come in the course of marching and fighting, constant since the early spring—and it was
now late summer. The infantry had marched out of their
shoes and very nearly out of their clothes, and out of most
of their equipment. The Confederate supply service, never
efficient, had utterly failed in the battle summer of 1862.
Thousands were barefoot. The poor gray jackets were in
tatters. Jackson's infantry had thrown away as useless, for
the most part, knapsack and leather gear. They carried, to
each man a haversack and a blanket-roll, and a canteen—
and to each squad a frying pan and a coffee pot, and their

cartridges were loose in their pockets. They were hairy and dirty and weathered black, and only their arms and their eyes were bright. Such ragged, miserable, and filthy wretches, observed a Yankee officer who was captured about this time and saw them close, you cannot possibly imagine. They lack everything . . . but as for marching and fighting——

Stuart's troopers were in little better case. The feathered hats, the shabracks, the jackboots, the braided jackets, the elegant accessories with which the young gentlemen rode first to war, had all disappeared. The hot-blooded Virginia horses, drawn and thin from hundreds of miles of riding, were about all that was left of the original equipment.

The physique and morale of the command was, however, remarkable. The Valley Campaign and the Peninsula had taken battle-toll of the best and bravest, but the ardors of the weather and the terrible marches had stripped away the weaklings. The men who remained in ranks were very hard men, seasoned and war-wise. Now they stood, 20,000 of them, in the midst of 100,000 enemies—with the enemy's food and stores in their hands. Every soldier present understood the situation and appreciated it. Their general, having placed the liquor under guard, and taken steps to secure as much ordnance material and public property as could be moved, loosed them on the depot, and they foraged jubilantly through the day.

The recorded scene is extremely jocose: Jackson himself was looking out for Pope's rear. His people had been living on corn and green apples, and they were sharp-set. One can hear across the years the wails of the Northern sutlers as the lank rebels gutted their choicest stores. The gray soldiers frolicked like bad little boys in a place they had no business being. Long-haired Georgians, Carolinians, Virginians, had never seen such plenty or such variety in their lives, and they gorged themselves to full capacity. What they couldn't eat they tried to carry off. Every cavalryman had a sack of coffee across his saddle. Infantry marched with bulging blanket-rolls, and hams skewered on their bayonets. Hatless fellows, men whose trousers were beyond redemption, men whose skirts had disintegrated to a button and frill, shoeless men, were all supplied. Major John Pelham, arriving late, deprived a sutler of four splendid draft-horses for his guns, and shared with Hill's and Ewell's chiefs of artillery the choicest animals in the army corrals. To Pelham, also, was given the detail of removing several batteries of artillery found in store. Ewell remained in observation down the road, and Stuart sent detachments of Fitz Lee's and Robertson's brigades to sweep the country toward Alexandria, where that morning they "had great sport chasing fugitive parties of the enemy's cavalry." Fitz Lee, with the 9th, 4th, and 3d Virginia regiments, rode as far as Fairfax Court House.

Alexandria reacted first; in the morning a New Jersey brigade, General G. W. Taylor, infantry without artillery, came down on a train of cars, alighted and formed at a safe distance, and moved by the railroad, on the Junction. Sufficient infantry was sent to meet him, and captured cannon were turned against him. He had not expected to find anything but raiding cavalry; he was mortally wounded and his command dispersed. Fitz Lee, on his line of retreat, cut up the remnants. Late in the afternoon Hooker's division appeared from Warrenton, and a brisk action developed against Kettle Run, beyond Bristoe. In the midst of it Jackson sent word to Ewell: Break off, and come in: he wanted no battle there. Ewell skillfully withdrew, Munford and Rosser covering his retirement, and fell back on Manassas Junction. Hooker had been so savagely received that he followed with great discretion, reporting merely that he had defeated the enemy and driven him five miles. Jackson had from Stuart the news that McDowell's corps was moving on the turnpike, from Warrenton, and that all the country to the southwest showed the dust of marching columns. He had also a message from General Lee, brought through Pope's converging masses by a trooper of the Black Horse in the 4th Virginia Cavalry, that Lee had marched with Longstreet the evening of the 26th, and was coming on by Salem and Thoroughfare Gap. The day was closing, and it was time to go.

The vast depot was set on fire, and blazed for miles along the railroad. Hooker's advanced elements watched the enemy retire northward, toward Centreville, toward Alexandria, in the direction of Washington; and Hooker, and presently Pope with him, come to see with his own eyes, were amazed. Hooker could not find out more, because Rosser and Munford covered the roads to the Junction, and fought from every coppice in the gathering dark.

Between the 24th and the 27th, Pope's divisions had done a great deal of marching and counter-marching. After the Catlett's Station affair he thought Lee might be getting ready to turn his left flank—his downstream flank, and he massed troops on Rappahannock Station, in his centre. Then he observed the activity of the Confederates on that flank, and decided that Lee was trying to mask a movement up-stream—in which he was correct—and he swung his centre of gravity toward Warrenton, which was not quite far enough. Longstreet, on the 26th, crossed the Rappahannock only three miles above him. Except the note on Jackson's marching column, the 25th, he had absolutely no information of enemy movements for these three days, and his first positive intelligence was brought by the train that escaped Stuart and Ewell at Bristoe Station, late on the 26th. Even then he did not realize how bad it was. On the 27th reports increased; he discovered that the Confederates had left the river on his front, and he issued orders for the army to fall back on the Manassas depot. It is queer that his great depot was left entirely naked to the enemy, so far as any adequate detachment for defense is concerned. In his reports he blames the corps commanders in his rear echelons for failure to guard it, but his orders to them had not been specific in this regard, and the simple fact is that the possibility of a Confederate raid on a corps scale never occurred to him.

Pope broke off movement for the night. All his army, except Banks, had left the Rappahannock during the day. Hooker and Kearney were on the railroad facing Bristoe Station, Fitz-John Porter behind them. Sigel was up at Gainesville on the turnpike, McDowell, with the rest of his corps, following close. Reno was between McDowell and Hooker. Bayard, with his cavalry, was north of Gainesville, and Buford's Brigade remained near Warrenton. Pope knew that he was between this enemy, now known to be Jackson, and the main body of the Confederates, and, sore and angry as he was, he did not see how Jackson could escape him.

Next morning, the 28th, he moved slowly forward, and came to smoldering Manassas Junction by noon. The place was deserted. Hooker's men pulled a few bloated stragglers out of the ditches; that was all. An occasional gray horseman was seen on the distant ridges. But Jackson had disappeared as though the earth had swallowed him. The early afternoon of the 28th was a period of profound bewilderment at Pope's Headquarters.

As for Jackson, he had marched ostentatiously on Centreville. There he had turned sharp to his left, to the west, and, favored by the same little ridges that hid McDowell's flank march at the First Manassas battle in July, a year ago, he had gone by the Warrenton turnpike and the Sudley Springs road to the position he had selected.

About two and a half miles west of the Stone Bridge, on the turnpike, is a little group of houses called Groveton. From Groveton a wooded ridge makes northward and north-westward for some miles, as far as Sudley Springs and Sudley Church. An unfinished railroad, some cuttings, and long, high embankments, passed along the east slope of the ridge, in the edge of the timber. The country to the east is open farm land, dominated by the high ground across the railroad workings. A road leads northwestward from the upper end of the ridge, toward Aldie. Into the thick forest on the ridge, early on the 28th, Jackson led his divisions, grouped his trains to the north, where the Aldie road debouched, set cavalry to watch the flanks, front, and rear, and lay concealed. Watching from the woods, his observers could see the thick dust clouds of marching infantry, rolling toward Centreville from the direction of Manassas Junction—and also coming from the west, on the turnpike, and along the Gainesville-Bristoe road. Seven miles away Pope was concentrating. But it never occurred to any Federal officer to scout the wooded country north of the Warrenton pike.

During the forenoon of the 28th, while Pope's corps approached Manassas by forced marches, already beginning to feel the loss of their rations, and Jackson's infantry lay unsuspected and unmolested in the forest above Groveton, cavalry was very active. Fitz Lee's brigade was riding up the railroad, past Fairfax Court House toward Alexandria, and Pope presently had a report that Burke's station, east of Fairfax, was being shelled. This and other reports, notably that Jackson was last seen at Centreville, impelled him to push on to the latter place. His columns, advancing, drove the Confederate picketing squadrons off the Warrenton turnpike, and away from Manassas Junction, which Rosser and Brien had been holding under observation. Meantime Stuart took a part of Robertson's brigade and rode west toward Gainesville, with the mission of opening communication with Longstreet. Moving clear of the Groveton forest, Stuart could plainly see the fires of the fighting at Thoroughfare Gap, where Longstreet was being feebly opposed by Rickett's division. At Gainesville, he found considerable cavalry and infantry drawn up—Bayard and some of McDowell—and he skirmished hotly with them through the afternoon. He sent also a message by a courier, who detoured widely to the north, informing Lee of Jackson's situation, and the courier got through. Stuart's people captured, in this fighting, a galloper with orders from Pope to McDowell: the army would concentrate at Centreville. Sigel, of McDowell's, had already marched southwest from the turnpike to Manassas, but King was still at Gainesville with his division, and this order had set him marching east, up the Warrenton turnpike, by the most direct route to Centreville. Jackson, to whom the order was immediately communicated, realized that King was almost the last Federal element which lay west of him, and, if Pope's concentration on Centreville was carried out, Lee's problem would start all over again: there would be Pope, united and ready for battle, in a position of prohibitive strength, with numbers accumulating behind him. Jackson's essential mission had been to draw Pope to battle on Lee's terms. Now King came marching across his front, along the Warrenton turnpike, and without hesitation Jackson threw at him the divisions of Ewell and Tallieferro. Pope's order, that moved McDowell from Gainesville, finally lost him his campaign. McDowell had 20,000 men, enough to have stood in Longstreet's way and held him from joining Jackson.

The fighting that followed was of the sternest order, and King's division, attacked in the late afternoon as it marched in route column, from a quarter believed to be empty of menace, acted in the most gallant manner. It formed front to its left and held its ground. Ewell and Tallieferro, both division commanders, were wounded as the Confederates came into action, and probably for this reason the gray attack was only half-developed and at no time pressed. The action turned into a fire fight, most of it in an apple orchard just north of the turnpike, where blue soldiers and gray volleyed in each other's faces at the closest range until dark. Jackson, who also had to form to a flank, found difficulty in getting his artillery placed, and his guns built up on the position seized by Major John Pelham, who took the Horse Artillery at a gallop through the Groveton woods, unlimbered in the open fields just north of the turnpike, and went into action at a range of two hundred yards, with double canister. Almost immediately he lost his horses, and so many of his men that the chief of Jackson's artillery sent him orders to withdraw. But, he reported, it was impossible to move his guns, so he stayed in action until night covered him. After dark King drew off in good order. About 3,000 men had fallen on both sides, and the fight was tactically indecisive. But the result was what Jackson wanted: Pope now knew where he was, and Pope would think only of destroying him, and could be held until Lee came with Longstreet. Through the night Pope gathered his army, and next morning his blue masses rolled over the ridges east of the Groveton woods and prepared to settle the matter. They drew also from the country between Groveton and Thoroughfare Gap, leaving it open for Longstreet's passage.

During the night Stuart reformed on Jackson, Robertson's brigade on the right, covering the turnpike, and Fitz Lee, returned from Burke's Station by a wide detour to the north, on the left, near Sudley Springs. Jackson made all things ready for the fight he expected. He relocated his batteries, massing them where the ground favored, and assigned Stuart the additional mission of opening communication with Longstreet. There had been a great weight of anxiety on Jackson this night: with 20,000 men, less the casualties and stragglers of the last four days, he stood to receive the assault of Pope's concentrated force. In case of disaster, he might fall back to the northwest, toward Aldie, and his wagons were gathered behind his left flank, ready to take that route.

Pause now and look at the Second Manassas Campaign, which is this day almost finished. It started with the detail of Pope to command the Army of Virginia at the end of June. It crawled through July with small unimportant operations. The first battle was at Slaughter Mountain (also called Cedar Mountain), on 9 August, where Pope had his first actual contact with the Army of Northern Virginia. After that Pope's fate began to close upon him. There was Lee, with Jackson in his left hand and Longstreet in his right, and Jeb Stuart going before. Once, behind the Rapidan, through Stuart's misadventure, Pope escaped. Again, behind the Rappahannock, by reason of the rain-swollen streams, Pope was saved. Then he was reinforced until he outnumbered his gray enemy, but the initiative had passed from him: since Lee came upon his front he had moved to meet Lee's ominous gestures—not Lee to meet his. Twice deflected from his purpose, Lee, with patience and consummate skill, had drawn him again, deceived him, baffled him, so that his own mistakes strengthened the Confederate strategy. Now, with a total incomprehension of his danger, he came down from the strong Centreville bridge, crossed Bull Run, and rushed to the final accounting.

Isaiah has said: "For every battle of the warrior is with confused noise and garments rolled in blood." It is not necessary to go deeply into Second Manassas. When Jackson came out of the Groveton woods upon King's unsuspicious column, on the 28th of August, he fixed the battlefield.

During that night Pope's tired divisions were brought into assault positions—and all through the 29th they pounded the inflexible Confederate infantry in front of the Groveton ridge. While they fought in front, Jeb Stuart rode to meet Longstreet, swinging down from Thoroughfare Gap: Longstreet, imperturbable and stolid, was with Stuart on the pike at Gainesville in the forenoon. Stuart rode south of the pike for a mile and made a base for the Confederate flank on a knoll (they call it Stuart Hill today) looking toward Fitz-John Porter's corps, which was advancing cautiously from Manassas Junction. Longstreet is deliberate, and Stuart, while he waits for the gray infantry, has an eye on Porter and sets his cavalry to dragging brush along the dusty roads. Porter sees the dust clouds and thinks: that is lots of rebels getting into line—and lay inactive, though ordered repeatedly by Pope to go forward, until, between noon and one o'clock, Longstreet was actually there. Lee has reunited his army, and now Pope is where he wants him. Pope can do his worst.

Jackson held his lines against six great blue assaults; 30,000 good troops were wrecked by Jackson's infantry and guns on this day.

During the forenoon two blue brigades, deflected from his left at Sudley Springs, slid around his flank and threatened his ambulances and trains. Stuart, just then starting toward Gainesville, saw and reported them, and sent John Pelham and Major Patrick, with six companies of cavalry, to hold them until Jackson could get up some infantry. But the infantry were not needed: Pelham met them with a blaze of canister, and the gray cavalry rode into their flank, making a great noise in the woods. They broke back and did not come again. Here Major Patrick, a very gallant officer of Stuart's, was mortally wounded. "He lived long enough to witness the triumph of our arms, and expired thus in the arms of victory. The sacrifice was noble, but the loss to us irreparable," Stuart noted in his report.

In the afternoon Lee wants a counter-stroke: orders Longstreet forward, but Longstreet demurs: he is not ready; he wants to reconnoiter; he wants this and that, and the day passes. He keeps his divisions out of sight behind the ridges; Pope does not know that he is there. Buford and Bayard are totally broken down; no scouts can pierce the screen Stuart has drawn around the flanks. Pope is confident; he has 30,000 more good infantry, or 50,000 if he needs them, and he concentrates again in the night, all on the front of Jackson. He will bag Jackson in the morning; he will then bag Longstreet, if Longstreet is up, which he doubts. Dawn discloses to him Jackson's old lines, empty except for the dead. Only a few gray batteries stand, impudent, in the eastern face of the raddled Groveton wood. The August sun rises; already the dead of yesterday are blackening under it. Go forward, says Pope, jubilant behind his troops—go forward and pursue.

Out storm the dense blue lines of battle, short and thick, brigade on brigade, division on division, with their bright flags and their bands, their mounted officers and their deep cadenced shouting. Bugles peal in the Groveton woods; a lean gray line, with a glitter of bayonets along it, and the red Southern battle flags above, shaken out in the early light, breaks from the woods and stands on the railroad line: Stonewall Jackson, where he stood before. Jackson's batteries, Stuart's Horse Artillery, the savage Confederate muskets, threaten from the ridge; the blue people come on magnificently; there breaks a shattering tumult, and white smoke, fire-hearted, rolls up from Jackson's line. The blue people drive home, reel back, reform, and come on again. Confusion, and strong crying: the Stars and Stripes and the Stars and Bars flap side by side in the battle smoke;

Jackson stands, but diminishing. In the afternoon, toward the right of his line, they break into him and he wigwags Lee for help.

His men are nearly out of ammunition; in the centre they run down between the blue assaults and glean cartridges from the dead, and hold their line with bayonets and thrown stones when the cartridges are expended. None of Jackson's officers thought about retreating—or, if they did, they put the thought firmly away: they remembered poor Garnett, a fine general, cashiered after Kernstown, because he very reasonably fell back. They put in their last reserves: every man of Jackson's was fought.

Lee sends to Longstreet; Longstreet, not yet engaged, sends Colonel Stephen D. Lee with a group of batteries, and they shred the Federal assault into fragments from the flank with long *rafales* of grape and canister. It is time for the counter-stroke: Lee's couriers gallop; Stuart's brigades get to horse on either flank; Longstreet moves at last; and Jackson's infantry rushes out from the railroad cut. From Sudley Springs down to Stuart's Hill three miles of yelling gray line goes forward, their shadows long before them in the level evening light. Pope's infantry gives way from right to left, recedes from the Manassas Plain, abandoning guns and wounded, prisoners and flags. But Jackson's much-enduring men were too spent to follow far, and Longstreet's pursuit ended about Bull Run, with the dark. Stuart, with Robertson on the right, Fitz Lee on the left, slashes at the skirts of the Yankees all night, riding over and behind the Centreville ridge.

There is preserved a glimpse of Stuart, this night, after the battle. Fitz Lee and Robertson were launched on their missions: to snap at the heels of the retreat, to urge it along, to capture and destroy where they could. The Major-General of cavalry, with his escort, elected to ride by the northern edge of the battle area, toward Chantilly, which is above Centreville, and after a night of large activity, in the very dark hours immediately before dawn, Jeb Stuart and his people came to a plantation where friends of the family lived —folks who had been hospitable to young cavalry soldiers last winter, before Joe Johnston fell back to cover Richmond in the spring. Stuart says, "Let's rouse them with a dulcet serenade—they've heard nothing but Yankees for so long that it'll be a treat to them"—and he led his group through the big gates and up to the side of the house. You imagine flowers of the old-fashioned garden kind, crushed under hoof, breathing small fragrances to mingle with the smell of sweated leather and unwashed men and animals, in the close, moonless dark. Sweeny spurred his horse to the centre, staff gathered, they all crowded in on the General, and Sweeny, with his banjo slung, struck a chord. Strong male voices, Jeb Stuart's ringing baritone, Von Borcke's mighty bass, and the croaks of anonymous cavalry officers and soldiers, bleared with dust and powder-smoke and battle-cries, swelled up in harsh, discordant chorus. The dogs of the household howled sympathetically under the porch. Windows rattled open, and alarmed heads were thrust out, and when the serenaders drew breath on the first strophe a quavering voice was heard: the gentleman of the plantation begged that the building and the lives of its inmates be spared, in accordance with the usages of civilized warfare . . . peaceful citizens . . . no military . . . every demand will be met— The Major-General, Cavalry Division, A. N. Va., had to identify himself. The household, delighted, and relieved also, lit its candles, dressed, and hurried down to make him welcome. It was a long time since last spring. They gave him breakfast.

Dawn on the 31st, the last day of August, finds Pope well posted on the high ground to right and left of Centreville, facing west, having come back seven miles. It began to rain. Stuart reconnoitred and reported: Pope was standing. Lee, Longstreet, and Jackson, rode close and looked at his lines in the rain, and Lee disposed Longstreet to occupy Pope in front while Jackson drew off and marched again by the flank, to turn him. The rain hindered all movements. Yet Jackson made ten miles through the mud, by the northeast, Stuart so covering him that Pope did not know he had withdrawn from the front. That evening and that night the Confederate cavalry was felt behind Pope's right, and he became alarmed. On 1 September he fell back rapidly, and Reno, on his northward flank, struck across Jackson's line of march, as the Confederate turning column came down by the Little River pike. At Ox Hill, near Chantilly, Reno clashed with A. P. Hill—just at dark, in a storm of rain and thunder. There was brief, angry fighting, and Hill lost men in blind rushes, and Reno had two generals killed, Kearney and the brilliant Stevens. There was some artillery fire, mostly Pelham's. Reno drew off toward Fairfax Court House. Ahead of him, Pope was making for Alexandria and the forts of Washington. He was utterly beaten, and he indicated it in frantic telegrams to Halleck. On the 3d, Stuart's brigades saw the last of him file into the Washington fortifications. And sent back to Lee the latest Washington papers: that day General George B. McClellan was entrusted with the defence of the Capitol City. August —July—June: sixty-odd days since, McClellan had been calling checkmate to the other capitol.

Lee might now appraise his campaign. With 55,000 men at his greatest strength, he had driven and manœuvred an enemy of 80,000 some sixty miles, defeated it in a pitched battle, and herded it into its last ditch. He had killed and wounded of that enemy 13,500 officers and men, and captured 7000 prisoners, 20,000 rifles, 30 guns, and many flags. He had destroyed the great Federal depot in Virginia. It had cost him 10,000 Confederate battle casualties.

* The campaign is an enigma to Pope: not while he lived, his after writings show, did he comprehend it. His preliminary movements were bold and not ineffective, but he showed more of aptitude in covering up against his antagonists than in attacking. Then he lost the initiative. Then he lost his head. He never dreamed that a soldier—as good a soldier as Lee—would divide his army in the presence of a stronger enemy. He never dreamed that Jackson would march fifty-two miles in two days, and lie tranquil in the midst of his host. He never dreamed that 55,000 would attack 80,000. And so disaster came upon him, and he passed, without the consolation of glory. He blamed his generals and he blamed his troops: he got cashiered perhaps his ablest lieutenant, Fitz-John Porter, which the Confederates rate high among the fruits of victory. Yet his soldiers, poor blue infantry who had already tasted bitter waters, in the Valley against Jackson, on the Peninsula against Lee, fought splendidly wherever they were put in action. There was no panic at Second Manassas. Except for details, the blue army held well together. It was Pope who was beaten.*

Lee beat him, and Jackson, and Stuart. The first two were always beyond his understanding. As for cavalry, Buford and Bayard were able and brave, and their sabres outnumbered Stuart's. But Pope's extravagant demands broke down his horses. The mounted strength was frittered away on a thousand details. In July and early August it had already begun to be expended; at the time the armies closed for decisive battle, it was utterly incapable.

Stuart had only to reproach his division for the mishap at Verdiersville, and for Fitz Lee's tardiness. Otherwise, the Southern cavalry was equal everywhere to the calls Lee made upon it. Wisely concentrated, it was always strong enough, at important points of contact, to ride down the Northern horse. And the cavalry screens, where screens were wanted to cover infantry movements, were impenetrable to the feeble blue squadrons. Outside the zone of operations, Stuart did not allow himself to be drawn: Bayard and Buford rode at will where it didn't matter for them to ride. And finally, Pope had little pertinent information from his mounted arm. Jeb Stuart, after Slaughter Mountain, then on the Rapidan, then on the Rappahannock, and then in final battle, kept his chief constantly advised of the adversary's movements, of his identities, and even of his orders. . . .

There was, except for the small clash at Brandy Station, little conflict of cavalry with cavalry. Along the Warrenton pike, late on the 30th, when the lines went forward, the 12th Virginia, of Beverly Robertson's brigade, and the First Michigan, of Buford's, charged each other, and in the *mêlée* Colonel Brodhead, the same who so nearly caught Jeb Stuart at Verdiersville, was killed in a combat of sabres by Adjutant Harman of the 12th. The Michigan regiment was dispersed, and 300 of the troopers killed, wounded, and captured. On that quarter of the field, also, Colonel Rosser of the 5th Virginia commanded the massed batteries of Longstreet's right and led that counter-stroke. There, says Stuart, "The Lord of Hosts was plainly fighting on our side." And on the 31st, going in front of Jackson to turn the Federal line at Centreville, Fitz Lee's brigade captured, near Chantilly, an entire company, officers and all, of U. S. regular cavalry—a former 2d Dragoon outfit, commanded by an old friend, Captain Tom Hight. Von Borcke was present, and found it very odd that, the formalities of the surrender being over, Captain Hight should give his parole, and ride off, talking and laughing in the friendliest fashion, with his good friend, Fitz Lee.

On 2 September Wade Hampton's brigade caught up, coming on from the James river, and Stuart sent Hampton and Pelham to harass Sumner's blue column, retreating through Vienna. The night of the 2d, cavalry headquarters were at Fairfax Court House, twelve miles from Washington, and Fitz Lee's points looked at the lights of the capital from the Virginia shore of the Potomac. Robertson's brigade was near Chantilly, and Munford's regiment of his was capturing Leesburg, up to the northwest. Longstreet was with Lee at Centreville, Jackson at Chantilly. It was time to think of something else.

Stuart's reports, covering the events of August, are thrilling reading; but everything he says can be proved. The records contain a controversy as to who took Manassas Junction, the night of the 26/27 July. General Trimble claims credit: Stuart has only to refer to Jackson, who placed him in charge. He concludes—containing his anger with a strong restraint: . . . "General Trimble does the cavalry injustice in his report. There seems to be a growing tendency, to abuse and underrate the services of that arm of the service, by a few officers of infantry, among whom I regret to find General Trimble. Troops should be taught to take pride in other branches of the service than their own. Officers, particularly General officers, should be the last, by word or example, to inculcate in the troops of their commands, a spirit of jealousy and unjust detraction toward other arms of the service, where all are mutually dependent and mutually interested, with functions differing in character but not in importance."

Good advice today, in any service. Ask the old officers of the A.E.F. Ask the regular army. Ask the Marines.

Cavalry losses were light, under 100. But Stuart had to mourn his nephew, Captain J. Hardeman Stuart, an undergraduate of the University of Virginia, and the signal officer of the cavalry division. During the confused little skirmishes behind Jackson, around Groveton on the 29th, Captain Stuart rode with a small detail to capture a Yankee signal station on a hill south of the turnpike. The station was heavily guarded, and young Stuart's detail was dispersed, his own horse being run off while he was dismounted. Failing to fall in with the cavalry again, he met Longstreet's column, picked up a musket, and marched and fought next day with the infantry. He was killed in the counter-stroke on the 30th, "among the foremost," his general wrote. "No young man was so universally beloved, or will be more universally mourned: moreover, a young man of fine attainments and bright promise."

Jeb Stuart would have to mourn many fine, high-hearted young men, dear to him, before he went himself. Here was the first of them.

On 4 September, the cavalry headquarters being then at Dranesville, Jeb Stuart wrote his wife—

"MY DARLING ONE—

"Long before this reaches you I will be in Md. [He means Maryland.] I have not been able to keep the list of battles, much less give you any account of them. Our present position on the banks of the Potomac will tell you volumes. . . . We captured Tom Hight's entire company of 2d Dragoons —Bob Clary was his lieut. We paroled them all. Parson Landstreet was captured and saw all their generals. Pope told him to tell me he would send me my hat if I would send him his coat. I must have my hat first. I recaptured Landstreet at Fairfax CH. We pursued the enemy beyond Annandale—We knocked Buford's (cavalry) brigade into Bull Run—captured 220, killing a colonel . . . Landstreet says all the officers on the other side speak kindly of me. May God bless you. In haste, ever yours, J. E. B. Stuart.

" . . . P.S. I send $200 in draft and $50 in notes. Can you pay my tailor bill?"

Also he wrote to her, in a brief pencilled slip, "The Horse Art'y has won imperishable laurels!"

XI

THE SHARPSBURG CAMPAIGN

AFTER Second Manassas, the Army of Northern Virginia had the briefest of rests. Between 2 September and 4 September it lay concentrated in the vicinity of Leesburg, thirty-five miles west of Washington. It was considered that the blue hosts, all alarmed behind their fortifications, were so disheartened and disorganized that no aggressive movement on their part need be expected until they were pulled together. It was known that Pope had been relieved, and that General McClellan was now entrusted with the defence of the Federal capital, and McClellan had established himself as a general who required lots of time.

D. H. Hill reported from Richmond with two divisions, and Wade Hampton had joined Stuart. These about made good the Confederate battle casualties, but all the areas, through which the Army of Northern Virginia had manœuvred in the last thirty days, swarmed with stragglers, fallen from the ranks in the terrific marches that had encompassed Pope's defeat. Except on tide water, at Hampton Roads, and at Aquia Creek, and except around Harper's Ferry, there were no Yankees left in Virginia. As early as 2 September, detailed and urgent despatches passed between General Lee and Mr. Jefferson Davis.

General Lee wrote, in effect: it is true that the army is much reduced by hardships and by battle, true that the commissary wagons ride empty and the ammunition wagons ride light, true that the men with the colors lack shoes and coats and blankets. But, in the nature of things, the Army of Northern Virginia cannot sit still and wait to be restored. Always, the Army of Northern Virginia fights against time.

Its adversary yonder, broken by defeat, is recuperating. Virginia is cleared, and the Confederacy must strike swiftly to take advantage of the opportunity its victories have created. To General Lee, it seems an excellent time to propose negotiations for peace, and in order that such proposals be pointed with material considerations, an excellent time to invade the territory of the United States. Just across the Potomac is the sister state, Maryland, believed to be powerfully Confederate in sympathy, and lately suffering the domination of blue armies. In Maryland there may be thousands of young men who would embrace the chance to join in the war for Southern independence—certainly there is food in Maryland, while there is little or no subsistence in these stripped northern counties of Virginia, and no rail connections with the Richmond bases whereby the army can be supplied. Striking north, across Maryland, at Pennsylvania, important enterprises might be carried out. One might penetrate as far as the great trunk railroads that cross the Susquehanna, and so cut the North in two, the West from the East. Capture or siege of Washington is not to be thought of— too many blue soldiers there—but Richmond is safe for the time being, and the Army of Northern Virginia can best prolong its safety by carrying the war to the enemy. Meantime, let work on the Richmond fortifications go forward, let any troops and supplies that can be found come on to the army, and we will see what we will see—under the blessing of God! So General Lee to President Davis. On the 4th of September orders were issued. That day the Army of Northern Virginia, Stonewall Jackson leading, crossed the Potomac north of Leesburg. The regimental bands played "Maryland, my Maryland." . . .

Stuart assembled his three brigades near Dranesville, between Leesburg and Washington, and his troopers had a day of rest. General Beverly Robertson is detached, to raise new cavalry in North Carolina, and his brigade is given to the senior colonel, Munford. From this brigade, also, is withdrawn Colonel Flournoy's regiment, augmented by the sick, broken down, and dismounted troopers of the cavalry division, with orders to remain at Gainesville and salvage the late battlefields, collecting all usable things for the needy Southern ordnance and quartermaster departments. On the 5th, the cavalry division crosses in turn, at Edwards' Ferry and White's Ford, and trots by the right flank to screen the marching infantry. There is no fighting of consequence: scattered Federal details scuttle east and south, to covert in Washington. Stuart draws a line twenty miles long, and faces southeast in the direction of the enemy. His right, Munford's reduced brigade, is at Poolesville. Wade Hampton has the centre, at Hyattstown. Fitz Lee is on the left, at New Market, and Stuart's headquarters are established at Urbanna, between his centre and Frederick City.

Cavalry, taking up its zone on the 7th, found a pleasant prospect, and had no immediate fighting to do. Some Yankee signal stations were destroyed among the hills north of the Potomac, and a few detachments of cavalry chased toward Washington—nothing important. At Urbanna, Jeb Stuart received calls of ceremony from the city fathers, and accepted, with his staff, a dinner invitation in the middle of the day. The story tells of a house guest where they dined, a spirited young lady from the North, who declared herself frankly secesh in sympathy, and was named by Stuart, our New York Rebel. Promenading, two by two, in the afternoon, the girls pointed out to their officers an academic building in Urbanna, then empty, and Stuart says, What a capital place to give a ball in honor of our arrival in Maryland! Major Von Borcke: you arrange it! Von Borcke has a talent for such things, and he sends details for sylvan decorations, and draws on the ladies of the town for roses, and hangs up the regimental battle flags by way of ornament. Stuart invites, from near Frederick, the colonel and officers of the 18th Mississippi infantry—who have a fine band— will they bring the band over too? The ladies of the Urbanna neighborhood co-operate excitedly, and the affair takes place on the evening of the 8th of September—brilliant in all respects: fair ladies and brave men. Von Borcke, master of ceremonies, selects the New York Rebel Queen of the Festival, in his courtly way, and opens with a polka. But, to his chagrin, when he turns to take his lady in his arms and waltz, she eludes him, and explains that she does not dance those round dances—gentlewomen don't do that, except with brothers or first cousins: an old Southern custom, she says.

Von Borcke, unabashed, orders the music changed, and the polka gives way to a lively quadrille. The evening proceeds famously . . . music, and candlelight on brass buttons against gray uniforms, and the fine women of Maryland . . . and spurs, and long swords, that are not worn for show, hung along the wall.

About 11 o'clock there is a stir at the door where the stags cluster, and an orderly, dusty and sweating, clanks in and reports to the General: Sir, enemy cavalry, beating up our pickets! Mississippi's music breaks, and in the hush, as the dancing stops, comes the crackle of pistols and carbines, from the east. The officers take their swords and go out, Stuart making, while his horse is brought, apology for this unseemly interruption: Be good enough to wait, ladies: we'll be right back. Just a little fuss on the picket line—these Yankees have no manners! They ride, and come upon the duty regiment, Baker's 1st North Carolina, toward Hyattstown, astride the Washington pike and fighting. The others of Hampton's regiments come up: John Pelham throws his horse guns ahead of the line and goes into action: the enemy

—patrols of Pleasanton's—are driven. By 1 o'clock it is over, and Stuart and his officers ride back to receive the tremulous admiration of the ladies, and to finish the dance. With dawn come the ambulances, and a score of wounded, to be laid in the hall on the polished floor and tended by the gentle ladies of Urbanna. The New York Rebel draws a youngster with a bloody shoulder wound, and faints: but she revives and insists on caring for the poor soldier. On the whole, a noble creature, decides Von Borcke, escorting her home to breakfast.

Frederick is the headquarters of the army, and there, between the 6th and the 10th, the commands of Longstreet and Jackson were concentrated. The good people of Maryland looked with all their eyes: these were the legendary gray soldiers who had been, up to this time, a rumor and a far-off thunder down beyond the border. They saw interminable columns of lean, hairy men, who marched with a long, free stride and bore useful-looking weapons, handled with the informal ease of veterans, but who lacked every outward detail of military show and smartness. Their uniforms were ragged remnants, in every shade of gray and brown. Their wagons and their canteens were mostly stamped, "U.S." They were incredibly dirty. They were bronzed and muscular, with bright, hard eyes, and there was a great air of victory about them, but on the whole, the young Marylanders were not attracted to the service of the Confederate States. A few—a very few—joined up, against the considered judgment of their more thoughtful friends. But all pressed to look at Lee, and Longstreet; and ardent Maryland girls, on an occasion, rushed Stonewall Jackson and cut the buttons from his uniform, and that fabulous hero further edified them by attending church on Sunday, bowing devoutly while the courageous preacher prayed for the President of the United States (why not? He needs it!

comments a bitter rebel general on a similar occasion) and then sleeping through the sermon. Maryland was relieved and touched by the excellent conduct of the Southern men—expressly forbidden by general orders, and by a vigorous provost—any kind of depredation: and Maryland received pay, in Confederate money, for all articles the quartermasters bought or requisitioned. Maryland read with respect the proclamation of General Lee, inviting them to make free choice between the Confederacy and the Northern yoke. But Maryland, on the whole, remained calm—sympathetic, but tranquil.

In effect Maryland disappointed the Southern army. They said, the tough, fighting regiments, marching to endless brassy renditions of "My Maryland," that Maryland had taken enough time to breathe and burn, and ought to be coming on to join up. . . . Lee saw, too, that Maryland was entirely conservative. At his headquarters they unrolled the maps that showed Pennsylvania. And there was further news from Virginia.

Confederate forces had taken Winchester from the Federals, and were herding the blue troops, who remained in the Valley, northwards toward Harper's Ferry. It had been urged by McClellan, on 1 September when he took command, that these now isolated forces be recalled. But Halleck said, no. In consequence, there remained 11,000 Yankees over there, and Lee must deal with them, for he desired to reroute his communications, which were trailing back to Manassas, too close to Washington; and to lay them in the Valley, behind the protecting wall of the Blue Ridge. Already he had the orders out, and army supplies were coming by way of Gordonsville, Charlottesville, and Winchester. On 9 September he issued a famous order, Special Orders 191 of the Army of Northern Virginia. That day Frederick saw the gray infantry march off, by the roads to the southwest and the west, and the gray cavalry came in. Frederick has left its impressions on record.

Blue cavalry, racking between Washington and Harper's Ferry—contract horses, under half-trained, uneasy riders, were no novelty to Frederick. But Stuart's men, they relate, were amazingly dirty, swore dreadfully in gentle, drawling voices, and sat their thin, spirited Virginia horses as circus riders sit. They impressed you as brash folk, dangerous on horseback, and they were much admired. Wade Hampton was a fine-looking man, they thought—and all the ladies took on over General Jeb Stuart—his quarters were banked with flowers, and he had callers all day long.

In Frederick there had been some Federal hospital arrangements for sick and wounded men, and among the sanitary attendants who remained with them when the Confederates came, was a medical cadet named Dwight Dudley, aged 20. He had duties, of course, but what he chiefly wanted was to see this rebel army. Ten years after the war, in 1875, he was moved to write a courteous letter to the widow of Jeb Stuart.

It is a long, pleasant letter, and the first part of it dwells in detail on the behavior of the gray soldiers: how they molested no private property, and treated the inhabitants with uniform kindness and consideration. Cadet Dudley saw General Lee, and furnished liniment to Stonewall Jackson's doctor when Stonewall Jackson was hurt by his horse, that reared and fell with him. And he mentions also the curious story of Barbara Fritchie: nothing of the kind happened, he says.

On the forenoon of the day that the Confederate cavalry came into Frederick, young Dudley, walking, in uniform, down the principal street, saw a group of officers on the porch of a private residence, where they appeared to be on friendly terms with the family. One of them, he noted, was evidently "a general of consequence," and hailed the medical cadet as he came abreast, calling him into the yard, and coming down the walk to meet him. The General invited the cadet's attention to the kindly attitude which the Southern army had preserved toward the Unionists of Frederick, and he asked that the cadet do him a favor. Certainly, Sir, says Dudley. "Then," says the general, "I want you to tell your commanding general when he comes that we have treated his friends here with great kindness, and that we expect the same treatment for ours, and unless they receive it, I will doubly retaliate at each and every opportunity. . . . I am General Stuart." Concludes Dudley, he was "struck with his noble and distinguished military bearing, and when I learned of his death, I felt that the Southern Confederacy had met with a great and irreparable blow."

While the infantry was inactive, Stuart's brigades began to be engaged on their outpost line. On the right, at Poolesville, the first Federal cavalry appeared under Pleasanton; General McClellan was throwing his old Peninsula regiments into the field, Bayard and Buford being still incapable. On the 8th, Pleasanton, with two regiments and some guns, drove Munford's pickets out of Poolesville. Munford brought up the 7th and the 12th Virginia regiments, and two guns; was overpowered, lost one gun, and barely saved the other. His last regiment, the 2d Virginia, was drawn in, and he finally stood at Barnesville on the Frederick road, five miles back. Pleasanton's objective was the hill called Sugar Loaf, a few miles west of Barnesville, a commanding eminence from which the movements of the Confederate Army might be observed, and Munford succeeded in saving it. No news of any kind had come to Washington through Stuart's cordon, since Lee crossed the Potomac—except frantic and urgent telegrams from the Governor of Pennsylvania, and press despatches to the Baltimore papers; and McClellan had no idea what to do. On the 9th and the 10th Munford had more fighting, and the unlucky 12th regiment lost its flag, but he still covered Sugar Loaf, from which Confederate signal officers watched the country to the east, now vexed with the dust clouds of a marching army. McClellan was coming slowly up from Washington, much in doubt, with 100,000 men. On the 10th, Munford was further weakened by the detachment of Colonel Jones' 7th Virginia and the 17th Virginia Battalion, sent for by General Lee. On the 11th, Pleasanton was joined by Franklin's blue infantry corps, and Stuart gave up Sugar Loaf, falling back on Frederick.

He had maintained his New Market-Hyattstown-Barnesville line, covering Sugar Loaf and the Washington-Frederick road, against increasing pressure, as long as his orders required. He withdrew to a shorter line in front of Frederick, sited behind the Monocacy River, Hampton at Frederick, Munford south of the town, and Fitz Lee to the north. The blue masses accumulated on his front, and he directed Munford to Catoctin Mountain at Jefferson, five miles southwest, and Fitz Lee to Liberty, about the same distance northeast. Thus Hampton and Munford faced the enemy's advance, and Fitz Lee was north of it, in position to operate on its flank. Meantime, Munford's brigade had been further reduced by the detachment of two regiments to accompany Jackson and Longstreet, leaving him only the 2d and 12th Virginia. On the 12th, the Federals approached Frederick, and Hampton fought them in the eastern edge of town during the day. The South Carolinians distinguished themselves in this, their first heavy action. They took prisoners and a gun from an Ohio regiment, but, they regretfully reported, they could not get the gun away, its teams having been killed. Late in the evening, Hampton retired from Frederick—Stuart being the last man to leave. He sent Hampton

on to Middletown, beyond Catoctin Mountain, and he ordered Fitz Lee to march around into the rear of the Federals, from the north, and see what they intended. He was
still in some doubt as to whether he faced a general advance,
or a reconnaissance in force.

From Fitz Lee, however, came no useful information. He
found the country east of Frederick too stiff with troops,
but he continued, hanging on the northern flank and adding
to McClellan's perplexities.

There are two ranges of hills west of Frederick, running
parallel to each other, about due north and south. Catoctin
Mountain is the first you come to, as you go west from the
town. The Frederick-Hagerstown pike, called the National
Road, begins to mount its slopes three miles out. Then you
dip into a pleasant valley, a region of apple orchards, substantial farmhouses, and fine large barns. In the centre of
the valley is the hamlet Middletown, and beyond Middletown, five or six miles from Catoctin, the ground begins to
rise again, and you come to South Mountain, which is the
prolongation of the Blue Ridge north of the Potomac. The
National Road, bending northwest to follow the contours of
the terrain, makes through South Mountain at Turner's
Gap. Just west of the exit from Turner's Gap is Boonsboro',
and the National Road, bearing more sharply north, leads
off to Hagerstown, near the Pennsylvania line, and thirteen
miles from Boonsboro'. At Boonsboro' another high road
comes up from the south, from Shepherdstown, on the Potomac, through Sharpsburg and Keedysville. Going back to
Frederick again, there is a road that leads southwest, passing
Catoctin Mountain five miles out, at Jefferson, striking the
Potomac at Knoxville, where South Mountain comes down
to the river, and going on to Harper's Ferry. In the valley
between the mountains, a fork of this road branches through
South Mountain at its other pass, Crampton's Gap. These

roads and hills must be borne in mind, if you would understand the operations that follow.

Stuart's orders had directed him to delay the advance of the enemy east of the mountains, and to keep him in ignorance of Lee's movements until the 12th, and if possible, for a day longer. As we have seen, the cavalry did not give up Frederick until the 12th, and on the 13th, it was in position behind the first range of hills, with the strong line of South Mountain still in the rear. But, so far, the Federals had covered themselves well, and only one infantry corps, the 9th, then commanded by Reno, had been identified. There was yet no reason to apprehend a general enemy advance, but the passes in South Mountain were important to the army on the other side, and on the 13th Stuart got in communication with the nearest Confederate infantry, D. H. Hill's division at Boonsboro'. Stuart thought that Turner's Gap had better be occupied and prepared for defence. D. H. Hill advised that he would send up two brigades. As long, then, as South Mountain was denied the enemy, McClellan must remain in ignorance of Lee's location and designs, and Stuart may well have counted on another five-day delay. The enemy's cavalry would not be able to drive him out, and he could force such infantry masses as appeared to slow up and deploy at each successive stand. So far, McClellan's cavalry had been heavily supported by infantry. But, Stuart reasoned, it might be a reconnaissance in force, a thing very likely, for McClellan must be desperate for information. This brings the situation to the morning of the 13th and it now passes beyond cavalry influence.

On the 13th, McClellan entered Frederick, and established headquarters. His army was closing on the city, and he had been entirely unable to estimate the situation, or to formulate a plan. From Washington came only fears, and the garbled news despatches of Pennsylvania. From Harper's

Ferry came word of an encircling gray enemy, and then
nothing at all. From his own advanced forces he heard that
Confederate cavalry, quite persistent in holding its ground,
was across his front. But of the Army of Northern Virginia
there was no word of any kind. Here fortune—continually
against Lee this year of 1862, broke again for a Northern
general.

The colonel of the 27th Indiana Infantry came in the
forenoon to headquarters in Frederick with a crumpled sheet
of foolscap: Private B. W. Mitchell, F Company of the
27th, had picked it up that morning, wrapped around three
cigars. Some of the names on the paper were known even
to privates, and Mitchell showed it to his first sergeant. The
Top thought that the colonel had better see it. The colonel's
eyes bulged, and he thought the Commanding General might
be interested. The Commanding General was. For it was an
authenticated copy of General Lee's Special Orders 191,
dated 9 September, and setting forth, in detail, the movements and intentions of the Army of Northern Virginia.
Briefly: it directed that the army march from Frederick, by
the Hagerstown road—the National road, on the 10th of
September. General Jackson's command, leading, would
turn off at Middletown—just west of Catoctin mountain,
proceed through South Mountain to Sharpsburg, cross the
Potomac at Williamsburg, turn downstream to Martinsburg, on the Virginia side, and approach Harper's Ferry
from the west. General Longstreet would move to Boonsboro', and halt with the trains of the army. General Mc-
Laws, with his own division and R. H. Anderson's, would
turn south from Middletown and approach Harper's Ferry
by Maryland Heights, from the east. General Walker
would cross the Potomac below Harper's Ferry and take
station on Loudon Heights, between the Shenandoah and
the Potomac, covering the town from the southeast. All

these detachments, after the capture of Harper's Ferry, would concentrate at Boonsboro' or Hagerstown. General Stuart would cover the rear of the army—detaching squadrons to Longstreet, Jackson and McLaws—and would round up the infantry stragglers on the lines of march.

There has been hot argument over the responsibility for the losing of this order. Longstreet memorized his copy, tore it up, and swallowed the fragments. Jackson memorized his and burned it with his own hands. He also made a copy

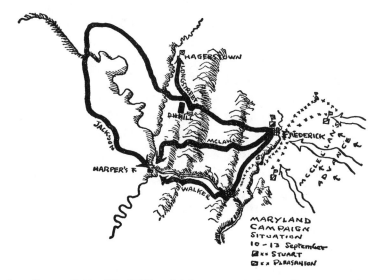

for General D. H. Hill, which never left Hill's possession, and was produced by him after the war. The copy McClellan received came from General Lee's headquarters: it will be remembered that the Confederate corps organization did not yet exist, and Jackson assumed that D. H. Hill was still under his orders, while Lee's adjutant-general did not so regard it, and made out a special draft for Hill's division. I suppose the lesson is that small administrative details are always important. But who wrapped Special Orders 191 around three cigars, and from whose pocket or haversack those cigars fell, and how they lay until the foraging Hoosier soldier picked them up—God knoweth!

From these orders, and from Lee's report, it is evident that he did not intend to fight near Frederick, or in the hills to the west, Catoctin Mountain, or South Mountain, which last is the prolongation of the Blue Ridge north of the Potomac. He felt that he would have been able, not only to defeat Pope at Manassas Plains, but to destroy him, had the Washington fortifications not been near enough to offer sanctuary to the broken army. Now he desired to draw the enemy as far as possible from these fortresses before he fought him again. He was going into Pennsylvania: then he would see. He had expected the Federals to withdraw from Harper's Ferry as he advanced between them and Washington, and he could not leave such a force in his rear when he went north, since his communications must pass that way. Therefore, he sent Jackson to clear the place. Longstreet was against the division of forces—against the movement further north: his idea was to bag Harper's Ferry and get back behind the Potomac without risking a battle. But Jackson agreed with Lee: further, there was the Maryland proclamation. Lee must show the people of Maryland that he could maintain his army among them. Finally, he knew that McClellan was commanding the Federal forces, and he counted rather heavily, I think, on McClellan. He believed that he could reduce Harper's Ferry, re-establish his communications west of the Blue Ridge, and reunite his army before McClellan became dangerous. Then he would fight his battle where he chose.

Bearing these considerations in mind, see how events had shaped themselves.

On the 10th, the infantry columns left Frederick by the Hagerstown road, northwestward. That day Longstreet and Hill reached Boonsboro', Jackson turned off at Middletown, toward Sharpsburg, McLaws turned southwest toward

Crampton's Gap, in South Mountain, and Walker marched east of the mountains to the Potomac, forded it, and proceeded up the south bank.

Next day, the 11th, Longstreet moved on to Hagerstown, drawn by the report of Pennsylvania militia assembling in that direction. D. H. Hill remained with his division at Boonsboro, guarding the trains. Jackson crossed the Potomac at Williamsport, and Walker and McLaws were marching. On the 12th, Jackson was at Martinsburg, coming south down the railroad, driving Federal detachments into the *cul-de-sac* at Harper's Ferry. McLaws and Walker were getting into position. Hill was at Boonsboro'. Longstreet was at Hagerstown. Stuart was in Frederick.

On the 13th, Jackson's investment of Harper's Ferry proceeded. His detachments were dragging guns to the mountain tops, getting ready for assault. Longstreet lay at Hagerstown, twenty-seven miles north of him, and these were the main elements of Lee's army. D. H. Hill, at Boonsboro', was fifteen miles from Jackson and twelve miles from Longstreet—these distances as the crow flies, but farther by the roads. It was Saturday, the day Lee had expected the Harper's Ferry concentration to be completed. Up to this time, everything had marched according to plan. McClellan had reached the vicinity of Frederick, advancing with his habitual caution. Saturday noon, McClellan had Lee's lost order, and from the 13th to the 16th the game was in his hands. What use he made of it will be seen. In a fumbling way, he had been pushing forward with intent to relieve Harper's Ferry, which he expected to hold out until he came.

Lee's order in his hand, McClellan spent the middle hours of the 13th in meditation. It might be a secesh trick. However, all his information indicated that the rebels had actually marched by the Hagerstown road, and that a great mass of them was at Harper's Ferry, and that some of them were close to Pennsylvania—there were Governor Curtin's shrill telegrams, relayed to him from Washington. In the meantime, his advanced elements were fighting the rebel cavalry on Catoctin Mountain. Finally, McClellan decided that the thing was authentic: Lee had widely divided his forces, and his army was spread from Harper's Ferry to Boonsboro'. McClellan refused to be misled by reports from Pennsylvania: Special Orders 191 placed Longstreet at Boonsboro', and McClellan decided that he must be there with all his command. When McClellan accepted a thing, he swallowed all of it.

You will note that the situation of the Confederates on the 13th differed only in one detail from the situation as laid out in the order: Longstreet was not at Boonsboro'; he was a day's march away. D. H. Hill was there, and his division, about 4000 men, and Lee's trains. So the only difference was vastly in McClellan's favor. Few generals have had, in all history, such an opportunity. The Confederates had notice, almost immediately, that something was wrong.

The morning of the 13th Hampton's rear guard—the Jeff Davis Legion—on Catoctin, and down to the south, Munford's brigade, had been attacked by cavalry and infantry. Catoctin Mountain was abandoned by the gray troopers shortly after noon, and there was fierce rear-guard fighting in Middletown and Jefferson, between Catoctin and South Mountain. Stuart had alerted Hill at Boonsboro', who sent two brigades to Turner's Gap in the evening, and later his whole division, because, contrary to reasonable expectations, McClellan was coming on, fast and hard. Columns of the enemy were seen from the heights, marching through Jefferson toward Crampton's Gap, immediately in McLaws' rear. Stuart warned McLaws, and sent full reports to Lee in Hagerstown.

Here, if McClellan had acted true to form, the matter

should have rested, with McClellan sitting reflectively before South Mountain and apprehending terrible mishaps. But McClellan had Special Orders 191, and he was acting. The evening of the 13th, he sent orders to his generals: Hooker to follow Burnside to Turner's Gap: Sumner and Porter to follow Hooker—four army corps against D. H. Hill over at Boonsboro'. And Franklin and Couch, two corps, through Crampton's Gap, to relieve Harper's Ferry. But— although there was a full moon, although the Federal troops had marched barely fifty miles in the past week, and the weather was fine—these corps were not ordered to move until morning, and the Confederates were granted another day. In the forenoon of the 14th, Reno and Hooker attacked D. H. Hill in Turner's Gap. To Hill, moving his division into position, and to Stuart, in the afternoon of the 13th, watching the blue masses—four strong army corps—pour over Catoctin Mountain, the thing began to look dangerous. Hill must stand at Turner's, to save the trains, and Longstreet might come to help him, but, Stuart reasoned—and he was right—the point of greatest danger was at Crampton's Gap to the south. There was the place where an alert enemy might actually drive between Jackson and Longstreet, and cut the army in two. Seeing Hill's leading brigades filing up, Stuart took Hampton's cavalry, about dark, and rode down to Crampton's. In the early morning of the 14th, he heard the fight at Turner's open fiercely, musketry and a cannonading that rolled like thunder through the hills, but at Crampton's, he was surprised to find no evident press of the enemy. Munford, out in front, was holding his ground against normal cavalry patrols, and there were two brigades of McLaws available over the mountain. We know—which he could not know then—that McClellan was delivering the weight of his thrust against Hill up at Turner's with four corps, and that only two corps were moving south, behind

Catoctin Mountain, at Crampton's. This was because Mc-
Clellan expected to find all of Longstreet on his front, and he
would take no risks. So Stuart, considering that Munford
and the supporting infantry could hold their gap, and understanding that McLaws was spread too thin to cover both the
eastern and the northern exits of Harper's Ferry, took
Hampton on to supplement McLaws, and placed him on the
river at Knoxville, covering the Harper's Ferry-Frederick
road.

This was a mistake. Hampton would have been of more
use with Munford, who was presently attacked in force. Or
he would have been of service covering the Keedysville road
that runs due north from Harper's Ferry, beyond McLaws'
up-stream flank. Stuart tried to have infantry sent across
that road, but McLaws had no troops to spare, and over it,
the night of the 14th, rode some 1200 blue cavalry, led by
an enterprising officer called Grimes Davis, who refused to
stay in Harper's Ferry and surrender, and who met Longstreet's wagon train in the night, falling back from Boonsboro', and destroyed it, and got clean away, eluding Lee's
scattered columns.

Couch and Franklin drove Munford in about noon. Mc-
Laws, alarmed, detached two brigades to help, for the fight
was squarely in his rear. This infantry, with Munford, was
slowly forced through the Pass in the afternoon, and the
gunfire, thundering nearer, brought Stuart up from Harper's Ferry on the run. Arriving at dusk, he met the fugitives, McLaw's infantry and Munford's worn out troopers,
streaming down from the mountain. With such fragments
as could be rallied, he formed a line across the western exits
of the pass and shot back the Federals so vigorously that
they halted for the night on the mountain. Up at Turners,
D. H. Hill, with some of Longstreet, 9,000 against 30,000,

had fought his hardest all day, and was whipped. Long-street, informed of the Federal drive, had come from Hagers-town by a forced march, arriving in time to cover Hill's withdrawal from South Mountain to Boonsboro'. General Lee was present there at dark: Fitz Lee's brigade came in also, from the north, over the mountain. It was apparent that McClellan was moving, and moving with amazing energy and purpose. Some time during the night, a trooper of Munford's picked up a civilian from Frederick and brought him to Stuart. This gentleman had learned, on the 13th, that McClellan had a copy of Lee's plan, and being a Southern sympathizer, rode to report it. Stuart took the man to Lee, and the thing was understood. General Lee sent Jackson orders to hurry with Harper's Ferry, and he ordered the rest of the army to assemble behind Antietam Creek, eight miles southwest of Boonsboro': there Jackson would come from Harper's Ferry, and the other detach-ments with him.

Early on the 15th, Stuart rode back to Harper's Ferry, in time to see the surrender: 11,000 Yankee prisoners and large stores. McLaws, with Hampton's cavalry on his right, faced about in line of battle toward Crampton's Gap, and Franklin, starting to roll out upon him from the Pass, heard the firing cease up the river, heard the jubilant yells of the McLaws' line, considered that it was too late to relieve Har-per's Ferry, and broke off the action he had started. Up at Turner's Gap, Hooker and Burnside had been so severely handled by D. H. Hill that they were relieved by Sumner's corps: the relief took time. On the whole, McClellan showed no energy on the 15th. But Jackson started his divisions marching as soon as the white flag went up in front of him. Walker started too, by way of the Ferry, and McLaws be-gan to withdraw from contact with Franklin and Couch,

Hampton covering him. Fitz Lee stood behind D. H. Hill, at Boonsboro'.

Fitz Lee had a heavy day. He took position facing the Gap, east of the town, from which the last of the gray infantry had marched. A heavy blue column, Sumner's corps, emerged from the mountain and approached. When it was near enough, he opened with the Horse Artillery, and forced it to deploy from column to line of battle. This accomplished, he began to draw off, sending the 3d Virginia to meet the blue cavalry that now passed the infantry line and rode at him. The 3d Virginia broke up a charge, and retired through Boonsboro', and the 9th Virginia stood in turn. The 9th was hard pressed, and brought to action in the town by a rush of Northern horse, and for a little while there was tumult and confusion in Boonsboro'. The last gray squadron was caught in the streets: the others were brought back to extricate it. Unhorsed troopers shot at each other from garden walls, and out of windows. A blue squadron pounded in, column of fours, and swept the main street clear. A gray squadron dashed around a corner and into the blue people as they halted, and drove them in turn. Colonel Rooney Lee, in this episode, had a misfortune: his horse fell and rolled on him by the roadside, and he lay dazed in the dust, while squadrons fought back and forth across him. His regiment finally got clear, to retire on the main body, and Pleasanton's regiments rode cautiously after them, Colonel Lee lying, unconscious and unrecognized, where they passed. Later, he revived, dragged himself off the road and out of town, and made his way on foot, with a pair of gray troopers in similar case, to Antietam Creek next day.

Beyond Boonsboro', the blue cavalry grew discreet, and Fitz Lee was not pressed further. His brigade came in good time, toward evening, to Sharpsburg.

Sharpsburg is a country town, of red brick houses, stone barns, and quiet, shady streets, a mile west of Antietam Creek. A mile and a half westward, winding generally north and south, is the Potomac river. The Hagerstown pike passes through from Shepherdstown on the Potomac. Harper's Ferry is seventeen miles south, by the roads. Lee fixed upon a line about two and a half miles long, facing east, between the town and the Antietam water. It was on high ground, traced across wheat fields and pastures that were cut up by country lanes and stone walls. On the left were some woods, and a great corn field, now about ready for harvest, and a knoll that gave good position for flank guards. The other flank rested on the creek where a stone bridge of three arches crossed—called now, Burnside's Bridge. The right flank was weak, because the creek was fordable below it. Although the Confederate line covered the highest ground, the terrain was full of small underfeatures, and on the centre and right the enemy, coming up from the creek, was covered from fire until he approached quite closely. East of the Antietam, the ground was higher, and to some extent dominated the country to the west. It is not a good battlefield. If Lee had been able to pursue, the Antietam creek would have been a protection to the enemy. If he had been obliged to retreat under pressure, the Potomac River, so close behind his front, would have been a death trap. Yet, he made the decision to stand here and fight, when, from the 14th of September through the 16th, he could easily have fallen back into Virginia, unmolested, with Harper's Ferry and its garrison in his pocket. His decision to fight is one of the most audacious he ever made, or any military commander known to history. We know some of the considerations that influenced him: we cannot know them all. It is hard to judge him, as to his wisdom here. But there is no doubt at all about the courage, skill, and resolution with which he delivered his battle.

The morning of the 16th, Longstreet was up, and Fitz Lee, and D. H. Hill—probably 12,000 men. Over the heights to the east came flooding the dense blue columns of the Army of the Potomac—six strong corps, 87,000 men, with a powerful artillery. But they were not aggressive: they deployed into lines, turning north from the Hagerstown pike, planting their flags on the high ground beyond the creek. Longstreet has recorded that nothing he saw in the war was so impressive as this slow up-building of the Federal host. By noon, Jackson was arriving, with his own division, and Ewell's, now commanded by J. R. Jones: Anderson and McLaws and A. P. Hill would follow. Toward evening, the first firing broke out: ranging shots of the artillery, then a spattering fire from the skirmishers, then a clash in front of the cornfield on Lee's left, where Hood's division met a dubious push of Hooker's corps. It was indecisive: under the pale moon Lee made his final arrangements: Jackson had the left, D. H. Hill the centre, Longstreet the right. Jeb Stuart, with some dismounted troopers of Fitz Lee's, and Pelham's guns, took station on the knoll beyond Jackson's flank.

The Confederate line was very thin. Marching and fighting had, in effect, whittled regiments down to battalions, brigades down to regiments, divisions down to brigades. The reports show no regiment over 300 strong: 200 muskets would be good average. Six hundred to 1000 would be a brigade: the strongest division was under 3000. But all the weaklings, the fainthearted, were somewhere on the back trail. Here were only the hardest, the people of steel and whalebone: the men who would not die. They knitted their lines together in the night, and when, at dawn, Fighting Joe Hooker came storming through the September mists that rose from the Antietam, Stonewall Jackson went fiercely down to meet him, and an unimaginable tumult rolled along the Confederate left.

Sharpsburg, called by the North, Antietam, is all shattering musketry and cannon smoke, shot through with a wild yelling. McClellan's plan was uninspired: you gather that he meant to crush the left, then the right, and finally to drive through the Confederate centre; and he withheld from battle all the infantry of two strong corps, Porter's and Franklin's. As it developed, his battle was a succession of pushes from the Confederate left to right, unco-ordinated each with the other. First, Hooker came, a splendid, headlong fighter in the direct way, when he had all his men under his eye, and no planning to distress him: Jackson held him, attack and counter attack, and broke him, and drove him. Then, Hooker finished, Mansfield and Sumner came successively against the left centre and the centre: won some ground, did great damage, but no vital harm, and were thrown back. Disengaged men of Jackson's—Hooker disposed of on the left—ran here to help D. H. Hill. McLaws came in with his division and R. H. Anderson's, on the road from Harper's Ferry and A. P. Hill was coming. There was dreadful fighting in the centre: there was the Bloody Lane, where the North Carolinians lay piled on top of each other, and there were killed the Federal generals, Mansfield and Richardson. The middle of the day passed, and in the afternoon Burnside advanced at the Bridge, on the right, defended by Toombs of Longstreet's. Much punished and delayed by Toombs, he got across, turned Toombs, crumpled him, and drove him into Sharpsburg—breaking up Lee's right flank. But, as Burnside's shouting brigades reached the town, A. P. Hill, come by forced marching, seventeen miles from Harper's Ferry since morning—come with his colors uncased, encouraging his laggards with the point of his own sword—

A. P. Hill's Light Division rushed screeching upon Burnside's flank, and Burnside fled back to the creek. McClellan
sent him frantic orders to hold the bridge—if the bridge was
lost the army was lost!

Behind the front, cavalry drew a provost cordon—Munford's decimated squadrons, sore from Jefferson and Crampton's Gap. "Show blood," was their grim word to tired infantrymen, walking wounded, straggling back, poor, demoralized fellows who shrank away from the consuming fires
of the shifting line. By noon, they were halting even the
wounded—if a man could walk, and carry a musket, he could
go back and fight. And in the late afternoon, they have
herded together a thousand or so, odds and ends of all commands. These are formed in companies, supplied with ammunition, and placed under casual officers, and Lee rides on
gray Traveller to look at them, and says: "Go back into the
fight, and show those people that the stragglers of the Army
of Northern Virginia are better than the best troops they
have!" Whereat the draggled fellows, with bloody bandages
and dry throats and lips all black from biting cartridges,
raised him a rasping cheer: but they were not needed. Mc-
Clellan is not going to fight any more, and the Army of
Northern Virginia cannot.

In the afternoon, while the surge of battle swept the Confederate centre and right, Jackson sought to gather his fragments and work around the Federal right flank. Some
troops were formed—breathless madmen, reeling with fatigue—and Stuart was ordered to command the advance.
He got to horse and scouted, up the Emittsburg road, toward the Potomac, and saw that Hooker's flank batteries
were very near an elbow in the river—only 800 yards, which
was too narrow a gap for Jackson's turning column to slip
through. He rode back and reported, and Lee, even then
watching the desperate fight against Burnside, gave up the

idea reluctantly. "General Stuart," he tells Longstreet, with regret, "says their right is secure on the river. . . . I didn't think so, but . . . Jeb Stuart has a good eye for ground."

Then it was sundown—a red sun descending, dilated, enormous, through drifts of smoke and dust. Lee's army was at its last gasp—Every man had been fought: there were no more reserves. Most of the generals were down, captains were commanding regiments and brigades: colonels led divisions: 10,000 Confederates lay dead and wounded. Stephen D. Lee had a battalion of thirty guns in the morning: now he has twelve. But Lee still had his army.

There was no cavalry fighting at Sharpsburg. Stuart, assembling his brigades in the evening of the 16th, emplaced the horse artillery on the little hill past the Confederate left, near the Emittsburg road, and formed some dismounted regiments in support. His pickets saw and reported the approach of Hooker's corps, but were not engaged in the infantry action at sundown. That night the General and his staff slept in a haystack by the road, and next morning, the horse artillery opened on Hooker's flank when the Federal First Corps advanced against Jackson. The immediate result was such a confusion in the Federal right that they veered away from Jackson's outer flank, toward his centre, and were unable to threaten an envelopment. Recognizing the importance of Stuart's position, Jackson sent Jubal Early's brigade to support the horse guns, and sent also batteries and odd guns to the number of nineteen, all reporting to Major John Pelham, who, with these and his own batteries, sustained the fire fight on the left all day. Early in the morning, when Hooker forced Jackson's line back from the corn field to the wood, toward the Emittsburg road, Stuart was almost separated from the Confederate line, and he moved down from his hill and gored Hooker's right with canister, while Jubal Early and the dismounted troopers of the support joined in the counter-stroke that restored Jackson's front. The crisis past, and Hooker receding, Horse Artillery and the supporting guns got back to their hill, and held there, making such a bold show that the Federal right now attempted nothing further in this part of the field.

Horse Artillery on the flank, with the cavalry regiments assembled and ready to meet opportunities, was Stuart's favorite battle situation. You think of him as a cavalryman, but he had a special genius for the guns, and, in young John Pelham, he had the finest horse artilleryist in the army. Says Jackson, of Stuart, "this officer rendered valuable service throughout the day. His bold use of artillery secured for us an important position, which had the enemy possessed, might have commanded our left."

The cavalry of Pleasanton was, by some strange concept of McClellan's, stationed behind the Federal centre, with the reserve, and had no part in the battle other than provost activity. Pleasanton's horse artillery, however, under Pennington, was engaged in long range shelling with the infantry batteries.

Most of Stuart's losses occurred when the ambitious Pelham, having finished with the infantry assaults, attempted an artillery duel with the heavy Federal batteries east of the Antietam—his little horse howitzers and 12-pounders fighting echelons of great blue rifled cannon. Guns and gunners, horses and caissons and timbers, were all smashed up in the Northern fire. Along the whole Confederate line the same thing took place: Lee's batteries were outranged and overwhelmed wherever they exposed themselves to the Yankee weight of metal. After Sharpsburg, the gray cannon engaged no more in artillery duels. In this respect the Confederates were increasingly at disadvantage: the strength was with the blue rifled guns, and the Southerners had to meet force by using, with greater daring and mobility, their inferior material.

*After night fell, in a field by Sharpsburg, the story runs that Lee stood under a reddish moon to receive the reports of his generals. They rode in from their shattered commands, with disastrous statements: their opinion was one that the army should retreat, get back across the Potomac, while it still existed. Not even Jackson had more hopeful counsel. . . . There was Longstreet, whose staff officers this day had served a gun of the Washington artillery, standing among the dead gunners, while Longstreet held their horses. There was Daniel Hill, who, his third horse killed under him, ran with a musket in his hand, and a battle flag, and 200 men, to enfilade the push of Richardson behind the Bloody Lane. There was tall Hood, honest enough to weep when he reports his brigades, his Texans and his Georgians, that now lie very still in the dreadful corn field. And there was Stuart, with the moonlight silvering his sword, and nothing at all to say. And the artillery chiefs, with despondent statistics— so many guns lost—so many caissons, so many horses.

Lee makes his own decision . . . Gentlemen, go to your commands . . . improve your positions . . . send officers back for stragglers. . . . If McClellan wants to fight in the morning, I will give him battle. Go!

Granted that the decision to fight at Sharpsburg was audacity, the decision to stay there on the 18th was sublime madness. Coldly considered, it is indefensible. But Lee knew the blue commander over yonder, above Antietam Creek. And the morale of his own army was important: that army had never yet been driven. It would not be driven now. *

The 18th came, and blue and gray confronted each other, at close quarters, inactive. There was occasional small bickering between the skirmishers, and desultory cannon shots. No fighting. Cavalry on both sides scoured the rear areas for stragglers. Fresh blue columns were seen to come in by the Boonsboro' road. Lee, and Jackson, lingered still on the idea of crushing the Federal right, by violent artillery and a rush of infantry. Stephen D. Lee goes and looks with Jackson: they will find him fifty guns. . . . "No, General Jackson, it cannot be done with fifty guns and the troops you have here." Finally, it is given up.

You cannot understand McClellan. He has lost in a day 12,400 officers and men, but almost that many reinforcements have reached him and more are coming. Meade, succeeding the wounded Hooker, reports bluntly that his troops are not to be depended upon to attack, and the other corps commanders, except Franklin, agree that the men might defend themselves, but are certainly incapable of aggressive movement. Only Franklin wants to fight, but Franklin has not been engaged. Pinkerton the detective—McClellan's Chief of Intelligence—says that Lee has 100,000 men over there. Staff officers examine rebel prisoners, and solemnly calculate, from their free statements, that there are at least 97,000 rebels across the Antietam. So McClellan does nothing, well content, again, to have preserved his army.

In the afternoon, Lee makes up his mind to retreat, and sends Stuart, with Hampton's brigade, to cross the Potomac in the rear, ride up-stream to Williamsport, and cross again, creating an alarm for McClellan in a new direction while he fords the river at Shepherdstown. Fitz Lee remains, to cover the rear of the army. Stuart rides for an obscure ford above Shepherdstown, misses it, and has to swim his horses, goes fifteen miles up-stream, and at dawn is chasing Federal pickets out of Williamsport. On the 19th, he demonstrates so successfully that McClellan sends cavalry to see what he means. Stuart had run out boldly, miles beyond the river, and for two days, with Hampton and a regiment of Munford's, and Pelham's guns, he maintained himself on the fringe of the enemy. There were endless small clashes of patrols, and wherever blue columns appeared, he slashed at them with horse artillery, dashed in and snatched pickets and detachments, and made a general nuisance of himself. He was rewarded by a growing interest on the part of the enemy, infantry began to appear against him, and presently he confirmed, through prisoners, the presence of an entire corps, Couch's Twelfth. The evening of the 20th he attempted to work Hampton through the converging blue columns and gain the open country up-stream, to draw McClellan's masses farther west, although he had already made as much diversion as his orders required. But the region was too stiff with troops for cavalry to get through. Hampton struck solid resistance everywhere, and somewhat sullenly, Stuart led his people back to the river, hard-pressed by the eager regiments of Pleasanton. John Pelham had to unlimber frequently, and slap them back with canister. A cold, blowing rain came on with the night, and they forded the Potomac at Williamsport, the horse artillery, passed ahead, covering them with salvos from the Virginia bank, and the way lighted weirdly by burning houses in the town behind them. He rejoins the army on the 22d.

McClellan's scouts, send forward carefully the morning of the 19th, had found the Confederate lines deserted. Cavalry, Pleasanton and Pennington, ride toward the Potomac, picking up one abandoned gun and 167 stragglers. Lee, with his mangled divisions, his trains, his wounded, and his sick, was south of the Potomac again. On the 20th there was rearguard fighting at the Shepherdstown Ford; some blue infantry crossed into Virginia and pressed Lee's rear—but A. P. Hill struck back viciously, and McClellan retired beyond the river with some loss. The Army of Northern Virginia moved on to the vicinity of Martinsburg, on the Opequon creek, and went into camp. The Maryland campaign was over. Six consecutive months of marching and fighting were over. You conceive the army drawing a long breath, and turning again, with a wrench, to such forgotten things as rest and food and shelter.

Says Stuart officially, of the cavalry operations, "My command did not suffer on any one day as much as their comrades of other arms, but theirs was the sleepless watch and the harassing daily *petite guerre*, in which the aggregate of casualties sums up heavily. There was not a single day, from the time my command crossed the Potomac until it recrossed, that it was not engaged with the enemy. . . . Their services were indispensable to every success attained, and the officers and men of the cavalry division recur with pride to the Maryland campaign of 1862."

He has also honorable mention of General Early, and Colonel Extra-Billy Smith, who fought with him to cover Jackson's flank, and he says: "The gallant Pelham displayed all those noble qualities which have made him immortal"; he is proud that his Horse Artillery Chief had under him at Sharpsburg "batteries from every portion of Jackson's command." Further, Major Von Borcke . . . "energy, skill, and courage. His example was highly valuable to the troops." And Cadet W. Q. Hullihen, C.S.A., aide-de-camp. And—I haven't been able to find out anything more about this fellow—"a young lad named Randolph, who, apparently about twelve years of age, brought me messages from General Jackson under circumstances of great personal peril, and delivered his despatches with a clearness and intelligence highly creditable to him."

I have found two letters to Mrs. Stuart, written during

the Maryland campaign. From Frederick, on 12 September, he advised that he "bought some shoes for you (size 2 1-2) and the children, and some kid gloves . . . some needles, white flannel. The ladies of Maryland make a great fuss over your husband—loading me with bouquets—begging for autographs, buttons, etc. What shall I do? I send a 'Secesh' agron for dear little Flora."

The other is from the Opequon on the 22d.—"We're again in Virginia but only for a short time. We hope to be in Pennsylvania very soon. The Yankees claim a glorious victory by our recrossing the Potomac, but it was necessary for a different reason. The result will show." In postscript, he wants a uniform jacket, like the last one, and a pair of gray pants, reinforced and one inch longer, from Douherty's in Richmond—will she see to it?

I have tried not to burden this narrative with statistics. Furthermore, every statement on Southern numbers is debatable. The staff work, especially the keeping of records, lapsed altogether in many formations, and was inadequate in all. Based on Lee's July returns, with deductions for known casualties, and calculated deductions for stragglers, Lee's strength must have been about 55,000, all arms, at the end of August. Numbers of barefooted men were allowed to fall out south of the Potomac, before the army marched into Maryland. Straggling not only by malingerers, but by honest men with no shoes and inadequate rations, weakened all formations before South Mountain was passed, and Jackson's sixty-mile march by Williamsport to Harper's Ferry meant more stragglers. D. H. Hill and McLaws lost heavily at Crampton's and Turner's Gaps in South Mountain on 14 September. Lee stated in his report that he fought Sharpsburg with less than 40,000 men. I think that 37,000 is a safe estimate of his strength.

McClellan's returns show slightly more than 87,000, all

arms, present for duty. This includes Pleasanton's five brigades of cavalry, and the two unengaged infantry corps of Porter and Franklin. He put into battle about 45,000 infantry. When this is considered, the real discrepancy between the opposed forces is not so great as would appear from the bare numbers on the field. Thirty-seven thousand Confederates, their unfit all eliminated by the previous stresses of the campaign, under Lee, Longstreet, and Jackson, made defensive battle from position against 45,000 men, who were handled in detail and unco-ordinated. The result is, therefore, reasonable enough. The real conflict was between the personalities of Lee and McClellan.

There are no cavalry returns from Stuart. I find one regiment entering Maryland with 75 troopers, another with 185. I calculate, in the three brigades, made up of ten regiments, and four legions or battalions, 5,000 sabres. I think that is high.

XII

THE CHAMBERSBURG RAID

IN the Valley of Virginia, the early fall is the loveliest season of the year. The air is like wine, and smells of apples, and in the afternoon the hills lie soft under thin, golden sunlight, their contours molded by the lengthening shadows. Hard outlines lose persistence, and take on a painted quality, and the brooding mountains run off to north and south, unbelievably blue. The grass is green, but the leaves are beginning to turn, so that the wooded slopes look as fine as Persian rugs, with their sharp colors blended to a softness. Ride there, and see why Virginians love Virginia.

After Sharpsburg, Lee's army made itself comfortable along the Opequon, a clear, musical mountain water that runs to join the Potomac above Harper's Ferry. The infantry was disposed in pleasant little valleys, Longstreet near Winchester, Jackson nearer Martinsburg, at Bunker Hill, and the cavalry placed to cover approaches from the north and east, paying due attention to the Potomac fords from Williamsport to Harper's Ferry. Stragglers from the summer marches and battles came in by droves, and some recovered wounded. On 30 September, the infantry strength was up to 62,000—although no replacement formations had been received—and ten days later, the strength was 70,000. There was a weeding-out of incompetent officers, a tightening of all commands, an improvement of discipline. Some shoes and uniforms came up from Richmond; new arms were issued, and the subsistence people began to provide regular rations. The army was full of spirit, regarding Sharpsburg as, in effect, a victory, so far as morale went. Certainly the

291

Yankees caught us in a bad way, and did their worst—and—
well, here we are, in pretty good shape and getting better!
Drill went forward mercilessly. General Lee had tested all
the parts of his weapon: now he is giving it the final welding.

The Commanding General is the busiest man in the army.
You read his correspondence with the President, with the
Secretary of War, with Longstreet and Jackson, and General Pendleton, chief of artillery, and with his cavalry commander, and you wonder how he got through it in the limited
number of hours a day has. There is a pleasant exchange of
letters with General McClellan, concerning the horse, saddle,
and sword of the late General Kearney, dead at Chantilly a
month ago: his widow wants these things, and General Mc-
Clellan forwards her request. It is found that the Quartermaster has the horse and saddle, as public property, and the
ordnance people have the sword: Lee convenes a board of
survey, Major-General Stuart as senior officer, to assess the
value of mount and horse-furniture; and he has the sword
appraised. He dutifully advises the Secretary of War, but,
pending formal authorization to return the articles, and
because of the uncertainty of future operations, he pays
from his own pocket the assessed price to Quartermaster and
Ordnance officers, and forwards all under flag without loss
of time. The horse, he writes McClellan, followed the march
of the army and may be somewhat under condition in consequence, but will doubtless pick up soon. The letters are
those of two courteous gentlemen—which both Lee and Mc-
Clellan were.

But most of all, above considerations as to stragglers,
complaints of depredated civilians bewailing stolen chickens
and broken fences, shoes for 8,000 barefooted soldiers, minute
directions as to morning reports, questions as to the Richmond defences, urgent requests from North Carolina for the
return of some several North Carolina brigades, ammunition,

food—all the housekeeping of a non-professional army—
General Lee must watch those people over there. Stuart's
cavalry guards the river, and scouts report a very careful
blue advance from Washington toward Manassas—a brigade—then a division, keeping one foot on the railroad all
the time. That is Sigel, who does not feel very strong. Mc-
Clellan, it seems, lies around Hagerstown and Sharpsburg,
recruiting and training and explaining to Mr. Lincoln that
he cannot, for a variety of excellent reasons, do anything
aggressive yet. What Lee wants is to maintain McClellan
in that frame of mind, where he is. If McClellan will stay
inactive until winter comes, it is likely that Virginia will not
be invaded again this year.

You like to dwell upon these days, the last of September
and the first of October, 1862, the happiest days that cavalry headquarters will have in the whole war-time. Jeb
Stuart's white tents were pitched under oak trees, on a hill,
within walking distance of the fine Dandridge mansion,
called the Bower, near enough for the General to offer
morning coffee to old Colonel Dandridge, who takes his constitutional while the dew is on the grass, and convenient for
the ladies to visit in the afternoons. Every night the Dand-
ridges kept open house, and there was dancing, sometimes
to the music of a regimental band: more often to stringed
instruments grouped around Sweeny's banjo. The ladies
came from all around, and solemn Major Edward McClellan
finds the social intercourse ennobling, while jolly Major Von
Borcke loses his heart to one fine girl after another, and finds
it perfectly delightful. Between dances, they acted charades, and Stuart reads his own anagrams, for which he
has a pretty turn, and Von Borcke and Colonel Brien pro-
duce an Extravaganza called: "The Pennsylvania Farmer's
Wife," in which the big Prussian acts the wife, gingham
mother hubbard, bonnet, stays, and all—so that Stuart

laughs until the tears run down his whiskers. Always, at the last, there is singing: the cavalry regiments send their chosen quartettes to raise those brave and tender tunes dear to the ardent Southern heart——

> "A hundred months have passed, Lorena,
> Since last I held that hand in mine,
> And felt the pulse beat fast, Lorena,
> Though mine beat faster far than thine,
> A hundred months——"

They relate, also, that the final song was always a crashing chorus, deep voices tuned to battle yelling, blending with the high, clear voices of the girls, and Sweeny's banjo thumping like a sardonic grin—this——

> "If you want to smell hell—
> "If you want to have fun—
> "If you want to catch the devil—
> "Jine the Cavalry——"

Cavalry headquarters, too, keeps open house—friends, officers, and civilians, drop in from meals. Mulatto Bob, Stuart's servant, rustles linen and silver for his Major-General, and the mess is supplemented by grouse and quail and wild turkey, bagged by Von Borcke and his hunting partner, Sweeny. There are many Ladies' Days in camp. Hampton's brigade, the nearest, South Carolina gentlemen, and sturdy Tar Heel riders, stages brilliant reviews. Cavalry, in general, enjoys life

The war is not too obstrusive, but on 1 October there is a rush by Pleasanton, with 700 troopers and six guns, across the Potomac at Shepherdstown. Along here, the river front was watched by Hampton's and by Fitz Lee's brigades, the last under Rooney Lee, his cousin having been laid up by the kick of a mule. The Opequon Creek was the brigade boundary line: Hampton up-river from the mouth, and Lee downstream. Pleasanton overpowered Lee's pickets on the river, and rode diagonally across his brigade sector into Hampton's, at Martinsburg. Lee and Hampton had planned for co-operation in such a case, but these arrangements failed of execution. Jeb Stuart, riding hard from the Bower to the sound of the guns, came up to find Pleasanton in Martinsburg, and Lee and Hampton standing off, forming their brigades. Stuart was angry: his blue eyes went black and hard, Pleasanton's snipers were shooting at him from the edge of town, and he said it wouldn't do: he would give his brigadiers just twenty minutes to throw Pleasanton out of Martinsburg. Whereat, Rooney Lee formed his squadrons on the Martinsburg-Darksville pike, in column of platoons, exactly filling the road, and led them in a pounding charge. Hampton bore in from the left. Pleasanton did not wait to meet them. He had gossiped with the citizens and learned that the Army of Northern Virginia was camped around Bunker Hill, and that was what he came for. He retired in good order from Shepherdstown, increasingly pressed by Hampton and Rooney Lee and Pelham's horse guns. At the Potomac, they were close upon him and he lost some men, wounded and prisoners. That night, in high spirits at Shepherdstown on the restored picket line, Jeb Stuart held informal reception, and traded with the pretty girls: buttons and locks of hair and autographs, for kisses. Staff is a little disgruntled because they are not invited to join in the transactions. Late, they ride back to a warm welcome at the Bower.

During this season, Jeb Stuart took thought regarding the old uniform coat of Stonewall Jackson, known to the army since the opening campaigns of the war. Contemporaries have loved to dwell upon that coat, by now become a thing in which no respectable officer would consent to be caught dead. Originally cadet-gray, from a provincial tailor in Lexington, dust and rain and sunlight, powder smoke, camp fires, and grass stains from fence-corner bivouacs in the field, had weathered it to a curious mottling of many shades, greenish to leaf-brown. Admiring ladies had cut away its buttons, only the most essential of which had been replaced, and those with horn. Furthermore, it is said to have been much frayed and torn and but indifferently mended. Jeb Stuart sent to Richmond, and on the 7th of October, he despatched Major Von Borcke, with an entourage appropriate to his rank and mission, on a call to Jackson's Headquarters over at Bunker Hill.

They relate that the day was fine, with cloud shadows sliding along the glowing hills, and the air full of vari-colored leaves, and there was a pleasant rustle under foot, in the oak grove where Jackson's tents were pitched. Von Borcke got through his affair, and the General said: Good: now we will have some dinner. But the Prussian says, first he has a little gift from Major-General Stuart, with his respects, and he would say, his love. Has he permission to open— A courier came smartly forward with a long box, wrapped like a Christmas present. From this, with an air, while Jackson looked mildly curious and Staff crowded eagerly to see, Von Borcke produced, out of swathes of silver paper, and displayed, a new general's coat, with sheeny facings of blue silk, sash, and snowy gauntlets. The buttons were fire-gilt, and the stars, wreaths, and *galons* of the most fine gold embroidery. A gratified murmur rose from Staff, and when Jackson, much moved, says he will keep it for a souvenir since it is much too fine for the hard use he must give it, Staff will on no account consent. He must try it on, and sit self-conscious in it through dinner, while his soldiers, among whom the rumor ran, pressed close by hundreds, to marvel and admire.

So they made merry among themselves in the war-time, these men who were fighting against destiny.

Meantime, Richmond becomes a little uneasy, and it seems good to send and see just what McClellan is up to, over there——

On 8 October, General Lee issues an order. Major-General Stuart is advised: "An expedition into Maryland with a detachment of Cavalry, if it can be successfully executed, is at this time desirable. You will, therefore, form a detachment of from 1200 to 1500 well-mounted men, suitable for such an expedition,"—and, in brief, pass the Potomac at Williamsport, ride north, bearing west of Hagerstown and Greencastle, to Chambersburg: cut the railroad there, do as much damage to transportation as found possible, and get all available information of the enemy, his position, force, and probable intention. Keep the movement secret—and—General John Pope having started the ugly practice of snatching leading citizens and civil officials as hostages—bring in some Pennsylvanians that we can exchange for Virginians these people hold.—Such persons to be treated, of course, with consideration.

Should Stuart's course take him east, the order warned, he might have to ride around the enemy's army zone, and cross back into Virginia near Leesburg. Finally, Colonel Imboden (who was operating with cavalry in West Virginia) has been desired to attract the attention of the enemy toward Cumberland, up-stream and away from Williamsport where Stuart would ford the Potomac.

These are such orders as Stuart loves. From his three brigades he selects 1800 men, about equally allotted, and John Pelham takes four guns, two of his own and two of Hart's. Headquarters, Cavalry Division, issues Orders No. 13, 9 October, over the signature of R. Channing Price, First Lieutenant and aide-de-camp: In the expedition about to be undertaken through the enemy's territory, horses, property of the citizens of the United States, were to be seized, and brigade commanders would arrange to have one-third of their commands engaged in gathering and leading horses. The led horses, grouped in threes, to go in the centre of each brigade. All horses to be exactly receipted for in the name of the Confederate States, that their owners might have recourse to their own government. No individual plundering, under the heaviest penalties. Other than horses, no property to be touched but public property. Public functionaries of towns in the United States to be seized and taken along by the Provost—and treated kindly: these as hostages to ransom abducted Virginians. No straggling; no looting; no foraging off the line of march. No seizure of anything authorized in Maryland. Thus Cavalary Division Orders: 13. They dealt with the methods to be followed. Stuart keeps the objective, which is information of the enemy, to himself.

This afternoon of the 9th, the designated cavalry assembles on Darksville. Wade Hampton leads his own brigade, Rooney Lee his cousin's, and Colonel William E. Jones—Old Grumble, recovered from his wound—the detachment of Munford's brigade. Toward dark, the column moves on McCoy's Ford, twelve miles north of Darksville, at the mouth of Black Creek, in Hampton's sector. There has been published to the troopers an address from the Major-General commanding:

"SOLDIERS: you are about to engage in an enterprise which, to insure success, imperatively demands at your hands coolness, decision, and bravery: implicit obedience to orders without question or cavil, and the strictest order and sobriety on the march and in bivouac. The destination and extent of this expedition had better be kept to myself than known to you. Suffice it to say that, with the hearty cooperation of officers and men, I have not a doubt of its success—a success which will reflect credit in the highest degree upon your arms. The orders which are herewith published for your government are absolutely necessary and must be rigidly enforced.

"J. E. B. STUART,
"Major-General Commanding."

Orders: 13 were distributed and communicated to all ranks. The troopers knew they were going to Pennsylvania: old timers—hoary veterans since last spring—told young recruits about another ride, on the Peninsula.

These orders, the address, and the manner in which the affair was presently conducted, speak volumns for Stuart's discipline.

Back at the Bower, there was the usual social evening— music, by Sweeny, and a white-armed girl who played upon the harp and sang; some dancing, and charades. Mr. Channing Price was not present: he was clearing the headquarters desk, preparing all the papers that required the General's signature. At eleven o'clock, Jeb Stuart raised his hand: the music stopped, and officers said good night. He spent an hour with Channing Price, closing up things, for he was exact in administrative detail. Then Headquarters got to horse, and rode to the Bower, where they rendered a serenade—something mournful and sentimental, perhaps:

"When the moon had climbed the mountains,
    And the stars were shining too,
    Then I'd take my darling Nellie Gray,
    And we'd float down the river
    In our little red canoe
    While my banjo sweetly I would play.

Oh, my poor Nellie Gray——"

. . . Horses, trotting on the hard stone road . . . you can't hear the sabres jingling against the stirrup-irons now . . . they go away so fast . . . you can't hear them any more. Oh,

they'll be back . . . oh, put out the candle and let's sit in the
dark . . . do you think—did you notice . . . Look at the
stars that shine in the north . . . the stars in the north. . . .

Up at McCoy's Ford there is a blue company on picket,
of vigilant habit, but when the October dawn puts out the
stars, the morning of 10 October, a thick mist rises from the
river. Lieutenant Philips, of the 10th Virginia, a notable
scout, and 25 men, dismounted, creep down to the water
and wade across, taking care not to splash. Colonel Butler's 2d South Carolina is in the saddle, waiting tensely.
The fog grows white, the river murmurs, and there comes a
crackle of pistol shots from the northern bank. Over
there, the picket is scattered, a man taken, and some horses.
Butler's people dash through shallow water, and behind
them crowds the column, quickly and quietly. Hampton
leads, with two guns of Hart's battery: Rooney Lee, Jones
and Pelham follow close. The friendly fog shrouds the
Potomac Valley, and they go six miles north to the Hagerstown pike, called the National Road. There is, at Fairview,
near Clear Spring, a signal station on a hill. Hampton rushes
it, getting close enough in the mist, and takes some
signalmen and horses and equipment; but the officers escape
in the brush. Flankers, pushed left and right on the National
Road, take ten blue infantry stragglers, and learn from them
that Cox's division of infantry was passing between three
o'clock and five that morning, marching west: Hampton's
advance guard missed them by half an hour. The column
rides in the growing day, north toward the Pennsylvania
line, by the Mercersburg road.

Already they had been observed. A citizen, living near
McCoy's Ford, had slipped off and warned a Captain Logan,
of the 12th Illinois Cavalry, that rebels were coming over.
This was at half-past five o'clock. It was Logan's picket at
the Ford: the rest of his small command was downstream.

He alerted his men and observed Stuart's advance from a respectful distance, estimating it at 2,500 mounted men, with guns. He kept the column in sight until nine o'clock, then fell back to the river line where he had been posted. But his gallopers had warned General Kenley, who had a force at Williamsport, a few miles down stream, by seven o'clock, and at ten o'clock Kenley advised Hagerstown that a rebel outfit was riding north.

It is interesting to note that the alert signal officer of the Army of the Potomac had, by noon of the 10th, set about the establishment of a chain of signal stations that covered the entire army area, the line of the Potomac, and South Mountain and Catoctin Mountain, in addition to the routine points of communication maintained. They saw nothing on the 11th, which was a day of poor visibility, but on the 12th, the signal people on Sugar Loaf, a little north of the mouth of the Monocacy, picked up Stuart's column, six miles away, and watched every step of the final phase of the raid.

The Federal Army, closely concentrated, lay in deep echelon from Hagerstown, through Sharpsburg, to the vicinity of Harper's Ferry. Army Headquarters were near the latter place, at Knoxville, down the river. On the 8th and 9th, Colonel Imboden, with a small, energetic command of gray horse and some infantry, had made a great stir to the west, up the Potomac toward Cumberland, and there had been a shifting of Federal forces in his direction—of which Cox's division was part. Averell's cavalry brigade had been sent into Virginia against Imboden on the day that Stuart marched up to the Potomac, for McClellan considered that Imboden might be the forerunner of a thrust from the west— exactly the impression Lee had wanted him to have. Pleasanton's cavalry division was at Knoxville, standing by, and Stoneman's mixed command over at Frederick. McClellan's Headquarters must have had a report, from Brooks at

Hagerstown, by eleven o'clock in the forenoon of the 10th. Very sensibly, McClellan held his cavalry in hand until Stuart's march was sufficiently developed to be estimated as to direction and intention. But the country into which Stuart was riding was without telegraph or railroad, and during the rest of the day, McClellan had no definite word. His next intelligence, at 9:10 P.M.—was from General Halleck, in Washington: "A rebel raid has been made into Pennsylvania today and Chambersburg captured. Not a man should be permitted to return to Virginia. Use any troops in Maryland or Pennsylvania against them."

To this McClellan replied at 10 P.M.: "Every disposition has been made to cut off the retreat of the enemy's cavalry, that today made a raid into Pennsylvania."

What McClellan had done was well enough as far as it went. Stuart would already be too well past the Hagerstown-Sharpsburg region to be headed off from Chambersburg, which, as a communication centre and a depot, would be his logical objective. But he would have to turn back to the Potomac either east or west of the route by which he advanced, and if he turned west he would have the shortest ride to the Potomac. To intercept him on this side, Averell's cavalry was ordered to counter-march from the west and to follow the route the rebels had taken; Brooks, at Hagerstown, was ordered to divert Cox's marching division to McConnelsburg, which is twenty miles west of Chambersburg, and Franklin, whose corps was at Hagerstown, would rush a division to the town of Hancock, where the McConnelsburg road crossed the Potomac. General Kelly, at Cumberland, would picket the upper Potomac between Cumberland and Hancock. Formations already on the river between Hancock and Harper's Ferry—the army zone—were strengthened. General Wool, at Baltimore, put a brigade on the cars and started it for Frederick, where Stoneman's cavalry division

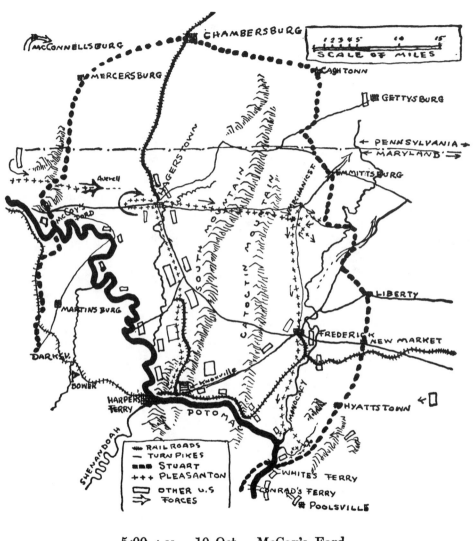

5:00 A.M.	10 Oct.	McCoy's Ford
9:00 P.M.	10 Oct.	Chambersburg
9:00 A.M.	11 Oct.	Chambersburg
9:30 A.M.	12 Oct.	White's Ferry

already stood, and he sent more troops to Harrisburg, Pennsylvania. The whole army was alerted, and by midnight the 10/11, the west and the south—all his back track—were closed behind Stuart. Frantic telegrams continued, through these hours, to be relayed from the Governor of Pennsylvania, through Washington, to the Headquarters of the Army of the Potomac. Despatches and reports accumulated on McClellan, estimating the rebel column at from 3,000 to 6,000 men. He put in motion after them three brigades of cavalry, and spotted about 12,000 infantry at strategic points.

At noon of the 10th, Stuart rode into Mercersburg, twenty miles from McCoy's Ford. The last ten miles he had been in Pennsylvania, with details out to right and left sweeping up horses. The quiet Mercersburg folk had not seen gray cavalry before, and refused to believe in such things until Hampton's squadrons reshod themselves on the merchants of the town, giving Confederate bills in payment. Here Stuart considered, and rejected, the idea of striking southeast to Hagerstown and beating up the army depots reported to be there, for there were too many Yankee troops at Hagerstown. After a brief halt, he turned east, by Bridgeport and St. Thomas, to Chambersburg. The column saw no enemy, moved in a wide zone of silence, arresting travellers who might report, and impressing horses—except those driven by ladies, which Stuart gallantly exempted—and jogging steadily. Toward dark it began to rain. Some way, the rumor of them had gone ahead, and as they reached Chambersburg, a deputation of citizens came out to surrender the place. Hampton was named Military Governor, the Provost Marshal, Colonel Hairston, mounted a strong guard, and the command concentrated in the town for the night, while the Quartermaster checked over the Federal army stores in the depot, and a demolition party vainly tried

to destroy the B. & O. railroad bridge—an iron structure—
and the horse details went out in every direction and cleared
the Pennsylvania barns for ten miles around. Some Federal
soldiers, sick and wounded in the town, were taken and
paroled. Stuart entered Chambersburg about 9 P.M., having
marched that day, by the road, thirty-five miles.

There was a Colonel McClure resident in Chambersburg,
a militia officer, liable to arrest if he had not kept quiet and
put on civilian clothes, who headed the surrendering com-
mittee. He was very anxious about his house and barns—
and indeed, his town, and he has recorded his impressions.
He found Wade Hampton "respectful and soldier-like." The
gray troopers entered town and camped without disorder or
violence of any kind. A regiment shook down in front of his
house—and wood and water details requested, with the utmost politeness, permission to enter his yard and use his
well. They also, with the utmost politeness, took his picket-
fence for fuel, and requisitioned all his riding horses. A
group of officers begged leave to shelter from the rain in his
house, sat before his fire, drank his coffee, and smoked his
tobacco, for which they offered pay in Confederate money.
He found most of them "men of more than ordinary intelligence and culture, and their demeanor was in all respects
eminently courteous." Colonel McClure drank a cup with
them, and they talked pleasantly of the war. Later in the
night he furnished tea to nearly a hundred enlisted men,
who came for it to his kitchen, and he observes that, not even
to the servants, was there a rude or profane word spoken by
a gray soldier. Outside, all night, he heard the long procession of led horses plodding into town, through the mud.

At four o'clock, the morning of the 11th, Jeb Stuart's
bugler blew Assembly, and Colonel McClure, following his
guests to the Market Square, had a glimpse of General
Stuart, who sat his horse in the rain and received the reports

of his brigadiers. "General Stuart is of medium size, has a keen eye, and wears immense sandy whiskers and mustache. His demeanor to our people was that of a humane soldier. In several instances his men commenced to take private property from stores, but they were arrested by General Stuart's provost guard . . . all our stores and shops were closed, and, with a very few exceptions, were not disturbed." As the column moved out, at dawn, Colonel Butler, now rear guard, blew up the Army Depot, destroying 5,000 rifles, much ammunition, and clothing stores. The rear guard cleared Chambersburg at 9 A.M.

Major McClellan says that Stuart had passed an anxious night: the rain was disturbing. If the Potomac went to flood stage in front of him. . . . Already, in his mind, he had decided where he was going to recross the river, and he had for guide one of his captains, White, of Poolesville, Maryland. Three times during the night he woke White up, and wanted to be reassured about the river. White thought, comfortably, that Stuart could march to the Potomac as rapidly as the rain water could run down to it, and that he would arrive in good time before the rise. But in the dawn, as they rode east, Jeb Stuart called his Engineer Captain, Blackford, to ride beside him, and said: "Blackford, I want to explain to you my reasons for selecting this route for return: and if I do not survive, I want you to vindicate my memory."

Then he spread his maps, and showed his reasons. The Yankees would expect him to strike back for the upper Potomac, because it was not so far for him to march, and farther from their main body. That route, he was sure, would be closely covered. And in this he had accurately read McClellan's mind. Therefore, he was going by the lower river. This meant, riding the eastern fringe of the Yankee army zone, between Frederick and Washington, three times as far as the other route. Nobody was likely to expect such a thing, because the distances alone would seem prohibitive. It was an even chance that the enemy would not be looking for him, and this was his best opening. Blackford said he understood.

His professional reputation and judgment thus provided for, Jeb Stuart became light-hearted again, and they passed the mountains, riding toward Gettysburg. Back in Chambersburg, the General had allowed himself to be overheard, and had designated individuals to talk loosely, giving Gettysburg as his next stop. This was all duly reported by the loyal Pennsylvania folk, and had the desired effect. But at Cashtown, eight miles west of Gettysburg, he turned sharply south, on the Hagerstown pike, for six or eight miles, then inclined southeast, and entered Maryland at Emmittsburg. He had come thirty-two miles since morning, and the day was getting on. Where the road crossed the Frederick-Gettysburg pike, there were many tracks in the mud, leading north. Stuart learned that 150 of Rush's 6th Pennsylvania Lancers—his old Peninsula friends—had passed a little while before, going north on a scout to find him. He says he regretted missing them. In Maryland, the column was closed up, and the horse details called in: there were to be no more seizures. One of the horse detail of the 9th Virginia brought in a full stomach and story. In Pennsylvania, this trooper—a gaunt, hungry-looking man—presented himself, all sabre, horse pistols, mud, and whiskers, at a farmhouse and asked if there was any food being put out. The men of the place had run off, and the women sat and rocked Pennsylvania babies and said, it was too bad, but there wasn't a scrap of food in the house. Well, drawled the Virginian, looking wolfishly at the little pink creatures, he had never, up to this time, eaten any baby meat, but it looked like he was going to have to try it . . . With that, the women rushed around and fed him bountifully.

At Emmittsburg, the kindly townspeople brought buttermilk and bread and meat, and some of the troopers ate, but the halt was very short. Stuart led his column, now short and compact, out the Frederick road, a little west of south. On this road they met and captured couriers from Colonel Rush to his detachment, and read his messages. These papers indicated, also, that there was a strong force in Frederick, and that Pleasanton, with 800 men, was marching from Hagerstown to Mechanicstown—the last place just four miles west of Emmittsburg. Also, whether Stuart knew it or not, there were two infantry brigades on the cars where the B. & O. crossed the Monocacy, engines with steam up, ready to jump in any direction. This, about five miles west of where he meant to pass. But it was at least encouraging to learn that they had no idea where he was, and Stuart pushed forward hopefully. All to the west of him, now, the country was full of blue soldiers. Eight miles short of Frederick, he turned hard east, at Rocky Ridge, crossed the Monocacy, and then bore south, all night, by Woodsborough, Liberty, New Market, and Monrovia, to Hyattstown, which the column entered with daylight on the 12th. Men and horses were getting tired, and the troopers were remounting themselves from the led animals. Relays of horses, changed frequently, kept the artillery up to the pace. There was no halt at Hyattstown. He had come thirty-five miles from Emmittsburg, and the Potomac was twelve miles away.

In the night Jeb Stuart did a characteristic thing: near Urbana, there lived a Mr. Cockey, who had been extremely hospitable to Cavalry Headquarters when he lay there in September, on the way to Sharpsburg. Leaving the region when the army moved, Stuart had assured the ladies of the Cockey household that he would call again. Now he rode from his line of march to New Market, roused the family, and paid his compliments from horseback, under their windows. Circumstances, he explained, forbade his tasting further their delightful hospitality, but as he promised, so he performed. And he galloped on to join his column.

Since midnight of the 10/11, McClellan had more reports, including hystɔrical despatches to the Baltimore papers, ringing with the rape of Chambersburg. But at noon on the 11th, word came from Colonel McClure, who told what he knew to Governor Curtin by telegraph as soon as the wires were repaired where Stuart's troopers cut them. He narrated events at Chambersburg, and said the rebels went to Gettysburg and that he thought they would try to get out by Frederick and Leesburg—a very close calculation, this last. At 3:30 P.M. the 11th, Fitz-John Porter, whose corps had the lower river area, was cautioned to be vigilant. Burnside had meantime been ordered to send additional troops to Frederick, for the safety of the army stores there. Throughout the army area there were brigades on trains, where the railroads served, ready to move by steam when Stuart should be reported. But at 5:30 P.M. Governor Curtin was positively assuring McClellan that the rebels were at Gettysburg, and this afternoon General Wool was moving troops into Harrisburg, which might be on Stuart's list—who knew? Troops were all around. But the only mobile cavalry force was Pleasanton's brigade, and during the night of the 10/11 it had been ordered to Hagerstown, from Knoxville, and it was at Hagerstown before noon on the 11th. There Pleasanton was told that the rebels were near Mercersburg, to the west, and he rode four miles that way before he was turned back to Hagerstown by fresh information. During this period, Stoneman's cavalry command, in the Frederick region, was drawn down to watch the Potomac between Knoxville and the mouth of the Monocacy. It was thought best to leave Stoneman posted, and the Gettysburg report was credited to Head-quarters. So Pleasanton was started, without rest, toward Gettysburg, by Mechanicstown and Emmittsburg. He reached Mechanicstown at 8:30 P.M. the 11th, and sent patrols out to the east and northeast, Taneytown and Middleburg. At Middleburg, about 12:30 the morning of the 12th, he learned that Stuart had passed an hour before, going south and trotting.

The play was now between Pleasanton and Stuart. Pleasanton had 800 men, and Pennington's Horse Artillery, and he rode south by the Frederick road for the mouth of the Monocacy. He made a splendid march, but before daylight his horses were giving out, his guns falling behind, and his men straggling off. By eight in the morning he reached the Potomac, where the Monocacy came in, saw much blue infantry alert and vigilant up-stream, and learned that no gray people had come that way. Which meant that Stuart was still to the eastward. He doubled back, crossed the Monocacy, and tried toward Poolesville. His force was now very small: Stuart would outnumber him, but, once the raid-ing column was located, he could delay it long enough to allow the fumbling, eager blue masses to close around, hem it in, and destroy it.

At Mechanicstown, Pleasanton had been an hour behind Stuart and four miles west of him. Both were heading for the vicinity of the mouth of the Monocacy, but Pleasanton could ride straight south, through Frederick, while Stuart had to detour eastward to avoid Frederick. Pleasanton's dis-tance to the Potomac was from twenty-eight to thirty miles, and Stuart's, less direct, was forty-two miles. Both columns drove horses and men for all they were worth, but Pleasanton took less time to cover his thirty miles than Stuart to cover his forty-two, and Pleasanton got there first.

The area around the confluence of the Monocacy with the

Potomac was under the immediate command of General Stoneman, who was held responsible for the Potomac from Point of Rocks, up-stream, to about Seneca Creek, below— a distance of nearly thirty miles. There were four good fords, habitually picketed: one at the mouth of the Monocacy, eight miles below Point of Rocks; then White's Ford, two miles below the junction of the rivers; then Conrad's Ferry, about five miles from White's; and Edward's Ford, six miles farther down. Stoneman stationed two infantry regiments, 600 men, between Point of Rocks and the Monocacy, two regiments, 700 men, at the Monocacy, and two regiments, 700 men, at Edward's Ford. His own headquarters were at Poolesville, the town about equidistant, five to seven miles, from White's, Conrad's, and Edward's fords, and here he held 2500 cavalry for patrolling and possible pursuit. The regiments at White's Ford were the 99th Pennsylvania and the 40th New York, but the 40th New York had been sent on reconnaissance south of the river during the 11th, and had returned to a point nearer to Conrad's than White's on the 12th. Pleasanton was in contact with these troops by daylight of the 12th, had a report from them, and rode east as fast as he could spur his tired horses. Soon after daylight, about the same time or a little earlier, Stuart was at Hyattstown. He had learned that the enemy was in Poolesville. That would be Stoneman, so he turned southwest, at Barnesville, leaving Poolesville to his left front. Stoneman's people came into Barnesville behind him, and pursued, but never caught up.

Now follow Pleasanton, coming desperately, with reddened spurs, from the Monocacy, on the Poolesville road. He had 400 troopers with him, all that have kept up, reeling in their saddles, for they have covered more than seventy miles since yesterday. A mile and a half from the Monocacy River, he saw a cavalry command, moving easily down from the direction of Poolesville. The October air is sharp, and these troopers wear pale blue army overcoats: in Pleasanton's advance, they think: some of Stoneman's. But they were Rooney Lee's 9th Virginia, with Rooney Lee and Jeb Stuart at their head—and the overcoats were U. S. stores from Chambersburg. They came on steadily, and the forward blue squadron commander sees the officer, leading, throw out his hand in what is taken for a friendly gesture, which is returned. He approaches them without suspicion. When they are near, they draw sabres and come at him with a croaking yell—Rebel cavalry! Pleasanton's people are knocked off the road. Farther back in the struggling column, the blue troopers whip carbines from the slings, and open ineffective fire. Behind the gray horse a section of artillery comes galloping; it is Pelham, and he opens fire. The blue troopers scatter, fall back towards the Monocacy, send in haste for Pennington. Pennington is behind a little ridge, and his spent teams are simply unable to drag the guns to the top of it, into position.

Up and down the Potomac, the picketing regiments hear the firing, and stand to arms where they are stationed. Pleasanton rushes couriers, flogging worn-out horses, to Stoneman at Poolesville, and to the fords, while he tries to build a line on the low ridge between the Barnesville road and the Little Monocacy Creek. But his command is dead on its feet: Rooney Lee's 9th Virginia, with Pelham, pushes rapidly toward the Potomac, while Stuart holds off Pleasanton, with one hand, as it were, and passes his compact column, gray cavalry, guns, and led horses, across the blue front. They get by safely, while the rear-guard regiment, Butler's 2d South Carolina, with the section of Hart's battery, cover them. Pleasanton sends for infantry, and waits for his guns.

Between Barnesville and Beallville there is a piece of timber. This covered the Confederates on the right, and they passed through it by a wood road. Just south of the woods, the road forks: one fork goes up, over the Little Monocacy, toward the mouth of the larger stream, and the other runs south, to White's Ford and the Potomac River. Rooney Lee rode south, the column after him. Stuart posts Butler and Hart on the other road, for this way Pleasanton must come when he gets in shape to follow. Rooney Lee, making what speed he can, is now in sight of the Potomac, and sees, on his right front, the 99th Pennsylvania infantry, drawn up in open order on the high ground commanding his path. Rooney Lee throws his regiments into line to his right, and sends for Stuart: those people yonder command the ford: the General had better come quickly! Stuart, back with Butler, getting his led horses and the prisoners past, tells Lee to use his best judgment: he himself is busy. Lee determines on an assault, by the front and left, with his regiment and one gun, under cover of which a detachment and the other gun will dash for the ford. While his people get into position, he tries a bluff: he sends a courier galloping, with a handkerchief tied to his sabre, and a note to C.O., comdg. U. S. troops: General Stuart with all his cavalry is your front: the hopelessness of your situation is apparent to you: to avoid unnecessary bloodshed, you are called to surrender: if you don't, we will charge you in fifteen minutes. Colonel Biles, 99th Pennsylvania, has this note. He sees Pelham's guns: he has no guns, himself. He sees the wolfish gray horsemen filing in on his left front, with a bright glint of steel among them. He takes serious thought of these things.

Rooney Lee hadn't really expected it to work: now he shuts up his watch and waves his hand to John Pelham. Horse Artillery fires rapidly: the gray lines ride out. And on the ridge yonder a Yankee drum beats the Long Roll: the gridiron flag goes back: Colonel Biles draws in his skirmishers and retires from sight.

The main body is up: Rooney Lee flings Pelham's section

through the ford, and the guns go into battery to cover the crossing. The main body, the led horses, the prisoners, splash over to safety. There is a breathless waiting for the rear guard: they can see, on the hills to the north and east, accumulation of blue forces, pressing angrily down, and finally Captain Blackford rides with an urgent message to Colonel Butler: Come on, for God's sake!

Butler is in line nearly a mile from the river, facing toward Barnesville, the enemy massing on his front. Hart's teams are about done: Butler is giving them a rest. Now, at the last possible moment, they respond to whip and spur and raise a gallop, on the river road, and Butler follows with the rear guard. Pennington, up at last, fires salvos from extreme range. Right behind him, Stoneman, and Pleasanton, and the watchers of the fords, toil down in line of battle, and Pelham volleys impudently from the south bank. The rear guard gets safely over. Jeb Stuart has escaped his enemies. He rides on joyfully, to Leesburg. In his rear, the river is rising, and the weather turns bad again. There is no pursuit.

Nobody was able to pursue. Stoneman, Averell, and Pleasanton were exhausted. Stoneman's command, infantry and cavalry, had worn themselves out with marching and counter-marching and night watches in a small area. Averell, recalled from the direction of Cumberland, had marched two hundred miles in four days and has never been anywhere near the Confederate column. Pleasanton was more effective and more dangerous. In the twenty-four hours preceding the contact at White's Ford, he had covered seventy-eight miles, and except for the unfortunate eight miles marched and counter-marched from Hagerstown, on the 11th, he might have intercepted Stuart far enough north of the ford to have held him. Stuart, from Chambersburg to

White's Ford, covered, in the same twenty-four hours, eighty miles, without a halt. Yet, when he met Pleasanton, his command had sufficient stamina to charge, and to throw him out of the way. Pleasanton blames his condition on the horses: he points out that Stuart was remounting himself as he went along, and that he was comparatively fresh. To an extent, this was true; but the final result lay with the men, who were, blue and gray, equally weary. The Virginia and Carolina troopers had fire in their hearts: the ultimate ounce, over and beyond any reasonable human endurance, that pushes the last assault home to victory.

In Virginia, there has been anxiety, for the risk was very great. General Lee learns, from a Baltimore paper, on the 12th, that his cavalry chief has reached Chambersburg. The same afternoon, Von Borcke, riding the line of pickets on the river, hears from them that the grapevine from the blue chaps on the north bank is, that Jeb has outsmarted them again, and gotten clean away. Telegraph and signal stations relay the news over the Blue Ridge in confirmation. On the 14th, they at the Bower hear horses galloping, and a weird, joyful music—cavalry bugles of Stuart's escort, in medley with the thrum of Sweeny's versatile banjo—and the General comes riding home. The evening of the 15th there is a ball at the Bower, by way of celebration, and it is Jeb Stuart's whim to send Pennsylvania teams for the conveyance of all the guests. Then these animals go to the quartermasters: they are for the most part too heavy and slow for anything but the trains and the artillery.

Stuart's report is brief and sufficiently modest, although the mere physical facts are remarkable. A well-mounted man may ride eighty miles in twenty-four hours, and think nothing particular of it, except that he has had a long ride. But to move a column of 1,800 sabres, with four guns, a number of prisoners, and all those led horses, eighty miles in a day and a night, and to have that column in spirit and condition to fight at the end of the ride, is something else again. I know of no equal exploit in the cavalry annals. Pleasanton rode almost as far, with fewer men, lost half his strength by straggling, and was incapable of action when the crisis called for fighting. Stuart accomplished his mission, which was reconnaissance on the largest scale. He left 60 broken-down horses of his own behind, and brought back 1,200. His loss was one wounded and two missing, and—a thing hard to bear, and curiously, not mentioned in any official records—two of his personal mounts, the horses Lady Margrave and Skylark. His servant, Mulatto Bob, had charge of them, and Bob tried to sustain the fatigues of the march with Pennsylvania and Maryland applejack, abundant in the orchard country at this time of year. Somewhere on the road, he fell out and was taken. The story goes that he returned, months later, after hard vicissitudes, to take his punishment, and that Stuart forgave him. Finally, Jeb Stuart concludes: "Believing that the hand of God was clearly manifested in the signal deliverance of my command from danger, and the crowning success attending it, I ascribe to Him the praise, the honor, and the glory."

All most true. But if you act with considered audacity, tempered with judgment and prudence, maintain rigid march discipline, keep your command concentrated and well in hand at all times, and go in person to the point of contact when there is danger—you advance a long way to meet the hand of God.

The reaction north of the Potomac, preserved in dusty files of official records, was more far-reaching than even Jeb Stuart, the ever-sanguine, anticipated. When, on the afternoon of the 12th, McClellan learned from Stoneman that the rebels had escaped his nets, he found the thing impossible to explain to Washington's satisfaction. Averell, Pleasanton, and Stoneman had ridden the legs out from under their mounts, and had nothing to show for it. McClellan blames the condition of his cavalry on a faulty remount service, and the Quartermaster General Meigs comes back hotly: he is furnishing horses, excellent horses, procured under strict government specifications, at the rate of 2,000 per week. McClellan's people are poor horsemasters and don't know how to care for their animals, he infers. McClellan counters with an explanation that most of his horses are sick, suffering from sore tongue, and grease, and sore backs. His cavalry was fatigued before the raid, and worn out by its exertions now. Lincoln takes a hand in the correspondence: he is insisting that McClellan cross the river and fight, and because of his horses, McClellan says now, he can't think of moving. So: "Will you pardon me for asking what the horses of your Army have done since the battle of Antietam that fatigues anything?"—A. Lincoln wants to know. McClellan answers hotly: his cavalry has done first-rate. He also promises to get what he has together, and cross the Potomac. A. Lincoln, having the last word, concludes: ". . . two considerations remain. Stuart's cavalry outmarched ours, having done more marked service on the Peninsula and everywhere since . . ." and he suggests that a movement south by the Army of the Potomac would be the best relief for the Yankee cavalry, by occupying Stuart elsewhere. This, by way of driving in the spurs. . . .

Finally, the last result of the raid was that the Federal mounted arm was rendered incapable for the rest of October. On the 16th, McClellan made a reconnaissance of the lower Valley, but he made it with a division of infantry, under Humphreys and Hancock. He forced the passage of the Potomac, brushed aside Stuart's cavalry pickets with infantry and guns, and advanced to about Martinsburg. Next day, the Federals retired to the river, escorted by Stuart and some brigades of Jackson's infantry, having learned what they came to learn: that Lee was still in the Valley.

October ran to its end without further event.

XIII

CAVALRY FIGHTS AND FREDERICKSBURG

ON the 26th of October there was a grand review of cavalry near the Bower: It was Hampton's brigade, drawn up in ranks for inspection, horses groomed, metal polished, flags and sashes and plumes all most elegant under the pale cold sun. Jeb Stuart rode the line and took the march-past, sitting his horse against a pretty background: the ladies of the Lower Valley, come out to see the last of their cavaliers.

Hampton had shifted down from the upper river, for Fitz Lee's brigade was being drawn eastward by reports of multiplied Yankee activities: over in Maryland, McClellan's Army of the Potomac was on the move from the valleys west of the mountains—moving toward the river. Intelligence, reports of spies, detailed stories from the Yankee war correspondents, as published in the Northern papers, all indicated that McClellan was being urged to do something. As early as the 6th of October he had received peremptory orders from the President: go south and bring the enemy to battle. As was McClellan's custom, he argued, protested, delayed. Then he expended his cavalry chasing Stuart on the Chambersburg raid between the 10th and the 13th, and delayed another two weeks. Finally, on 26 October, Fitz Lee's people, watching eastward from the Blue Ridge, saw his pontoons thrown across the Potomac at Berlin, downstream from Knoxville and Harper's Ferry. That day, two divisions of the Ninth Corps, Burnside, and Pleasanton's cavalry, entered Virginia. Farther down, about Leesburg, the main army was crossing.

320

Invasion again; east of the Blue Ridge. By Manassas Plains?—by the Upper Rappahannock?—thinks Lee, and sends Longstreet's Corps, marching from Winchester to Culpeper, on the 28th. Jackson's Corps he leaves in the Valley, moving it up the Shenandoah from the Martinsburg area to the vicinity of Winchester, headquarters at Millwood, behind Ashby's Gap in the Blue Ridge.

Presently, forty miles divides Lee's two corps. Between them, cavalry will maintain a contact.

The Army of Northern Virginia had been reorganized: James Longstreet and Stonewall Jackson were promoted lieutenant-generals, and the nine divisions of the infantry were grouped under them in permanent corps, the First to Longstreet, the Second to Jackson. So ordered, it was vastly more efficient than the loose associations of divisions, batteries, and brigades which had hitherto carried on the war; it was become the army that history knows. Lee has 72,000 men, with his cavalry division and three battalions of artillery. Invasion of the North is not to be thought of so late in the season: he must confine himself to confronting the enemy, delaying him, if possible, until winter stops operations, and watching always for a chance to shift to local offensive. Jackson he will leave in the Valley, on McClellan's flank, while he stands before him with Longstreet. The two corps must, it is understood, unite for battle. Otherwise, Lee, going on to Culpeper, leaves Stonewall Jackson a free hand.

Cavalry's mission will be to watch the enemy, and to prevent the enemy from finding out just where we are and what we are doing.

There is the Blue Ridge, the mountain wall, passing across the state, from the Potomac River to the southwest. One to two thousand feet its heights mass themselves above the rolling country to the east. As you go up from the Potomac, east of the Blue Ridge, you have on your right hand its several passes, the gaps in the wall through which the roads lead to the Valley of Virginia. First, Snicker's Gap, where meet the roads that come from Leesburg and from Aldie, going to Winchester. Next is Ashby's Gap, and the direct road to Aldie in the little Bull Run Range to the east: Middleburg and Upperville are towns beside this road, and there are secondary roads that take you up to the Snicker's Gap highways—the villages of Bloomfield and Union lying on them. Above Ashby's is Manassas Gap, where the railroad from Manassas Junction to Strasburg pierces the wall: the town of Markham is in the eastern entrance of the Pass. Next south is Chester Gap, where the hills break down, opening a wide passage to Front Royal on the Shenandoah. Out to the east, at Barbee's Crossroads, the Front Royal highway intersects the road that passes from Warrenton and Waterloo up to Manassas Gap. The last gap with which we are concerned is Thornton's, where the direct road goes through from Winchester to Culpeper, by way of Sperryville, and the little towns on the headwaters of the Rappahannock.

From the Potomac to Thornton's Gap is about fifty miles. It was this line that Stuart had to watch. The passes and the heights must alike be denied to the enemy: he must not be allowed to get through, or to get high enough to see, the camps of Jackson.

In the last days of October, the weather changed, and winter settled down, with cold rain and a bitter wind, and skim of ice on pond and ditch in the morning. At the Bower, on the 29th, they broke camp, and Headquarters packed its modest possessions into the escort wagons. They relate that the occasion was sad, and a mean drizzle came out of the leaden clouds, and the bleak October wind harped

mournfully in the naked branches from which the bright
leaves were now all whipped away, and the companions were
heavy-hearted at this severing, both those who stayed, and
those who rode away. Yet those ride singing: Headquarters
and the escort, cavalry division, in their dripping oil-cloth
capes, the General leading——

> "O let the world wag as it will—
> I'll be gay and happy still——"

On the 30th, Jeb Stuart, with Fitz Lee's brigade, rode
east through Snicker's Gap, and saw, far out and far below
under the gray sky, the heavy blue marching columns, and
the long white wagon-trains of the Army of the Potomac,
feeling their way south.

Fitz Lee's brigade was under Colonel Wickham, for both
Fitz Lee and the senior colonel, W. H. F. Lee, were incapacitated for duty. There were, the reports say, less than 1,000
sabres present, and Pelham with a six-gun battery. The
nearest return, of October 30, shows 8,000 in the cavalry division, but the same horse maladies, that were
ravaging the Federal cavalry, had appeared in Stuart's
squadrons; sore tongue and greased heel—foot-and-mouth
evils of sorts—were prevalent among the horses. There are
no exact figures, but nearly half the cavalry must have been
dismounted. The vexing institution called Company "Q"
swelled to distressing proportions.

From high in the hills, the Federal mass had been seen
rolling southward. But on the 30th, Stuart's command, taking the road southeast toward Aldie, made no contact with
this advance. Scouting developed, however, that some blue
cavalry was further east, at Mountsville, Bayard's cavalry,
which had come from up the direction of Washington—not
down from the Potomac. Stuart could deduce that Mc-
Clellan's left was ahead of his right, and that the body of

the Northern horse was still up toward the river. He turned his back on them, and struck boldly across, about daylight on the 31st, at Bayard near Mountsville. There he found a Rhode Island regiment; and the 9th Virginia, supported by the 3d, drove the Rhode Islanders and their supporting echelons, in a running fight, to and beyond Aldie in the Bull Run Mountains. Penetrating to the eastern slopes, the gray horsemen saw all the country, from north toward Leesburg to southeast toward Centreville, crawling with the blue army. Here, then, was McClellan's true mass of manœuvre: the columns, immediately east of the Blue Ridge, would be flank elements only. Stuart dropped back, with some prisoners, toward Bloomfield and Philomont, certain that Pleasanton would be coming hard from the north.

The strip of country in the shadow of the Blue Ridge, from Philomont and Upperville, down to Warrenton, is peculiarly adapted to cavalry fighting. It is a country of fine vistas, with bare, rolling hills and little clumps of trees. There are infrequent wheat fields, and some orchards, and numerous little streams. Fences of stone and rail lay off the pasture lands. The villages are small and old, tranquil, tree-shaded places. The people are sturdy folk, small farmers, notable horse-breeders. Most of the young men are, this year, in the Confederate Army—very many of them in cavalry regiments. Over the length and breadth of it, the first week in November, ran the fighting, Stuart and Hampton and Rosser, Pleasanton and Averell and Bayard, and the Horse Artillery of Pelham and Pennington.

You conceive a placid farmer, going out to his milking in the early dawn, blowing on his hands and cocking an eye at the weather, by his barn. He hears, on the road, a trampling and jingling, and goes to the fence to watch a cavalry detachment pass, the troopers sitting easy in their saddles,

wrapped against the cold, and the breath of their horses
jetting white. Perhaps a sergeant falls out to ask questions,
getting much information or little, according to the uniform
he wears. The detachment trots on, their noise diminishing
up the road—and there comes a shout, and a crackle of
firing. The patrol has put its foot into something: now it
thunders back, frozen clods flying, the rear files shooting
over their shoulders as they run—the whole affair sudden
and sharp and loud in the quiet morning. A squadron goes
by in pursuit, formation lost, bright flags whipping, and
the sabres out. Bullets whine across the barn-yard, and make
gray lead splashes on the stone walls, and the farmer takes
cover and watches cannily, his blood astir: all Virginians love
a sporting event. Now he hears cavalry bugles, silver-clear,
blaring behind the hill. A regiment, in column of squadrons,
trots over the crest and down through the cow pasture. Out
in front of them an officer in a red-lined cloak shakes his
sword, and commands peal along the column. The bugles go
again, and the regiment pounds, yelling, at the people on
the road. Pursuer becomes pursued, the thing changes in
moments, formations disintegrate to individual chases over
the frozen fields. Salt smoke of powder hangs about in
patches. Finally, from some hill-top, horse artillery opens
with a red flare of sound, and the wall of the Blue Ridge
yonder throws it back in a long roll of thunder. Away the
fight streams, off by the roads, trampling the winter wheat,
spilling the limp dead from its skirts, until yelling and carbine shots and horse hoofs recede to a far-off murmur, punc-
tuated by the bumping detonations of the guns. The farmer
gets on with his milking, and presently his women folk are
patching up such damaged heroes as may be lying around,
and later, decent burial is given to any dead persons found
on the premises. Near Warrenton, widely affirmed tradition
locates a grave of the period, inscribed as follows:

"The Yankees came in thousand bands
To ravage our Virginia lands,
This lonesome and secluded spot
Is all this Goddamned Yankee got——"

Pleasanton came, with his brigade, 2,000 sabres or so, and drove hotly on the 1st of November toward Snicker's Gap. That day, and the next, Stuart, with Wickham and Pelham, fended him off, fighting at Bloomfield and Union—as Pleasanton, held from the mountains, extended his thrusts to the south. Wickham, who was always getting wounded, had a shell fragment in his neck on the 2d, and Colonel Rosser took Fitz Lee's brigade after him. On the 3d, Stuart was crowded close up to Snicker's Gap, and Pleasanton saw, beyond him, the bayonets and battle flags of D. H. Hill's infantry, sent by Jackson to stand in the Pass. He drew off, and edged south again, and the fighting was heavy around Upperville, and eastward toward Middleburg, before sundown. In the night, Pleasanton was reinforced by Averell's brigade, and he sent Averell by a detour south, toward Manassas Gap, while he hammered at Ashby's. That night, also, Stuart rode through to Millwood, and conferred with Jackson.

Von Borcke makes a special story of the visit.

While they ride to Jackson, the Prussian, a great hero-worshiper, talks with feeling of old Stonewall's greatness, and how he is moved at the thought of him—and he says, in his halting inverted English, that when that General talks to him, it makes his heart to burn— Late in the freezing night, Jackson receives them, and Stuart livens the company by poking fun—nobody else, on record, ever made jokes at Stonewall Jackson—"Unfortunate, the effect you have on my officers, General! Old Von Borcke, here, says you give him the heartburn! Ho! Ho! Ho!"—Von Borcke flushes hot, but Jackson touches his arm gently and says, "Never

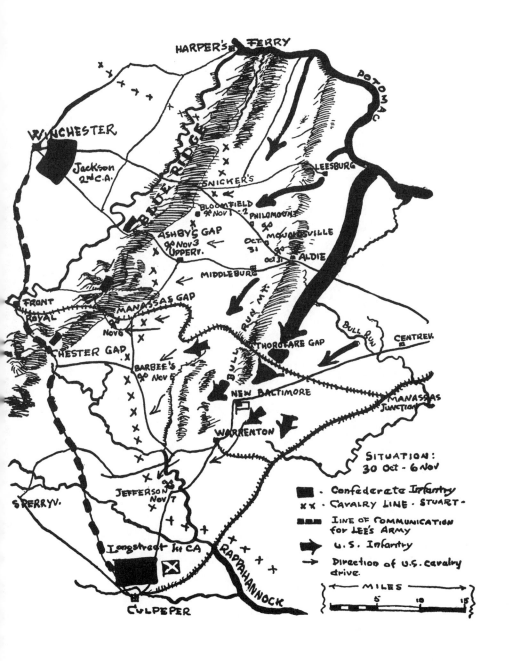

HARPER'S FERRY

POTOMAC

WINCHESTER

Jackson 2ND C.A.

BLUE RIDGE

SNICKER'S

LEESBURG

BLOOMFIELD
9% Nov 1

PHILOMOONT

ASHBY'S GAP
9% Nov 3
UPPERV.

MOUNTSVILLE

Oct
31

Oct 31

ALDIE

MIDDLEBURG

MANASSAS GAP

FRONT
ROYAL

CHESTER GAP

Nov 6

BARBEE'S
9% Nov 5

BULL RUN MT.

THOROFARE GAP

BULL RUN

CENTREV.

NEW BALTIMORE

MANASSAS
JUNCTION

WARRENTON

SITUATION:
30 Oct - 6 Nov

JEFFERSON
Nov 7

S. PERRYV.

■ · Confederate Infantry
x x · CAVALRY LINE · STUART ·
▬▬▬ LINE OF COMMUNICATION
for LEE'S ARMY
➡ U.S. Infantry
→ Direction of U.S. Cavalry
drive.

Longstreet 1st C.A.

RAPPAHANNOCK

CULPEPER

MILES
5   10   15

mind Jeb Stuart and his jokes, Major—we understand each other—" and Stuart is a little miffed. Most of his jokes that they remember had no sting in them.

Getting to business, Stuart reports his deduction: that Pleasanton's persistent effort indicates an intent, not only to pierce the Confederate screen and to spy out the land, but to cover something behind his own front, and he thinks that the main Federal effort is toward the Rappahannock, and not toward the Blue Ridge. Hampton's brigade has turned over Jackson's outpost area to Jones' brigade from up-river, and is now available. Jackson could hold the passes with infantry, and a few horse detachments would suffice to watch the crests. Therefore, Stuart would leave Hampton to cover the upper passes—Chester Gap and Manassas Gap and Thornton's—and take Fitz Lee's brigade eastward, to guard the approaches to the Rappahannock. By morning, Hampton was through Manassas Gap and covering it, and Chester Gap, and on the 4th he received Averell and thrashed him— most of the fighting around the village of Markham. Stuart worked eastward and bickered all day with Pleasanton, and next morning Stuart and Hampton, Pleasanton and Averell, clashed at Barbee's Crossroads. This was the heaviest fighting of the week, both sides losing men and horses, killed, wounded, and captured. To Stuart's left, the blue horse broke in far enough to see Confederate infantry, waiting grimly between the hills, and to feel some of Jackson's batteries. To his right, in open country, Rosser fought his regiments dismounted toward the close of the day—and these—high tribute to their steadiness—were taken for more infantry by Pleasanton. The battle ended with Stuart thrown back all along his line, but his thin brigades intact, and the screen they had interposed still unbroken. This was the 5th: on the 6th, and for three days more, there was no important fighting. Stuart extended his picket line to Warrenton, and discerned the slow, cautious approach of Mc-Clellan's main army upon that point.

The cavalry reports of these operations are voluminous, and contradictory, and highly confusing. They are bright, also, with a fine knightly valor, lavishly displayed on both sides. You find agreement on two points only: each opponent invariably overestimated the force brought against him; and the localities are the same. By the last, the course of the actions can be followed: you see that Stuart opened on the 31st with the fighting between Snicker's Gap and Aldie, then drew back to his left rear to cover the passes, then extended his right to the eastward to guard the Rappahannock. In six days, the Northern advance was about fifteen miles, against nothing but cavalry, and he opposed to them an unbroken front, and he had discovered and held in observation the main blue body, accomplishing his mission as his orders required. Pleasanton, with Averell, accomplished nothing. They got to the mouths of the passes, and saw infantry—presumably Jackson's—inside. They never reached the Rappahannock, or came within striking distance of the Winchester-Culpeper roads, to see for themselves: they had the gossip of the country folk, the impressions of stray refugeeing negroes, and statements from one or two deserters of Longstreet's, all of which conflicted and confused. The sum of their information was that Jackson was reported in the Valley, and Longstreet down behind the Rappahannock—matters already affirmed by McClellan's secret service. But where the main Confederate mass was, where its communications ran, whether Lee had his weight in the Valley—on McClellan's flank—or on the Rappahannock, across his front—cavalry could not tell at all. Characteristically, McClellan ceased to move and sat down to ponder. If he turned and struck through the mountains, Longstreet would come up at him from the south. If, on the other hand, he pushed down toward Longstreet, Stonewall Jackson might leap at his flank from the Blue Ridge, or, worse still, invade Maryland again. And if he tried to drive in between them, he would offer his flank to both. Finally, he was utterly uncertain as to which was strongest, and most dangerous, and there was always the possibility that somewhere, around the wide angle between Winchester and Culpeper, Lee might be lurking with a major concentration, yet undiscovered. It was McClellan's unfailing habit to believe Lee had 200,000 men, and when he couldn't find them, he was convinced, not that they did not exist, but that they were hidden and laying for him.

By 6 November the situation is static, and the cavalry reports set the period. Averell and Pleasanton complain mightily about bad horses and sick horses: Stuart considers himself, in that regard, no worse off than the enemy, and regards his mission—that of covering the movements of the army—well accomplished; which it was. The upshot of his approval goes to Major John Pelham, in Stuart's winged words: "The Stuart Horse Artillery comes in for a full share of this praise, and its gallant commander (Major John Pelham) exhibited a skill and courage which I have never seen surpassed. . . . I was more than ever struck with that extraordinary coolness and mastery of the situation which more eminently characterized this youthful officer than any other artillerist who has attracted my attention. His *coup d'œil* was accurate and comprehensive, his choice of ground made with the eye of military genius, and his dispositions, always such in retiring as to render it impossible for the enemy to press us without being severely punished for his tenacity. His guns only retired from one position to assume another. . . ."

Indeed, it was mainly with Horse Artillery that Stuart

had maintained himself, for none of his regiments are more than 100 sabres. We learn of Pelham, unsupported, attacking a Yankee regiment with a howitzer section and scattering it; and another time, he aims a gun with his own hands and brings down a Yankee color bearer at eight hundred yards. Pleasanton's greatest triumph was the day at Middletown, when Pennington hit and blew up one of Pelham's caissons.

The Army of the Potomac fell so quiet, after 7 November, that Lee and Stuart wondered—until they got, next day, some prisoners and Northern papers. McClellan was relieved, and General Ambrose Everett Burnside, ruddy, affable, bewhiskered, stepped from the Ninth Corps to command the army. Lincoln wanted a battle before winter set in, and there was no assurance that McClellan would give him one. There are two Lincoln stories of this time:

In late October, Lincoln, talking to a group of friends after a visit to the army, is asked by some one: Drake De Kuy—"Mr. President, what about McClellan?" Lincoln looks around humorously, "Well—" he pauses and traces reflective circles, two of them, with the point of his umbrella, and continues in his high, thin voice—"when I was a boy, we had a game—three times around and out. Stuart's been around McClellan twice. One more time, gentlemen, and McClellan's out——"

And the other story is about Jeb Stuart——

Up in Michigan, at Ann Arbor, they raised a new cavalry regiment for the Army of the Potomac. It came down to Washington, was much admired, and ordered to the field. One day before its departure, one of the Michigan Congressmen took the officers to the White House to shake hands with the President, and Mr. Lincoln received them, acknowledged their presentation with a preoccupied air—for indeed, there was much on his mind these days—and shuffled out, having said nothing. This the Michigan Congressman could not countenance: he submitted to the President that these splendid gentlemen were going South to lay their lives on the altar of their country, and deserved more consideration. "Yes, Mr. President," declaimed their colonel, "we're going after Jeb Stuart, and being true Wolverines, we'll hang on to him until we pull him down." Lincoln halted by the door and heard them through, looking quizzically. And he said, "I'll tell you one thing, gentlemen: I'd far rather see Jeb Stuart a captive in this room than see you here!——"

While cavalry was watching the region between the Blue Ridge and the Rappahannock, enjoying daily clashes with the enemy, little Flora Stuart, sick in Lynchburg, died. She had been very ill for weeks, and her mother had written urgently for her General to take leave and come to see her. The letters, pitiful and tender ones, are preserved: he would not, at such a time, ask for leave of absence. On the morning of the 5th of November, Von Borcke, opening the Headquarters' mail, comes upon the telegram: she was dead. With German thoroughness and sentiment, he describes the General's grief, and there remained a gloom on Headquarters. Left alone at night, his desk cleared and the orders issued, the aides would see their leader's head bowed on his arms, his wide shoulders shaking miserably. And they thought, in skirmishes, he rode more recklessly in front. But the cavalry division sees him always with his head high and his bearing splendid, as a chief's ought to be. I have not found a soldier who loved his family more than Jeb Stuart, or one whose sense of duty burned with a clearer flame. And duty came first. Heartbreak was unofficial: you kept on soldiering. His letters to his wife are beautiful, and tender and sad. They are not my affair or yours. . . . From the Gettysburg campaign, next year, he sends his wife pressed blue flowers:

corn flowers, maybe: they reminded him, as he strode, of little Flora's eyes.

The snow came, about the end of the first week in November, and officers and men, insufficiently clothed, suffered from the cold. There was a dearth of overcoats, and you saw men in every variety of blankets, worn like shawls, or poncho-wise, with a hole for your head in the middle, huddled close to their fires in the snow. There was an anxious time at Waterloo Bridge, where the guns, the ambulances, and the cavalry wagons had to pass, and all movements were clogged by the necessity of saving Company "Q," which now was vastly increased by men whose mounts were breaking down under the exacting service of the past ten days. Fortunately, Pleasanton showed no disposition to venture far from his infantry supports, and cavalry got safely behind the Rappahannock, and lined up on the fords it had fought across in August.

Headquarters were established at Culpeper, with Lee and Longstreet, and there followed some days of light activity, during which the General rode, with one or two of his staff and a few couriers, to take part in affairs of outposts, squadron actions, on the Hazel River and the debated Rappahannock line. On the 11th, with Fitz Lee's brigade, he fought Pleasanton near Jeffersonton, at the little place called Emmittsville. Pleasanton had too many men for him, and drove Fitz Lee's advanced squadrons back on their reserves, who lay dismounted in the edge of the woods. Jeb Stuart, very angry at the troopers who would not stand, rides out into the clearing, and takes the fire of a blue skirmish line, coming hotly at him. Staff remonstrates—General, this isn't a proper place for you—won't you please— If, Stuart tells them, ill-naturedly, you find it too hot, you're at liberty to leave it. Suits me— Quite close now, the blue riflemen are taking deliberate aim—you heard their officers, directing them: Kill that rebel colonel; kill that big rebel! Muskets crackle excitedly, and they see Jeb Stuart pass his hand across his face. Then he rides back slowly, with a queer expression: a slug has cut away one of his cherished mustaches, clean as if a barber had snipped it with his shears.

In this fight, the Federal cavalry picked up a deserter from Hood's division, who had killed a man, was sentenced by court-martial to be hung, and elected to escape North. They also took a Marylander who had joined Stuart in the Chambersburg raid and found the rebel cavalry service too exacting. Whatever information they had came from these captures. Stuart pressed them so hard that they found no leisure to reconnoitre.

Otherwise, mid-November was quiet, and Stuart took advantage of the tranquil days to issue orders reorganizing the cavalry division. It received another brigade, Rooney Lee, finally promoted, commanding. W. E. "Grumble" Jones received permanently the old Robertson brigade. Fitz Lee came back to duty. The Horse Artillery was reduced from five batteries to four.

To Stuart's headquarters, near Culpeper, comes, for a few days, Mrs. Stuart, with little Jemmie, now their only child, to draw strength in her sorrows at her General's side. And little Jemmie, aged 3 but most active, has a man detailed as personal orderly, and is spoiled by the whole cavalry division, or such of it as is not on the line. The visit does not last long.

Along the Rappahannock, the pickets reported decreasing Federal movement, and on the 18th of November, Lee ordered Stuart to make a forced reconnoissance. Stuart, with Wade Hampton and Fitz Lee, rushed the picket line across the river and penetrated to Warrenton. He found that the Army of the Potomac had turned its back, and was marching on Fredericksburg. Lee at once put Longstreet in motion from Culpeper, and Jackson, advised that events were shaping toward a battle, marched down from the valley with his corps. You conceive that he was loath to leave the Valley: the scene of his first triumphs, the theatre of his greatness. He was never to go there again, while he lived.

Now the game trended east, Lee south of the Rappahannock, Burnside north of it. The Blue Army appeared on the Falmouth Hills, across from Fredericksburg. Stuart's cavalry was divided: Rooney Lee rode to watch the crossings below Fredericksburg: Hampton and Fitz Lee occupied themselves in small raids across the upper river on the Federal communications, that were being shifted from the Manassas plains toward the Potomac. The records preserve notable enterprises of Hampton's: with 208 sabres, carefully selected, he crossed Keys' Ford on 27 November, rode thirty miles to Hartwood Church, and captured and brought back 84 of Averell's Pennsylvanians, surprised on picket: again, on 10 December, with 500 sabres, he raided up to Dumfries, and took and brought back 50 prisoners and a train of twenty wagons. This last adventure was made in the snow, and Hampton's South Carolinians had never seen such weather.

Burnside had taken command on the 7th, and forwarded, as ordered, a plan of action. He would, as was expected, drive for Richmond; this was the common error: Lee's army and not the city was the true objective, but U. S. Grant had not yet come east. The Manassas route, by the Upper Rappahannock, had been tried. He, Burnside, would thrust directly through Fredericksburg, across the lower Rappahannock. That way, the Potomac would cover his left flank and serve as a line of communications, safe from cavalry raids.

He had on his rolls present for duty, 201,351 men, and he would drive through or brush aside the rebel army. On to Richmond!

Lincoln and Halleck agreed in principle, and it seems to have been expected by them that Burnside would cross the Upper Rappahannock and come down astride the stream, turning the strong position south of it at Fredericksburg. But Burnside had a yearning for the water route. There is evidence in the records that his plan may have developed into a move, by the Potomac and the James, against the Confederate capital.

Burnside made his first movement by the lower river, about Port Royal, seventeen miles below Fredericksburg. Here the Rappahannock is 1000 feet wide, and he proposed to get over on pontoons. But Rooney Lee was vigilant: one of his regiments crossed, lower down, by ferry, and saw the pontoon trains moving east on the roads, so that, when Burnside's army massed opposite Port Conway, Jackson's corps was discovered in position on the south bank, waiting for it. Burnside prudently drew off and concentrated again on Falmouth.

The temper of the Army of the Potomac, after a month of Burnside, was good enough. He adopted an organization of three grand divisions, two corps to each—and re-equipped the troops: you discover the field quartermasters quarrelling with the depots over the sizes of shoes and coats: some of the soldiers were not properly fitted. Letters of the rank and file disclose a doubt and a bewilderment, but Sharpsburg had raised their spirits from the despondency of the Seven Days' and Second Manassas, and, as they presently proved, they were willing and able to fight. Only the cavalry seems to have been ineffective: Pleasanton and Averell and Bayard still complained of horse diseases, and Hampton rode around them at will. On the other hand, Burnside made no intelligent use of his cavalry arm: probably did not understand its functions.

South of the river, with Jackson's corps joined up, Le: commanded the largest army he ever had in the field: 78,000 men, now efficiently organized and compactly grouped. Some thousands were still without shoes, and there was a shortage of blankets, and there were no overcoats; so that considerable suffering came with the snow and cold of early December. But the spirit of the troops was excellent: they were ready for anything. We know now that Lee did not want to hold the line of the Rappahannock: he wanted to draw Burnside farther south, twenty miles, at least, to the North Anna river. Then, if he whipped Burnside—as he expected—he could cut him up in retreat. At Fredericksburg, the river, dominated by the powerful Falmouth Heights, would save a beaten enemy from close pursuit. But Mr. Davis disliked to give up ground, and the army was held to the Rappahannock. Meantime, Burnside draws to his fate, at Fredericksburg.

You know the place: steep hills march down to the north side of the river: Falmouth Heights. Over them come the Telegraph road, which is the Washington Highway, and the railroad from Richmond to Aquia Creek Landing: there had been a railroad bridge, the broken piers of which stand in the tawny water, like old stumps of teeth. The little town, with its church steeples and its stout brick houses that entertained George Washington and Lafayette, is built on flattish ground along the south bank. Up-stream, a mile or two, rises a line of hills, that curve off south and east, drawing back from a mile to two miles south of the town, in line parallel to the Rappahannock and dominating the river plain. Troops on these hills are like persons disposed along the upper tiers of a great ampitheatre. Marye's Heights, where there is now a cemetery of dead blue soldiers, is the hill directly south of town. East of it the Telegraph road goes on toward Richmond, where Hazel Run flows through to the river plain, and just east of this road is the height from which Lee watched the battle. Farther east are more hills, wooded and commanding, curving gradually back to the river, three miles below the town. They end at the creek called Massaponax. You cannot imagine a military position stronger in front, or more readily turned from the flanks. A few miles up-river there were numerous fords, easy of access and hard to defend: a few miles down, the river plain is wide and clean, favorable for pontoon bridges and accessible to supporting gunboats. A general need not fight at Fredericksburg unless he wants to. Burnside elected to fight there.

It is the second week in December. The snows have melted, but it freezes most nights and the ground is iron hard. Burnside's powerful artillery, emplaced, hub to hub, on Falmouth Heights, has shelled the town, from which the civilians are evacuated. Lee's headquarters are on the Telegraph road, Longstreet with him, and Stuart, his brigades above and below, widely divided, but his Horse Artillery in hand, is in the pine woods just east of the highway. Jackson was down at Port Royal, but is marching up when Burnside's deliberate movements give notice that he will fight at Fredericksburg. On the 11th, in the fog, Burnside crossed at and below the town, on pontoons. Lee does not go beyond a show of resistance, Barkdale's Mississippians skirmishing on the river bank, and retiring. On the 11th and on the 12th, the Army of the Potomac masses men and guns; occupies the town, and digs in below it, on the river. On the 13th, they fight.

There was no cavalry action at Fredericksburg: it was infantry and artillery. To Stuart, Jackson assigned the protection of his right flank, on the Massaponax, and Stuart put John Pelham there, with the Horse Artillery. John Pelham ran a Blakeley gun out, some hundreds of yards in advance of everything, enfilading the railroad track where the R. F. & P. left the river and turned south toward Richmond. From that point the railroad, on a high embankment, traversed the river plain toward the town, and behind the embankment Burnside's Left Grand Division was formed for the assault. Only at one place, on the right centre of Jackson's front, is there a dubious sector: where a little stream goes down to the river through a triangular wooded area, quite marshy, which Jackson does not think it necessary to occupy. . . . It is related that Von Borcke, riding the lines with Stuart, and Stonewall, and Lee, on the 12th, volunteers the opinion that the strip, thrusting like a fang into A. P. Hill's line, should be held: if the Yankees are fighting men—and Von Borcke thinks they are—they can get into it. But no one regards his judgment: Jackson has plenty of reserves.

The 13th of December broke foggy, with nothing to be seen from the Confederate hills but rolling mist, down in the heart of which the skirmishers are popping away. The skirmishers come running back: out of the fog rises a vast, growing sound: thousands of hobnailed boots on the frozen ground, an explosive shouting of commands, bugle calls, military music. Lee, Longstreet, and Jackson stand on Lee's Hill in the Confederate centre—Jackson wearing, to the admiration of the army, the coat that Stuart gave him. Stuart has been there, but he has ridden off at a long lope toward his guns on the right. The fog thins a little, and a pale sun shows in the gray sky. You feel a wind against your cheek. The Confederate Army, careless, confident, lies and peers, like an audience waiting for a curtain to go up. Down the river, towards Massaponax, breaks a burst of cannonading

—John Pelham's Blakeley gun. "I think," says Lee, looking that way, "that the young Major-General"—as gray Lee called his cavalry chief—"is opening fire too soon." The racket grows: whitey-blue cannon smoke rolls up out of the fog. Five Federal batteries are searching for Pelham, because the blue flank, all formed and ready, is being shot up at close range, and much disarrayed. Jackson takes his horse and rides that way. The wind grows stronger: the fog shreds out and vanishes, and the wintry sunlight glitters on the bayonets and the bright flags of the Army of the Potomac, rank on rank, coming up from the river, flowing over the plain. Their bands play, their lines of battle lift a deep, cadenced shouting, and Lee says, his hand on Longstreet's arm, "It is well that war is so terrible—if it were not, we would grow too fond of it!"

Burnside may have planned this and that: his battle developed into senseless frontal rushes, at Longstreet on his right and at Stonewall Jackson on his left. Never in any war have attacks been made with such stubborn, gallant courage as by the blue waves that broke around the base of Marye's Hill and the Confederate left. There was a sunken road behind a stone wall "breast-high to a man." It was brim full of infantry: Longstreet's guns crowned the heights. No enemy with weapons in his hands reached that wall, but the dead presently lay out in front like tide drift on a beach. Down where Jackson stood, there was harder fighting. Meade's steady Pennsylvanians breached through the marshy strip, the frozen ground bearing them up, where Von Borcke thought there should have been a line. Jackson's reserve came and threw them out, but Jackson lost 3500 men, and gallant Maxcy Gregg. Up in the centre, by Deep Run, the blue people made no headway, and on the far flank, Pelham's guns, increased to fifty pieces by batteries Jackson sent to the Chief of the Horse Artillery, stood out in front and enfiladed the Federal left, so that it never got forward at all. Pelham lost men and horses and had guns knocked out, but he stayed. Once, even Jackson ordered him back—the message relayed through Stuart, went, Get back from destruction, you gallant fool, John Pelham!—but Pelham stayed. That night, Jackson says: "General Stuart, have you another Pelham? If you have, I wish you'd give him to me." And Lee, in his official despatch, refers to "the gallant Pelham"—the only mention of an officer so junior that you will find in his reports.

Through the day, Jeb Stuart was on the line, with the batteries for the most part, taking, on his big horse, in his red-lined cloak, infantry fire at 300 yards. They came close to him, the Yankee sharpshooters, looking for fair targets. One bullet whipped away the fur collar of his cloak—made by his wife to replace the one lost at Verdiersville and admired by General Lee. But Jeb Stuart's word was, that he never feared a bullet aimed at him, although stray shots might be dangerous.

Burnside's battle ended at dark, and the night settled, bitter cold. They remember, who stood on Marye's Hill, that all the plain beneath them seemed to moan. In the morning the field was quiet: the first thing a wounded man wants, in any weather, is a blanket, and this night most of them died of cold. The Federal loss had been 12,644, Lee's, 5,309. Only four of Lee's nine divisions had been engaged, and the Confederates had no idea of the thoroughness with which Burnside was whipped. Jackson, it is true, wanted a counterstroke at once: sends Stuart word to stand by with his guns to support him, and discusses with his surgeon the feasibility of issuing bandages for brassards, so that his troops will know each other in the dark. Stuart goes forward with Pelham from the left, on the river plain, and opens an artillery duel, each adversary firing at the gun flashes of the other.

Downstream Rooney Lee, with his cavalry concentrated by Massaponax, sends a courier: What's up? "Tell General Lee it's all right," says Stuart. "Jackson has not advanced, but I have, and I am crowding the enemy with artillery." Jackson hears from the Commanding General, gives up the idea, recalls Stuart. It is Lee's opinion that the enemy will renew the fight tomorrow—the Army of the Potomac, he thinks, will not acknowledge defeat after one attempt, and we can damage him more by waiting for his second attack, and then following it. During the night, a Federal courier is taken, carrying orders from Burnside to the corps commanders, providing for fresh assaults in the morning. Burnside, a gallant man, much distressed by the casualties of the day ("Oh, my poor men yonder! My poor men!") is going to form the Ninth Corps and lead it himself, after daylight on the 14th. He is capable of it. But, in the slack morning hours, his generals dissuade him. The 14th comes, foggy and dark, and there is only skirmishing and long range artillery. The Confederates wait in their lines. Toward evening, the weather breaks: a south wind brings rain. In the storm and the dark, Burnside draws off his army, leaving the dead on the field. The Confederate infantry, picketing his front, do not discover that he is moving until after daylight: then they see him on the other bank. You have occasion to remark, again and again, the utter helplessness of the infantry, gray and blue, in all the aspects of scouting and patrolling.

At Fredericksburg was killed the Federal General, Bayard, by a shot of the Horse Artillery. In the gray lines they lost General Cobb of Georgia—and with him, wounded by the same shell-burst, was General John R. Cooke, Jeb Stuart's brother-in-law. Where Meade breached Jackson's position, fell General Maxcy Gregg, an officer much beloved and admired. There is a letter of General Lee, to Wade Hampton, offering Gregg's South Carolina brigade, thus vacated. It seems that Hampton's assignment to cavalry had been temporary, because, in the spring, no infantry command was open. But Hampton, now growing into great reputation as a cavalry brigadier, elected to remain with Stuart.

So ended Fredericksburg, on the 15th of December, and with it the important fighting of 1862. Fredericksburg stands as a battle induced by political considerations: the pushing hands of Lincoln. It had no bearing on the military situation: Lee missed his chance to follow it up; his army was vastly elated by it, and had some shoes and blankets from the Federal dead. The Army of the Potomac could afford the loss in battle casualties: otherwise it was plunged into black despondency, and the North was horrified at the butcher's bill. Federal desertions multiplied: General Joseph Hooker began to intrigue for high command. Both armies went into winter quarters. Some humorous rebels, billeted in Fredericksburg, painted and erected a great sign, at their end of the broken railroad bridge; it read, to the Yankee pickets on the northern bank: "This way to Richmond."

XIV

THE WINTER OF 1862-1863: COMPLAINT TO U. S.
QUARTERMASTER GENERAL

FOLLOWING Fredericksburg, the main armies went into winter quarters, their repose broken only by some ineffective gestures of the energetic Burnside. It was a time of appraisal. In the year now closing, the Confederacy had maintained its fronts with various fortunes. The sea was gradually being closed to the South by the Northern blockading squadrons, and the blue forces were gnawing into each end of the Mississippi line. The western border states were the theatres of shifting battles: out there little generals of the South, chief among them the loyal, incompetent, and unlucky Bragg, were accomplishing nothing in particular, while the stars of Grant, of Sherman, and of Sheridan, were rising. In Virginia the outlook was more cheerful. Lee has fought four campaigns in the year and won three of them. The Federals hold the mouth of the James, the country between the Rappahannock and the Potomac, and the lower Valley—but all of their holdings, except where the main army sits, are debatable, a wide No-man's land where the distracted civilian population entertain blue cavalry one day and gray the next, and are plundered by both.

In the Army of Northern Virginia, the effects of faulty military legislation, and inefficient finance and supply organization, began to be felt. The original enlistments of the first volunteers were expiring, and men rated furloughs home before signing up for the duration of the war. The conscript material, now coming forward, was poor. Supply broke down, so that the army around Fredericksburg could not be fed. An immediate result of this last was the despatch of most of Longstreet's corps to the vicinity of Suffolk, down southeast of Petersburg, in a country offering abundant subsistence. This was well enough, under the maxim "disperse to feed—" but when, in the spring of '63, the time came to apply the other half of the maxim—"concentrate to fight" —Longstreet had involved himself in a fumbling siege of unimportant Northern forces at Suffolk, and Chancellorsville had to be fought, against the most dangerous odds, without his veteran divisions of Hood and Pickett.

The condition of the cavalry was distressing to its officers. Long forage failed utterly, corn was increasingly scarce, and you could tell where a cavalry detachment had picketed by the gnawed trees, which the wretched animals stripped of bark and of every small limb they could reach. Improper food distended the horse's barrels, and brought on mange, and increased the ravages of sore-mouth and foot-evil. The creatures looked grotesque, with their swollen bellies and bare bones.

Cavalry headquarters was located, after Fredericksburg, in a pinewoods near the Telegraph road, south of the town. Jackson was not far away—toward Corbin's Neck, where the General lived in the little one-room plantation office of the Corbin place, in which, as was his habit, he forbore to disturb any of the owner's appointments. Among these— Mr. Corbin being a sporting gentleman—were numerous prints of race horses and of game chickens and of rat-killing terriers, famous in the annals. Jeb Stuart, visiting there, made endless fun of these ornaments. One day, at table, they brought on a gift of molded butter, stamped, in one of the cedar butter presses of that day, with a rampant fighting rooster. "Gentlemen," says Jeb—"we ought to have them make a drawing of this interior, the picture to be labelled 'view of the winter quarters of Stonewall Jackson, affording an insight into the tastes and character of the individual'— why, the man even has his favorite gamecock stamped on his butter!—" There were jests in plenty, in the Army of Northern Virginia. Snow came, and the soldiers staged wide battles, marching on snow forts, in formation, behind their officers, giving and taking clouds of missiles. There must have been rocks in some of the snow balls, for the records mention eyes knocked out, serious injuries. It was a great season of revivals: regimental chaplains, reinforced by evangelicals from all over the South, instituted a mighty saving of souls, and the woods rang to powerful exhortations, and to deep-chested singing of hymns. There was, say the chaplains, particularly the Reverend J. William Jones, a very bountiful outpouring of grace upon the army. In this the generals led: most of them were praying men, and waited earnestly upon their God. Orders of Stuart's exist upon the subject, and there is a memory of him, riding one snowy day by an outpost regiment to which had come a parson for the holding of prayers. Stuart and his staff, including "his big fighting Dutchman," alighted from their horses and knelt humbly in the slush. There is also an order of the Commanding General, in which he takes notice, with pain, of the spreading practice of gambling throughout the army. He appeals with noble words to the better natures of his soldiers, and says that gambling will not be tolerated.

Otherwise, there was shortage of shoes and blankets: men rolled themselves in carpets and made rawhide moccasins, and divisional generals, noting bloody footprints in the snow where the soldiers mounted guard, do not fail to draw favorable parallels with Valley Forge.

The army entertained visitors: journalists from England and from France, and officers on missions of military observation. All these worthies visited cavalry headquarters, for Jeb Stuart was the first cavalier of the South, and the impression he made was cast across the world. We have in a letter to his wife, his own description of his establishment: It was called, by his whimsey, "Camp No-Camp," and was, he says, the most luxurious he ever occupied. The couriers built a chimney to his tent, and he lived in great comfort on the rare days he spent in camp. A sad thing happened: his personal flag, always displayed at his headquarters—"the beautiful one you made—fell from the tent into the fire and burned. I send you the fragments. It had proudly waved over many battlefields and if I ever needed a motive for braving danger and trials, I found it by looking upon that symbol placed in my hands by my cherished wife, and which my dear little Flora so much admired. . . . Poor Hagan was greatly distressed at our darling's death. He had gathered chinckapins and hickory nuts for her on the mountain. . . ." This letter speaks also of the death of Redmond Burke, a Virginia gentleman, not young, who had served on Stuart's staff, volunteer aide, since the war broke out. "He was killed by the Yankees on the 25th (November). He died as he lived, true as steel. . . . His child-like devotion to me is one of those curious romances of this war which I will cherish next to my heart while I live. He has three sons in my command, worthy of such a father." Stuart briefly discusses in this letter the foreign visitors—and matters of policy—particularly that fatal expectation of the Confederacy—armed aid from abroad. "I have strong hopes of France but depend most on our own strong arms and His aid Who can accomplish *all*."

Thus, in camera, the hearts of these fighting men. Ardent soldiers, of a great piety. Dreamers, more than a little. Cherishing their friends and remembering their graves, and making sport among themselves while they lived, finding time for thought and love and laughter and tears in the grim business of war.

But Stuart is not much at headquarters. Great preparations had been made for Christmas. Wagons had been sent, out through Hampton's area, on the upper Rappahannock, to forage in Loudon county, and these had slipped through the Yankee cavalry fringe and returned with a-plenty: hams, and some thirty dozen eggs, and good Virginia apple brandy (Von Borcke's thought) and a number of turkeys: cavalry headquarters had acquired some turkeys from a Fredericksburg refugee, but Hood's Texans, who camped near by, get credit for stealing most of them before they could be eaten: these new ones are put under heavy guard. Mrs. Stuart came up from Richmond, to a near-by plantation, to spend the holidays with her General. Von Borcke, master of ceremonies, provided for music and minstrelsy, and invited his friends all around. There is, General Stuart permitting, to be an enormous eggnog. Christmas Eve arrives. And Stuart, having orders from General Lee to ride behind Burnside and see what he is doing, assembles 1800 troopers, drawn equally from the brigades of Hampton, Fitz Lee, and Rooney Lee, with Pelham's guns, goes off, up the river.

This was the famous Christmas raid. Its object was, primarily, reconnaissance, and, as always, to make trouble on the enemy's communication line. The column crossed at Kelly's Ford, eight miles from Culpeper, on Christmas Day, rode east to Morrisville, ten miles, and halted there, the night of the 26th. The weather was bitter cold, the Federal troops not alert—relaxed, also, for the season—and Stuart planned a division of forces. Accordingly, on the morning of the 27th, they headed out fanwise, Fitz Lee toward the Telegraph road about Chopowamsic Creek, south of Quantico, Rooney Lee toward Dumfries, above Chopowamsic, five miles, and Hampton ten miles farther north, to Occoquan.

This would cut off a fifteen-mile strip of the main Fredericksburg-Washington highway, and after that, Stuart would see.

Matters went according to plan: early on the 27th Fitz Lee struck the highway at Chopowamsic. Rooney Lee came in above him at Dumfries, and they felt out the place, finding it heavily garrisoned. Snatching away some prisoners—the Federals reported 68 missing—they detoured north to join Hampton at Occoquan, coming up to him after dark. Hampton had taken wagons and prisoners, and gotten through with some sharp skirmishing: he was at Dumfries on the 19th of the month, you remember, and since that visit more troops were stationed on the Telegraph road. At Cole's store, up the Occoquan, the column concentrated, and the prisoners, the captured weapons, and two of Pelham's guns which had expended their ammunition, were sent back to the Rappahannock with a squadron of the 9th Virginia in escort.

Next morning, the 28th, the column swept westward along the south bank of the Occoquan toward Brentsville, beating up small blue cavalry and infantry detachments, which were everywhere surprised and outnumbered, although several of them had been sent out expressly to run down the enemy who had attacked Occoquan the day before. Some weapons and more than 100 prisoners were bagged during the 28th, and there was sharp fighting along the creek, notably by Rosser's 5th Virginia and Butler's 2d South Carolina, and late in the evening Stuart led them north of the Occoquan and rode to Burke's Station. Burke's Station, on the Orange and Alexandria railroad, is between Fairfax Court House and Washington—not fifteen miles from the capital. Stuart surrounded it during the night, seizing everything so quickly and silently that the telegraph operator, who was transmitting messages from General Heintzelman, at Alexandria, directing measures against Stuart by commands in that vicinity, did not get off an alarm. Jeb Stuart, who travelled with a telegraph operator of his own—among the diverse talent in the escort—put his man at the key and received General Heintzelman's orders with interest, checking on his map the disposition of blue forces so disclosed. When he had learned all he could, he broke off, and sent a caustic telegram to Quartermaster-General Meigs of the U. S. Army, signed J. E. B. Stuart—"in reference to the bad quality of the mules lately furnished, which interfered seriously with our moving the captured wagons." Then he cut the wire.

This telegram is one of the classic jokes of the war. I could not find in the old records the original of it—hardly expected to, in fact, because from Quartermaster-General Meigs' papers, you deduce that he was deficient in humor, and probably threw it on the fire. There are many versions of it, given by contemporaries; the foregoing is from Stuart's report.

After destroying the Accotink bridge, near Burke's, Stuart rode by Fairfax Court House and alarmed the blue infantry there, but they opened fire on him with guns, and showed too much force, and he went on past. He knew now where they were looking for him—all along the Occoquan and the Rappahannock to the south—so he led north and west to Vienna, thence above Manassas Plains to Aldie and Middleburg, and thence, by easy stages, far outside any pursuit, to Warrenton. He was back in Culpeper Court House on the last day of the year. The result of his movement to the north and west was to draw large forces after him, away from the main blue army, and to create an uneasiness about a new invasion of Maryland. Heavy detachments were also sent from the Rappahannock to the Occoquan-Aquia Creek region, and all the guards on Burnside's line of supply were increased. The Confederates captured 200 prisoners, and a number of wagons, and lost 1 killed, 13 wounded, and 14 missing.

Only in the division of forces, to reunite in the presence of the enemy, does the Christmas raid differ from his previous raids, while the fact that he was able so to disperse and come together again, illustrates forcibly the skill and excellence now attained by his cavalry. Otherwise the tactics are the same: swift, secret marches, wide observation, the main body always in hand, under control, able to overwhelm any resistance. In the aggregate, he invariably had many times his own strength chasing him. But at the point of contact, which he was always able to select, he was the strongest. This is the essence of the Military Art.

XV

KELLY'S FORD—THE DEATH OF PELHAM

THERE was little movement of any kind in the violent cold and mud of January, and in February, 1863, one spectacular raid, by Fitz Lee, was the only incident. The army line remained on the Rappahannock. Longstreet went off, with three divisions of his Corps, to Suffolk. Jackson extended through his old camps, from Port Conway up to Fredericksburg, a seventeen-mile line. Rooney Lee's brigade held to the lower river: Hampton led his Carolinians south to recruit and remount: Fitz Lee's brigade took over the upper river, operating from Culpeper Court House. On the north bank, Hooker—Fighting Joe—succeeded Burnside, renovated the Army of the Potomac, restored its normal corps organization—in place of Burnside's clumsy grand divisions—reduced desertions, granted furloughs, put some heart into the sad blue soldiers. He had 130,000 men; and his cavalry corps, 12,000, was given to General Stoneman and made independent, after the pattern of the Army of Northern Virginia. Lee watched him from across the river, shepherding his shrunken divisions. About 45,000 infantry was left to Lee, and some 4000 cavalry, in Stuart's two brigades—Jones was detached to the Valley.

Lincoln and Halleck wanted fighting, but Joe Hooker was not to be forced as Burnside had been. The only episode in the opening month of 1863 was Averell's thrust at Culpeper, by the upper flank. On 14 March, in the clearing weather, Averell set out with 3000 sabres and some guns, and headed for Kelly's Ford. Next day was a Saturday, the 16th. Averell's mission was "to attack, and rout or destroy" Fitz Lee's brigade at Culpeper.

In Culpeper a court-martial was sitting, to which Jeb Stuart was summoned as a witness. He went up on the train from headquarters of the army, taking with him Major John Pelham, for he liked company when he travelled, and also, John Pelham was paying his addresses to Miss Bessie Shackleford of Culpeper, and was eager to go there on his own account. While they lay in Culpeper, on the sessions of the court, there came a note and a gift from that "Miss Nannie" of Stuart's letters, who was down in Orange Court House, very near:

"Dear General: we had a little candy stew last night, and knowing your fondness for 'sweets' of all kinds, I send you some of it this morning. Miss Brill sends some of it for the 'Gallant Pelham,' which you must be sure to give him. If you could see the burns on our fingers I am sure it would seem much sweeter——"

The trial was finished on Saturday, but Pelham wanted to stay over Sunday, which has ever been in the South the best day of the week for courting, and Jeb Stuart indulged him. Also, on Saturday, Fitz Lee had a telegram from the Commanding General, giving notice that scouts of the army had discovered the movement of a large body of blue cavalry, which had left Fredericksburg, and was marching up the Rappahannock. This telegram made Stuart more willing to remain: he never went away from a fight in his life. Fitz Lee had the wire before noon on Saturday, and sent some scouts galloping, who found and reported Averell's column between Morrisville and Bealton, about four miles north of the Rappahannock. They might, reasoned Fitz Lee, be going to Warrenton, or they might attempt the river at either Rappahannock Station or Kelly's Ford, points equidistant from Culpeper Court House. Accordingly, he alerted his river pickets, but held the main strength of his brigade in hand near Culpeper, until Averell's intention was developed.

At this time, Fitz Lee's brigade had 1900 sabres on its rolls. But many horses were unfit for service, and many troopers had been furloughed home to remount themselves, and his effectives, in the 1st, 2d, 3d, 4th and 5th, his Virginia regiments, numbered 800. Half of his strength was in the 2d and 4th alone. He had also Breathed's battery of horse artillery.

Averell's advance was cautious. Fitz Lee's scouts, during February and early March, had been so active north of the river that the Federals believed a large rebel force to be maintaining itself above Warrenton, and Averell detached 900 sabres to watch his right and rear as he advanced, but most of the riding and shooting which caused Averell to make this detachment was due to John Singleton Mosby, now holding the President's commission as Major of Partisan Rangers, and a great favorite of Jeb Stuart's. On 7 March, Mosby had ridden out of Stuart's lines with a party of 29 rangers, intent upon an enterprise he had. That night he left Aldie, riding east, and slipped through the Federal pickets at Chantilly. Then he rode, favored by darkness and rough weather, to Fairfax Court House, the headquarters of Brigadier-General Stoughton, whose command was covering the roads to Washington from the west. Acting quietly and boldly, he went straight to the General's billet, pulled him out of bed, and took him off, prisoner, plucked from the midst of his men. There was a great hue and cry after him, and among the Secesh sympathizers arrested by the angry Federals was that Miss Antonia Ford whom Stuart had commissioned; the authorities sent her to Old Capitol Prison on the chance that she might have communicated useful information to the rebel raiders. . . . No doubt she did. . . . Mosby's numbers were, of course, vastly overestimated, and Colonel Wyndham broke down a brigade of cavalry, chasing the rumors of him. The event was still fresh when Averell moved. The evening of the 16th, his own points reported rebel infantry at Rappahannock Station—they heard the drums—saw the camp fires—so Averell decided to cross at Kelly's Ford, where reconnaissances disclosed only a small cavalry picket. Incidentally, there was no gray infantry nearer than Fredericksburg.

About daylight, Sunday morning, the 17th—St. Patrick's Day—Averell's advance rushed Kelly's Ford. The picket, twenty men of the 2d Virginia, was overpowered. Their support, forty men, were hurried forward dismounted, and also broken up, and some of them captured, because, the records say, the horse-holding numbers would not bring the led horses forward when the blue line began to be dangerous. From this dates an order of the cavalry: the Number Fours —the horseholders—must be good men, carefully selected as to valor—not sorry fellows, left in the rear because they were of less use on the firing line. The picket overthrown, Averell began to cross his command, and his advance guard pushed slowly out, along the Culpeper road, toward Brandy Station. Gallopers fled back to brigade headquarters, and Fitz Lee got his men to horse. Jeb Stuart and John Pelham borrowed mounts and went along to see the show—the local tradition running that the young Major waved good-bye to Miss Bessie Shackleford as they loped by her father's house on the edge of town. Ahead, and with them, Fitz Lee's regiments were going at a trot, but the ground was so heavy that Breathed's guns fell behind. Averell has written, in his report: "From what I had learned of Lee's position, and from what I knew personally of his character, I expected him to meet me on the road to his camp." And Averell had been deliberate. He appeared at the ford about 5:30 A.M. He took two hours, after the fight there, to cross his command. Then the horses were fed and watered. It was well into the forenoon before he was ready to move, and Fitz Lee, alerted

at 7:30, rode nearly seven miles and met the blue advance
before it had made a mile from the ford. The fight was
opened on the Wheatley farm, Fitz Lee hurling his 3d regiment at Averell's advance guard, which was deployed across
the Brandy Station—Kelly's Ford road, and partially dismounted. The 3d Virginia, supported a little later by the
5th, Rosser's regiment, involved the Federal front and broke
into it near the road. Averell brought up his main body,
disclosing his entire force. Too many Yankees! Fitz Lee's
bugles drew off the 3d and 5th: he had outdistanced his
guns, and he must hold together until they came.

Meantime, there had been a pretty little fight. When the
3d regiment charged, they went by column of fours down a
lane and out through a wheat field. With them rode John
Pelham, on a raw-boned black mare—enjoying himself immensely, for he usually has responsibilities in a fight, and
now he is free of them. They who noticed him relate that he
wheeled clear about halfway to the enemy, and stood, shouting encouragement to the rear fours of the 3d, who were
lagging a little. His horse pranced about, and he waved his
hat, and the watery March sunlight touched his yellow hair
with brightness. Out in front, the Virginians were slicing
into the Rhode Islanders and the Maine cavalry: there was
a great rattle of carbines and pistols, and on the blue flank
a horse battery went into action. A shell burst near John
Pelham, on his black mare. . . .

Two Pennsylvania regiments, the 16th and 4th, of Mc-
Intosh's, rode out and struck the 3d Virginia, then the 5th,
on the flank. The fight streamed back across the wheat field,
and by Wheatley's house the adjutant of the 3d Virginia
drew rein to assist a trooper who was straining to get a soldier's body across his saddle—a limp man whose face was
masked with mud and blood. The blue troopers, shooting
and shouting, were very near, but the adjutant and the

trooper flung the body up, head on one side and legs on the other, and got away down the road toward Brandy, to the point where the 3d and 5th were reforming on Fitz Lee's remaining regiments. Behind the line, they lifted the casualty off the horse, wiped its face, and looked at it. It was Major John Pelham. A shell splinter, a long, narrow sliver of steel, had driven into his skull. He was still breathing. An ambulance was brought up, and they took him to Culpeper and carried him into the Shackleford house. His sweetheart helped to dress his wound, and chafed his cold hands. In the afternoon, he died.

Back in the trampled mile between Brandy Station and the approach to Kelly's Ford, Fitz Lee has Breathed's guns up, and his brigade reformed. Averell has advanced slowly for three-quarters of a mile, but shows no disposition to press matters. The action is degenerating into a fire-fight. Fitz Lee, making his own battle under Jeb Stuart's eye, orders a general advance. From left to right they ride at Averell, the last troopers in line, Breathed's gun teams galloping to new positions, not a sabre left in reserve. Averell's line is short and thick, but it gives way generally, only a few formations—notable among them the Rhode Islanders—standing to meet the shock. Men were killed with sabres, shot at such close range that the pistol flashes burnt their jackets. Yet Averell's men were steady: commands held well together, and the Confederate regiments lost cohesion and drew off to form again. Averell had a large reserve, not yet engaged, and the Confederate officers anxiously expected that it would be flung upon them—nor do they see how they could have held against it. But, to their relief, Averell formed it as a rear guard, and drew off rapidly toward Kelly's Ford with the main body. Fitz Lee followed with what he could get together, and saw Averell north of the Rappahannock by dark.

Averell had lost 80 men, killed, wounded, and captured—half of them from the 1st Rhode Island—out of 2,100 on the field. Fitz Lee's loss was 133, of whom 34 were led away, prisoners. In horses alone—almost as valuable as the men—his loss was 71 killed and 87 wounded—which shows the close and savage nature of the cavalry fighting. To sum up, Averell, with 2,100, had advanced three-fourths of a mile into Fitz Lee's territory, driven 800 Confederates another mile, and then retired. The dispassionate and critical Confederate commentator has recorded his opinion: "We cannot excuse General Averell's conduct. He ought to have gone to Culpeper Court House."

The affair did not please Fitz Lee, although he considers that he drove his enemy from the field. If, he says, he had been able to mount all the troopers on his rolls, and if his horses had not been, by reason of overwork, scant forage, and exposure, in such poor condition, not a man of Averell's would have been allowed to recross the Rappahannock.

There were some hard men in the ranks, that day: we read of Sergeant Kimborough of F Company, 4th Virginia. He took a flesh wound early in the day and stayed in ranks. In the last charge, he was twice slashed over the head with sabres, had his arm broken by a pistol ball, and was captured and carried over the river. But he escaped from the Yankees, four miles beyond the ford, and, that same night, walked twelve miles to Culpeper and rejoined his regiment in the morning.

Averell returned to Falmouth with his thirty-odd prisoners, having failed to accomplish the rout or destruction of Fitz Lee's brigade. The Confederates counted it a victory, and the Federal cavalry officers studied the reports, observed the statistics on dead horses, and hopefully concluded that the blue cavalry was learning to fight—which is true: it was. And they killed John Pelham.

Captain Harry Gilmer writes that Jeb Stuart, riding with one of Fitz Lee's regiments as a volunteer sabre, bowed on his horse's neck and wept, when they told him of Pelham's death. There was love and mutual admiration between the two of them, and no abler combination, sabre and light artillery, has ever been arrayed for battle. Pelham had fought through every general engagement in Virginia; his battles and skirmishes numbered nearly sixty, and he never lost a gun, although he was accustomed to charge with the cavalry and to go into battery at infantry ranges. He took his guns and caissons where single troopers on horses hardly ventured, through streams and over mountains. He had maintained, with his material, the fierce pace of Stuart's raids. At Sharpsburg he personally commanded nineteen guns, and at Fredericksburg, fifty. Stuart's consistent praise in his reports, and Lee's accolade in despatches, show how he was rated professionally. Jeb Stuart wrote mournfully to his wife on the 19th of March—one of the few sad letters he ever sent her:

"The noble Pelham . . . killed. You know how his death distresses me." And Stuart thinks ahead: sees his own death: "I wish an assurance on your part in the event of your surviving me—that [Stuart's italics] *you will make the land for which I have given my life your home and keep my offspring on Southern soil.*" And, later, "Poor Pelham's death has created a sensation all over the country. He was noble in every sense of the word. I want Jemmie to be just like him."

His order to the cavalry division has in it a great grief and a great pride:

"The noble, the chivalric, the gallant, Pelham is no more. How much he was beloved, appreciated and admired, let the tears of agony we here shed, and the gloom of mourning throughout my command, bear witness. His loss is irreparable. The memory of the 'gallant Pelham,' his many virtues, his noble nature, and purity of character, is enshrined as a sacred legacy in the hearts of all who knew him. His record has been bright and spotless, his career brilliant and successful. He fell, the noblest of sacrifices, on the altar of his country, to whose glorious service he had dedicated his life from the beginning of the war."

Von Borcke was detailed to escort John Pelham home to Alabama: the body went in an open casket, and at every stop the people thronged to see him, lying dead with the pleasant, smooth face of a boy.

Young Chew, Breathed, Beckham and Pegram, able and gallant horse artillerymen, carried on his work. The light arm continued to be well served and gallantly fought to the end. But with Pelham, there passed from the army something youthful and golden. They would have no more like him. . . .

XVI

CHANCELLORSVILLE:
JEB STUART LEADS THE SECOND CORPS

STUART'S letters, in the first months of 1863, show a thoughtful tinge. In March, he is writing his final reports of the battles of 1862, and finds it dull work: they remember that he would spring up from his desk and wrestle a fall with some lively fellow of his staff, or have in Sweeny and the banjo and make uproarious music for half an hour, then return, much freshened, to his compositions. He tells his wife to keep a scrap book, of all the articles and pictures that seem pertinent—"which we will prize and our boy will prize in after years. . . ." This same letter suggests that "Her Bright Smile Haunts Me Still" is a very fine song, especially applicable to her. And he wishes that he could settle her in "a nice house, quiet, secure, and lovely, such as I have often pictured in my infancy. . . ." He sees her moving in such surroundings—ideal, because just now she is living between Lynchburg and Richmond, very inconveniently—and "bless that pretty figure, the pattern of grace. . . ." He is, he notes, messing alone, in the state that becomes a Major-General, but he always has some one drop in for sociability's sake. She has written sadly on the death of Pelham, but he tells her—"You must not give way to gloomy forebodings, and remember *fortitude* is woman's *specialty* and *patience* her most shining virtue . . . be ever hopeful and up-hearted, and laugh croakers out of countenance!"

Toward the end of April, he writes—from Camp Pelham—"How I miss you this beautiful Sabbath morning—and yet before yonder sun reaches the zenith, our blades may be

362

gleaming brightly on the warpath. . . . I am going to church, but I go equipped for the field——"

And the first campaign of 1863 opens with a rush.

Hooker is confident, his orders spirited and resonant. He had, he said, the finest army on the planet—the man enjoyed a gift for large, mouth-filling phrases. May God, he remarks, have mercy on General Lee: he, Joe Hooker, will have none. On the south bank, Lee, with 60,000 gray soldiers, spread very thin from Port Conway up to Fredericksburg, watches Falmouth Heights, and writes anxiously to the President that Longstreet had better join him. Down at Suffolk, Longstreet is happily fighting a small war of his own—and, as always with Longstreet when he did not want to move, finds abundant reasons for delay. His wagons are dispersed, gathering forage: transportation is not good: he will come when he can.

In the middle of April, Stuart's cavalry—Fitz Lee's and Rooney Lee's brigades—picketed a line that extended—in Stuart's words—from the Chesapeake to the Blue Ridge. This was almost literally true. Rooney Lee watched the Rappahannock River, as far up as Kelly's Ford and Culpeper. Fitz Lee was flung out to the north, through the Warrenton region, to Salem, between Bull Run Mountain and the Blue Ridge. W. E. Jones was off in the Valley, and Hampton had not come back from the south. Stuart's two available brigades numbered, Fitz Lee about 1500, and Rooney Lee about 1200—a total of 2700 sabres. Correspondence, between Lee and Stuart, and Lee and the Richmond government, indicated that the condition of the cavalry caused them grave concern. The horses had wintered badly, many troopers were dismounted: the gun teams were reduced, and there were no remounts available. A call had been sent for all the unemployed cavalry in the Carolinas and Georgia, and some regiments came forward, but not until the urgent need of them was past. The Secretary of War had authorized, it may be noted, the purchase of 1000 horses in Texas, but nothing ever came of it, as far as re-mounts for Stuart were concerned. He applied himself cheerfully to the making of bricks without straw.

The news from across the Rappahannock was ominous. Lee's intelligence agents, supplemented by the well-served Northern newspapers, kept him fully informed. Hooker had drawn up, in March, a plan of invasion: he would feint at Falmouth and cross up-stream, turning Fredericksburg and forcing Lee to defend the road to Richmond somewhere south. The plan seeped through to Lee. He had Jackson's four divisions of the Second Corps; two—McLaws and Ander-son—of Longstreet's; and Stuart's Horse. He knew that 130,000 were arrayed against him—12,000 of them, under Stoneman, blue cavalry. He waited anxiously at Fredericks-burg, and wished for his three divisions off with Longstreet.

On the 13th of April, Stuart's scouts brought news of a great blue cavalry concentration at Morrisville, near War-renton Junction. This was Stoneman, with the most ardent orders from his chief. Stoneman would force the Rappahan-nock at the upper fords, and ride for Gordonsville, and the line of the Virginia Central. He would swing down east along the railroad, toward Richmond, cutting Lee off from his cap-ital, and drawing the enemy cavalry after him. Then Hooker would cross, above Fredericksburg, and turn the lines that had ruined Burnside in December. Lee would, of course, re-treat, only to find Stoneman in his rear, blocking his roads and burning his bridges. Stoneman would be able to delay the rebels, then, until Hooker caught up with them, some-where between Fredericksburg and Richmond, and destroyed them. "We've got the men, we've got the guns, we've got the finest army on the planet." Gay and bold was Fighting Joe Hooker in these opening days of spring, and from him the blue army drew a brittle confidence. Stoneman went, with Averell's division, Gregg's, and John Buford's, to his task, leaving Pleasanton's three brigades—a few sabres above 3000—to serve the main army. Behind Stoneman, the Army of the Potomac is ordered to strip itself for action, and take eight days rations in haversacks—Hooker is going to move fast: he will not be bothered with trains.

Morrisville is four short miles from Kelly's Ford. Stuart had, in the region, two regiments of Rooney Lee, the 9th and the 13th Virginia; a squadron, 116 men, of the 2d North Carolina; and 143 dismounted men of "Company Q." He reinforced Kelly's Ford with sharpshooters of the 9th Virginia —Captain Bolling's company—and one gun of Moorman's. At daylight on the 14th, Buford with the U. S. regular cavalry, thrust at Kelly's Ford, an attack not pressed, and Bolling beat Buford off with the forces on the ground. Under cover of Buford's move, Gregg's division attempted the passage at Rappahannock Station, up-stream. Here were some of the 9th Virginia in a blockhouse, with the 2d North Carolina and a Whitworth gun in support. Gregg, there and at Beverley's Ford, two miles up, attempted a crossing, but was also beaten off, although his was to have been the main attack. Stuart's general reserves—Rooney Lee and his two Virginia regiments, held near Culpeper—were not needed.

Next day, the 15th, Buford moved up to Rappahannock Station, to the railroad bridge, and some of Gregg's men went up to Welford's Ford, got over, and turned Beverley's, and for a while the way was opened. But Stoneman moved very slowly, and Rooney Lee, with the 9th and 13th, moved very fast, and the river line was restored, in a sharp fight that drove Stoneman's advance back across the fords and caused him some loss in men and horses. Hooker sent angry and urgent orders: get on over, you!—and the river began to rise. By the 16th, the fords were swimming-deep, and

Stoneman, with the whole army behind him, lay inactive for eleven days, until the waters had subsided. Jeb Stuart improved the granted respite to draw in Fitz Lee, and concentrate Rooney Lee's brigade.

Stoneman endured the caustic comments of Hooker, merely explaining that the roads were too muddy for rapid movement (just as muddy for the enemy as they are for you, says Hooker, sagaciously) and continued to make preparations for his raid. Lee and Stuart understand, now, what he intends, and Rooney Lee is told off to watch him, and to save the railroads and communication centres if he can. On the 28th, Stoneman gets over, Gregg and Buford and Averell with him, above Stuart's flank. He rides for Orange Court House, Rooney Lee following and nipping at him, but too weak to hold him. Stoneman has 6700 sabres in his main column.

The same day, Stuart was watching the Army of the Potomac. Leaving, at Falmouth, its camp standing, and Sedgwick's corps, with details, some 35,000 men, in plain sight of the Confederate watchers south of the river, the main Army of the Potomac, 90,000, marched rapidly up-stream, behind the hills, and concentrated three corps of infantry at Kelly's Ford. Stuart's pickets were brushed aside, and pontoons laid. That night, the Fifth, the Eleventh and Twelfth corps crossed, a bold and skillful operation. Two corps marched south toward Germanna Ford on the Rapidan, and one followed the river road toward Ely's Ford, further down. Stuart, with Fitz Lee in hand, lay at Brandy Station, behind his picket line. On the 29th, when the reports were in, he rode east toward Germanna, pierced the Federal line of march, and took enough prisoners to identify the three corps, and to ascertain that the main army was behind them. This information despatched to Lee, he turned his back on Stoneman, leaving Rooney Lee to do what he could with him, and

rode with Fitz Lee across the front and flank of the marching blue masses. From that day, Hooker was blinded. Pleasanton was not strong enough to do more than cover his front,
leaving his flanks open. He never had another report from
Stoneman, launched off into the blue. And it was at his
flanks that Stuart persistently struck. One gray regiment,
the 3d Virginia, got in front of Hooker at Wilderness Run
on the morning of the 30th, fought briskly with the 6th New
York of Pleasonton's, and retired through Chancellorsville
to the east, to meet Lee's advance guard. Stuart hung on,
with the rest, in a course parallel to the Germanna Ford
road, and annoyed the blue march with carbines and horse
artillery. Early in the afternoon the blue advance reached
Chancellorsville. Its intention was fully developed: marching on Fredericksburg from the west. Stuart drew off;
swung southward, and rode toward Spottsylvania Court
House, intending to bivouac on the enemy's flank at Todd's
Tavern. Reaching that point with his regiments he took his
staff and trotted eastward to report to his Commanding
General.

For Lee was coming. He had Stuart's reports, detailed
and exact. Sedgwick had crossed on pontoons at Deep Run
below Fredericksburg, and Jackson would come into line in
front of him by the 30th. Anderson's and McLaws' divisions
had been pushed west of Fredericksburg on the turnpike.
The night of the 30th, Lee and Jackson considered the crushing of Sedgwick, against whose 35,000 they could bring
overwhelming force. But the idea was rejected: Stuart's
messages showed that Hooker was the real menace. Early's
division, 10,000 men, was left to hold the Fredericksburg
position, and the night of the 30th, Lee's order put Jackson
in motion, out the Chancellorsville road.

Hooker had three balloons up in front of Fredericksburg,
U. S. Balloon *Eagle* and two others. These saw little of the

Confederate movement; much of it was by night, and the 30th April and 1st May were days of poor visibility. But what they reported was disquieting to Joe Hooker, who, the night of the 30/1, established his headquarters at Chancellor's House. For all the gray columns were marching west—not south, in retreat on Richmond, as Hooker expected. This was contrary to the rules. Turned, and outnumbered, Lee ought to be running. Hooker felt bemused. His orders, issued in the early morning of the 1st, were not energetic. Columns would advance by the river road, by the turnpike, and by the Plank road, from Chancellorsville. The remainder of the army would close on the Chancellorsville clearing. There was a doubt in Hooker's mind. Except for the fragmentary reports of the balloon service, he knew nothing of what went on in the nine-mile gap between his main body and Sedgwick, at Fredericksburg. Sedgwick reported gray lines of battle on his front, on Marye's Hill, on Lee's Hill—bad and bloody locations. Gray cavalry had been in contact with his marching columns since he crossed the Rappahannock. Some deserters had come in, who said that Longstreet had joined from the south, with Hood and Pickett and Wade Hampton—deserters, it is related, carefully instructed by Stonewall Jackson before they absented themselves from their regiments.

And the battered remnants of the 6th New York cavalry, carrying their colonel's body across a horse, had reported confusedly at dawn from the south.

These people had an adventure the night of the 30th. That afternoon they rode from Chancellorsville toward Spottsylvania, and were returning, under a fine spring moon, by way of Todd's Tavern, where a right-hand fork led, five miles, to Chancellor's House. Just before they reached Todd's Tavern, walking their jaded horses, they met a party of horsemen, trotting, who rode very close, hailed, wheeled, and galloped off. That, if they had known it, was Jeb Stuart. He spurred back to Todd's, found Fitz Lee's nearest regiment, the 5th Virginia, unsaddling, and led it toward Spottsylvania, while staff officers went for the rest of the brigade.

Lieutenant-Colonel McVicker, commanding the 6th New York, was a prudent officer, and he deduced that Stuart's party were rebels, and that they would return with more rebels. He moved his regiment off to the right, and formed line facing the road, in the dark shadows of the trees. The 5th Virginia, looking for a fight, pounded across his front without seeing him, and he dashed out at their rear, upsetting the last squadron, taking some prisoners, and creating a great confusion. Much puzzled at finding the enemy behind instead of in front, the 5th Virginia scattered, and fled toward Spottsylvania. Some very lively accounts of this contact exist. Stuart, riding ahead, was whirled away in the panic rush of his troopers from behind, and his staff and small escort driven in every direction. Swords and pistols were out; men shot and thrust and hacked in the dark, and the orders and entreaties of the cooler-headed officers were unavailing. The rout swept a long way eastward before it could be stopped.

Meantime, the 6th New York pushed rapidly toward Todd's Tavern, but on the way there, collided headlong with Colonel Carter's regiment, which was galloping hotly to overtake the 5th.

A bewildering dog-fight followed. The captured troopers of the 5th, herded for safe keeping in the head of the blue column, cried out to their friends to be careful! Gray troopers and blue were all mingled, and at just that point, tall, thick timber along the road cut off the moonlight, and it was too dark to see anything. But the well-trained 6th New York knew that safety was generally to the right, to the north, and most of them ran off independently to the cover of the trees on that side. Colonel Carter, uncertain as to whether or not he had actually charged the 5th Virginia, got his regiment off the road to the left, where the country was more open, to reform and to estimate the situation. The captured troopers of the 5th escaped, in the melee, and rode around and added to the ambiguity of the case.

The whole affair lasted but the fewest minutes. Lieutenant-Colonel McVicker was killed. But his regiment held together, and gained the road to Chancellorsville, losing only their rear guard, which the rallied Virginians took. They came in and reported to headquarters that they had met rebel cavalry, lots of it, coming from the west! Hooker had time to think it over. There shouldn't have been any cavalry from that direction. It ought to have been drawn after Stoneman. Did it mean, the advance of some infantry, not yet suspected, from over there? You can see, in Hooker's next orders and correspondence, the growing vagueness in his mind.

In the forenoon, they at Chancellorsville, waiting, heard firing to the east, and reports came in: rebels in force across the turnpike, this side of Zoar Church, three miles from here! A little later, that column reports itself as being flanked by the right, from the south: and coincidentally comes a report from the column on the Plank road, we are up against a rebel line of battle—and later, we're being turned—rebels south of us! What happened was this: Anderson, at Zoar, entrenched across the pike and stood in the way of Meade, whose Fifth Corps seemed disposed to come on. Fighting began, but Jackson rode up and ordered Anderson to extend his left, to the south. A little later, McLaws, on the Plank road, met the enemy, and he had similar orders: he side-stepped around toward the unfinished railroad. Up on the river road, the same thing happened. About noon,

Hooker recalled these columns and ordered them to dig in, with the left on the river, toward United States Ford, behind Mineral Springs Run, and the line curving to face south around the edge of the Chancellorsville clearing. Thence, during the day, he built it up toward the west, through the Wilderness, south of and parallel to the turnpike, out to the far side of Dowdall's Clearing. Late in the afternoon he pushed a strong column down toward Catherine Furnace, and found the enemy there, due south of his centre. Through the day and the night, his troops worked steadily on field fortifications. From the head of the army came no further instructions, Joe Hooker was growing numb.

There is no campaign in which psychology plays so strong a part as Chancellorsville. General Hooker was not an indifferent soldier, and his movements in the first three days, from the 28th of April to the 1st of May, had been bold and skilful. His great army had crossed two rivers, threaded the difficult narrow ways of the Wilderness in good order and without loss, marched forty-six miles, and gained a position which effectively flanked out the dreaded Fredericksburg hills. So far, so good: no army has done better. But one fatal mistake had been committed, the detachment of Stoneman's cavalry. On the 1st of May, the effect of this error began to be felt, and Hooker's campaign started to go to pieces.

Chancellorsville was an old, white-columned mansion, facing south on the Orange Turnpike, nine miles west of Fredericksburg. It was a crossroads in a wide clearing in the eastern face of the Wilderness. The Orange Plank Road forked off to the southeast, passed south of the pike, and came back into it six miles to the east. A road ran north, forking a mile and a half from Chancellorsville, the right hand road taking you three miles to United States Ford on the Rappahannock, and the left hand, four miles to Ely's

Ford on the Rapidan. A little west of south, three miles, in the Wilderness, was Catherine Furnace, an old smelter: there were ancient gold mines in the vicinity. Across the Wilderness, east and west, passing about four miles south of Chancellor's House, was the line of an unfinished railroad. As you went west on the Turnpike, you plunged, a mile from the mansion, into the Wilderness again: just to your left rear would be Fairview Cemetery, and a mile to your left Hazel Grove—points on a low ridge of cleared ground, with Chancellor's House at one end and Hazel Grove at the other. Proceeding by the Plank Road, for about another mile, you open the Dowdall clearing, in which stood Dowdall's Tavern, Wilderness Church, and Talley's Farm. Then—nearly a mile of open ground, and the Wilderness closed upon you again. Here it was not so dense, along the road, as farther to the south and east. At Wilderness Church, the Orange Plank Road left the Turnpike and branched southwest. Three miles from Wilderness Church and five miles from Chancellorsville stood Wilderness Tavern.

The Turnpike, it will be seen, traverses the region from east to west, following generally the highest ground. North of it are the streams that feed into the Rappahanock, Wilderness Run, and Hunting Run, and Mineral Springs Run, and south of it the streams go toward the Peninsula; the Ny river at Catherine Furnace leads you, eventually, to the Pamunkey and the York.

Consider Hooker, ruddy, handsome, splendid in his blue and gold, by the Chancellor's House in the mild spring afternoon. West and south and east rolls the Wilderness, like a sea, new green leaves and white dogwood flowering. His artillery and columns of sturdy infantry move in the open fields around him. Smoke wells up from the woods to the

south, Catherine Furnace-way. He has just issued to the troops resounding, congratulatory orders on what has already been achieved: but I imagine that his face, turned toward the forest walls that shut off the east and the southeast, was anxious. He knew certain things: Sedgwick was immobilized at Fredericksburg. There were rebels across the river road, the Turnpike, and the Plank Road, and out the unfinished railroad at Catherine Furnace. And last night they were coming from the southwest, at Todd's Tavern. How many, he did not know: those deserters mentioned Longstreet, thought to be at Suffolk. But Stonewall Jackson, certainly, and Jeb Stuart, certainly, and General Lee! There was a dangerous feel . . . Jackson, Jackson, in the soft May air. Joe Hooker abandoned his offensive and began to cover up. Some of his fighting generals came, amazed at the orders to stop, when everything was going well, and have recorded (after the event) that this day their Chief seemed a beaten man. Indeed, the thing had passed from him, with those collisions on the roads to Fredericksburg. Lee had it in his hand.

During the afternoon, Lee's last elements are arriving from Fredericksburg, and Fitz Lee's Brigade, now with gray infantry close behind, is feeling Hooker's front, exactly locating his lines. South of Catherine Furnace, Jackson, riding in advance, sends for Stuart; he thinks he has found a position from which the blue line can be enfiladed, but Wright's Brigade of Anderson's, which is up, has no guns, and he asks Stuart for some. Stuart brings four of Beckham's Horse pieces, and with Jackson, rides down a narrow road to the little timbered knoll selected. So thick is the brush that only one gun can be emplaced, and it goes into battery, the others standing in the road behind. It opens through the screen of leaves, and at once two Federal batteries, unsuspected and very near, beat it down with a blizzard of shell and cannister. Horses and men are knocked over, kicking, the terrified gun teams plunge and rear in the narrow way, and nobody understands how any person came from the place alive. As for Stuart and Stonewall Jackson, their work is not yet done, but Stuart loses here his adjutant, young Major Channing Price, a good officer and very dear to him.

Night falls, and Stuart collects the reports from the regiments and from Fitz Lee, and goes to the Commanding General, whom he finds with Jackson, three miles east of Chancellorsville, on the Plank Road, in an oak wood. Lee has thought that Hooker's left, near the Rappahannock below United States Ford, is vulnerable: but Jackson's staff had reconnoitred Mineral Springs Run, which covers it, and reports it too strong. In the center, Jackson has seen the strong earth-works and abatis, already rising. Now Stuart brings Fitz Lee's report, and they plot his information on the map: the Federal right trails in the air, in Dowdall's clearing, on the Turnpike. There, without question, is the place.

Lee and Jackson sit on hard-tack boxes with the map between them, in the ruddy fire light, and staff and couriers look from a respectful distance. Around them in the Wilderness, 90,000 men in blue, and 50,000 gray soldiers, all within a few miles, squat at their camp fires, gnaw field rations, hold the outpost lines, write letters, look at the slow-climbing moon, or sleep. The lean cavalry horses nibble at the bark of trees; keen gray videttes, carbines on thigh, watch the roads to Chancellorsville. After a while, Jackson rides to his headquarters, farther up the Plank Road, and has some orders for his staff. Jackson sleeps an hour or two, on the ground. They remember that he had a heavy cold in his chest this night, and when, before dawn, he rises and drinks coffee, his sword, leaned for the night against a convenient tree, untouched by anybody, falls to the ground with an iron clang. . . .

At four o'clock in the chill gray dawn, Jackson's corps, three divisions, is marching west through the Wilderness. Jubal Early is back at Fredericksburg. A. P. Hill's Light Division, D. H. Hill's division, under Rodes, and Trimble's division, with the Second Corps artillery, made up his column, 25,000 men. McLaws and Anderson, perhaps 12,000, remain with General Lee, under his personal command. Another detachment lies back on the roads to Fredericksburg. Jeb Stuart rides with Fitz Lee on the right of Jackson's column, between the infantry and the Federal front. General Lee has divided his forces again, in the immediate presence of 90,000 men, and his back is turned to Sedgwick, who stands with no mean force, in his rear.

The 2nd of May is fine, and sunny, and the air fresh and cool. Hooker's people do nothing, except in their centre, where Sickles is pushed down by Catherine Furnace, and starts a brisk local battle that crackles and smolders, by turns, through the morning, into the afternoon. So boldly and so skilfully does Lee dispose his two divisions that the Federal centre is greatly impressed, and sends to the Federal right for help: a brigade, Barlow's, is marched that way from Dowdall's Tavern. The hours pass, and a certain slow stream of information trickles back to the blue corps headquarters, and to Chancellorsville. From Hazel Grove they see a column, all arms, and trains, maching southwest. Lee retreating, decides Hooker, and orders more activity, out from Catherine Furnace. Pleasanton's cavalry moves forward, and gets into Jackson's rear, so that Jackson's last brigade has to face about and fight. But neither Sickles nor Pleasanton press matters. They take a Georgia infantryman, a hot-headed fellow of Jackson's, indignant at being captured. Just wait, he says, till you see what Old Jack does to you. Old Jack's going to take you all apart! This is reported, but Headquarters considers that the intentions of the enemy can hardly be calculated from this mere statement of a straggler or a prisoner!

They observe, throughout the day, gray troopers moving to the left, just in view of the blue outpost line. In the afternoon, a German Colonel, von Gilsa, who has the extreme right element of Hooker's right, gets a report from his patrols—a mile west of his line, astride the Turnpike: the rebels are forming lines of battle, facing east. Von Gilsa takes his horse and gallops furiously for his corps commander, Howard, at Dowdall's Tavern, and tells him about it. Howard is preoccupied, listening to the far-off fighting at Catherine Furnace, whither he despatched Barlow. "Colonel von Gilsa," he says, not at all impressed, "you will put your trust in God." And von Gilsa, amazed, angry, starts back to his brigade.

At two o'clock this day, Stonewall Jackson, riding ahead of his infantry, has come nearly twelve miles by devious, covered ways; the Plank Road partly, the unfinished railroad partly, and by wood paths, and finally by the Brock Road, to the Orange Plank Road, two and one-half miles southwest of Dowdall's Tavern. Here he had planned to form line to his right and attack. But Fitz Lee, who has ridden with his screen all day, comes up and begs the Lieutenant General to ride with him and look. They trot to a point on the Plank Road from where, on a hillock, you look down into Dowdall's clearing. They saw, a few hundred yards north, the right end of Hooker's line—strong earthworks, guns emplaced—and the Eleventh Corps, lying about at ease in the golden afternoon, the rifles mostly stacked. The Turnpike runs beyond them, quite empty. The line

faces south. To the west there is nothing—no intrenchments, no guns, no troops formed that way. Fitz Lee relates
that a brilliant light grew on Jackson's face, and that his
lips moved, but he said nothing for some minutes. Then he
gave orders: his leading division would continue on the
Brock Road across the Plank, to the Turnpike, and receive
orders there. Two more miles of marching.

The Second Corps marched that day fourteen miles—
ordered: no talking or unnecessary noise, no straggling,
men who fall out of column are to be bayonetted. At 4:00
P.M., Rodes, leading, reached the Turnpike, half a mile
east of Wilderness Tavern, and Stonewall Jackson began
to form line of battle to left and right of the highway, facing east.

He sat on the grass, under a tree, his staff and Jeb Stuart
with him. The gray infantry came up, and deployed to left
and right. They came by one narrow road, 25,000 men, and
it took two hours to form the first division, Rodes, then
Trimble after him. A mile to each side of the road, in two
waves, at four hundred yards distance, their troops took
station and dressed their lines. A. P. Hill came upon the
Turnpike and headed east, remaining in column. It was
nearly six o'clock. Jeb Stuart's work is done: there is no
more need for cavalry here: he gets Jackson's permission
to take a regiment and a battery and ride up to Ely's Ford,
where some small enterprise may be carried out against a
wagon-park there reported, and he rides off, humming a
little tune to himself. By the Turnpike, at six o'clock, Jackson orders Rodes forward.

A mile of the Wilderness intervenes, unbroken, before you
reach the first Federal troops. You cannot walk in a straight
line through that wood today, without tearing your clothes
and clawing your path through dense underbrush. Try
marching fourteen miles, first, and then struggling through

on a given course, in formation, and loaded down with military gear. The Confederate regimental officers relate that they kept direction by pocket compasses—a thing not yet seen in this war—leading with compass instead of sword. Yet the lines went swiftly. A little before sunset, flocks of turkeys, hares, deer, and foxes, broke from the Wilderness into Dowdall's clearing. Close behind, with the brazen pealing of bugles, and the high, screeching rebel yell, swept the gray infantry, with their bright bayonets and their red battle flags. Von Gilsa's brigade, at Talley's farm, took the first impact: he had two Maine regiments and two German regiments. The American half dispersed: the Germans stood and fought, and were very quickly overrun. By Wilderness Church, there were some guns in park, and several of these were gotten into action. A few scattered groups resisted bravely. But for the most part, the attack stamped over Howard with the completeness of a nightmare, and the Eleventh Corps disintegrated. The débris rolled, in frantic rout, down the Turnpike towards Chancellorsville. For nearly three miles, almost without check, Stonewall Jackson drove his enemies. A little east of Dowdall's Tavern, the darkening Wilderness intervened an arm, and here the gray assault began to slow down. About this place, a wood road debouched upon the Turnpike from Hazel Grove, and out of this road, into A. P. Hill's marching column, rode in twos the 8th Pennsylvania Cavalry, sent up from Hazel Grove to see what the shooting was about. Gray and blue cavalry were equally amazed: then the blue horse were engulfed. On the high ground three-quarters of a mile west of Chancellorsville, the gray people halted. Rodes and Colston were so intermingled that it was imperative to reform. Hill, still fresh, and in column, was ordered to deploy. It was about eight o'clock, and Stonewall Jackson with some staff officers and couriers, rode impatiently to the front, to reconnoitre, while Rodes and Colston straightened out their commands. After a few hundred yards, he ran into blue troops from the Federal centre, unshaken except by rumor, organizing a line just this side of the Chancellorsville clearing. The Lieutenant-General rode back, first along the south side of the pike, for the blue skirmishers were firing up it; then, near his own troops, about where a track runs from the Turnpike toward United States Ford, he turned diagonally across the highway and continued up the north side. On to the road to United States Ford stood the 18th North Carolina Infantry, formed in line. They had heard the firing out in front. They were keen and alert. They saw a body of horsemen approaching from the direction of the enemy. A voice called, Yankee Cavalry; and another voice called, Fire! Their volley struck down Stonewall Jackson, and most of his staff with him. A. P. Hill, next senior, held command a few minutes and was wounded. Command devolved on young General Pender, and Hill, from his litter, sent a staff officer galloping for Jeb Stuart.

Jeb Stuart had ridden to Ely's Ford, and found Averell's blue Cavalry, returned from Stoneman, and very tired, but in position to guard the passage. While he made his dispositions to attack, Captain Adams, aide to General A. P. Hill, came to him on a panting horse: General Jackson wounded, General Hill wounded, you are senior in the Second Corps. Stuart turned over his little force to Major Von Borcke: you fire three rounds into them and draw off. He sent Fitz Lee orders to hold the Ely Road, in case Averell should grow aggressive; and he rode at a gallop to take up his responsibilities.

I think he rode with a lifting heart, for all his distress at Jackson's wounding. There had been murmurs: you find them in old letters, in the newspapers, and, hinted a little,

in the reports: young Jeb Stuart is a fine cavalry soldier
—yes! But he's never handled any infantry, and after
all— . . . Jeb Stuart was sensitive to such things. Arriving about midnight, he established himself on the Turnpike, and took hold with a strong hand. Since the wounding
of Jackson, about nine o'clock, a number of things had
happened. Jackson's last orders were, to Hill as he deployed: "Press them, Hill! Press them. Cut them off from
United States Ford!" Jackson's last information, when
these orders were given, was that there existed no organized
enemy line of battle on his front—this, from an officer who
had made a hasty reconnaissance. Then he went to see for
himself, but when he came back, he was shot, and gave no
more orders. The next event was a storm of artillery, from
blue guns, very near, at Fairview Cemetery, which caused
loss and disorder in Hill's troops on the Turnpike, and
wounded Hill himself. Then an abortive blue attack—one
of Sickles' Brigades—had materialised against the Confederate left, glanced across Hill's front, lost direction, and
turned upon its own lines between Hazel Grove and Fairview. Stuart had these items when he took over. He issued
instructions for all formations to be closed up and put in
readiness for further movement. He sent his staff—stran-
gers to the divisional officers of Jackson's Corps—to gather
exact data. He sent Major Sandy Pendleton, of Jackson's
staff, to the wounded Lieutenant-General to see if he was
able to give advice or directions. Jackson, it developed, was
in a hell of pain, his senses dulled with the opiate they gave
him, and he couldn't collect his thoughts: he said, feebly,
"I don't know: I can't tell: say to General Stuart that he
must do what he thinks best."

As was his habit, he had told nobody in his Corps what he
intended. There were no written orders. Rodes, Colston
(commanding Trible's division), and A. P. Hill had con-

ferred, and agreed that the troops were not in shape to
deliver a night-attack, and their officers were engaged in
sorting out their commands and preparing for what the
morning might bring. These efforts were going forward
when Stuart arrived. He quickened them with his own un-
flagging energy. The men were much exhausted, and had
not been fed, and were scattered and intermingled, but
order began to reassert itself. Jeb Stuart sent Colonel Alexander, acting chief of Artillery since Crutchfield was
wounded—to reconnoitre the front, and Alexander did his
work thoroughly and quickly. The Confederate line was
nearly two miles long, astride the Turnpike, and back several hundred yards from the edge of the woods, where the
Federals were industriously entrenching themselves all night:
Alexander saw the Yankees, heard their axes, heard them
talk. They had infantry and guns in position, good breastworks, and abatis: their engineers this night accomplished
miracles. Stuart wanted to use his artillery: Alexander
found but two roads on which it could be moved, both narrow, and commanded by the enemy. One was the Turnpike,
running straight to Chancellorsville. Immediately south of
it, four hundred yards from the point where it debouched
upon the clearing, was Fairview Cemetery and a blue battery of twenty-seven pieces. The other road was the wood
track from the Turnpike to Hazel Grove, out of which
the 8th Pennsylvania had ridden to be destroyed by A. P.
Hill. Their infantry and guns held Hazel Grove, which
now thrust out in something of a salient, but if you took it
from them, you enfiladed the line up to Fairview, and stood
at the end of the ridge which dominated all the Chancellorsville clearing. Stuart considered that Hazel Grove, then,
was the key to the Federal position, and he massed his reserves behind his right, giving that sector his personal attention. Meantime, the moon went down, and the front was

quiet, except for the ringing of the northern axes at Fairview, and the small noises of stray soldiers looking for their commands. The wagons of the Second Corps began to arrive, and the officers came to apply for permission to feed the troops, who had not eaten, now, for twenty-four hours. And there came a message from General Lee at about three o'clock—and in forty-five minutes, a second one. He was over in front of Chancellorsville, to the right of Hazel Grove, on the south. He was going to attack as soon as it was light enough to see. He wanted Stuart to press the battle vigorously, and connect with him. The lines would join, Stuart calculated, about Hazel Grove, or a little east. He sent swift orders, which stopped the arrangements for food: rations could wait. The sky, down the Turnpike, was taking on the dawn-look. He made the last adjustments of his line, and ordered the gray infantry forward. Unlike most movements in this war, his attack got under way as a unit, exactly when he ordered it. His staff officers and couriers had galloped the lines to good purpose, and there was a rare *zero hour* touch to the thing.

Jackson's hard-bitten brigades, reduced by casualties and manœuvre to some 20,000, responded as a good horse leaps to the spur. High and clear, their yelling pierced the misty Wilderness, and their musketry shattered the dawn. They knew, now, that Stonewall Jackson was wounded, and Stuart gave them a watchword—he loved such things:—"Remember Jackson!" And riding himself to their front, he gave them a song—to the ancient fiddler's breakdown, the "Old Dan Tucker" tune——

> "Old Joe Hooker, won't you come out' the Wilderness—
> Come out' the Wilderness—
> Come out' the Wilderness—
> Old Joe Hooker, won't you come out' the Wilderness—
> Come out' the Wilderness now.' "

Very steadily the Northern men stood to meet them—the guns at Fairview, the guns at Hazel Grove, the strong blue lines between—the Third Corps, Sickles, and the Twelfth Corps, Couch, and some of Pleasanton's dragoons. North of the Turnpike, there was charge and counter-charge, in the woods and out of them, and a young Yankee Volunteer Colonel, Nelson Miles, gained the admiration of his friends and the respect of his adversary by the stand he made. Across the Turnpike, blue and gray volleyed into each other's faces for hours. But on the right, the fight grew gigantic. In less than a mile of front, a hundred guns contended. There was five hours of hard battle. Twice the gray infantry, having gained the edge of the woods, rushed up to the breastworks in the clear, and twice the Yankee canister and musketry threw them back. The reports here grow almost lyrical: sober colonels describe Jeb Stuart, on a great bright charger, leading the infantry waves, with a voice that dominated the tumult, and that song. . . . He rode with the first guns into the open where the Turnpike entered the Chancellor clearing. Twice he led the 28th North Carolina regiment in a charge. His fine horse Chancellor is killed early in the day: he mounts another, a big blood-bay, and dashes into a regiment that has broken under the Northern rifles and is running back: snatches their battle flag from the color bearer, turns them about with a ringing, brazen voice, and leads them against the flaming breastworks with their flag in his hands. He rides ahead of the last assault, leaps his big horse through the drifting smoke, over the Yankee fortifications, and the animal stands, with flaring nostrils, above the dead and the débris, between two silent guns. The gray infantry flood up behind him. Jeb Stuart halloos his people forward to the chase, and the fight streamed across the clearing, up from Hazel Grove.

Confederate gunners, hot with whip and spur, ran their

guns into battery on the ridge, and swept the Fairview lines. The flank elements of the Second Corps were aware of blue fragments that fled across their front, and of a growing racket to the south. Out of the woods, down there, broke the red battle flags of McLaws and Anderson: Lee's army was united again, and Lee rode upon the field in the midst of his troops.

They say, who saw it, that the moment was such a one as lives in the hearts of men through any after-life of dullness or of glory. The line was everywhere in the open, with its fierce flags swooping on. White smoke of musketry fringed the infantry advance, and white smoke shot with red flashes swirled about the guns. The shells howled overhead, and the small arms made a crackling tumult, and there was wide outcry. The Wilderness to the south was burning, and a long smudge rolled up from its depths. Chancellor House had taken fire and was wrapped in flames. The army of Northern Virginia, swung as a keen scythe is swung, saw its chief, and raised a wild triumphant shouting. Under Lee's eye, they hustled the last of Hooker from the open ground into the Wilderness to the north.

Now it was ten o'clock in the morning of 3 May. Lee did not rest, for the thing was yet incomplete: always he was feeling for the Cannæ-battle—the battle of annihilation. North of Chancellorsville, from a mile to two miles, Hooker's Army stood. It had been driven, but it still existed. Lee proceeded rapidly to reform his divisions, get his guns forward, and prepare the final blow. He proposed immediate assault. The blue people were in great strength, but they were huddled in small compass, and were a beaten strength. Then, at eleven o'clock, before he could begin, word came from Early: Marye's Heights were lost, and Fredericksburg. Sedgwick was moving on

Lee's rear. And Sedgwick had nearly as many men as Lee. The attack was suspended. McLaws, in line of battle on the right, was drawn off and sent by the Plank Road to Salem Church; Wilcox, of Anderson's, at Bank's Ford, was started to join him. At Salem Church they met Sedgwick, in the late afternoon of 3 May, and checked him. Lee came up with the rest of Anderson, and on the 4th, Sedgwick was driven slowly back on Bank's Ford, while the Second Corps, now less than 20,000 men, held Hooker's 60,000 to his lines. Hooker thinks that Sedgwick—one corps—should have come to help him.

He is badly beaten, is Joe Hooker, although only half of his army actually has been engaged. The morning of the 3rd, while they fought at Fairview, half a mile away, and he watched from Chancellor House, a shell stunned him. But, since the 1st, his thoughts have been all defensive: he thinks now only of getting away. His engineers, and his veteran troops, on the 4th, strengthen mightily his lines: the enemy must come at him across the open, in front, and he lies in good cover. On the 4th, there is a truce for some hours, and gray officers and blue meet between the lines, all very pleasant and gentlemanly. Carl Shurz, the German soldier of the Union, now a division commander, writes in his diary that he could not help feeling attracted to General Stuart, "the young enemy who seemed so gay and brave."

The gray intention is plain. Obvious reconnaissances, and steady, harrassing fire of artillery, all indicate that Lee will attack him when he is through with Sedgwick. And on the 5th, Lee is at liberty to attend to Hooker, against whom he can array perhaps 45,000 men. His generals are dubious: staff says, it can't be done—frontal attack on fortified lines, they in cover, we in the clear—no! What Jeb Stuart says is not recorded. The blue generals were calm and confident.

But there were, apparently, two men on the ground who thought Lee would attack successfully—they were General Lee and General Joseph Hooker.

The 5th breaks dark and stormy, with wind and a driving rain making the roads too heavy for his guns, and Lee waits, perforce, for clearing weather. The 6th comes, and the gray lines go forward. Hooker's works are empty. Cavalry comes in from the flank and reports him crossing the Rappahannock: he was entirely over by eight o'clock the morning of the 6th.

In the period, from the 29th of April to the 6th of May, Hooker lost 16,844 men and thirteen guns, out of 130,000 on the field, and he returned on 8 May to the old camps behind Falmouth. Lee's army lost, out of 57,000 engaged—every man put into battle—12,777, and, more than all of them, Stonewall Jackson. For on the 10th of May, at Guiney's Station, Lieutenant General Thomas Jonathan Jackson died, he being in his 40th year. He had stood, well enough, the amputation of his left arm, and the bullet wound in the chest was healing. He was thought to be nicely on the mend. Then pneumonia took him. "Any victory," says Lee, "would be dear at such a price. I know not how to replace him."

Chancellorsville was a barren victory. A tactical masterpiece, up to a certain point, bold surpassingly in conception, possible only for veteran troops of the highest valor and skill, it had no effect on the situation in Virginia, or on the strategic aspect of the war. The Confederates had the gleaning of the field—some 20,000 muskets, stores, 13 guns; and 6,000 prisoners to feed. Otherwise, Joe Hooker still stood on the Rappahannock. There was no pursuit, no drawing of the enemy, as Lee drew Pope, on to destruction. Perhaps it was because Jackson was not there any more. But the evidence is that the Richmond Government held Lee's arm:

the Richmond Government could not see the difference between a victory and an incomplete victory, and Mr. Davis and his advisers hoped for a northern anti-war reaction, and for European aid, quickened by Hooker's disaster. So, Lee went back to Fredericksburg, and they buried the dead, and Captain Melzi Chancellor, whose father owned much of the property over which the battle was fought, took a wagon down to Ely's Ford and got a big whitish rock, something that looks like quartz, and placed it where Stonewall Jackson fell. There you can see it to this day, just east of the Jackson monument, by the Orange Turnpike.

On the 5th of May Jeb Stuart wired his wife: "God has spared me through another bloody battle and given us the victory yesterday and the day before. I commanded Jackson's corps yesterday. He and A. P. Hill were wounded the day before . . . Hullihen wounded. My horse killed."

On the 7th, he wired again: "All well. I am again in command of the cavalry, A. P. Hill having reported for duty. Enemy cleared out yesterday. I go now after Stoneman. He is said to be crossing the Rapidan going back. A glorious victory at Chancellorsville."

But he did not catch Stoneman: that morning, Stoneman got over at Raccoon Ford and rejoined the blue army. He had made a good deal of trouble on the Virginia Central, burned bridges and water tanks, and torn up the track in places. But in his mission, which was to draw the Confederate cavalry after him, he had failed, and his absence from Chancellorsville was the circumstance that made possible Jackson's flank march. Cavalry took up the familiar posts along the river: Hampton's Brigade rejoined, much refreshed, from the south, and things fell quiet for some days.

Stuart drew up and sent in his report on the campaign. It is a report sufficiently modest, in view of what the young

Major General had accomplished. His little cavalry regiments, confronted by the weight of Stoneman's sabres, had kept their equipoise, and held fast to the true function of cavalry: to be the eyes and ears of the army: to screen movements that the enemy must not see: to guard the flanks and rear, to be in readiness for special missions. Then, the night of the 2nd, Jeb Stuart had been summoned in anxious haste to pick up the sword that fell from Stonewall Jackson's hand. Seldom has there been a situation so obscure, so full of potentialities for success and failure. Jackson had struck a tremendous blow, and his Corps was like a wave, halted in mid-career: it might gather impetus and roll forward again, grinding matters small; or it might collapse upon itself, impotent. The gray formations were disorganized by the very speed and force of their attack. Darkness, and the tangled Wilderness all around, hampered the efforts of the regimental officers. A brave and by no means demoralized enemy, not yet involved in disaster, was in close contact on the front. Alexander, the artillery colonel, a trained soldier and the sanest of the Confederate commentators, describes the condition of Jackson's command, in the hours between the fatal volley that struck down the Lieutenant General, and the arrival of Jeb Stuart, as dubious at best; and he makes it plain that the surviving gray generals were not only against pushing the battle that night, but were apprehensive for the safety of their troops. And Alexander thinks there was "no more brilliant thing done in the war than Stuart's extricating that command from the extremely critical position in which he found it, as promptly and boldly as he did." Hear Alexander again, "We knew that Hooker had at least 80,000 infantry at hand—" (Hooker did have 60,000)—"and that his axmen were entrenching his position all night, and in that thick undergrowth, a very little cutting gave an abatis or entanglement that a rabbit could hardly get through. . . . We had little chance in the night even to hunt for the best place to make our attack. But Stuart never seemed to hesitate or to doubt for one moment that he could crash his way wherever he chose to strike. He decided to attack at daylight, and unlike many planned attacks that I have seen, this one came off promptly on time, and it never stopped to draw its breath until it had crashed through everything and our forces stood united around Chancellor's burning house."

It is true that there appears, in the reports of colonels and brigadiers, a certain inference that the infantry of the Second Corps, on the morning of 3 May, was handled a little recklessly by the Cavalry General. Thrown too carelessly, perhaps, against cannon and strong entrenchments. But when Stuart hit, with horse or foot or guns, he hit hard, and the answer to his critics is that the thing worked, and that the gray infantry, in spite of losses, had spirit and stamina enough to pen Hooker in his last ditch through the 4th and the 5th, and were quite ready to assail him again on the 6th. The simple soldiers, who carry the war to the flaming point of contact, stand killing better than their generals do—or most of their generals. Yet, Stuart was supersensitive, and always rose to criticism, whether just or not. We have a calming letter to him, from Lee, written evidently in answer to a hurt note of Stuart's: Lee assures him of his entire satisfaction with Stuart's conduct of the battle. And Lee, courteous always, and kind, never used words idly, or gave praise without sound cause. Another echo lies in a letter of Stuart's to his brother, William Alexander, written after Chancellorsville: he says proudly that his battle dispositions had the approval of General Lee and of his own conscience, "whatever else others might say. Nor am I forgetful that we are not fighting for fame, however gratifying the approval of our own countrymen may be—" But Jeb

Stuart likes fame. So does any soldier, worth his rations
—any man.

In the days after Chancellorsville, it became necessary to
make a new Lieutenant General for the Second Corps,
vacant on the death of Stonewall Jackson. The decision lay
with the Commanding General: it is pleasant to note, in the
full and free correspondence between General Lee and
Jefferson Davis, that the Richmond government thrust no
unwanted officers upon the Army of Northern Virginia,
however queer the appointments might run elsewhere. For
a time the Generals of Brigade and Division, conscious of
merit—it was a proud, touchy, and individualistic service,
this gray army—were much astir. There were several out-
standing officers: D. H. Hill, a very fine and skilful leader,
and A. P. Hill, of splendid reputation, were the most discussed. Also, the name of the Major General of Cavalry had
its supporters: who could better succeed Jackson than the
man who fought his Corps when he fell? Jeb Stuart writes
his wife, "there has been a great deal of talk of my succeeding General Jackson, but I think without foundation in
fact." And a letter from Lee to Stuart thanks Stuart for
"your views on General Jackson's successor—" Stuart's
letter, here referred to, is not preserved, and I cannot find
what his views were, but he must have recommended
somebody. I cannot find that he himself expected the commission.

Lee, keeping his own counsel, chose Major General
Richard S. Ewell, "dear Dick Ewell," who is this month out
of hospital, with a peg in place of the limb he left at Groveton in August, '62, hopping around on crutches, more like a
bird than ever. It was said that Jackson, before he died, discussed the matter and gave out as his opinion, that Ewell deserved, by service and seniority, to have the Second Corps.
Ewell was Jackson's favorite division commander, and they

had worked well together. He was loved by his troops, looked after them, and fought them well, in the Valley, on the Peninsula, and in the Second Manassas Campaign. But he was a man not young: he had been maimed, with attendant shock and stress, and he seems, after that, to have lacked vitality. I think D. H. Hill would have been in all respects a better corps comander, and A. P. Hill was a better corps commander, on the same ground. And I think that Jeb Stuart would have come nearest to swinging Jackson's sword than any of them. Take some contemporary evidence: Alexander's again; "I always thought it an injustice to Stuart and a loss to the army that he was not from that moment" (after Chancellorsville, he means) *"continued in command of Jackson's corps. He had won the right to it. I believe he had all of Jackson's genius and dash and originality, without the eccentricity of character which sometimes led to disappointment. For instance: Jackson went into camp near Shady Grove Church before sunset on the 26th of June, 1862, when he might have participated in the battle of Mechanicsville. This, and his feeble action at White Oak Swamp, on the 30th of June, 1862, show that Jackson's spirit and inspiration were uneven. Stuart, however, possessed the rare quality of being always equal to himself at his very best."

One more word on Jackson, with all admiration and respect: his biographers feel that he was struck down with his job but half completed, and that, if he had continued on the field, he would have encompassed Hooker's utter destruction. This is based on his last utterance—"Press them! Cut them off from United States Ford!"

It could not have been done. To reach United States Ford, Jackson's corps would have had to batter through miles of the Wilderness, with no roads for the artillery, and to stamp over 60,000 blue infantry behind strong fortifications. Only a general panic would have made it possible. Nor, I think, would Jackson have tried to do it.

It is hard to criticise Lee's judgment. The weight of his responsibility was to him not only official, but personal. He did the best he could, from every aspect. No man ever had less cause to reproach himself, for things done or undone. But it seems to me that in passing over Jeb Stuart— if indeed he passed him over—he committed one of his few grave mistakes. Stuart was junior to many officers in the army, both in rank and service, and very young, we know Lee thought, for a Major General. That may have worked against him in his mind, but we do not know. I think, myself, that it was a question, with Lee, of making the best use of the tools he had. His dependence on the cavalry—Jeb Stuart—for his services of security and information, was very great, and increasingly, as the war went on, the Commanding General relied on his mounted arm. In Jeb Stuart he had a lieutenant who could be trusted. And there did not exist in the Confederacy, so far as Lee knew, another who could replace him. And Cavalry is mostly over the horizon, while you can keep your eye on an infantry corps. Stuart might have led the gray foot as dashingly as he ever led his troopers. But Lee kept him where he was, and Ewell became Lieutenant General, commanding the Second Corps, A. N. Va.

XVII

THE BATTLE OF FLEETWOOD HEIGHTS

CAVALRY, after Chancellorsville, had a few weeks of reduced activity: Hooker lay quiet, and made no movements south of the river. About the end of May, Stuart's command received, in addition to Hampton, the brigade of Beverly Robertson, made up of new levies from North Carolina; and W. E. Jones came from the Valley. Dismounted men of Fitz Lee, W. E. Jones, and Rooney Lee came back from furlough with remounts. Several hundred carbines were sent up from the ordnance depots of Colonel Gorgas. Presently there were between 9000 and 10,000 effectives in the cavalry division, the largest force that Stuart had yet commanded, and five batteries, twenty guns, in his battalion of horse artillery.

The infantry underwent its final reorganization. A. P. Hill was promoted Lieutenant-General, and three corps were formed, of four divisions each. The order ran, Longstreet, the First, Ewell, the Second, and A. P. Hill the Third Corps. Artillery was redistributed: Colonel Pendleton was made Brigadier-General and Chief of Artillery, and there was a battalion to each corps, with a reserve battalion under the hand of the Commanding General. The rolls show, present for duty in the Army of Northern Virginia, 72,000 men, with 287 guns. At Fredericksburg the previous winter Lee had commanded a few more soldiers than this, but the army he now had was in all respects the strongest and ablest force he ever led to battle. The spirit of the troops was high and exultant: whatever else Chancellorsville accomplished, it raised the morale of the gray people to a peak: they were ready for anything. Correspondence goes between Lee and his Presi-

dent; it is time to invade the North again. Lee will go by
the Valley, with the long wall of the Blue Ridge to cover his
communications, from the rail head of the Virginia Central
at Staunton, up to the Potomac, thence through Maryland,
and into Pennsylvania. The army of Hooker, all the blue
forces in Virginia, would be drawn after him, to cover Washington. Up there, he could choose his objective: perhaps the
Susquehanna bridges, perhaps Baltimore—Philadelphia—
he would see. The main objective was, as always, to free
Virginia: the ultimate mission to bring to battle and destroy
the Army of the Potomac. Otherwise, all plans were nebulous.
Lee thinks, and suggests it, delicately—for a general must
speak delicately to Mr. Jefferson Davis, commander-in-chief
of the combat forces of the Confederate States, and working
at it—that a reserve should be formed, to advance from
Richmond to the Rappahannock line, and maintain the
menace against Washington from the south. The troops can
be found, he hints—and indeed, they exist: the South is spotted with small detachments, dispersed on obscure and idle
missions—and Beauregard, who never lost, in the North, at
least, his great prestige, might command them. Should Lee,
as he expects to, make good his lodgment north of the Potomac, Beauregard and such an army would make it possible
for him to stay there. These things you see in Lee's careful
letters, of May and June, 1863. But Mr. Davis, ignoring
his interior lines, never seeing his war in its large perspective,
was thinking in water-tight compartments. So the Confederacy launched on its last high adventure. The rank and file
were confident. The Commanding General kept, in his strong
gray head, whatever misgivings he may have had. We come
to the Gettysburg campaign.

In the early days of June, Ewell's Corps withdraws from
his camps and marches to Culpeper: A. P. Hill, in line on
the river, stands fast, where Hooker can watch him, and

Ewell is unobserved. Longstreet's Corps has marching orders, and leaves Fredericksburg. Traffic, trending westward, is reported by Hooker's balloons: he falls into doubt and perplexity: thinks the enemy may be getting ready to strike at him by the upper fords of the Rappahannock: more fighting on Manassas Plain. He begins a slow shifting of corps toward Centreville. Patrols that he sends to the upper river are driven back by vigilant gray horsemen. All his services of information fail. He has Pleasanton up, and gives him orders.

These days, the gray cavalry division, basing on Culpeper, undergoes a great burnishing and polishing. The Major-General commanding puts on his West Point manner, harassing plain combat colonels, southern gentlemen who prefer informal war. The negro servants, the spare shirts, the Day and Martin boot-polish, with which the gentlemen rankers rode to battle in '61—they are forgotten things. You see elegant young men greasing their own leather, and shining their metal with wood ashes, and grooming their horses. Jeb Stuart hopes that the Commanding General will come over and review his brigades. Letters pass, but Lee is very busy, and on June 5, Jeb Stuart holds his own review, in the open fields between Brandy Station and Culpeper. It is a brilliant occasion, with ladies and gentlemen from all over the region banked behind the reviewing stand. Eight thousand cavalry, Hampton, Fitz Lee, Rooney Lee, Jones and Robertson, all the men who can be spared from the outpost line, pass in review, in column of squadrons, first at a walk, then at a thundering gallop, Jeb Stuart taking the march-past. Opposite the reviewing stand, the massed horse artillery battalion fires salutes, a noble, war-like noise, with highly decorative white smoke clouds curling up the blue heaven. Stuart indulged to the full his taste for pomp and panoply, and even the hard-worked troopers, cursing the spit-and-polish ideas of their chief, record that it was a good show. Then, on the 7th, a note was received from headquarters of the army: the Commanding General would, on the 8th of June, be pleased to review his cavalry division.

Much harassed, the brigades spent another day in feverish preparation, and assembled in the same fields under the eye of Lee, who came with his staff and some distinguished personages from Richmond. It was, however, less of a spectacle. General Lee excused the artillery, in view of the work he had laid out for them, and did not desire the regiments to gallop: it was better to spare the horses. But it was still a very fine occasion, all the sabres, the groomed horses of a riding people, the bright flags, and the lean, bronzed troopers, ardent for the war.

" . . . I reviewed the cavalry in this section yesterday," Lee wrote his wife. "It was a splendid sight. The men and horses looked well. They have recuperated since last fall. Stuart was in all his glory. Your sons and nephews were well and flourishing. . . ."

Over at Culpeper, Longstreet has marched in, and Ewell is headed northwest, for the Valley.

On 8 June, following the cavalry review, the Commanding General gave Stuart his orders: he was to cross the Rappahannock next day and cover, on the right, the northward movement of Longstreet and Ewell, the first stage on the road that led to Gettysburg. That night, instructions were issued to the cavalry: camp would be broken and the brigades conducted to position at daylight on the 9th. Headquarters were on Fleetwood Heights, and had been for some days. The evening of the 8th tents and camp furniture were stored in the escort wagons and sent off to Culpeper to follow with the trains of the army. That night, Stuart and his staff bivouacked on Fleetwood, with a pair of tent flies against the dew.

Fleetwood Heights is a low ridge, partly wooded, partly pasture, on the Barbour Farm, running north for a little more than a mile from the Orange and Alexandria railroad. Brandy Station is at its southern foot, and it takes its name from Fleetwood house, that looks down on Brandy Station. Eastward, about three miles, is the Rappahannock, and the road to Beverly Ford skirts east of the ridge and turns to the river at its northern end. Half a mile north is the little Hazel River. A mile east of about the centre of the ridge is St. James Church. Six miles southeast is Kelly's Ford, and six miles southwest, Culpeper Court House. From Fleetwood, the valley of the Rappahannock lies before you, but a hill to the west, Barbour's Hill, cuts off the view toward Culpeper.

The ridge was about in the centre of Stuart's distribution.

As late as the 8th, the region north of the river had been empty of blue patrols, and Hooker, down the Rappahannock, lay apparently quite tranquil. Stuart's orders directed concentration for movement to a new station, and that night, Fitz Lee's brigade was assembled near Oak Shade Church, five miles from Fleetwood, north of Hazel River, with a battery of horse artillery. Immediately east of the north end of the ridge was Rooney Lee's brigade, which maintained an advanced picket on Welford's Ford, north of Beverly's. Next in line was W. E. Jones, his brigade camped in the woods by St. James Church, and his pickets watching Beverly Ford, two miles east of the church, and Rappahannock Station, on the railroad crossing. South of the railroad were Wade Hampton's camps, between Brandy Station and Stevensburg. Somewhat in advance of Hampton was Robertson's brigade, watching Kelly's and the fords below, and charged with the defence of the direct road to Culpeper. The battalion of horse artillery, four batteries, with Major Beckham's headquarters, was parked in the woods near St. James Church. This, as events developed, was the weak point in the dispositions. The brigades were generally in supporting distance, but the horse artillery—less the battery with Fitz Lee—was grouped too close to the Rappahannock. Stuart expected no immediate fighting south of the river.

Now, there was some alarm at Federal headquarters, unknown to the Confederate camps. Hooker had urgent rumors that Jeb Stuart had collected 20,000 sabres over at Culpeper, and was preparing a grander raid than any yet seen. Washington had the same rumor, and was inclined to think there might be something in it. It was ordered that Hooker send his cavalry over to break up Stuart's concentration. Stoneman had passed, one of the scapegoats of Chancellorsville, and Pleasanton led the blue horse. His picture shows a handsome man, with a thoughtful, somewhat heavy face. He and Stuart had been at West Point together, and Von Borcke says that Stuart never liked him, because of his foppish ways.

North of the Rappahannock, through the quiet afternoon of the 8th, a strong blue cavalry force was approaching. It was commanded by General Alfred Pleasanton, and formed in two columns, the 2d and 3d Cavalry Divisions, and Russel's Infantry Brigade, under Gregg, and the 1st Cavalry Division, the Reserve Cavalry Brigade, and Ames' Infantry Brigade, under John Buford. It numbered 10,000 men, with five batteries of horse artillery.

This Pleasanton, for more than a year, has been studying the art of war with his schoolmate Jeb Stuart, and he is capable of learning. His orders from Hooker, down at Fredericksburg, were to cross the Rappahannock at the upper fords, find Stuart, and whip him. Pleasanton moved rapidly and skillfully, so that no gray scouts saw or reported him, and he camped the night of the 8th without fire or bugle. His points crept out to the Rappahannock fords and ascertained that the Confederate pickets were entirely unalarmed. In view of his projected movement, everything had been drawn in from the north bank by Stuart: only the watchers of the crossings remained. Pleasanton estimated the situation, and issued orders. One column, Buford, would cross at Beverly Ford, above the railroad. The other, Gregg, would cross below, at Kelly's. Both columns would converge on Brandy Station. Gregg would have the longest distance to go, moving indirectly, by the Stevensburg detour, and Buford would move first to keep attention from him.

At dawn, Davis' Brigade of Buford, headed by the 8th New York, rushed Beverly Ford, which was guarded by a company of the 6th Virginia of Grumble Jones. The road was narrow, and the company, although surprised, resisted vigorously, long enough for the alarm to go to the regiment, some distance to the rear, and for the regiment to alert the parked artillery, at St. James Church. But Davis drove hard, and came up from the ford with all his strength behind him. The 6th Virginia, led by Major Flournoy, charged down the road at a gallop, and crashed into the head of Davis' column, the fences and ditches there preventing either force from deploying. There was vicious fighting: Davis was killed by a lieutenant of the 6th Virginia; but the weight of his brigade forced the 6th Virginia aside, with a loss of thirty men and horses—heavy casualties for a cavalry regiment. The fight came up to the very edge of the artillery camp, and Stuart was near losing his guns. The artillery trains galloped to the rear in great confusion, and the field desk of the artillery commander, Major Beckham, bounced out of the headquarters wagon, and was picked up by Buford's men. It contained Beckham's official files, and on its capture Pleasanton based his claim, in his report, of taking Jeb Stuart's headquarters documents.

The batteries got off under the cover of canister from two of Hart's howitzers, and drew clear to unlimber beyond the fields, west of St. James Church. While this went on, the 7th Virginia, led by General Jones in person, just from his blankets, without coat or boots, came into action, charged, and was repulsed, and Jones and Flournoy, all mingled with pursuing Yankees, rode over Hart's howitzers. Hart's gunners defended themselves with pistols and sponge staffs, and, miraculously, got their guns away. The rest of Jones came into line, and from up-stream, Rooney Lee, like a good soldier, marched to the sound of the guns. Behind Davis' brigade, Buford came on in force, dragoons, horse artillery, and the plodding brigade of infantry. When Jeb Stuart, galloping from his morning coffee on Fleetwood Heights, reached St. James Church, he found Jones and Rooney Lee in line of battle, the sharpshooter companies of each regiment dismounted, and the sabre companies formed in readiness for developments, while the blue people built up to the front. Stuart's position made a deep re-entrant, the angle at St. James Church, Jones to the right, his back to the railroad, facing generally north, and Rooney Lee facing east. Hampton, with four regiments, was riding from Brandy Station, and formed to the right of Jones. Three regiments of Rooney Lee were out on the left, in a commanding location, just south of Hazel River, and a regiment of Fitz Lee's came down to help. Buford faced the centre of the angle, and was effectively blocked, and Jeb Stuart redistributed his guns and improved his position, with intent to drive the enemy.

Back on Fleetwood Heights was stationed Stuart's adjutant, Major McClellan, maintaining headquarters with a force of couriers: to him all messages were routed, and there was still Robertson and part of Hampton, unengaged to the south, beyond the railroad. Hampton has two regiments near Brandy Station, detached by Stuart's orders to watch the rear. With Robertson, these numbered 1500 sabres. Robertson, about dawn, had moved with his brigade out the direct road to Kelly's Ford, and as he went, his pickets ran back to meet him, reporting that a strong Federal column had forced Kelly's and were moving, around to his right, on Stevensburg. Robertson reported this fact, and asked for instructions, falling back, meantime, toward Brandy Station, with some idea of covering Hampton's flank and rear. And here, Robertson's part of the battle ended. His brigade did nothing all day. Up to its left, and around in its right and rear, the hottest kind of fighting raged. Robertson's original orders placed him along the direct road from Kelly's Ford to Brandy Station, and on that road he remained.

Gregg's column had no difficulty at Kelly's Ford. It bore left, on Stevensburg, rode two miles to the fork, and divided: Gregg, with the main body, turned northward toward Brandy Station, and Duffié, with a detachment, bore west to Stevensburg. The plan was for Gregg to assail Stuart's right flank, while Duffié rode around into his rear, and also watched toward Fredericksburg, from which direction might come gray reinforcing infantry.

But Hampton's regiments were across the Stevensburg road, above the fords; Colonel Butler, with the 2d North Carolina, and Colonel Wickham, with the 4th Virginia. They met Duffié's detachment, and made a very stubborn fight in front of Stevensburg, and then north of Stevensburg, where they finally checked him. By that time, Gregg with his main column was having all he could handle, and ordered Duffié back by the road he had come.

It was Gregg who made the trouble. While Buford was firmly held, and Duffié slowed up, Gregg's column passed around Robertson, by empty roads, toward Fleetwood Heights. Major McClellan, watching the cannon smoke that rolled up from the woods at St. James Church, was hailed by a breathless courier: the Yankees were coming up to Brandy Station, right down there! McClellan says he was not acquainted with this courier—a trooper of Robertson's —and Yankees in that direction were absurd! He told the man to go back and make sure. He could, he was informed, ride to the south end of the ridge and see for himself. He rode, and saw Gregg's thousands, already within cannon shot. He sent a courier to General Stuart: kill your horses! There was at hand a gun of Chew's, a 6-pounder, under Lieutenant Carter, come back from St. James Church to replenish ammunition, and standing now east of Fleetwood. He sent for it, and it came upon the ridge at a gallop, and began industriously to brown Gregg's column down to the south. Gregg halted, formed line of battle, unlimbered three rifled guns, and subjected the vacant Heights to a thorough shelling. He had been fired on from that commanding point, and he reasoned that it would be, naturally, held in force. He made elaborate preparations for a decisive attack.

There followed an anxious time for Major McClellan. He sent his last courier to the General, a mile away, with the most urgent expressions. Except for the single gun crew, he was alone. And down at St. James Church, Stuart turns angrily and incredulously from the first galloper. The Yankees simply couldn't be coming down that direction—he had not yet heard from Robertson, and Robertson would be in their way. He told a staff officer to "ride back and see what that foolishness is about!" and turned his attention to Buford. Then he heard Carter's 6-pounder, and the blue rifled guns, and was convinced. He withdrew a regiment and a battalion of Jones', the 12th Virginia and the 35th Battalion, and sent them on the run. They had a mile and a half to go, but they rode upon Fleetwood as Carter was withdrawing, his last load expended, and as the Englishman, Colonel Percy Wyndham, with the 1st New Jersey Regiment, was mounting the slope to seize the crest. Major McClellan dashed to meet Colonel Harmon of the 12th: for God's sake, charge! They're right on you! Harmon charged, taking no time to go from column into line, and the 35th Battalion charged, but only the leading files were effective, and both commands were ridden off by Wyndham. Forced to the left, they reformed and came on again, while Gregg, regiment on regiment, stormed up from the south. Jeb Stuart, realizing, when he heard the guns at Fleetwood, that he was turned, had delayed long enough to despatch orders to Rooney Lee, Jones, and Hampton. That done, he followed Harmon's 12th, and galloped upon the ridge as Wyndham broke his cavalry.

It was between ten o'clock and eleven in the forenoon, and for the next few hours the heaviest cavalry fighting of the war raged at Fleetwood Heights. Hampton came in first, then Rooney Lee, and finally Jones, who, with great skill and courage, kept such a resolute face turned to Buford's front that Buford did little more than follow his orderly retirement. Gregg attacked hotly. His guns advanced to the foot of the slope, on the west side, and his horse went up by squadrons from the southward end. Colonel Harmon, reformed, drove at them from their left, was wounded in personal combat with a Yankee colonel, and saw his regiment broken again. The blue lines began to advance astride the ridge, a horse battery aiding from their left. But two of Harmon's squadrons got together and rode down the three rifled guns, Martin's battery, that had done well at Chancellorsville. There was desperate fighting around the pieces:

Martin's blue cannoneers defended themselves with pistols and linstocks and sponge staffs until thirty out of thirty-six were killed or wounded. Blue cavalry came up and drove off the Virginians, but the gun teams had been shot or run off, and the guns could be neither moved nor put into action.

Hampton arrived, four regiments in column of squadrons, and Stuart, watching from the ridge, ordered him to charge Gregg's right. The Carolinians and Mississippians, yelling, swept around the Heights, and struck Gregg's flank, riding through and beyond it as far as a battery which he was holding in reserve. The battery opened, and scattered them, but they rallied and rode over it, taking their losses. All of Gregg's right and centre was involved, and for some minutes the fight swayed back and forth in clouds of smoke and dust, so thick that those who watched from the hill could not see who was winning and who lost. Finally, it was apparent that the tumult was rolling eastward: Gregg was giving ground. The observers note that this conflict, between Hampton's four regiments and about as many of Gregg's, was one of the most important hand-to-hand combats between the two armies in the four years of the war. Hampton's men used the sabre only. His right echelon, a little behind the main body, charged up the Heights from the northeast, and cleared them of Wyndham's men who had lodged there. These were driven off, to the west, and took refuge on the high spur of Fleetwood called Barbour's Hill. Then Hart's battery, supported by sections of McGregor and Chew, galloped to the crest, and opened plunging fire on Gregg, below them. With this, Gregg's attack ceased: the last incident at Fleetwood was the escape of the Jerseymen of Wyndham's, who rode out through Hart's unsupported battery and cut their way back to Gregg.

Meantime, Rooney Lee and Jones had fought a rear-guard action, falling back from the line of St. James Church. Buford pressed them hard, worked a brigade around by the north, and got behind Rooney Lee. The big Brigadier led his regiments in a dash to clear the way, and fought with Buford's regulars on the northern slopes of Fleetwood. Rooney Lee was shot from his saddle, badly wounded, and one of his colonels was killed. Munford came across Hazel River, with two regiments of Fitz Lee's, and got into Buford's right. By this time, the fight had rolled away from the other end of Fleetwood Heights: Gregg had manœuvred into touch with Buford at St. James, and Duffié had rejoined from Stevensburg. Pleasanton had reports of gray foot, approaching Brandy Station. He sends orders: they are too strong for us—come away! He drew off in good order, along the railroad, and crossed the Rappahannock at the railroad bridge, late in the afternoon. Down at Stevensburg, with Duffié, Colonel Butler had fought sharply all day. He was wounded, and Stuart's aide, Farley, was mortally wounded. Lieutenant-Colonel Frank Hampton, son of General Wade Hampton, was killed there in hand-to-hand fighting. Wade Hampton had a younger son, an aide on his staff, who was wounded during the fight with Gregg. The boy recovered. But Wade Hampton, spartan on the field, said that his surviving son must transfer into another command: such a strain on him, in addition to his military duties, was too great to be endured. . . . Captain Farley, who died the evening of the fight, deserves more than passing notice. His status was the queer one of volunteer aide: he had been in the war, on his own, since the beginning, found his own horse and arms, drew no pay from the government, and was unequalled as a scout. Since the autumn of 1861, he had served on Stuart's staff, and gained frequent mentions in reports, and was esteemed as a gallant officer and a good companion; gay and whimsical. When wounded, he was talking to Colonel Butler, both of them mounted. A projectile riccocheted from the ground beside them, carried away Butler's leg, about the ankle, went through his horse, then through Farley's horse, and took off his leg at the knee. As they picked Farley up to carry him from the field, he pointed to his leg, which lay near by, and asked for it. One handed it to him. He hugged it in his arms, and laid it gently down, saying, with a smile: "It's an old friend, gentlemen, and I do not wish to part with it." He said good-bye to all the friends he could reach, and so died, lamented and admired. Colonel Butler recovered, and served his state as U. S. Senator long afterwards.

At Brandy Station this day the Federals lost 936 officers and men, of whom 486 were prisoners, six flags, and three pieces of artillery. Pleasanton had 10,981 men, of whom all, except one brigade of infantry, were engaged. He saw some infantry—Ewell's, but he did not identify it, for he withdrew before it got into action; and this was the only piece of information he brought back as to Lee's movements: Confederate infantry near Culpeper. How much was there, what it was doing, where it was going, he did not learn, so Hooker remained as much in the dark as ever. And he did not whip Stuart.

Jeb Stuart had—by his return of 30 May, 9,536 sabres, five brigades, twenty-one regiments. Of these, he engaged fifteen regiments, most of Fitz Lee and all of Robertson's brigade being unemployed. Although forced back, locally, he kept his fighting forces together, and remained in possession of the field, accomplishing his routine mission, which was, here, to shield Lee's movements from observation. His total loss was 523 officers and men, the wounded including Rooney Lee and Colonel Butler, two able and valued veterans. One of his regiments lost a flag. Considering the fact that he suffered a tactical surprise—one of the few that the blue cavalry achieved—his recovery was praiseworthy, and his fighting through the day as good as he ever did. The important failure of the battle, on the Confederate side, lay with Beverly Robertson, and it would have been fortunate for the Confederacy if he had been relieved from command. But events crowded fast upon the cavalry, and he was allowed to continue with his brigade. State politics seem to have entered into the affair: Robertson was important and esteemed in North Carolina, from which state came most of his regiments, and just then Jefferson Davis was having as much trouble with Zebulon Vance, the Tar-Heel war governor, as he could conveniently handle. Stuart's judgments on Brandy Station were unusually mild, for him, and he seems to have considered that everybody did as well as they could. But he must have felt—although his letters do not show it—that Brandy Station was an ominous fight. For the first time in the war, blue cavalry had come over in dangerous force, provoked combat, inflicted heavy damage, and gotten away in good order. The gray troopers would no longer have it all their own way. Those Yankees, they conceded, could always fight: now they were learning to ride and fight at the same time. In Brandy Station, Gettysburg was foreshadowed, and Sheridan, and the last scene at Yellow Tavern.

A few days before the battle, a correspondent from a Richmond paper reported to Jeb Stuart's headquarters: the writing fellow proposed to accompany the cavalry through the next campaign, "which," writes the General to his wife, "I politely declined. He returns tomorrow with a flea in his ear. Look to see me abused for it." He was right, about the abuse. Three days after the fight, he wrote her: "God has spared me through another bloody battle and blessed with victory our arms. . . . It will be called the battle of Fleetwood Heights. . . ." (Wrong: he so reported it, but it is called by the mellow name of Brandy Station, north and south.) He goes on to give her news of the staff: Farley killed, Captain White wounded, Lieutenant Goldsborough captured. Then—he has seen the public prints—"the papers are in great error, as usual, about the whole transaction. It was no surprise. The enemy's movement was known and we defeated him. The *Examiner* of the 12th lies from beginning to end. I lost no papers—no nothing. I will, of course, take no notice of such falsehood. . . ." As a matter of fact, the *Examiner*, cut off from news at its source, had simply rewritten Pleasanton's account of the fight as set forth in the northern press, and Pleasanton's claims were extravagant enough. He made a great fuss over that field desk of Beckham's. If you are interested, you can find, in the files of the *Examiner* a few days later, a long, indignant letter, signed *Veritas*, or some such name. It purports to be from the pen of a staff officer of the cavalry division, and gives the Stuart side of it, and breathes a splendid indignation against slander, envy, and so forth. Tradition ascribes it to Stuart's good staff surgeon, Talcott Eliason. But the style is much like Stuart's own.

After Brandy Station, we see no more of Rooney Lee. He was shot dangerously in the thigh toward the end of the fight at Fleetwood Heights. As soon as he was well enough to move, they carried him down to Colonel Wickham's place, Hickory Hill, near Hanover Court House, where his wife could nurse him, and where he was thought to be safe from raiding Yankees. His brother, the youngest son of the commanding general, Robert, Junior, recently discharged from the ranks of the Washington Artillery to serve on Rooney's staff as lieutenant and aide-de-camp, was sent with him, and no other soldier. At that time, the Federals had captured some Confederate naval officers, in a status held dubious on the seas, and proposed to hang them as pirates. Jefferson Davis had set aside a corresponding number of Federal officers, prisoners of war, and proposed to hang them in retaliation. While matters stood so, the location and condition of Brigadier-General W. H. F. Lee, oldest son of the Commander of the Army of Northern Virginia, became known to the Washington authorities: and, the gray army being absent Pennsylvania-way, and such enterprises, in consequence, practicable, a raiding column was formed, and dashed to Hickory Hill, and took big Rooney Lee away on a mattress, captive, to Fort Munroe, where his jailor was the ineffable Benjamin Butler. Washington, then one up, announced, in some triumph, that, if the Federal officers were hung, Rooney Lee would hang. But the case lapsed into the correspondence phase, and stayed there until late in the year 1864, Rooney Lee being denied exchange—although Davis offered any one of a number of brigadiers for him, and agreed to throw in a quantity of lesser officers. Eventually, nobody was hung, and Rooney Lee came back to his brigade—but not to Jeb Stuart. During his detention, his wife, a gay gentle lady, beloved of General Lee, her father-in-law, fell sick and wanted to see her husband before she died. Custis Lee, Brigadier-General and aide to the President, offered to give himself up as hostage if Rooney was allowed to visit his wife; President Davis took every possible step to arrange the matter. But the Yankees held their prisoner, while his wife died, calling for him. It is one of the bitter stories of the war, an affair ordered and controlled by the Northern Secretary of War from first to last. The only pleasant aspect bears on Ben Butler: when Rooney Lee came home from captivity, to be swamped with sympathy in Richmond, he stated unequivocally that General Butler —Spoon Butler of New Orleans—had treated him with every courtesy and all consideration. It took courage and character to say that in the Richmond of 1864.

XVIII

THE GETTYSBURG CAMPAIGN

JEB STUART writes his brother, William Alexander Stuart, after Brandy Station, "I am standing on the Rappahannock, looking beyond . . . and feel not unlike a tiger pausing before its spring . . . that spring will not be delayed much longer . . . I ask now, my dear brother, and best friend, that you will pray for me in the coming struggle. . . . The great and good Jackson was the dearest friend I had, and I feel that I possessed his full confidence and regard. His messages were always: 'give him my love.' His example, his Christian and soldierly virtue are a precious legacy to his countrymen and to the world."

Just after that, he, as he would say, sprang.

Lee had already begun to move, Ewell, then Longstreet, and A. P. Hill to follow. The first stage, as you have seen, is from Fredericksburg to Culpeper.

While Ewell marched toward Winchester, Longstreet lay at Culpeper, and A. P. Hill stood fast at Fredericksburg. Three days after Brandy Station, the 12th of June, Lee's corps were spaced twenty-five miles apart—fifty miles from his advance to his rear. This day Stuart's scouts reported Federal infantry, a corps, on the railroad just north of Rappahannock Station, and A. P. Hill, at Fredericksburg, saw Sedgwick cross for reconnaissance in force. Two things were apparent, that Hooker now understood Lee to be moving toward the Valley, possibly to strike across the Potomac, and that Hooker was feeling for a counter-move. We know now that Hooker desired to drive south across the Rappahannock, perhaps at Hill, or to move by the upper river and thrust across Lee's line of march to the northwest. But

Washington had decided that Hooker was not to be trusted with another battle, and Halleck's order confined him to covering the Capital.

On the 13th, Ewell's Second Corps was driving Milroy out of Winchester, Longstreet was preparing to leave Culpeper, and Hill was marching west from Fredericksburg—this last because Hooker had left Falmouth, three of his corps dropping back to keep the base at Aquia Creek safe from rebel cavalry while he evacuated it, and the other half of his army moving to the Centreville area.

With the departure of Hooker from Falmouth, both the great masses of manœuvre, gray and blue, were in motion, and the two opposed cavalry corps took up their missions— Stuart, to cover the right flank of Lee's army and deny knowledge of it to the enemy: Pleasanton, to pierce Stuart's screen, and find out where Lee was and what he did.

Ewell had marched with his own cavalry protection, picking up Jenkins' Independent Brigade in the valley. When Longstreet moved from Culpeper, his long, slow column extending for miles on the dusty roads, he went east of the Blue Ridge, pointing for Ashby's and Snicker's gaps. In the gray cavalry division, Hampton and W. E. Jones were left on the Rappahannock to maintain connection with A. P. Hill, and Stuart, with Fitz Lee, Robertson, and Rooney Lee's brigade—now under Colonel Chambliss, took station on Longstreet's front and right. Hooker was building up a concentration around the Manassas Plain, between Centreville and Warrenton Junction, and Stuart, brushing the westernmost of his pickets as he passed, sent the regiments trotting to occupy the roads that led through the Bull Run range, and south of it.—Robertson to Rectortown, covering Manassas Gap in the Blue Ridge, Chambliss to Thoroughfare Gap, east of Robertson, and Fitz Lee's brigade, under Munford, to Aldie, covering Middleburg. West of the gray troopers, on the lower benches of the Blue Ridge, trailed the dust clouds over Longstreet's foot. East of Bull Run meantime, Pleasanton has orders to push west and look.

Now the record runs of little cavalry fights, days of them, exploding northward like a train of fireworks. The first collision comes in the forenoon of 17 June: Munford, with some of Fitz Lee's regiments, has picketed Aldie in Bull Run Mountain, and takes the rest of the brigade on a circuit out the Snicker's Gap road, where some corn has been reported to him. While he rides, there is a burst of firing east of Aldie: it is hot-spurred Kilpatrick of Gregg's division, driving in Munford's pickets. Rosser's 5th Virginia, Munford's nearest regiment, swings around and meets Kilpatrick's advance, charges with the sabre, and drives it through the town. He places his sharpshooters, about a squadron, under Captain Boston, in a strong position north of the Snicker's Gap road, and sends for Munford. Munford comes, with three regiments, and, charge and counter-charge, the battle rolls out the road to the west, away from Boston's dismounted squadron, which has peremptory orders from Rosser to stay where he left it. Gregg's main body surrounds Boston, cuts him off, and Boston surrenders; wherefrom comes a very bitter court-martial procedure when poor Boston is exchanged. Confederate officials there present think Rosser's orders at fault, and hold that Boston did as well as he could: but this does not save him from Stuart's wrath. It is the only formal surrender by an element of Stuart's cavalry that I have found recorded. Toward evening, Munford brings Gregg to a stand. He has lost 119 men, half of them Boston's, but he has captured 138 Yankees, and Gregg reports a total of 305 casualties. As the fight died down, the still evening air bears up the noise of firing from the south.

Chambliss, ordered to Thoroughfare Gap, had been slow

to move his main body, and Stuart, with a few of Munford's troopers, had ridden to Middleburg. Early in the morning, Colonel Duffié, the fiery Frenchman, with the 1st Rhode Island, rushed Thoroughfare, chased off Chambliss's pickets, and turned north on Middleburg: he was a flank detachment from Gregg—and his orders were to go to Middleburg and await the main body, coming from Aldie. But, as we have seen, Gregg had been detained just west of Aldie, and was content to stay there after his fight with Munford, leaving Duffié to his fate. Duffié was a *beau sabreur*, and the 1st Rhode Island a fighting regiment. By 9:30 A.M. he had passed Thoroughfare Gap, and turned north, ignoring or not seeing Chambliss, who was coming up from the south. He rode as his orders directed, to Middleburg, meeting nobody. Here, about 4 P.M., he closed up and galloped the town, upsetting with sudden violence the few gray pickets he found outside.

In Middleburg, much at his ease, lay Jeb Stuart and his staff. Munford has reported from Aldie that he is doing well, and Stuart has sent a runner to Robertson, who rides from Manassas Gap, and Chambliss is reported coming from Thoroughfare. We do not know what Stuart was doing, but Major Von Borcke, in a resplendent plumage and highest spirits, was seated on a cool porch in the pleasant afternoon, relating, to a circle of wide-eyed young ladies, hero-tales of Chancellorsville and Brandy Station. Then, firing, sudden and loud: the pickets pound in, low on their horses' necks: "The Yanks are coming!" Von Borcke leaps for his horse without farewells: all of staff gets to saddle, and with Jeb Stuart in the midst of them, they get out of town to the west, toward Robertson, pursued by the shouting Rhode Islanders. But Duffié calls in his men—he has about 300 sabres: he is in a bad place, and knows it: he sends gallopers to Gregg—who are immediately captured on the road by

Munford—and he goes to work barricading the ways into town, and to putting himself in position for defence. His orders are mandatory, and he is a brave man.

Jeb Stuart is very angry: they drove him, and drove him while the ladies looked. His eyes are bright and hard. Robertson is quite near, and Stuart meets him, and orders him to go and retake Middleburg. Also, he makes sure that Chambliss is in position to the east, and he detaches squadrons to cover the other roads. It is no time for finesse: he has enough men to bludgeon Duffié, and he does.

It is near sunset. Enormous, with the low light behind it, amplified in smoke and dust, and yelling, Von Borcke riding in front as guide, with his long sword out—and Von Borcke always makes good his gestures—Robertson's column charges in by the turnpike. The flanking squadrons open fire from right and left. Duffié's slight defences are ridden down: the gray troopers leap his barricades: the Middleburg girls run out of their houses and clap and wave, and Duffié is hurled out, broken and scattered. Chambliss gathers up his fragments that flee southeast: Duffié gets off in the dark, returns to Pleasanton, and reports that his regiment no longer exists. Eventually, about a hundred Rhode Islanders straggled in, stray individuals, but 200 were shot or taken.

Stuart spent the night in Middleburg, and they danced to Sweeny's music and the country fiddles, and sang "Lorena," and "Sweet Evelina," and all made very merry. Major John S. Mosby was there, with his quiet, secret look. He has brought Jeb Stuart a present: a fine sorrel horse, late the property of a Yankee officer, and he has been this day on top of Bull Run Mountain, and reports Hooker moving north: from every road to the east goes up the dust of his marching. This news has gone to the Commanding General, and Mosby, who lives by habit, with his Partisan Rangers and his little gun, within the Yankee lines, is meditating further schemes. Stuart has sent some orders: Munford, with Fitz Lee's regiments, to drop back on Union—ten miles west of Aldie: Robertson to hold at Middleburg, and Chambliss to join Robertson.

Early on the 18th, Kilpatrick's brigade appears before Middleburg, and does not press. But Mosby, slipping around behind Kilpatrick, held to the woods and gained a position on the Fairfax turnpike, four miles east of Aldie. All afternoon he lay and watched the corps of Hooker flood by, going north. At dark—it was a time of no moon—he and three men of his mingled with the Yankee columns on the turnpike, lay for a while near Hooker's Headquarters tents, spotted some officers bearing despatches, following them until they stopped for refreshment at a house by the road, and took them quietly, using a pistol and the name of Mosby, which was a name of power. They were three, a major and two captains, with messages from Hooker to Pleasanton.

The despatches were important. They showed that Pleasanton, with all his cavalry corps, was holding Aldie, and that he was to force a reconnaissance toward Warrenton and Culpeper—and resolve Hooker's doubts as to how much of Lee had left the Rappahannock—from which, we know, A. P. Hill was now marching, after Longstreet and Ewell. Stuart had the despatches before daylight, Mosby's messenger riding to him through the Yankee camps, under a sky that glowed in every direction from their fires. The despatches went to Lee, and Hampton, who had performed his duties with A. P. Hill, and was coming to Stuart by Beverly Ford, was turned off to meet Pleasanton and stop him.

On the 19th, there was heavy cavalry fighting, along the turnpike from Middleburg, toward Upperville. Stuart, realizing that he could not disperse his three brigades to hold the gaps in Bull Run Mountain, decided to draw back to the west and concentrate, giving battle where the weight of

Pleasanton's force developed. He formed line a mile west of Middleburg, having three batteries of Beckham with him. Gregg's division drove at him along the pike. The blue horse, blocked in front, extended to the north and turned his shorter line. Shifting about, moving his guns from ridge to ridge, leading everywhere, with his sword out, and a great, war-like appearance, Stuart held off Gregg and saved his flanks, and at evening had given up only half a mile of ground, and still stood across the roads to the Blue Ridge. Gregg has only his fighting for his pains. In the afternoon, at Stuart's side, falls Von Borcke, shot through the neck by a Yankee sharpshooter as they direct the withdrawal of a regiment too much exposed. The lead slug went through the Prussian's collar, driving bits of cloth and braid into his windpipe and lungs. A man less hardy would have died, and they think he will die, and Stuart is very sorrowful for him: writes him after Gettysburg that he missed his long sword and his strong arm there. Von Borcke is never able to do field service again: he has, eventually, the thanks of Congress, and was abroad on a Confederate mission when Lee surrendered. Back in the German service, his health restored, he fought in the Prussian wars, and in his old age visited again the Virginia battlefields. You will see him once more, by a death bed. In him, there passes from this narrative one of the most picturesque and gallant men of all the gray cavalry that followed the plume of Stuart. A trained soldier, a valuable and accomplished officer, and a good companion.

The night of the 19th, W. E. Jones joined from the south, having escorted A. P. Hill behind the Blue Ridge. Hampton this day has fought and driven off the blue reconnaissance at Warrenton, and is coming on. Stuart posts Jones at Union, moves Munford to the left, to cover Snicker's Gap, places Chambliss to support Jones, and, when Hampton arrives, the morning of the 20th, stations him across the pike, in front of Upperville. He holds Robertson in reserve. He has three roads to cover: the road from Leesburg to Snicker's Gap, and the road from Aldie to Snicker's Gap, and the road from Aldie through Middleburg and Upperville, to Ashby's Gap and Manassas Gap.

The 20th is quiet, but scouts discover heavy infantry supports behind the squadrons of Pleasanton, moving out from Aldie. On the 21st, Buford's division attempts the left of Stuart's line, Chambliss and Jones, while Gregg makes at Hampton and Robertson, in front of Upperville. Buford is checked, but Gregg, with Kilpatrick, and some infantry and guns, forces Hampton and Robertson slowly back upon Upperville, then through the town, and into Ashby's Gap. In the Gap stands Longstreet's gray infantry, but the day closes with Stuart's line intact, Chambliss and Jones in contact on the left, and Pleasanton definitely checked at the entrance to the pass. This day the horse artillery lost the first gun it ever lost: a Blakeley piece, the axle of which was broken by a shell as it moved to a new position under a blue flanking dash. They note that, in the last stages of the action, Stuart draws off and watches, leaving the tactical conduct of the affair to his brigadiers—contrary to his custom, which was always personally to direct. He is asked why, and says he wants them to feel their own responsibilities, and to gain whatever honor the field may bring. Was he already turning in his mind a division of forces, you wonder? Hampton did superlatively well, handling his brigade like a sword. And old Grumble Jones conducted his fight with Buford ably, and there are words of praise for all the others, Robertson as much as any.

In these battles, Stuart's loss was 510, and Pleasanton's 827, of killed, wounded, and missing.

Next day, the 22d, Pleasanton pulled in his pickets and withdrew. He had failed to gain the passes, or the crests, and

his report says so. Stuart followed him, pushing feelers out
to Middleburg. If Pleasanton could have looked into the
Valley beyond the Blue Ridge he would have seen the Confederacy moving north—miles on miles of gray infantry,
guns and trains. The Valley was cleared of the enemy: only
at Harper's Ferry a blue force stood, arrayed, for safety,
on the Maryland side of the Potomac, but covering the town.
Hooker's information of the enemy began to come from
Pennsylvania.

These are the stages:

On the 17th, when Hooker started Pleasanton to see, he
knows that Ewell is on the Potomac at Williamsport, and he
believes that A. P. Hill is at Culpeper—seventy-five miles
south of Ewell. As Lincoln put it, if the head of Lee's army
was on the Potomac, and the tail at Culpeper, the animal
was mighty thin somewhere. Hooker has a correct feeling
for attack, but he is not allowed a free hand, and has been
marching dutifully north, to keep between the enemy and
Washington. There is a nine-day period in which he has no
reports of any kind of Lee's activities; then come the frantic shrieks of the Pennsylvania towns: Ewell is upon them,
and for fifty miles south of him the gray people are marching. Stuart has, up to this point, done his work perfectly.
What now remained for him to do, the simple thing, the obvious thing, was to continue to screen, from hostile eyes, Lee's
great mass of manœuvre that was crawling down the Shenandoah Valley. Ewell, far to the north, had with him Jenkin's
cavalry brigade, enough for the needs of the Second Corps.
Once the army was over the Potomac, every sabre of Stuart's
belonged on its front and eastward flank. Lee was looking,
of course, for a battle on Northern soil. But it must be a
battle of his choosing, when and where he pleased, and for
such latitude, Lee's dependence on his cavalry was absolute.
The only complication was, where could the division of cav-

alry, now about 8,000 men, cross the Potomac? Blue forces
were still at Harper's Ferry, but this time Lee was going to
pass them by—no dangerous detachments, as in the Sharpsburg Campaign. His infantry and trains were fording at
Williamsport and Shepherdstown, up-stream. For Stuart
to swing in, behind these slow columns, would take him on a
detour of forty miles from his flank station. To cross the
cavalry over the Potomac east of the Blue Ridge was, just
then—the 23d—dubious: the blue people at Harper's Ferry
might well keep a contact with Hooker's masses to the east.
Time and convenience might have to be sacrificed, but, in
all events, cavalry should hold in touch with the main army.
So reason and prudence directed. Of Hooker, Stuart knew
where he was, and that he was not moving. He had discussed
these matters with Lee on the 21st, at Paris by Manassas
Gap.

About that time, Major Mosby, with a considerable bag
of captured men and horses, snatched from the very camp
fires of the Federal corps, had come into Stuart's lines. He
was a man of pushing, active mind, and had a scheme for
the crossing of Bull Run Mountain, at Glasscock's Gap,
south of Aldie, with the cavalry, then a dash through the
centre of Hooker's army area, to pass the Potomac at Seneca
Creek, between Washington and Leesburg. The advantage
would be the upsetting of Hooker's trains, the breaking of
his communications with Washington, and the consequent
delay of Hooker while he deals with raiding cavalry on his
disengaged flank and on his rear. Mosby tells this himself.
Stuart's report does not mention Mosby's name. But the
idea Stuart presented to the Commanding General is
basically the idea outlined by Mosby.

He suggested a plan: "of leaving a brigade or so in my
present front, and passing through Hopewell, or some other
gap in Bull Run Mountain, attaining the enemy's rear, and

passing between his main body and Washington, to cross into
Maryland and join our army north of the Potomac." Lee
mulled the matter in his careful mind. His thought had been,
to leave a few cavalry regiments in the Blue Ridge passes,
against raiding Yankees in the rear, and to keep Stuart's
main body with him on the advance. He orders Ewell, on
22 June, well over the Pennsylvania line, to York; and Ewell
may take Harrisburg, "if it comes within his means." He
talks to Longstreet of Stuart's suggestion, and Longstreet
ponders heavily and thinks well of it. Then, on the 22d, he
writes to Stuart, a letter full of "if's." "If you find that he
is moving northward [Hooker], and that two brigades can
guard the Blue Ridge and take care of your rear, you can
move with the other three into Maryland and take position
on General Ewell's right." Ewell will go, he adds, in two
columns, toward the Susquehanna by Chambersburg, and
by Emittsburg. Later this day he advises Ewell that Stuart
will cross the Potomac with three brigades and report to him
in Pennsylvania, to cover his right. The letter to Stuart
went through Longstreet, senior officer present along the
Blue Ridge line, and was subject to Longstreet's approval,
which it received.

Longstreet, forwarding Lee's order with covering note,
thinks definitely that Stuart should go, not by the rear of
the Confederate Army, but by "the proposed route in rear of
the enemy—" On the 23d, Lee, anxious about the matter,
wrote again to Stuart:

"June 23, 1863, 5 p.m.

"Major-General J. E. B. Stuart, Commanding Cavalry.

"GENERAL:

"Your notes of 9 and 10:30 a.m. today have just been
received. As regards the purchase of tobacco for your men,
supposing that Confederate money will not be taken, I am

willing for commissaries or quartermasters to purchase this tobacco, and let the men get it from them, but I can have nothing seized by the men. If General Hooker's Army remains inactive you can leave two brigades to watch him, and withdraw the three others, but should he not appear to be moving northward, I think you had better withdraw this side of the mountains tomorrow night, cross at Shepherdstown next day, and move over to Fredericktown. You will, however, be able to judge whether you can pass around their army without hindrance, doing them all the damage you can, and cross the river east of the mountains. In either case, after crossing the river, you must move on and feel the right of Ewell's troops, collecting information, provisions, etc. Give instructions to the commander of the brigades left behind to watch the flank and rear of the army, and, in the event of the enemy leaving their front, to retire from the mountains west of the Shenandoah, leaving sufficient pickets to guard the passes, and to bring in everything clean along the Valley, closing upon the rear of the Army. As regards the movements of the two brigades of the enemy moving towards Warrenton, the commander of the brigades to be left in the mountains must do what he can to counteract them, but I think the sooner you cross into Maryland after tomorrow the better. The movements of Ewell's Corps are, as stated in my former letter. Hill's First Division will reach the Potomac today and Longstreet will follow tomorrow. Be watchful and circumspect in your movements.

"I am very respectfully and truly yours,

"R. E. LEE, General."

The fatal sentence is: "You will, however, be able to judge whether you can pass around their army without hindrance, doing them all the damage you can, and cross the river *east of the Mountains.*"

Probably Lee meant: *Immediately* east of the Mountains.

But, at the time this order was sent, no passage immediately east was practicable. From Harper's Ferry down to Edward's Ferry the enemy concentration commanded the approaches to the Potomac from the south. Stuart's first movements made it appear that he thought he could get through to this stretch of the river, but there are no direct statements bearing on this matter.

Lee's order was delivered the night of the 23d, cavalry headquarters and some of the regiments lying in bivouac at Rector's Crossroads, between Upperville and Middleburg. It was pouring rain, and officers and men were bedded down in the open, under their oil-cloths, the Major-General out with them in the weather. There was a house near by, and on its porch Major McClellan, the division adjutant, was allowed to shelter, in order to receive and handle messages; all other officers were in the wet with the men; it was a principle of Stuart's: what his troopers endured, their officers bore also.

McClellan woke the General and read Lee's order to him by the light of a lantern. Jeb Stuart lay quietly, saying nothing, and made his own decision. Before daylight, McClellan sends the gallopers with orders. Ewell is beating up Pennsylvania this night: Hill is in Maryland, on the Antietam: Longstreet's columns are turning their heads north, to follow Hill. Confused and doubtful, squabbling angrily with Washington, Joe Hooker lies a few miles east of Bull Run Mountain, his army compactly grouped. And here, at Rector's Crossroads, crop up the first of the events that lose for the South the Gettysburg Campaign.

On the 23d of June, Jeb Stuart found time to write to Flora Stuart: "send my letters to Custis Lee if you hear of me being in Penna." (Custis Lee was the President's Aide.) "The 1st Dragoons tried very hard to kill me the other day.

Four officers fired deliberately at me with their pistols several times, while I was putting a regiment at them which routed them. . . ." His wife has instructions about communications: it seems that the poor woman, receiving such letters as the foregoing, had taken to telegraphing the Commanding General, when her general's letters were late, and he tells her: "Don't be telegraphing General Lee's staff or anybody else. If I am hurt you will hear of it very soon. . . ."

* * * * *

Now, we are judging men who were laboring to the best that was in them for the things they believed. Our after-knowledge is complete: they could know only a little of the situations then. You sit coldly in your study, removed from the haste and violence and responsibility, and say: there he did wrong: there he erred greatly: there his judgment was unsound. So, of necessity, history is written: to be valuable, it must be critical. Jeb Stuart was a trained and experienced officer; so was Lee; so was Longstreet, and they were all loyal and devoted. Lee, the Commanding General, had a doubt, but passed it on, conditionally, to his subordinates for decision. Longstreet affirmed the matter, and passed it on, still conditional, to Stuart. Stuart understood as well as any man the functions and uses of cavalry. But he did not concede its limitations, and, if he saw obstacles, he did not allow that they might turn him from his course. Personally, he admitted no limitations, took never any counsel of his fears.

He had his orders. He must guard the passes. Good. He will leave his largest brigades, Jones and Robertson, to do it. Jones, for all that he is eccentric and unpopular, is regarded as the best outpost officer in the army. Robertson will do well enough with a strong man to watch him: he is senior to Jones, but Jones has the largest brigade and no regard for seniority, and can be depended upon to direct matters in emergencies. Other cavalry with the army is Jenkins, 3,000 sabres by the last return, and Imboden, from West Virginia, 2,000 strong. Actually, Jenkins had joined Ewell with only 1,800 effectives, but Stuart did not know this. Robertson and Jones, remaining in contact with the army, will receive subsequent orders from General Lee. He sends Robertson a careful order, covering every contingency, and tells him that he will receive further directions from the Commanding General, with whom Robertson is enjoined to maintain constant liaison. So much for the routine cavalry mission.

Himself: he will take Hampton, Fitz Lee, and Chambliss, three brigades, three batteries, and ride into the rear of Hooker's army, alarming and delaying it, and cutting its contact with Washington, and then he will rendezvous with Ewell's right at York, Pennsylvania. Early on the 24th he issues orders: Hampton, Fitz Lee, and Chambliss to Salem.

The brigades of Hampton, Fitz Lee, and Chambliss were between 4,000 and 4,500 men (the returns are not definite as to unit strength), and in the passes, under the orders of the Commanding General, the brigades of Robertson and Jones were 3,000 sabres. With Ewell, already in Pennsylvania, was the cavalry brigade of Jenkins, 3,000 strong by its latest return, and on the left of the army was Imboden's West Virginia cavalry, 2,000 men. An infantry report, that of Rodes, with whom Jenkins worked during the campaign, gives Jenkins' strength as 1,800 effectives. Accept, if you like, that figure, and you find that Lee now had, under his orders, or under his designated corps commanders, 7,800 sabres—considerably more than Stuart took away. On the 24th, they were distributed, a brigade, Jenkins, with the outthrust right corps of the army, Ewell's corps, a brigade, Imboden, coming up on the left, about abreast of Hill's corps, and two brigades, Robertson and Jones, down at the right rear, in touch with Longstreet.

It is said, after the event: Stuart was the chief of cavalry, and he should have known better than to take any of the cavalry away. One of the people who says this loudest is Longstreet, that solemnly approved the detachment and the project of passing by the enemy's rear. And Lee authorized it, as Commanding General, and Stuart's subsequent course, although modified by circumstances which he could not control—notably the movement of Hooker's army—was well within the discretion extended by his instructions.

It is a principle of the military art, that orders should be clear, direct, and open to that interpretation, only, which the commander desires. Lee's instructions to Stuart do not conform to the principle. They fall outside, even, of that latitude which a general may with propriety extend to a trusted subordinate. Questions affecting vitally the operations of the army are the affair of the commander-in-chief—not any lieutenant, no matter how able. Whatever Stuart's error in judgment, the responsibility lay with Lee, nor, let us add, did Lee in his final report evade it.

And consider another thing: the Gettysburg Campaign failed. No one cause broke it down: Lee was poorly served by all his corps commanders, and full credit must be given to General Meade, and seventy-odd thousand Yankee soldiers. If—as he might well have done, and came breathlessly near doing—Lee had won his battle, Stuart's conduct of the cavalry force would certainly stand in the annals as a great and daring operation. Success justifies itself. Failure is wrong in the first place!

* * * * *

With his great bay horse Virginia between his legs, and three brigades at his back, no gloomy thoughts oppressed

Jeb Stuart, when, at one o'clock in the morning of the 25th of June, he rode from Salem toward Bull Run Mountain. At dawn he was through the pass at New Baltimore, ten miles on his road. Five miles farther on, at Haymarket, with the Manassas Plain to the east and the pike to Leesburg, which he meant to use, opening on his left hand, he came upon Hancock's Federal corps, crowding the road he wanted. Hancock was marching north, and Stuart fired into him with artillery, keeping his brigades out of sight, until Hancock turned, deployed, and moved against him. Then he withdrew, for it was plain that Hancock had the right of way. He sent a courier to Lee with the information: Army of the Potomac heading for the river about Leesburg—but the messenger does not appear to have gotten through. And he had a final decision to make: he must go back the way he had come, and ride to Shepherdstown, in rear of Longstreet, or he must swing very widely to the east, to cross the Potomac on the far side of Hooker's army. The place appointed for his rendezvous with Ewell was York. Shepherdstown— looking at your map—is forty-five miles from Haymarket, a little west of north, and sixty miles from York—one hundred and five miles, with South Mountain to negotiate, and all that time the Yankees would be marching. York is one hundred miles, northeast, from Haymarket, and he could go faster, any given distance, than the Yankees. (These distances are by airline: the road distance to Shepherdstown, alone, was more than sixty miles—nearly a two-day march, if he kept up his guns.) He consulted nobody, and set his face toward York, in the direct route, with only the necessary detour eastward to clear the skirts of Hooker's army, now vexing all the sky with its dust to the north of him. The night of the 26th, he bivouacked at Wolf Run Shoals on the Occoquan, after a forty-mile march. On the 27th, at Fairfax, Hampton's advance struck and destroyed a squadron of blue cavalry riding from the Capitol to Centreville, and there was some delay to feed the horses. By dark, Hampton was on the Potomac at Rowser's Ford, where the river is nearly a mile wide. The water was high, but he found the ford and crossed. Chambliss and Fitz Lee, with the guns, got over after him, but slowly and with great trouble. The night was moonless, and the caisson and limber chests had to be emptied on the Virginia shore and the ammunition taken over by hand, so deep was the water. By three o'clock the morning of the 28th, the command was in Maryland, and you hear the troopers singing, irreverently:

> "—Oh, Bob Lee's heel is on thy shore,
> Maryland, my Maryland—
> You won't see your old horse no more—
> We'll ride him till his back is sore—
> And then come back and get some more—
> Maryland, my Maryland."

In Maryland the usual strict discipline applied: only the appointed officers requisitioned on the country for subsistence, paying in new Confederate bills. The canal was cut and some blue soldiers taken, and about noon, bearing east, the column entered Rockville, fifteen miles from Washington, on the Frederick road. While they destroyed the telegraph, and gathered supplies, a party thrown out toward the Capital discovered, and gave chase to, a wagon train: army stores bound through Rockville to Frederick. It was alarmed, and turned about, but Colonel Thomas Lee and the 2d South Carolina took after it and captured it, snatching it away under the guns of the fort at Tenallytown. This occurred in sight of the Capital, and was shocking to the heads of Government. Colonel Lee returned to Rockville with one hundred and twenty-five wagons of subsistence, which were, with drivers, animals, and loads, eventually turned over to the quartermaster of the army at Gettysburg.

It was an unfortunate capture. It would have been far better if Stuart had never seen these wagons, or had contented himself with destroying them where he found them. But Stuart kept what he had set his hand upon. His swift, light column now becomes convoy to a lot of commissary stores: his raiding pace is cut down to the plodding speed of the Yankee mules. You calculate his distances: after he took the wagons, his best day's marching was about twenty-five miles; before, he could do forty; and without the wagons he would have gone over the route he followed and joined Lee by the 30th of June. As it turned out, two days were added to his time, and the entailed escort duty was exhausting to the command. Old Jubal Early, discussing the campaign long afterward, says that holding on to the wagons is the only point he finds to criticize; but, he adds, one hundred and twenty-five wagon loads of grub would be mighty hard for a lot of hungry Confederates to leave in the road. Much burdened, the column formed at Rockville, with the wagons in the centre of Hampton's brigade, and moved north through the afternoon of the 28th of June. Fitz Lee rode ahead to cut the Baltimore and Ohio Railroad at Hood's Mill and Sykesville. The rear elements delayed some time near Rockville, paroling 400 Yankee prisoners, rather than bring them along. Marching all night, Fitz Lee reached the railroad, twenty miles from Rockville, at daylight on the 29th, and broke the link between Washington and the Army of the Potomac, which had now crossed into Maryland and was moving on Frederick, although Stuart did not know it. At 5 P.M. of the 29th, Stuart closed his column on Westminster, and the advance guard rode down a squadron of the 1st Delaware cavalry, which lost 67 men out of 95 present. Stuart moved the head of his column out to Union Mills, five miles from Westminster, on the Gettysburg road, and rested all night, finding food for men and horses. Scouts came in, who

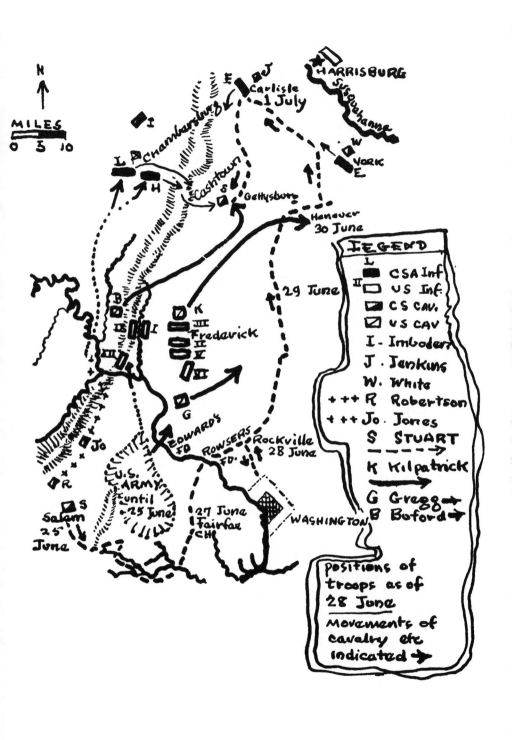

reported Federal cavalry bivouacked at Littletown, in Pennsylvania, seven miles west of Hanover. Hanover, ten miles north of Union Mills, was on Stuart's route, and he proposed to gain Hanover and intercept the blue cavalry there. Orders were issued for an early start.

Already he had made an impression on the Federal mind which would have gratified him. With the report of Hancock, on the 25th, Hooker had shifted Kilpatrick and Gregg around to his rear and right to watch for gray cavalry, and they had followed the rear of the blue army up to the Potomac. Then—Meade having taken over command of the Army Hooker relieved, came the alarm from Washington: Jeb Stuart, raiding under our very noses! And Gregg and Kilpatrick were ordered to ride east and northeast and intercept him. Kilpatrick was, the night of the 29th, about to cross his path in front, while Gregg was pounding along somewhere behind him. Only the division of Buford was left to do the scouting for the Army of the Potomac.

Stuart's brigades were astir early the morning of the 30th, but the captured wagons caused delay, and imposed a certain dispersal of the brigades to front and rear and flanks. So it was ten o'clock before Hanover came in sight, with Kilpatrick's division entering the town from the west. The advance guard, the 2d North Carolina regiment, dashed in with more valor than judgment, routed the blue rear-guard regiment, of Farnsworth's, and had some minutes of success. The blue people rallied, and faced about, and the 2d North Carolina was driven back on the main body. Fitz Lee was off to the left flank, and Hampton had the wagon train on his hands, so the advance guard could not be immediately supported.

Stuart, with his staff and a brace of couriers, had ridden off the road into a field to watch, and when the North Carolinians were driven by Farnsworth, the General and his party joined in the fight with their pistols, until a blue squadron wheeled from the road and ran at them. Jeb Stuart, retiring, loped across the field, found a water jump, a deep, wet ditch, very wide, and his long-sparred Virginia cleared it easily, although some of his staff and couriers fell. Farnsworth's people, who were not jumpers, had to look for a crossing, and Stuart's party got off safe.

Meantime, Hampton checked Farnsworth, and got into line as Kilpatrick brought up the rest of his division. There was some brisk mounted combat. Kilpatrick lost 197 men, most of them Custer's, and let the matter rest. He stood, however, across the road, and there was a flicker of fighting through the rest of the day, each watching the other for an opening, and keeping well covered up. They relate a story of this afternoon: Stuart rode near a regiment, which was waiting orders under some cherry trees, beautifully loaded with ripe fruit. The gray troopers were not eating regularly, and while their lean horses cropped the grass, a squad or so swarmed into the nearest trees, and began to fill hats and haversacks. Out in front, a blue dismounted line was worming forward, and they see the gray jackets in the branches, bunched against the sky. They begin to fire, and minie balls whine among the cherries. Down tumble the gray troopers, in frantic haste—no good horse soldier wants to be shot out of a tree, like a 'coon—and Jeb Stuart's laugh peals joyously —"What's the matter, boys? Those cherries sour?"

As the day declines, Stuart passes the wagon train—which has been, for some hours, drawn up in a field, ready to be burnt if Kilpatrick gets too close to it—around to the east, Fitz Lee taking it over, while Hampton faces Kilpatrick. As soon as it is dark, Fitz Lee detours east, to Jefferson, and then straightens out for York. Chambliss took the advance, Hampton withdrew from Kilpatrick's front and passed around his left, and they all moved on. Kilpatrick let them go, and followed at a respectful distance. There would be no more contacts with him.

That day, the 30th, while Stuart was at Hanover, Confederate elements of Ewell, Early and Gordon were in Gettysburg, eleven miles west of him, Kilpatrick had left the road open, and Stuart might easily have joined the army, in good time, with all his plunder. But his orders were for York, and he marched that way. The gray troops then in Gettysburg left it, for it was a place nobody wanted. Buford's cavalry entered it behind them, and Jenkins felt him, learned what he was, and reported him to Lee. Lee, that day, was with Longstreet and Hill, at Chambersburg. Meade had pushed one corps, the First, Reynolds, up toward Buford. His army lay generally west of Frederick, facing more northeast than north. From his reports, Stuart rather than Lee was worrying him. No general could endure having rebel cavalry plundering and burning in his rear.

Both Meade and Lee have a plan. Meade—in case the enemy comes at him from the west or north, thinks he will fight about Pipe Creek, between Gettysburg and Emmittsburg. Lee has selected the Cashtown vicinity to the west, near the mountain wall, as good holding ground. Neither is quite ready to attack the other.

Ewell, on the 30th, has left York, and turned back to the southwest, recalled by Lee, who knows now that Meade is north of the Potomac. The last Meade heard, before Stuart cut the wires behind him, is that Ewell was in York and Carlisle. Late on the 30th, he is notified, from Harrisburg, that Ewell has turned south, and he thinks that means a Confederate concentration. He orders Reynolds to continue toward Gettysburg.

Jeb Stuart knew nothing of this—any of it. He moves on from Jefferson.

The night march from Jefferson was bad. There was now

an accumulation of 400 prisoners in the column, bagged on the 29th and the 30th. The wagon mules were wearing out, and there had been no opportunity to feed or water. The drivers—also prisoners—were not full of cheerful help. The wagon guards were growing careless, simply through fatigue. It took everything that Staff could do, and Stuart's own untiring drive, to keep the column moving. At daylight, they were all at Dover, six miles from York, only to learn that gray soldiers had been at York, and marched westward the day before. Local rumors located a Confederate concentration at Shippensburg, thirty miles west of Dover. This was Stuart's first news of the main army since the 24th, and very annoying to him. He sent staff officers galloping southwest and west, on Early's track, to find where Lee was, and what was happening off beyond the hills. He led his column then toward Carlisle, twenty-five miles northwest, an important town and a U. S. Army depot.

Late on 1 July, Stuart was at Carlisle with Fitz Lee. Federals were in the place, and they refused to surrender. Stuart deploys, sends for his horse guns, and prepares to storm. Then two of Stuart's officers catch up, Major Venable and Captain Lee, who have ridden hard. They have found the army, and bring orders from General Lee: Concentrate on Gettysburg. Fitz Lee, in position, flings some shells, sets fire to the U. S. Cavalry Barracks at Carlisle, and they draw off. The stumbling horses turn patient heads southwest, to Gettysburg, thirty miles.

The blue forces at Carlisle were a strong division sent from Harrisburg to harass Ewell. Stuart burned their supplies at Carlisle, and they lay immobilized for four days. Otherwise, they would have come in on Lee's left flank during the battle. This was one of the most valuable achievements of the cavalry detachment.

• Down at Gettysburg, on the 1st of July, things have hap-

pened which were outside the calculations of both commanders, and Meade and Lee are alike annoyed. A. P. Hill's
corps lay out a few miles east of Cashtown, and in the early
morning he sent Heth's division toward Gettysburg. Heth's
report says he went to reconnoiter, although the presence
of Federal cavalry was known and reported the day before.
In Heth's later writing, he says he went on some rumor of
shoes in the town; but, you remember, Jubal Early and Gordon had already been in Gettysburg, both necessitous persons, and if Heth expected to glean behind the Georgians, he
was singularly optimistic. At any rate, he collided with
Buford, west of the village. Buford put his regulars behind
the stone fences, and held him off until Reynolds came up
with some infantry. Heth drove in hotly, had two brigades
shot to pieces, and lost a flag and a brigadier. Pender's division was sent by Hill to support him, and some artillery—
Hill was always a headlong fighter, and he urged the battle.
Miles away, toward Cashtown, Lee hears the guns, and is
visibly annoyed—he had given no orders for any fighting.
He puts Traveller to a gallop and rides to see what Hill is
doing. Up to the north, Ewell hears the guns, and hastens
his long columns. Howard marches from the southeast to
support Reynolds. The battle grows, in the blazing July
weather, and by dark, two Confederate corps and two Federal corps are involved. Hill and Ewell kill Reynolds and
drive his men back through town. In Gettysburg, Howard's
Eleventh Corps is shattered, and 5,000 prisoners captured.
Lee is on the field in time to see the gray jackets sweep forward with jubilant yelling, while long files of dusty blue
prisoners plod back. Hancock, sent by Meade, is also present, and decides that Gettysburg is a fine place to fight a
defensive battle, and Meade, receiving his report, orders
his army to march to Gettysburg. Lee calculates that
he has destroyed, to all practical purposes, two corps of the

enemy, and that he will do as well tomorrow. He, too, sends orders: march on Gettysburg. He wishes he had more cavalry, because, when he breaks them yonder, he will need cavalry to ride down the fugitives and harry the retreat. On the 29th, he had sent for Robertson—that day still in the Virginia mountains, where Stuart left him—and he had expected to hear from Stuart before this time. And at daylight, on the 2d, he realizes that Ewell let a fine chance slip, the evening before. Just beyond Gettysburg, as the Confederates faced it, is the end of Cemetery Ridge, and Culp's Hill. He had ordered Ewell, "if practicable," to take possession of them. Ewell, however, did not find it practicable, and Lee did not press him. Culp's Hill and the end of the ridge were the bastions of the Federal right: if Ewell had taken them from the fragments of Reynolds and Howard the evening of the 1st, there would have been no further battle at Gettysburg.

At the time Jeb Stuart joined the army, noon of the second day, the battle had taken form and the lines were in the trace that they held to the end. The well-known simile of a fish-hook is the best one, if you would visualize Meade's position. Immediately south of the town of Gettysburg is Cemetery Ridge, running straight south for a little more than a mile, with the Taneytown road sited along its crest. This high ground was Meade's centre. As you look south along it, there is on your left hand, a high hill, rocky and wooded—Culp's Hill. This marked the Federal right through the battle. To it, and to the north end of Cemetery Ridge, the remnants of Reynolds and Howard fled in the evening of the first day, and Hancock's supporting troops formed there as they came up.

Continuing south along the Taneytown road, you see, on a line inclined a little west of the ridge, two small hills, wooded and rocky, like Culp's Hill, but steeper; they are

Little Round Top and Round Top, and they were the corner posts of the Federal left. They were not occupied until noon of the second day, and were, from the early dawn of 2 July, within Longstreet's hand, if he had cared to take them. From them, you can look straight down the Federal centre, which they dominate.

So you have your fish hook, Culp's Hill the barb, Cemetery Ridge the shank, and the Round Tops the end where you make fast your line. From end to end of this curving position was about three miles.

The positions taken up by Lee were without such excellent natural features. His centre was about Seminary Ridge, running southwesterly from Gettysburg. Ewell's corps curved around to the right, containing Culp's Hill. A. P. Hill lay along Seminary Ridge. Longstreet prolonged the line to the left, as far as the Round Tops. The Emmittsburg pike, running a little west of south from Gettysburg, marked the front of Longstreet's first position, and in the later stages lay within his lines, after he had made some advances. Lee's position was, from end to end, more than five miles. His guns were clumsily emplaced, none of them closer than one thousand yards to the blue infantry. You see, at a glance, that, had he concentrated his artillery just south of Gettysburg, opposite the angle in Meade's lines, he could have enfiladed both Meade's right and left, and here was the place for the weight of his attacks. But the guns were employed in frontal fire, and the Confederate infantry attacked frontally, left, right, and centre, piecemeal and unco-ordinated for three days, until they were used up. The gray troops never fought better, in any battle. Nor, in any battle, was the staff work worse.

At noon on 2 July, Jeb Stuart rides into his own army, and his hard-driven troopers have brief rest, sleeping like the dead. Their horses—half of them miscellaneous animals gathered from the Pennsylvania farms as their Southern hot-bloods wear down, stand with hanging heads and trembling legs. Inside the arc of Stuart's riding, Kilpatrick and Gregg have come in also, and about the same hour they draw behind Meade's flank. The one hundred and twenty-five wagons go to Lee's Quartermaster: the prisoners to Lee's Provost Martial. Jeb Stuart goes to the Commanding General, to report. "Well, General Stuart, you are here at last!" says Lee, austerely. Indeed, he has sufficient to trouble him, and Stuart's name has been much in his mouth, the last few days. This noon, he is listening and watching anxiously for the attack on the Federal left, which he ordered James Longstreet to make, in the early morning. Yesterday was a good day: two blue corps destroyed—Reynold's and Howard's. Today promises well, but Longstreet is hard to move—hasn't attacked yet——

The rest of Gettysburg is not Jeb Stuart's story. Of it, Lee says, afterwards:

"Its loss was occasioned by a combination of circumstances. It was commenced in the absence of correct intelligence. It was continued in the effort to overcome the difficulties by which we were surrounded, and it would have been gained could one determined and united blow have been delivered by our whole line."

Had Stuart been up, and not the width of Meade's army away, it is unlikely that the battle would have been fought at Gettysburg: Meade's scattered corps might well have been crushed in detail before he could concentrate his army. On the other hand, if Stuart had been on Lee's front, Pleasanton would have been there, too, and Meade would have had his own information. It is idle to speculate about Gettysburg. Maybe it is as I have heard pious old men say who think much on these things, seen and unseen, in the quiet South: there was a current in the universe that set against the Confederacy. God did not mean for it to win the war. In the event, they shocked together on the iron-ribbed hills by the little town and fought as fiercely as men have ever fought— Hancock, Doubleday, and Sykes—Gordon—Hood—Garnett —Pettigrew—George Pickett. The armies, attacking and attacked, saw fall, or led off as prisoners in that three days, nearly a third of the strength of each. In the words of Froissart, "They were very noble: they did not value their lives——"

On the third day came the cavalry fight, off to the northwest, beyond the Hanover road. Pleasanton has Gregg, Buford and some of Kilpatrick. Stuart has Fitz Lee, Hampton, Chambliss and Jenkins. Blue and gray, horse and man, they move numbly, in the mist of fatigue. The efforts are convulsions: the shouting cracked and strained, almost to hysteria.

* * * * *

It is the noon of the third day. On the right Culp's Hill raises itself, fringed around with the smoke of Jubal Early's fighting. Beyond Culp's Hill is Cemetery Ridge, and the thick blue lines, and the centre of Meade's strength. A hundred and sixty-two Confederate guns are shelling it: two hundred and twenty Federal guns are answering. Pickett is marshalling the Virginians, the North Carolinians, the Alabamians, to charge. Over the field is a sense of breathlessness, a gathering of all strength to the ultimate effort. Lee is trying, the third time and the last, to put home a killing blow, his right and his centre swinging together.

There are no written orders for the cavalry, and the messages are not preserved, and we cannot tell exactly what orders Stuart had from his Commanding General, or what arrangements were made for liaison, between the cavalry and the Confederate infantry. We know that Lee planned a great stroke at the Federal centre, on Cemetery Ridge, 15,000 men, led by Pickett, to be timed and co-ordinated by Longstreet. The memoirs and the comments indicate that Pickett was to be supported by other troops, sent forward in echelon on his right flank as he struck the Federal line—but here again there are no orders; Pickett's report was destroyed by Pickett himself, at Lee's wish, and the other reports are reticent. Lee expected, however, a break-through, and he sent Stuart to pass around the blue flank on Culp's Hill, gain their rear, and disorder their echelons while Pickett battered in their front. Since the three brigades joined the army, yesterday, they have been stationed on Lee's right, and now Jenkins is added to them.

About noon, Stuart led his brigades out the York pike, while the artillery battle mounted to crescendo behind him. For two and a half miles, he followed the pike, then turned to the right, into the fields, where a long ridge ran up from the south, with woods on the northern end of it. Behind these woods, he placed Hampton, Fitz Lee, and Chambliss, while Jenkins' men, dismounted, ran forward as skirmishers: they had Enfield rifles, but, by some odd mischance, only ten rounds of ammunition per man. Jeb Stuart himself rode through the woods and along the ridge to reconnoiter. There is no sign of war here. The ridge falls away to a level valley, down which, a mile and a quarter south, is the Hanover road. Pleasant farmhouses dot the landscape; stone fences, and stake-and-rail fences traverse the fields. Over all is the great sun of July, and the distance dulls the battle roar, three miles off, to your right hand. Stuart sees that he is in position to strike across all the roads that lead to Meade's line. Down in the flat behind the fences there are some dismounted blue troopers. Across the flat, three-eighths of a mile to the east, is a long stand of timber, in which wait, out of sight, the squadrons of Gregg, Kilpatrick, and Custer: Custer is just receiving an order to take his brigade to Meade's left, where trouble is expected; but about noon, a message came that a large body of gray cavalry was marching on the York pike, and Custer has waited to see.

Stuart shells the woods a little, and Jenkins' troopers run out and engage the Federals in the flat, on the left. The blue people come forward dismounted, and Fitz Lee is involved. Stuart has planned to move two brigades, mounted, farther to the left, and try for the flank of the blue dismounted lines, but before his couriers can find Hampton, Hampton is drawn in, too. Well, he is in good position: it is 2:30 P.M.: the artillery firing back yonder is at its loudest, and it is time—he will attack where he is.

Beckham's guns run out, Griffin's battery first, to be beaten down by Pennington and Randol. Beckham brings more guns: Chambliss, Fitz Lee and Hampton ride down—in array very splendid, Yankee observers note: flags and guidons in place, bright sabres at the carry. Then, a straight, pounding fight. The blue dismounted lines are driven from the flat. The squadrons of Gregg and Custer and Buford come charging and cut up Jenkins. Hampton and Lee meet them furiously, and the battle sways in a dense dust cloud, up and down, now toward the Hanover Pike, now toward Stuart's wood. Wade Hampton, fighting among his troopers, is slashed terribly, to the skull, with a sabre. Flags are lost and taken, formations broken up and formed again, and, after some hours, the dust subsides, and the squadrons draw off, Fitz Lee, Hampton, and Chambliss to the ground from which they started, and Gregg, and Buford, and Kilpatrick to their old line. Dead horses and dead men lie in the trampled flat between. Stuart has seen no sign of a gray break-through yonder.

Stuart's loss is 119 in three brigades; Jenkins did not report. The Federal loss is 252, killed, wounded, and missing.

Both outfits are tired, and quite intact. Pleasanton's troopers have done what they should have done: kept Stuart off of Meade's rear. Stuart has nothing but the glory of fighting.

It is near sunset, the 3rd of July.

In the centre over there, on the other side of Culp's Hill, the shooting and the yelling fall to a murmur. Pickett has been among Doubleday's guns, and come back with a remnant to his lines. General Lee has made his cast, and missed, and presently he must retreat. But Meade is too much mauled to follow him.

You must think of the battle, called Gettysburg, as an event that began to take form the day after the fight at Brandy Station, the 9th of June. Then Lee moves behind the long rampart of the Blue Ridge, and follows it, on the west side, up into Pennsylvania. The Army of the Potomac is drawn after him, on the east side of the mountains. Neither commander has planned a battle, at any certain place or time. Each means to fight when and where he finds it most advantageous. Quite accidentally, they collide at the town of Gettysburg, a place of no strategic or tactical importance to either. They fight three days, Lee attacking, Meade attacked. At the end, Meade stands where he stood on the second day, and Lee about where he began. Their losses are nearly equal. Lee is too used-up to attack any more, Meade too much expended to molest him. After another day, Lee retires; he has failed to destroy the enemy, he has used up the local subsistence for his army, he is at the far end of a line of communications two hundred miles long, and he needs ammunition, and—if he is to stay, more troops. The ammunition is doubtful and the troops are out of the question.

Go briefly over the period between the 25th of June, when Stuart was detached, and the 2d of July, when Stuart rejoined it. The records are not complete, and most of the memoirs and comments are from interested parties who have cases to prove. Consider the records alone:

Robertson's cavalry reports to Lee for the period 25 June—2 July are not preserved. But Robertson says, officially, that he was in daily communication with the Commanding General, and his instructions from Stuart are available today, and are perfectly adequate. He lacked energy, but always did what he was ordered to do. On the 23d of June, Hill's corps marched to the Potomac at Shepherdstown and crossed that day and the next. On the 24th, Hill was seen by the U. S. signal stations on Maryland Heights and South Mountain, and promptly reported to Hooker. Hooker then proceeded to cross the Potomac and his pontoons were in sight of the outpost area of Jones' cavalry brigade, and of the heights south of the river, in the Confederate zone. It is reasonable to suppose that Lee was notified that day, whether he was or not. Jones was an officer of admitted ability, and no complaint was made of him. It was his mission to watch Hooker—not Stuart's, now detached.

On the 25th, Hooker ordered infantry and cavalry to the passes in South Mountain. Lee made no attempt to hold these passes. Jones and Robertson were not ordered north of the river. It would have suited Lee for Hooker to come through the mountains. His trains were drawn in, and he was living on the country in Cumberland Valley.

From the 27th to the 29th, Lee was with Longstreet and Hill at Chambersburg. Ewell was at York. Jenkins was along Ewell's line of march, and Buford, on the 29th and 30th of June, reports the roads between Emmittsburg and Gettysburg infested with rebel cavalry. Lee knew that Buford was on his front. From that he could deduce that infantry was in support of the cavalry. The uncertainty was Meade's. He had reports from Buford, but Kilpatrick and Gregg were away. His anxiety was about Stuart—not about Lee.

The night of the 28th, Lee had news of the change in command from Longstreet's scout, Harrison. Longstreet says Harrison's report was more comprehensive than anything cavalry could have brought in.

The collision at Gettysburg was brought on by A. P. Hill and Heth, who provoked an action where Lee did not desire, nor expect one. In their reports, Hill and Heth say they were on reconnaissance looking for the enemy. Lee knew Buford was there, if they did not. In his post-war memoirs, Heth says he was looking for shoes. Early had been through Gettysburg on the 29th. If Heth expected to find any such gleanings behind Early, he was silly. He went looking for a fight. That contact was not brought on by the absence of cavalry.

Lee had already selected a position, in case he had to fight: Cashtown, four miles west of Gettysburg. Meade had selected a line: Pipe creek, ten miles east.

The engagement between Heth and Buford drew in Heth's support—A. P. Hill—and Buford's—Reynolds. The main armies were then drawn in.

None of the foregoing argues that it would not have been better for Stuart to be up: his presence would, at least, have removed the excuse for irresponsible wanderings on the part of Heth and Hill.

To repeat: It was within Stuart's discretion to cross the Potomac east or west of the Blue Ridge. He chose to cross east—approved specifically by Longstreet, Senior Officer Present. When the decision was made it was then his mission to harass and intercept the Federal army lines of supply and communications. He did this so effectively that he drew after him two cavalry divisions, and caused Meade to retain a corps of infantry on the line of communications. He took an army supply train of one hundred and twenty-five wagons, and brought it off safely. He captured nearly 1,000 prisoners. He rode two hundred and fifty miles, lived off the country, whipped Kilpatrick, burnt Carlisle and immobilized 15,000 men in that region who were under orders that would have brought them upon Ewell's flank and rear, and he rejoined his main army—this with a loss of 89 men, killed, wounded, and missing.

The cavalry failure in the campaign was not Stuart's. Ewell made good use of Jenkins. He does not complain of lack of cavalry. Buford was too weak to do anything on Longstreet's flank, so Longstreet did not suffer for lack of cavalry.

Hill went outside his orders to pick a fight with Buford. And Robertson received no orders to come forward until 29 June, three days after Hooker had crossed, and one day before the scout Harrison reported. Then, although Robertson rode fast, he was one hundred and fifty miles behind the army, and took nearly three days to reach the zone of operations. Lee seems to have forgotten Robertson, whose usefulness south of the river ceased with the withdrawal of Hooker from his front, and he wasted Robertson during the next four days.

What Lee missed at Gettysburg was not cavalry: he had plenty of cavalry. He missed Jeb Stuart.

You come now to the last phase of Gettysburg.

Lee's problem, the night of the 3d, was to extricate his army, with its trains, and thousands of wounded, from the perilous position in which the failure of the campaign now placed it.

He was east of the mountain wall that has covered his communications, and behind which he must retire. His wounded, a procession of agony, seventeen miles long, in

springless wagons, were started on the 3d for Cashtown,
thence to head down the Cumberland Valley to Williamsport.
Imboden, with his brigade, 2100 cavalry and twenty-three
guns, was in charge.

On the 4th, the gray army aligned itself on the ridges west
of Gettysburg, Stuart covering the left. East of Gettysburg, the blue masses crowned the heights they had held so
valiantly, and made no aggressive gestures. Meade had, for
the time being, no idea of taking the offensive. He had lost
almost as many men, defending, as Lee lost attacking, and
at least three of his six corps were incapable, so far as offensive power went. It began to rain. But in the afternoon,
Meade despatched Buford and Kilpatrick to ride south,
pass the mountains between Frederick and Boonsboro', and
snatch at Lee's trains that would be coming down the Cumberland Valley ahead of his army.

At dark, beyond Seminary Ridge, Lee began to retire off,
his corps marching west and southwest, by parallel roads as
much as possible. Ewell's 2d corps on the left. To Stuart
was assigned the task of guarding the left flank and rear.
Beverly Robertson, with his own brigade—reduced by detachments to two regiments—and Jones' brigade, had crossed
the Potomac on the 30th and had been in action on 2 July at
Fairfield, southwest of Gettysburg, against small Federal
forces that were feeling around to the south of Lee's army
during the battle. Robertson had done well enough, but a
blue detachment had taken a courier with a letter from Davis
to Lee, advising the latter that he could look for no supports
from Virginia. The officer who brought this letter to Meade
was Captain Ulric Dahlgren, and so vitally did the letter
affect Meade's future plans that Dahlgren was rewarded
with a colonel's commission. Of him, more hereafter.

Robertson and Jones were unable to, or did not, hold the
passes in South Mountain, and on the 5th, Kilpatrick forced

his way through them and captured 1000 men and forty-five wagons of Ewell's. Stuart, riding all night from Gettysburg, with Fitz Lee and Chambliss, had a shorter distance to cover than the blue horse, but started later. On the afternoon of the 5th, beyond Emittsburg, he found Monterey Pass in the possession of Kilpatrick's rear echelons, and had to force his way through. Kilpatrick, pressing Jones back on Hagerstown, now felt Stuart in his rear and was greatly alarmed. He turned hastily south, to Boonsboro', where he lay until, on the 6th, Buford came through the hills and joined him.

This day, you will visualize the long gray mass of infantry and guns, twenty-five miles from head to rear, sloshing through the mud between Cashtown Pass and Hagerstown. Behind it is an empty interval, and then the sore blue mass, following sluggishly. The gray columns are through the mountains, and go along southward with the protecting ramparts on their left hand. Down to the south, the Federal cavalry have come through with intent to head them off and harass, and lie between Hagerstown and Boonsboro', but the gray horsemen are through the mountains also, and are shaking out into a screen in front of the infantry. Finally, at Williamsport, on the Potomac, blocked by the swollen river, stout Imboden, with his ambulances and his wagons and his thousands of racked miserables has turned about to make the best defense he can.

Over at Boonsboro' Kilpatrick and Buford agree upon a plan: Jeb Stuart is at Hagerstown: Kilpatrick will engage him there, while Buford dashes west and hits at the cornered Imboden. The 6th passes, with nothing more than little cavalry skirmishes around Hagerstown. But Jeb Stuart, too, has taken his measures. The Confederate infantry is marching steadily toward him, and that will be a help: he leaves Chambliss and Robertson at Hagerstown, sends Jones and

Jenkins to support them, and with Fitz Lee, and Hampton's brigade, now under Gordon, he rides for Williamsport to save Imboden.

The 7th comes, another day of rain, and Kilpatrick rides furiously at Hagerstown. The Confederate cavalry is roughly handled in front of the town, and forced back through it, Colonel J. Lucius Davis being captured, pinned under his fallen horse: he gratifies his captors by saying that somebody ought to stop this useless war. But the thin gray brigades re-form, and cling to the skirts of the town, and the leading divisions of Longstreet appear on the Hagerstown pike—grim infantry, quite anxious to fight somebody. Kilpatrick is forced away, to the south.

Over at Williamsport, Stuart has been riding to the sound of the guns, for Buford has involved all of Imboden, and is pushing matters: Imboden has armed his teamsters, and such of the wounded as could sit up and hold a musket; has put his wagons in stockade, and is going to fight. Fitz Lee appeared, with his own and Jenkins' brigades, and Jeb Stuart in person urged the fight. There were two of Beckham's guns. Buford was vigorously attacked, and hustled away from Williamsport, down river. As he fell back, his right echelons came in contact with the left elements of Kilpatrick, retiring on his own account from Hagerstown. The cavalry loss in this phase of the operations—the race for Lee's trains and the fight to save them—was about 400 Federal officers and men of the three blue divisions, and 254 Confederates. Mounted and dismounted, the fighting was fierce and sullen. The horses were too exhausted for wide manœuvring, or charging. It was, for all, stand up and fight—in the mud, and the rain that fell without ceasing.

On the 7th, the first of Lee's infantry appeared, and from the 8th to the 11th it was arriving, by easy marches, not pressed by Meade. Cavalry skirmishers, at Boonsboro', and at a dozen points along Antietam Creek, took place almost hourly. In three days, Stuart reports a further loss of 216, the Federals 158: Stuart held his chosen ground by aggressive tactics, hitting hard wherever the blue people showed themselves. His mission, to cover the infantry and delay the enemy until Lee was ready for him, was efficiently performed. On the 12th, he drew his slim squadrons away to the left, up-stream, and Meade, whose army was assembled, found himself facing a fortified line six miles long, with Lee's veterans behind it, quite ready to receive his attack. He did not deliver it.

On the 10th of July, in the field, near Hagerstown, Jeb Stuart wrote his wife: "Upon the eve of another battle I write today. God has mercifully spared me through many dangers and bloody fields. My cavalry have nobly sustained its reputation and done better and harder fighting than it has since the beginning of the war. Pray without ceasing that God will grant us the victory. We got the better of the fight at Gettysburg, but retired because the position could not be held." You need not comment. It was Jeb Stuart's conviction, also, that a man couldn't be whipped until he admitted that he was whipped.

This letter is written in pencil, and it shows exhaustion. The characters are waveringly formed and almost indecipherable, unlike his bold, clear hand in all his other letters. He was, according to McClellan, about dead on his feet, and McClellan tells how he went to sleep, sitting at table, in Hagerstown, finished his meal, joined in some singing, and then dictated orders, all without waking up. This is McClellan's story, and he makes it sound plausible. Certainly, the record does not show where, or when—except for one night—he rested during the whole campaign.

On the 13th, he was able to write at length to Flora Stuart.

"I am all right thus far, and all the staff have thus far escaped. . . . I made several purchases for you, having received your list just in time. Many things, however, could not be had. I got most of the small articles but no black silk could be had. . . . I had a grand time in Penna. and we return without defeat to recuperate and reinforce when no doubt the rôle will be reinacted. I shelled Carlisle and burned the barracks. I crossed near Dranesville and went close to Georgetown and Washt. cutting four important railroads and joining our army in time for the battle of Gettysburg with 900 prisoners and 200 wagons and splendid teams. Starr" (old friend of the family) "of the 2d Dragoons was captured. I have been blessed with great success on this campaign and the accidents and losses in the way of captures" —I think he means Ewell's train, toward Monterey, which Robertson and Jones should have covered—"are in no way chargeable to my command. I had another horse shot on the 10th.

"We must invade again. It is the only path to peace. . . . Genl Lee manœuvring the Yankees out of Virginia is the grandest piece of strategy ever heard of. If they had sent 10,000 reinforcements and plenty of ammunition to join him here our recrossing would be with banners of peace. . . . I am so sorry for Dundee—" (house in Virginia, near Fairfax, where he had visited) "but Penna. has well paid for it. . . . Got Maria a dress but could not get you any needles."

No need for comment on that, either. What he believed, he said out loud, and wrote down. There was no special reticence about Jeb Stuart in any relation.

The first phase of the withdrawal ended on the 11th of July, with Lee in position for battle, on the Maryland bank, his back to Williamsport. Conococheaque Creek covered his left: his right was on the river in front of Downsville, and the thin squadrons of Stuart were to either flank. Meade came and developed his position and found gray infantry and guns in strong lines, eager, if you believe the letters and memoirs, to pay him in his own coin for the repulse at Gettysburg. And Meade believed that he would be repaid. The armies faced each other, inactive except for snipers, and for continuous cavalry skirmishes on the flanks. Meantime, the swollen Potomac was going down. The 12th passed, and the 13th. Prodding telegrams come from Lincoln and from Halleck—go on and get him! Don't let him escape. But Meade, on the ground, had no battle in him. The night of the 13/14, Lee forded the Potomac, taking off every gun and every wagon, and every wounded man. The files crossed, singing,

"Carry me back to Ole Virginny,"

and Lee, sitting Traveller in the shallows, as the sky downstream lights up with dawn, receives the report of the rear guard: "They're all over, General." "Thank God!" said General Lee.

It is his last thrust. He will come that way no more. Lee, the flaming attacker, must turn his genius to the hard business of defense.

* * * * *

There are two reports from Lee on Gettysburg: one is dated 30 July, when the army was hardly reassembled, and before all the data could have been in. It was written when Lee, behind his unchanging mask of coolness, may well have been sore and angry. It names a specific cause for the Gettysburg misfortune: absence of the cavalry. It was published in the papers by order of the Government. It makes

Jeb Stuart scapegoat for the army. Stuart's preliminary reports, written, doubtless, under the sting of the publication, were then turned in—but were not published. The final report, submitted by Lee in 1864, with full data, is fair to Stuart. But it was never published, until the United States Government collected and issued the official records of the Union and Confederate armies.

Across the Potomac, on the 15th, Stuart was for a few hours at the Bower, the scene of the pleasant autumn encampments of 1862. You imagine him riding thoughtfully under the wet clouds of this rainy July . . . Pelham, von Borcke, Burke, Farley, Rooney Lee, Frank Hampton, young Channing Prince—all the good companions, all the gallant young men, gone from him. But there was no time to sit and mourn: there was a report of blue horse crossed at Shepherdstown, and he sends Fitz Lee, Chambliss, and Jenkins after them, and they retire. Lee says he wants Stuart to cross the Shenandoah and move over the mountains to Loudon with the cavalry division. Lee wants another fight: Meade is on the Potomac, and he will follow Stuart with the army and strike those people on the river.

The Shenandoah stops this. Stuart's scouting parties, forwarded immediately, have to swim its swollen fords: no chance for guns or trains. And Meade, spurred hard by Lincoln and Halleck—now you've let him get away! Go on over and destroy him!—is moving rapidly. Before the Shenandoah subsides he has thrown pontoons over the Potomac and moved his army south of it, and has the lower passes— Snicker's and Ashby's gaps. Lee has to send Stuart, and Longstreet, by hard marching to save Chester Gap and Manassas Gap. Meade pushes south, toward the Rappahannock. Lee follows Longstreet with Ewell and Hill. Jeb Stuart takes station on the left, and skirmishes again through the familiar region between Upperville and Warrenton, to the line of the Upper Rappahannock. By the 24th of July, the Army of Northern Virginia is concentrating around Culpeper, and the Army of the Potomac looks across from the north bank of the Rappahannock, both, less some 30,000 fighting men struck from each, exactly where they were six weeks before.

In the west, Vicksburg was fallen. A General Grant was well launched upon his career. The last chance of foreign intervention was dead, although a few infatuated politicians in the Richmond Government still hoped. The Confederacy had no more any likelihood of winning military decision: it was over the peak, starting down to the shadows. Sensible men, thoughtful men, must have realized it. It was a trait of Jeb Stuart's, that the cold shade of discouragement never touched his heart.

There was good grazing around Culpeper, in the pastures and the old grain fields. Cavalry rapidly recuperated, both men and horses. The sick and wounded rejoined.

In the campaigns just concluded—Chancellorsville and Gettysburg—the achievements of the cavalry division had been remarkable enough, in skill, valor, and endurance, to satisfy any commander. There had been 400 miles of marching and fighting: the main army had been at all times covered and informed, and, except for the faulty employment of the command in the Gettysburg movement, criticism can find no opening in the conduct of operations. Fleetwood Heights and the combat on 3 July had been great cavalry battles, in which Stuart at least inflicted more damage than he had received. But you sense, in his orders, that he was not entirely pleased. His material was running down in quality, horses, men and arms, while that of his adversary was rising. The splendid Virginia mounts of 1861 and 1862 were gone, or wearing out. Very many of his best and bravest officers and men were dead, or wounded, or lay in prison. The ardor of the faint-hearted element—always present—was definitely on the wane—and over there, under such good soldiers as Pleasanton, Gregg, and John Buford, the Yankee morale was improving.

Stuart's cavalry comes in for a thorough shaking up. General Order 25, of 29 July, 1863, is a blistering pronouncement. It opens:

"That nondescript irregular body of men known as Company 'Q' which has so long disgraced the cavalry service and degraded the individuals resorting to it is hereby abolished.

"The sick or disabled men requiring hospital treatment will be sent as heretofore to the General Division Hospital in Hanover where they will receive the kindest treatment and care known to the army.

" . . . The Major-General Commanding is convinced that unless a more sure means of detecting & punishing the guilty, and preserving the strength of this command, can be devised, all discipline is gone, and with it the efficiency of the cavalry division. By prowess in action, by vigilance on the outpost, and by patient endurance on the march, it has won a name of which its members can be justly proud, but owing to the inefficiency of a portion of the company officers and the forgetfulness, on the part of many of the men, of their high duty, and the patriotic resolve which has heretofore been the rule of their action, its numbers are rapidly diminishing and its efficiency becoming consequently impaired.

"The Maj. Gen'l. appeals hopefully to the brigade commanders, regimental officers & to the men of his division, to aid him in arresting this growing evil.—He is determined to spare no effort to rescue his command, in which he feels so much pride, from the impending fate. Let the straggler be disgraced in the eyes of all honest and patriotic men; let the artful dodger on the battlefield receive the retributive bullet of his gallant comrade. Let every man recognise his duty to his oppressed country as his sole motive and vengeance on a ruthless invader, his constant aim.

"By command of Maj. Genl. J. E. B. Stuart:

"H. B. McClellan,

"Maj. & A. A. Genl."

XIX

THE BRISTOE CAMPAIGN—THE BUCKLAND
RACES—THE DAHLGREN RAID

AT the end of the summer, attention swung to the west. The Richmond government comes around to the idea of using its interior lines, and proposes to Lee that he go out, with a suitable detachment of troops, take command of the forces in the Georgia-Tennessee sector, and see what he can do. But Lee does not want to leave Virginia. He sends Longstreet by rail with two divisions of his corps to Georgia, and Longstreet joins Bragg in time to win, with a great, smashing attack, the barren victory of Chickamagua. Longstreet is a strange character. I think that he took better care of his troops than any other corps commander in the Confederacy, and held them better in hand. When he put his heart into an attack—which means, when he had conditions exactly as he wanted them, and was able to lend his personal approval to the general scheme of operations—not even Jackson could strike a blow more powerful and sustained. The familiar accusation, that he was slow, is not justified by the records. And there is a comment of Lee's, on excellent authority, that Longstreet was a better marcher than Jackson, and that Jackson had the bad habit of being never on time. You do not find Longstreet's Corps making those terrific swift movements which characterized Jackson's command, and which littered Jackson's line of march with exhausted soldiers, fallen from the ranks. When Longstreet reached a place, he arrived with his whole corps, unbreathed, and ready to put in its full weight. As a defensive fighter, he was, I think, without superior in either army, and hardly with an equal. But he was stubborn; he lacked the splendid faculty of giving up his own plans and lending his loyalty to a plan which differed: he thought that his own ideas were better than the ideas of any other person—even the Commanding General's. And when he was overruled, he confined himself to an exact and perfunctory obedience, following the letter, but not partaking of the spirit at all. He always aspired to independent command, and his independent operations—Suffolk, and East Tennessee—show him quite incapable of it. Such a general never won a war—but no war is won without its Longstreets. Lee loved him, and showed, most conspicuously in his case, his fatal unwillingness to discipline a trusted subordinate. Longstreet, at Second Manassas, hung back exactly as he did at Gettysburg, until conditions suited him: then he hit like a thunderbolt across the Manassas Plain. But, at Gettysburg, affairs never shaped themselves to meet his requirements, and the result was bad. If a Wellington or a Stonewall Jackson had been in command of the Army of Northern Virginia, Longstreet's connection with it would have ceased at Second Manassas, and another might have led his corps at Gettysburg. You are forced to the conclusion that the Confederacy would have gotten a better quality of obedience and of co-operation from its Generals if it had shot one or two of them.

August passed without incident in Virginia, and some well-merited promotions were dealt out from Richmond. The cavalry division becomes a cavalry corps, and Jeb Stuart writes his wife that there is great talk of his being made Lieutenant-General, but that he builds no hopes upon it, and she is not to discuss it herself. Just then, he was being blamed for the loss of Gettysburg; the fire-eating Richmond editors were spreading the loosest sort of talk, and he dismisses the Lieutenant-Generalcy with the fewest words, and quite without sulking. He had other traits of Achilles, but not this one, which, in a man of his mercurial temperament, is remarkable and fine. Wade Hampton and Fitz Lee were promoted Major-Generals, and given divisions. To Hampton was assigned W. E. Jones' brigade; and Baker's brigade —formerly Hampton's—and Butler's brigade which was made up of parts of Hampton's old brigade and a regiment of Robertson's; and to Fitz Lee, Rooney Lee's command, under Beale, Lomax's brigade—and Wickham's—the last two being reorganized elements of Fitz Lee's old brigade, with parts of Munford and Jenkins. In the two divisions there were six brigades, twenty-four regiments, and six batteries of Horse Artillery under Beckham. Beverly Robertson had asked for detachment and was sent to North Carolina again. A few weeks later, charges were preferred by Jeb Stuart against W. E. Jones—the two never got along, and the records show much praise of Jones' professional attainments by Stuart, and many recommendations that he be sent to serve elsewhere—and old Grumble was ordered to Southwest Virginia where, 1864, he was killed in battle.

On 13 September opened the Bristoe campaign.

Both Lee and Meade were reduced in numbers: Longstreet went west with his corps, and troops were detached from Meade to serve Grant's growing requirements. With no very exact reasons for it, both Meade and Lee now indulged in some manœuvring.

Meade moved first. On the 13th, Kilpatrick crossed at Kelly's Ford and struck for Culpeper. Stuart, forewarned, was ready for him, and there was another fight around Brandy Station, Stuart maintaining a delaying action and retiring toward the Rapidan, which was Lee's army line. The Horse Artillery lost three guns, but there are no detailed reports from either Kilpatrick or Stuart, and the affair led to nothing. On the 22d, Buford's division, swinging

Vidette 1863

Sapper

Infantry CSA 1863

widely to the west, came down on the Rapidan from the direction of Madison Court House, by Liberty Mills, and Kilpatrick advanced at the same time from the north. Stuart crossed the Rapidan to meet Buford, and engaged him: there was never any finesse about Buford: he was an unsubtle man, who hit straight in front. While they fought, Kilpatrick developed sudden force, turned Stuart's right, and gained the ford behind him at Liberty Mills. By the rules of the game, Stuart should have been broken up, or at least lost his guns. His regiments had not been fighting well against Buford; now, with Kilpatrick turning them, they struck back furiously. Buford was held in front—for a while, the story goes, two gray horse batteries on the same knoll were fighting back to back, in opposite directions—and a determined rush drove Kilpatrick away from the ford. Holding Buford back with one hand, and Kilpatrick off with the other, Stuart withdrew his guns and got safely away. There are no detailed reports on the fight, and I mention it to show how vigorously Stuart reacted when things looked worst. Nothing discouraged him, and he was never so dangerous as when his command seemed to be involved in hopeless difficulties. You find case after case: the bold attack at White's Ford by the mouth of the Monocacy, the furious assault on Gregg at Fleetwood Heights. His idea for the solution of most situations was attack. If that failed——

There is a conversation in point, related, I think, by Wickham. They were discussing either the Chickahominy raid, or the Chambersburg raid, and possibilities: "Well, if we hadn't been able to get across the river, there would have been just one thing left to do—" says Jeb Stuart. "You mean surrender on as good terms as possible?" they asked. "No," says Stuart. "To die game." I think he was always ready to die game, and the Federal officers at White's Ford sensed it, and Kilpatrick sensed it at Liberty Mills. The average person gets out of the way of the person who is perfectly ready to die. You find testimony in the Bible—

After this engagement, Meade felt out the Rapidan lines and considered them too strong, and while he studied the situation, Lee, who had 45,000 infantry to Meade's 60,000, started a series of moves around Meade's right, the reverse of the manœuvres directed at Pope, but over the same ground. Stuart's mission was, to screen the thrust until it could be unmasked, and he left Fitz Lee at Raccoon Ford, and moved with Hampton's division, by Madison Court House, across the Robertson River, to James City. It was the 9th of October, and the weather was clear and cool, the year just turning. On the 10th, they drove in Kilpatrick's pickets, and on the 11th, following, they came upon Kilpatrick, standing on the old Brandy Station battlefield. Behind him, Lee's infantry was now well under way, northwest of Culpeper, while Meade, unsuspicious, lay to the east. Stuart skirmished heavily with Kilpatrick, while, at Raccoon Ford, Fitz Lee's time had come for action: he was over the Rapidan and assailing Buford. In the afternoon, Fitz Lee drove Buford slowly up to Brandy Station, and after some delay caused by faulty liaison arrangements, the commands united close to Fleetwood Heights. That day, the main army crossed the Rappahannock, and moved on Warrenton, while Meade, still deceived, directed three corps to advance to Culpeper—considering that Stuart and Fitz Lee would be closely supported by Confederate infantry. . . . On the 12th, Stuart went north to cover the advance of Ewell's corps, and Rosser, with a small force at Brandy Station, was attacked by the blue infantry, and fought a very creditable delaying action. The afternoon of the 12th, Stuart was sent by Lee to secure the ford at Warrenton Springs on the Rappahannock, and he attacked here, and routed, a force of Gregg's cavalry. These carried an alarm to Meade, advising that Lee was past his right, and he countermarched and hurried to gain the Orange and Alexandria railroad, and the plains of Manassas. Lee, who had planned to fight him on the line of the Rappahannock, followed, and the morning of the 13th, Stuart was sent from Warrenton to reconnoitre toward Catlett's Station, scene of the Pope raid. Lomax (who succeeded W. E. Jones) and Gordon, with seven guns, moved to Warrenton Junction, about eight and a half miles, and found the enemy in possession. Thence they turned to Auburn, five miles east, where the column concentrated. Lomax was left at Auburn, and Stuart pushed on, three miles, through the fine autumn landscape, toward Catlett's Station. The country around Auburn is rough, hilly, and wooded, but three miles southeast it becomes open: low, rolling hills and pasture land, the visibility extending for miles. The railroad passes across southwest to northeast, from Hanover Junction on your right to Catlett's Station on your left, and there, closely parked, Stuart saw the wagon trains of the Army of the Potomac, with an unbroken column of all arms marching along the railroad, as Meade retired toward Bristoe Station.

Stuart, halting where the Auburn road debouched from the forest, looked yearningly: the wagon trains were very tempting, but there were too many Yankees in sight. He sent an officer to Lee, suggesting that the army come and hit Meade here, and he waited, as dark drew on, for any opportunities that might come to him. His messenger, Major Venable, at Auburn, rode into some miles of blue infantry, the Second and Third Corps, marching from Fayetteville, by way of Auburn, toward Bristoe Station. They had already driven Lomax off toward Warrenton, to the west, and the messenger Lomax despatched to Stuart was captured by them, although he kept his message to himself. Major Venable escaped them, going on to Lee, and about dark, Stuart reluctantly turned back toward Auburn. Almost immediately, his advance discovered the approach, on the Auburn road behind him, of the blue infantry column, and about the same time, his rear elements were discovered by flank detachments of the columns on the railroad, and fired at. The main body lay in the road in the forest, just above the place where the Auburn-Catlett's road crosses Cedar Run.

Jeb Stuart had no time to ponder, and took no time. His staff officers cantered down the column—everybody off to the right of the road! Quickly! Front and rear elements were drawn in: fire of the enemy not to be returned! A low ridge passed along the road here, on the north side, and the command hurried over and behind it, and lay close in cover, 300 yards from the marching blue infantry, which immediately filled the road. It became dark, and there was no moon. Along the road the blue infantry corps halted and bivouacked. And 300 yards from the Yankee camp fires, Jeb Stuart, two brigades of cavalry, seven guns, and five ordnance wagons, squatted for the night—every trooper and teamster with his hand on his animal's muzzle, lest some gregarious horse or mule let out sociable bray or nicker. When a man moved, he lifted his sabre carefully, and managed his spurs. The officers discussed plans in whispers. The men sat on their heels and waited. Old Jeb had taken them in and out of many a tight place, but this looked the tightest.

The colonels advise an expedient: the abandonment of guns and ordnance wagons, and a concerted dash for safety. Better that, than to lose the two brigades. But Jeb Stuart will not discuss the abandonment of anything. Another scheme—his own—was to ride down and order out a Federal wagon train, in the dark, fall in column behind it, and turn off to the west—Major Mosby, on a smaller scale, does such things. But the brigades would be certain to attract attention. Stuart sent picked men to creep through and reach Lee at Warrenton, advise him of the situation, and ask him to attack the Federal column from the direction of Warrenton: in the attendant confusion, Stuart hoped he would get clear. Meantime, some miles of blue infantry lay between him and safety. The night passed in the light of the Yankee fires, to the murmuring of their encampments. During the night, some strolling officers walked into the gray cavalry and were seized. Men who remember say it was a very long night, and, for the only time in his career, Jeb Stuart appeared to worry.

Very slowly, the sky grew pale. Down on Cedar Run, the Yankee soldiers began to stir, set cooking fires alight, and going to the Run for water. The smell of coffee and fried bacon drifted up to the gray troopers. What was going to happen would happen soon.

By hand, Beckham's people eased his guns to where they commanded the nearest camps. A few dropping shots were fired from the west, indicating—maybe—a diversion by Lomax, or some gray infantry sent from Warrenton. Jeb Stuart gives the word: Beckham's guns go off, double canister at the closest range. A regiment, the 1st North Carolina charges, yelling, and rides down the Yankees at the Cedar Run crossing—it breaks through, spreading confusion, but loses its colonel, Ruffin, killed. The brigades swarm out, and the road is abandoned to them. Stuart breaks clear to the west, and forms his line, keeping up some artillery fire, hopeful that a solid attack may develop in which he can be helpful. But there have been sent only a few of Ewell's infantry, who are uncertain where he is, and he does well enough to come away, without much loss, and with a good story to tell: he reports it briefly and humorously, concluding that his blast of canister upset the enemy's "coffee pots and their cooking arrangements, to their great confusion."

But it was plain that Meade's idea was retreat and not fighting. Lee threw Stuart out to his left flank, toward Manassas Plains, and pushed east from Warrenton with his infantry, A. P. Hill leading. A. P. Hill, following recklessly, as was his custom, ran without reconnaissance against a strong Federal line on the railroad by Bristoe, and the head of his corps was shot to pieces: he lost a thousand men and five guns in fifteen minutes. With this incident, the Bristoe campaign closed. Nothing had happened, except in the hearts of several thousand next of kin to dead soldiers of the two armies.

Cavalry was to have a final adventure, the affair called the Buckland Races. Stuart followed Meade toward Washington, and Manassas Junction and Groveton saw the gray jackets again, and heard small, noisy skirmishes of no consequence, up to the 18th of October. That night, Stuart, with Hampton's division, was at Buckland Mills, a few miles west of Gainesville, on the Warrenton Pike. Fitz Lee was down in Auburn, a little on the right flank, and in supporting distance. Early on the 19th, Kilpatrick trotted from the east, and Stuart formed a line along Broad Run to resist him. During the forenoon, they fought an uninspired action, Kilpatrick rushing frontally, and being beaten back, while Fitz Lee came up from the south to the sound of the guns.

About noon he is near enough to see the field, and estimate the situation. He sends Jeb Stuart a suggestion: fall back, by the Warrenton Pike. Old Kilpatrick is sure to follow you. I'll lie off to the right of the road, and hit him when he gets by me. You turn and come at him when you hear my guns. We'll gobble him up, and everything with him!

In consequence, a little later, Kilpatrick is gratified to observe the rebels retreating—falling back from Broad Run, by the Warrenton Turnpike. He sends orders to Davis and

Custer, his brigadiers: Get to horse, and pursue vigorously by the Warrenton Pike—Davis obeys, forms a column, closes up, and pushes toward Warrenton, the rebels just ahead, so that his advance keeps their rear in sight. But Custer wants to feed his men, and water his horses. He goes to Kilpatrick, and makes representations, and carries his point. His colonel, Kidd, who served in the 1st Michigan, gives it as an instance of Custer's military instinct: Custer acted on no information, Kidder says: he had what is called a hunch. At any rate, he delayed, killing time for no obvious reason on the south side of Broad Run, and when he was almost ready to move out—no excuse to remain longer—his left elements saw, in the edge of the woods to the left, out in front of Broad Run, something moving. The Michigan brigade, now mounting, began to file right toward the Turnpike, to follow Kilpatrick and Davis. But those on the left watched suspiciously. They saw a trooper come into the clear, a few hundred yards away, but the light was wrong to show the color of his uniform. Then, a thoughtful Wolverine said: that fellow's a rebel! Look, he's circling his horse—that's rebel signal when they see the enemy! Our fellows don't do that— And then the rebel shot at them. Forthwith, a gray skirmish line, dismounted, ran out of the woods over there, and opened fire. A battery of Horse Artillery was close behind it, and opened fire. Fitz Lee, expecting to find himself in rear of Kilpatrick's entire division, was driving to interpose between the blue jackets and Broad Run, and he came dismounted, to make his lodgment certain. Recovering from a momentary confusion, the Michigan regiments formed front to meet him, their backs to the stream, not where he expected them at all. They think, the Michigan people, that if Fitz Lee had attacked them mounted, he would have knocked them into Broad Run.

Simultaneously, a great uproar broke out toward War-

renton: that way, Jeb Stuart, as soon as he heard Fitz Lee's
guns, whirled around and flung himself furiously at Davis,
with whom was Kilpatrick in person. Davis did not stand
it long. Gordon's brigade, the 1st North Carolina leading,
thundered at him on the Turnpike, and crashed into the
head of his column as he changed formation. Young and
Rosser obliqued to left and right of the pike and upset his
squadrons as they opened out. At the same time, the rear
elements heard rapid salvos of artillery behind them, toward
Broad Run. Davies' troopers were veterans, and they struggled desperately for a few minutes, but it was too much to
endure: they broke, and it was every man for himself, a frantic steeplechase, for five miles back along the Turnpike, from
Buckland Mills to Broad Run. All the transport of Kilpatrick's division, including Custer's headquarters wagons
and personal baggage, was taken. And the fugitives of
Davis, stampeding through Custer's flank to the left of the
Turnpike, apprised him that he was in danger. He had been
holding his own against Fitz Lee; now he drew off, hastily
but in good order, getting his guns away, and fell back on
Gainesville. Stuart and Fitz Lee followed until they came
upon the infantry lines of Meade's 1st corps, behind which
Kilpatrick took refuge.

Camp Chickamauga of the gray cavalry corps celebrated
the event in doggerel poetry, some of which got into the
papers, and sounds remarkably like Jeb Stuart's phrasing,
and the affair took its place in the annals as the Buckland
Races. On the event, there is a report of Custer, who did
very well, and no report whatever from Kilpatrick or Davies.
Yet I found the best account of it in the memoir of Colonel
Kidd, the Michigan cavalryman.

During the Bristoe campaign, the casualties in the Confederate cavalry corps were 408 officers and men, killed,
wounded, and missing. During the same period, the Federal

cavalry report 390 killed and wounded, and 885 missing, believed captured—most of them from Kilpatrick's division. Stuart turned over, incidentally, 1370 blue prisoners to Lee's provost marshal.

In the last days of October, the Army of Northern Virginia retired behind the Rappahannock. Cavalry took up its vigils on the fords; and north of the Rappahannock, around Warrenton and along the Orange and Alexandria, settled the Army of the Potomac.

There was brief flare-up in November: Meade advanced on Kelly's Ford and forced the crossings with his main army, on 6 November. Lee retired behind the Rapidan. On the 26th, Meade advanced again, crossing the Rapidan at Germanna and Ely's Fords, and thrusting toward Orange Court House. Hampton's cavalry division covered the front of the army, while Stuart, supported by Early's infantry—for the main armies were in close contact—felt out Meade's intention and his axis of advance. Lee considered that Meade meant to attack, and took a strong position behind Mine Run, a few miles west of the old Chancellorsville battlefield. Meade came on, reconnoitred the Confederate works, and decided that he might storm them, but that it would cost 30,000 battle casualties, too many to think about. Four days the armies confronted each other; then, on the night of December 1, Meade moved north of the Rapidan again, his retirement marked by a series of little cavalry fights. Meade north of the Rapidan, Lee south of it, the two armies settled into winter quarters, after the agreeable fashion of that war.

Kilpatrick was a West Pointer, a man of positive traits, not unpicturesque. He was one of the young captains who came to regimental command under McClellan. His portrait shows a lean, slab-sided man, with a thin nose, a hard eye, and a straight, thin-lipped mouth, his long face framed in lightish side-whiskers. He affected, and prescribed in his commands—the type of hat that came to be called by his name—the Kilpatrick—with the left side turned up and the right side down. His character was a mixture of uncalculated recklessness, and caution. Nobody, up to a certain point, was a more dashing leader. Then, prudence would assail him, and his resource was never adequate to the emergency. He was quite likely, upon occasion, to rush out of danger as precipitately as he rushed into it. And he was one of the worst horsemasters the blue squadrons ever had: his raiders usually returned on foot, leading their broken-down horses, and the name his troopers had for him was Killcavalry. Yet, for some reason, he had the confidence of Meade, and while, under Meade, the cavalry corps had its chief in General Pleasanton, that officer functioned more as a member of the staff than as a commander. John Buford, the Old Regular, and David McM. Gregg, were cavalrymen of ability, but you hear little of them in the winter of 1863-1864. Kilpatrick was Stuart's chief opponent. After Buckland Mills fight, he had part in one more conspicuous episode.

In February of 1864 occurred the Dahlgren raid.

It was known that Lee had sent Longstreet away to the west, and that other large detachments of the Army of Northern Virginia had been withdrawn to meet emergencies on the coasts, and in the interior, which were now multiplying upon the Confederacy. With the main army facing Meade, around Orange Court House, and the only other considerable body of gray soldiers stationed on the lower James, Richmond was lightly garrisoned during the winter, and in Richmond some thousands of Federal prisoners of war lan-

guished. It was proposed to organize a raiding column of
sufficient strength and mobility to strike through from the
Rappahannock to Richmond, enter the city, free the prisoners, and take them off to the Union lines, or to some point on
the York or the James where they could be covered by the
naval echelon. The conduct of the operation was entrusted
to General Judson Kilpatrick, and it marked his last important part in the Virginia scene.

Kilpatrick organized a force of about 5000 sabres, composed of the effective elements of his division. The Federal
intelligence service provided, through spies, perusal of newspapers, and occasional captures, details of the Confederate
army dispositions. Stuart was known to be covering the
Rapidan front, Fitz Lee on the left, Wade Hampton on the
right. Small pickets were on the fords, their supporting
regiments in permanent camps to the rear, and the divisional
concentrations further back, close to the infantry camps.
All forces were much reduced. The Horse Artillery had been
sent to Charlottesville to winter: so that the horses might be
fed from the railway. Light guards watched the line of the
Virginia Central, Lee's artery of supply.

Kilpatrick's first preoccupation was to draw Stuart away
from his intended path. General Meade co-operated to the
extent of furnishing two corps of infantry for a feint at
Lee's left, and Kilpatrick told off Custer, his most energetic
and capable brigadier, with 1500 men and a battery, to dash
around the Confederate left, as if to beat up Charlottesville
—where there was only the demobilized gray artillery. Stuart should go after Custer while, with his main column, 3500
sabres, Kilpatrick would ride for Richmond, around the
Confederate right. Approaching Richmond, he planned another detachment, Colonel Ulric Dahlgren, 500 men, to detour west of the city, cross the James, and assail Richmond
from the south, while the 3000 left to Kilpatrick rushed in

by the Brook Turnpike, from the north. The plan was fundamentally unsound: it called for a division of forces, to be reunited at the point of contact, and the reunion depended on both forces, which would take different routes, and meet obstacles that might well differ widely in effect, maintaining an exact time schedule. No allowance was made for enemy interference, and no means would exist for communication after the initial division.

It can be briefly dealt with. The 28th of February, 1864, the weather being clear and cold the Sixth and part of the Third Corps were thrown forward from Culpeper southwest toward Orange. Fitz Lee was immediately involved, and Stuart rode to the front in person, and the cavalry skirmished with Sedgwick through the short winter day, yielding Madison Court House to the blue infantry pressure. About midnight, Custer, with his 1500 sabres, jumped off from Madison Court House, and rode west toward Stannardsville, about ten miles, to clear the gray cavalry fringe, then south toward Charlottesville, about ten miles, making steady progress, unresisted. He approached Charlottesville, at noon on the 29th, found the artillery camps on the Rivanna, three miles north of town, and attacked them. Captain Moorman was in command, and there was no infantry or cavalry available, although Lee, about the same time, was despatching infantry by train from Orange. Moorman resisted vigorously with such artillerymen as he could arm with rifles, got a section of guns in action, and managed to save his batteries, although Custer broke in and burned the camps of Chew and Breathed, destroying most of the private effects of the unfortunate gunners, and capturing two men and nine horses. Custer, having done what he came to do, retired about dark toward Madison Court House.

There seems to have been some fault in Stuart's service of information, because Custer was not reported until the forenoon of the 29th, and it was afternoon before Stuart, with Wickham's brigade, could get off in pursuit. He rode, first, directly on Charlottesville, until despatches indicated that Custer was retiring north. Then he turned west to Stannardsville, calculating that Custer would come out the way he went in—which was correct—and when he reached Stannardsville, after dark, he found that Custer's advance had already passed through, going toward Madison. On this information, he placed Wickham's brigade in ambush on the Charlottesville road, and waited for Custer's main column. Toward dark, the weather had grown foul, and rain began to fall, which, after dark, turned to sleet, and continued through the night. The shivering Confederates squatted by the road, their wet clothes freezing on them: Jeb Stuart held them in place, and allowed no fires. Custer was a long way behind his advance guard, and for three hours the miserable gray troopers waited for him. When Custer came, he came compactly grouped, with his men warm— comparatively—from the saddle. A few hardy fellows got off shots at him, but most of Wickham's brigade were utterly benumbed, and Custer rode over them and went on out. Jeb Stuart had no luck on this turn.

As for Kilpatrick, at the same time Custer started, he had left Stevensburg, skirted Hampton's flank, and overpowered the picket at Ely's Ford, which he captured to a man. He took the road to Spottsylvania, by the west of Chancellorsville. Colonel Dahlgren, with his detachment, free of guns and wagons, pushed rapidly ahead, passed Spottsylvania Court House at three o'clock the morning of the 29th of February, and, by noon, was at Frederickshall, where he captured a Confederate court martial, prisoner and all, and glanced by the camps of the Second Corps artillery. Proceeding south, he rode all day and all night, and reached the James at Dover Mills in the morning of 1 March. He had come sixty miles in some thirty hours, with very little rest. And he found that he could not cross to the south bank, as his orders directed. He continued down the north bank, ten miles or so, and in the late afternoon he reached the vicinity of Richmond. There were abundant signs that the country was alarmed, and roused against him, and small detachments hung off and harassed him through the day. But if he hoped to find Kilpatrick at Richmond, he was disappointed: Kilpatrick had left him to his fate.

Bearing more to the east from Spottsylvania than Dahlgren bore, Kilpatrick, with his main column, struck the Virginia Central at Beaver Dam, burnt some cars, marched to Ashland, and followed the Fredericksburg railroad in toward Richmond, where he appeared at ten o'clock in the morning of 1 March, before the outer defenses, on the Brook Turnpike. Since the evening before, gray troopers had been snapping at his flanks and rear, and Wade Hampton was after him, following fast. Also, Richmond was alarmed, and 500 infantry manned the outworks and opened on him with artillery when he appeared on the Brook Turnpike. Forthwith, his ardor cooled: he had led at such a pace that his command was exhausted. Now he drew off—formed line of battle, studied the scene for some hours, and fell back about three miles, to Atlee's Station, where his squadrons made an uneasy camp. Dark came; he may, or may not have heard a spatter of firing, miles off, at the western gates of Richmond, where Dahlgren, just come down the River road, made a brave dash at the edge of town and was repulsed with musketry. But he had trouble nearer at hand: Wade Hampton, with his leading regiment, had sighted his fires and attacked him. Kilpatrick got his weary men to horse and turned east in the dark, and rode off by the Williamsburg road, Hampton following, the gray force slowly accumulating strength as the regiments caught up, and taking prisoners and horses. Next day, Kilpatrick found refuge in the Yankee zone at Williamsburg.

As for Dahlgren, the sharp resistance he met in the west face of the city advised him that there was no hope of surprise. He had no way of knowing where Kilpatrick was, and he was losing men and horses, both from sniping and exhaustion. He turned north, was headed off by Confederate cavalry coming from the direction of Beaver Dam, turned east, crossed the upper waters of the Mattaponi, and the Pamunkey, and directed his march on Gloucester point, where he would find Federal forces. He made tortured progress through the 2d, and that night, near King and Queen Court House, rode into an ambush of home guards and was killed. His detachment, now reduced to 135 troopers, surrendered.

On Dahlgren's body were found certain interesting papers: his orders, directing him to free the prisoners at Libby, and other orders, addressed, over his signature, to his command, indicating that the burning of Richmond, and the killing of the high officials of the Confederate Government, were additional objectives of his enterprise. There was great scandal over the publication of the papers, and the Federal Army and Government disavowed all knowledge of any intent to burn or assassinate.

When the Federal cavalry next took the field, it had a new commander, Major-General Philip Sheridan.

XX

THE WILDERNESS—AND YELLOW TAVERN

THE winter of 1863-1864 set in. Cavalry Headquarters were east of Hanover Court House, at a camp called The Wigwam—Stuart's choice of names was always outside the ordinary. You may have noticed some of them—Camp Qui Vive—Camp Pelham—Camp Chickamauga—Camp No Camp. The official records, between the middle of November, when Meade went away from Mine Run to seek his own winter lodgings, and the first part of May, offer little in the way of incident, except the Dahlgren Raid. It may be noted that, from now on, it is the Yankees who are raiding; Grant is going to follow Lee too hard, and hold him too close, from the Rapidan to the Petersburg lines, for many detachments, and he sends Stuart away no more.

Still, there are the newspapers, and the letters, and the contemporary memoirs, from which something of the scene may be constructed.

Except for the lack of food and clothes, winter was not such a bad season, the army thought. Infantry and artillery were snug enough, and even cavalry enjoyed the luxury of permanent bases, and the volume, if not the ardor, of their toils diminished. And the Confederate soldier was learning to do without food and clothes, to an astonishing degree. He kept well and, on the whole, cheerful with very little, and some Federal officers who saw rebel prisoners taken in small operations during the winter—notably Colonel Lyman of Meade's staff—say that they were the hairiest, most weather-beaten, and muscular set of fellows imaginable—like wolves of the forest, Colonel Lyman decides.

Jeb Stuart's letters run from grave to gay. Flora Stuart is expecting a baby, and the General writes his lady all manner of loving, anxious things, about her health, and her dress —she is not, on any account, to wear black, he insists, no matter who dies—and about her spirits, which she must maintain high and cheerful. Regarding this last he scolds her, gently: "There is an old lady here, Mrs. ——, who danced a jig with my great uncle (Sam Pannill), at my mother's wedding. She wears a turban and is an elegant old lady. Major Venable remarked the other day that she is never so happy as when she is miserable. It reminds me of my darling, when she will insist on looking on the dark side in preference to the bright. . . . Have you heard the words of *When This Cruel War Is Over?* Captain Blackford has written *The Cavalier Glee.* . . ."

There was singing, around Cavalry Headquarters, but not so much of it, you fear. Sweeny is dead of pneumonia in the winter-time. Fitz Lee has a minstrel troupe, jolly black faces, who travel through the army area and put on shows, and the revivalists are among the troops again. Another letter to Flora gives a hint as to cavalry activities: "Venable is getting a great name as a staff officer. He obeys my injunction: 'Cry aloud, spare not, show my people their transgressions. . . .' I think I will make Cooke [John Esten Cooke, novelist, and Ordnance officer of the Cavalry Corps] write my reports when he comes back, I am so behind on them. I have brigade reviews every day. . . . Saw Ewell's whole corps under arms the other day . . . every General and Colonel in the infantry appears to have his wife along. . . . When will you be on my Maryland again? . . ." This Maryland was a fine horse, a gift to the General, and about the only mount he had that was gentle enough for his wife to ride when she visited him. This winter Maryland takes the glanders, and has to be sent away. Virginia dies with distemper. Cavalry loses a great many animals, and the officers are, as usual, frantic over the remount question. No hope of horses from Texas now: the Yankees patrol the Mississippi.

The reports are on the General's mind until along in February, 1864. He says he hates to write reports, but the testimony of his adjutant, McClellan, is that he wrote his own in every instance—and they all sound like him. I have a scrap of paper that was among his effects. It is dated 28 January, 1864, and on it he started some official writing or other, then lost interest, and inked out what he had set down. He drew some elegant capitals, shaded and illuminated with delicate pen-strokes, and drew a rudimentary little house. Then, after several false starts, and with much interlineation and erasure—you imagine his great beard brushing the paper as he bent to it—he got this verse out of himself:

> "While Mars with his stentorian voice
> Chimes in with dire discordant noise,
> Sweet woman in angelic guise
> Gives hope and bids us fear despise.
>
> The Maid of Saragossa still
> Breathes in our cause her dauntless will
> Beyond Potomac's rockbound shore
> Her touch bids southern cannon roar. . . ."

After which, refreshed and relieved, you imagine him returning to the Gettysburg report. Colonel Marshal, of Lee's staff, says he was very late with that report, and had to be asked for it repeatedly, from which Colonel Marshal concludes that he felt guilty about it. But the report shows no such feeling. It is straightforward: "In obedience to such orders, I did so and so—" No excuses, no complaints, nothing controversial. The file of reports for the actions of the Army of Northern Virginia contains some very lively writing, and very few of the generals failed to state, in their accounts of each action, how the writer—had his advice been followed—had General —— on his flank, met his responsibilities, had this happened, or that—would have won the war. You find nothing of this in Stuart's papers. Once in a great while, to his wife, or to his brother, he expresses himself, but in the army I am sure that he was an influence for harmony.

Toward the end of the winter the baby came, and they named her Virginia Pelham Stuart, a war-name, gallant as a cavalry sabre. Perhaps the General saw her three times or so, before the opening of the Wilderness Campaign. Flora Stuart could not come up to Orange, and the General could take little leave of absence from the front.

There is one record of such a leave, however, spent, in January, in Richmond. His brother, William Alexander, came on from Saltville, where he administered the salt-works of the army, to see Jeb Stuart, and brought along his son Henry, eleven years old. Across a long lifetime, more crowded with events than the lives of most men, the gentleman who was that boy, Henry, remembers Uncle James, seen for the last time in the Confederate capitol—Uncle James, standing among other generals in the parlor of the Ballard House, taller and more magnificent, to Henry's opinion, than any man on earth. Next day he and his father, walking, met Uncle James on the street, and William Alexander, who was a man of affairs, began to talk of important matters, while Henry admired the sword of Uncle James and the fringed ends of his silken sash. And Uncle James said, "No, before we go into that there is something I must attend to first." And he addresses young Henry with the gravest politeness and concern; begged, and solemnly considered, his ideas on refreshment at that time of the day, and conducted him forthwith to Pizzinni's Palace of Sweets, a very elegant establishment of old Richmond. In Pizzinni's he ordered for young Henry everything that a boy's heart could wish, or his stomach yearn for. And when young Henry couldn't eat any more, he filled his pockets and loaded his arms. And he remembers, does young Henry, that Uncle James was the first man in his life who talked to him as an equal, as a man among men himself. And went home on the cars next day, sobbing from a broken heart, because he couldn't get across a horse and ride with Uncle James to fight the Yankees.

When spring approached, Jeb Stuart had, through careful husbandry and extraordinary exertions, 8,000 sabres in the divisions of Hampton and Fitz Lee. Among them were boys of fourteen and sixteen, whose mothers write him letters —which he scrupulously answers, in his own handwriting.

Here is one of those letters, that hangs, framed, in a room in Georgia, never having been out of the possession of the family which received it. The young cavalryman in question had entered the service at the age of fourteen, and being adjudged a little youthful for the rigors of the ranks, was serving as courier at Cavalry Headquarters, and his mother wanted the General, please, to keep an eye on him, which is the fashion of mothers.

> "Hd Qts Cav Corps A. N. Va.
> "Feb'y 25th, 1864.
>
> "My Dear Madam,
> "You need have no apprehensions about your son Jacquelin, who is still with Major Fitzhugh, and has won golden opinions from all who know him.
> "If it should be in my power to assist him, be assured that it will be cheerfully done.
>
> > I have the honor to be
> > very Respectfully
> > yours
> > J E B Stuart."

Besides these, there were a few old men, and a saving backbone of the veterans, the unkillables, hardened and war-wise. Eight thousand sabres, and the Horse Artillery. The Confederacy is running down.

You remember the Wilderness, rolling like a sea from the forks of the Rappahannock down, southeasterly, to Spottsylvania. This spring of '64, the dogwood flowers in it, and the violets bloom, and the wild life follows its obscure affairs, as it did last year, when Stonewall Jackson was marching, and all the other years. Spring is always spring, and the heart lifts at the end of winter, but this year, over the green leaves and the new grass, there played a menace, like a chilly wind. Last year, the Confederacy was attacking, carrying the war to the enemy. This year—Stonewall Jackson's grave is turning green in Lexington, so many graves are green, and the gray ranks are growing thin, and the army that looked always to attack must stand now and fight for its existence. From the west comes only bad news, and from the coasts, where the blockade strangles, one by one, the seaports, comes only disaster. No hope, now, of a military decision—perhaps, if we can kill enough of them, they will falter and negotiate . . . but we have killed so many, and they keep coming on. . . .

Jeb Stuart, watching the Rapidan, his gray pickets at every ford, is hopeful; writes his brother that he thinks the chances of the Confederacy are as good as they ever were, if we learn from our mistakes and make the most of our resources—but he was always hopeful. Some 60,000 zealots in the ranks, the gray army of Lee, are hopeful; but they are infatuated people, possessed of a dream, and there are no more where they came from, and there will be no more like them when they are gone. And as for General Lee, if he is not hopeful, he keeps it to himself, and shows the same calm front that he invariably presents to victory and to calamity. It is May again, and they stand up to meet the war.

Over yonder, across the Rapidan, around Culpeper, where Stuart's cavalry horses grazed fat last year before they went to Gettysburg, is the Army of the Potomac, under a new man, Grant. He has come out of the West, with the habit of winning, and he has studied the matter with his pale cold eyes and his simple, clear-thinking brain behind them. . . . Here are a lot of people who have been fighting back and forth for three years. They are still fighting, but they must be mighty tired, and their stuff is wearing out. We've been fighting, too, and had no luck at this end, but there are more of us than there are of them, and we can outlast them, that way. Now, the thing we've got to do, to whip them, is to go where they are, and fight, and keep on fighting until we've used them up. No use talking about Richmond—about any-thing else at all—there's Lee's army, yonder. Break it down, and then you'll have it all in your hand—Richmond and the whole concern. . . . He saw the war, and I think he saw it as simply as that—from the Red River to the Atlantic, from the Potomac to the Gulf. Already he has sheared away much of the Confederacy, opened the Mississippi, cleared the border States in the West. He plans for the whole war—not for any battle, or any one campaign. He has Sherman in his right hand and Meade in his left. Then there are little gen-erals: Thomas, Sigel, Butler. And the blockade. Himself, he is Lieutenant-General and Commander-in-Chief, and he elects to go with Meade's army, in Virginia.

North of the Rapidan, he has a hundred thousand men, the Army of the Potomac, restored and vastly cheered since Gettysburg. He has a fine cavalry corps, nearly 13,000, under another new man—Sheridan; and the cavalry are armed with Spencer carbines, breech-loading repeaters. He is going to cross the Rapidan, pass through the Wilderness, and bring Lee to battle on the other side. He rather expects that he will have to fight Lee for the river crossings, but the important battle will be in the open, on the way to Richmond, when Lee tries to interpose.

The gray army, 60,000, has not yet concentrated; bad supply, and the wornout country had forced Lee to wide dispersion through the winter. Longstreet has come back from his adventures in Tennessee—from Chickamauga and Knoxville; and two of his divisions are down at Gordonsville, and the third, Pickett's, at Petersburg. Ewell's Corps is on the Rapidan, above Mine Run, and A. P. Hill's is farther west, toward Orange Court House. Lee's Headquarters are at Orange, and so are the Headquarters of the Cavalry Corps. All of them have come through a lean winter, but they are good soldiers, and they have seen much war, and they will fight. On 2 May, it is related, Lee went with his corps commanders to the top of Clarke's Mountain, and they swept with their glasses the rolling land toward Culpeper and the camps of Grant. Lee thinks that Grant will cross at Ely's Ford—signs are plenty, that he will move soon—and he is not going to oppose the crossing. But—when he gets into the Wilderness—where the thickets mask his artillery, and entangle his heavy corps of infantry, then we will hit him! Longstreet; old Ewell with his crutch; slim, red-bearded A. P. Hill; Jeb Stuart with his cavalry swagger—they stand, and look at the country spread out like a map beneath them. Perhaps they think of Stonewall Jackson, who was with them the last time they gathered here, before Second Manassas. And they do not know yet, but the signs are that Grant, yonder, is not like John Pope. . . .

Facing east, and a little north from Clarke's Mountain, you see two roads, that run straight from Orange Court House to Fredericksburg. The first is the Orange Turnpike.

A little south, and parallel, is the other, the Orange Plank Road: you remember them from Chancellorsville, which stands just west of where the highways meet. This side of Chancellorsville is spread the mat of the Wilderness, reticent and wide, but you know that down through it, on the diagonal, from Germanna and from Ely's Ford, pass the Germanna Plank Road and the Brock Road, intersecting the Turnpike and the Orange Plank, and leading toward Spottsylvania. Lee, you conceive, points, and talks quietly.

The 2d of May passes, and the 3d: much activity over yonder in their camps, Stuart reports. After midnight, in the morning hours of the 4th, the cavalry pickets on the fords send gallopers: the Yankees are crossing, in force. ... Cavalry is brushed aside, and comes sullenly away, fighting from every thicket, hovering dangerously, and dashing in to sting—record the Federal officers—like hornets. Lee has the reports, and sends orders to his corps: come on at once. Longstreet, the farthest off, is alerted before noon, and is marching by 4 P.M. with forty-two miles to go. Hill, who is twenty-eight miles away, marches earlier, by the Plank Road. Ewell, who is the nearest, has to cover eighteen miles, by the Turnpike. Longstreet will come in behind Hill. The march is timed so that Hill and Ewell will go along abreast. You wonder why Lee did not, in the day of grace he had—the 3d of May—move his corps closer to each other. The 4th was a dangerous day for Grant, with his troops in column, and his extended trains, but he moved with energy and good engineering sense, and that night he was all across the Rapidan, and his advance had made twelve miles, to Wilderness Tavern. Five miles west of his bivouacs was Ewell, and thirteen miles southwest, Hill. Across his front was the screen of gray cavalry, which gave ground to the plunging Sheridan, but did not break. And all about him was the Wilderness.

Into the Wilderness, at dawn on the 5th, went Grant, and Ewell struck his flank where the Turnpike intersected the Brock Road. A little later in the morning, where the Plank Road passed across his front, at Parker's Store, on the Germanna Road, Stuart's troopers drew off, and the blue cavalry of the advance ran into A. P. Hill's Corps, Jeb Stuart himself guiding the head of the column. Grant had not expected to be attacked in the Wilderness, but he knew that Longstreet was away, and that he had only to contend with Ewell and Hill, and he turned resolutely to destroy them before Longstreet could come on the field. Hancock, Warren, and Sedgwick, 72,000, formed line of battle to their right, and drove; Ewell and Hill, 40,000, put in all their strength, and the fight flamed for five miles through the Wilderness, on the left and the right of the roads that go to Fredericksburg.

If you had been on the ground that May morning, behind the centre of either army, you would have known little, save that a very great combat was raging. It was an infantry battle; hardly anywhere was there enough cleared space for the employment of the guns. You would have heard a crackling hell of musketry, rising and falling, running off for miles on either hand. Now you would catch the ordered, deep-chested shouting of the Federal soldiers; now the high, ardent yelling of the gray people. The Wilderness labored, and yielded up a shrieking tumult, and a long, low smoke of powder, and presently the dark, rolling smokes of burning timber. So the 5th passed, and Ewell did better than hold his own, but A. P. Hill, on the right, against whom Grant directed most of Meade's strength, held on, but hardly. The 6th dawned, and Hill was driven—and, at the last instant, with Hancock pressing through, exultant and shouting, Longstreet ground down upon his flank, and restored the battle, attacking violently, by the Brock Road and the unfinished railroad. Hancock was rolled up and driven in his turn. For a little while, there among the flaming thickets, it looked like disaster for another blue General, and Lee was very close to overwhelming victory. But Longstreet was shot by his own men as he rode ahead of them—much as Stonewall Jackson had been shot, last year, just a few miles from this place—and the opportunity passed. During the 7th the battle subsided, with little sputtering flames and a drift of smoke, as a fire burns out. Grant was definitely checked. He had lost 18,000 men. Lee had held him, and gained local success, at the cost of 7,700 casualties—more than he could afford.

The night of the 7th, Jeb Stuart sent his wife a telegram, the last she is to receive from him out of battle:

"I am safe and well tonight—Saturday. We have beaten the enemy badly but he is not yet in full retreat." . . . This enemy is not going to retreat.

When the Wilderness battle joined, Jeb Stuart drew his cavalry to the Confederate right, and on the first day had hard fighting with Sheridan in the woods, dismounted action, in places where a squadron could not form. Rosser whipped Wilson, over at Todd's Tavern, and so alarmed the flank division of blue infantry—Barlow's, of Hancock—that Barlow drew in his left and stood inactive through the 6th, while Meade, fearing another Chancellorsville-thrust, vetoed Sheridan's plan for a massed cavalry drive around the Confederate right, and held out the blue squadrons to meet a possible emergency in his rear.

Late in the evening of the 7th, the miles of infantry fallen strangely quiet, Stuart lanced through, past the Federal left, and had a glimpse of Yankee wagon-trains moving east.

The word went quickly back to Lee, who thought, and deduced: Grant is trying to turn my right: the next place is Spottsylvania. He sends Stuart with Fitz Lee's Division to stand across the way and slow those people down, and he draws off his battered infantry, and his lean columns go southeast through the Wilderness. Fitz Lee rides by forest roads on the direct line to Spottsylvania Court House: Sheridan, leading the blue advance, goes by the Brock Road, each stretching out an arm to feel the other as they go. The Confederates have the shorter route. At daylight, on the 8th, Torbert of Sheridan's arrived, and finds Fitz Lee in position, and cavalry engages around the Court House, and Fitz Lee holds his ground, taking some loss, until R. H. Anderson, with Longstreet's infantry, comes up. Just a little later, Warren arrives to help Torbert, but the gray people are settled firmly, and the battle of Spottsylvania Court House builds up around them. Stuart takes position on Anderson's right, and finds space to put his Horse Artillery in the action. The country here is thick, but not so thick as the Wilderness back to the west. They relate that, this day, Stuart sat his horse for hours, at the edge of a clearing where his dismounted troopers joined Anderson's infantry. He was conspicuous, and the infantry officers beg him to come down: they don't want to see him killed, and besides, he is drawing fire. . . . Only one of his staff is with him, Major McClellan, and he has many messages for McClellan to take to Anderson, some of which, McClellan thinks, are idle and unnecessary, and he is wearing down his horse. All the General is doing, he decides, is sending him out of danger. Finally he says—returning to the place where Stuart sits, his eyes on the blue line firing yonder, and the pine twigs drifting down around him, and the bullets whining by—"General, my horse is weary, and you are exposing yourself, and you are alone. Let me stay here with you." Jeb Stuart smiles at him, and gives him another order to carry back.

Meantime, at Meade's Headquarters, General Philip Sheridan is angry and shouting. His cavalry has been dispersed on idle missions. His combinations have been broken up by the doddering schemes of Meade. He has not been allowed to do anything. He tells Meade to go on and give his orders to the cavalry, direct—he, Sheridan, is out of it! Meade is conciliatory, but Sheridan will not be pacified. Give him a free hand, he says, and he will go off, draw Jeb Stuart after him, and whip him. Grant, listening, says: "Go ahead."

Sheridan moves fast. Such of the cavalry as is engaged is withdrawn. He forms a column of 12,000 men, Wilson, Torbert, Gregg, three divisions. He is going to ride toward Richmond, fight Stuart, if he can, and march to Butler, on the James River, where he will re-provision, and then return to the army. He concentrates between Spottsylvania and Fredericksburg, and Grant will neither see nor hear of him for eighteen days. Early on the 9th he moves clear of the flanks of the armies, to Hamilton's Crossing, then wheels south and marches by the Telegraph Road. Formed up in fours, his column is thirteen miles long, and he holds that formation, because he is far enough east to evade all but the extreme right fringe of Stuart's pickets. And he sets a level, unhurried pace, going mostly at a walk, a gait of confidence. Old troopers, who rode this way with Kilpatrick in February, are mightily impressed: Kilpatrick's progress was a process of headlong, killing rushes and unreasoned halts; Sheridan plods as steadily and as relentlessly as fate. The diminishing clangor of battle behind his right shoulder, Spottsylvania-way, tells him that Lee is fully occupied, and he is not going to manœuvre—he is going to ride through. He has enough men to do it.

There were gray pickets near Massaponax Church, and these run to Stuart and report. Wickham's brigade of Fitz Lee is available, and Stuart sends it, while he makes quick arrangements to withdraw the rest of Fitz Lee from the line, and to bring Hampton's Division from the left. Wickham rides hotly, and at Jarrald's Mill he overtakes rear-guard of Sheridan, and attacks it. He has about 1,000 sabres, and he makes a few prisoners, and upsets a regiment or two, but Sheridan's main body goes on, unhurried, and the blue rear-guard confines itself to holding him off. Below Jarrald's, where the Telegraph Road trends a little east, Sheridan turned due south, by the Groundsquirrel Road, by Chilesburg, toward the Virginia Central at Beaver Dam station. Close to Mitchell's Shop on this road his rear-guard selects good ground and stands, and Wickham's desperate charges recoil from it, with loss. Here Stuart joined in person, bringing General Fitz Lee and the brigades of Lomax and Gordon. Including Wickham, he has between 4,000 and 5,000 sabres. It was about dark on the 9th. Stuart sent Fitz Lee and two brigades to follow, and took Gordon and rode, himself, by the right of Sheridan's march, to Davenport's Bridge on the North Anna, and thence to Beaver Dam, where Sheridan's rear, with Fitz Lee hanging on, passed through, in the early morning. Sheridan did damage at Beaver Dam, to the railroad and a depot of stores, and liberated a long file of prisoners who were being taken to Richmond. He continued south, toward Negro Foot, and Stuart calculated that he was aiming for the Old Mountain Road, which runs from Louisa Court House to Richmond. He called Fitz Lee in, this morning of the 10th, for he now had a closer road to Richmond than the route Sheridan had chosen.

While his brigades assembled, and the men ate such scanty rations as they carried with them—flour and water, mixed to dough, and fried in bacon fat, or stuck on a ramrod and seared in the fire—he rode to the house of Doctor Edmund Fountaine, near Beaver Dam, where his wife and little Jemmie and the baby were living. He had an hour with them, and he was not to see them again. He may have divined, now, that he was Sheridan's objective: it was not a raiding column, that strong blue force winding down over the hills. He would not waste his forces trying to save the railroad, or the bridges. It was perfectly evident that Sheridan was going to Richmond. Jeb Stuart has said good-by to Flora and to his children. You know that in his mind, when he turns his back and rides, he has unrolled his map of the country around Richmond, the hills and rivers that he knows so intimately. There is a line of hills at Yellow Tavern, where you can stand, facing north and west, and with a few men hold off many. Major McClellan, who has received Flora Stuart's parting injunction to take care of her General, is with him, and relates that he was thoughtful and quiet as they rode, talking of little personal things, of friends, and places that he loved. The rising sun is in his face; he will see one more sun, while his horse is under him, and his men behind, and his sword in his hand. He takes Fitz Lee, with Wickham, and Lomax, leaves Sheridan's trail, and goes southeast to Hanover Junction, twelve miles. Gordon is detailed to follow Sheridan's rear.

He reaches Hanover in the night, and proposes to keep on south, by Telegraph Road. But Fitz Lee insists that his men and horses are spent, and Stuart grants rest until one o'clock the morning of the 11th, two hours or three. He sends Major McClellan with Fitz Lee; McClellan is not to

Contraband .
on the picket line

Gun Teams — Horse Artillery

close his eyes until he sees Fitz Lee's brigades in the saddle and on their way: then he is to report. With the rest of the staff, Jeb Stuart lies down under the stars and sleeps. Fitz Lee is moving promptly, and tired McClellan reports back, sits down to rest while the horses are being saddled, and falls asleep himself. As they mount, one will awaken the Major, but Stuart says: "No. He was carrying orders while we were resting. Leave a courier to tell him to come on when his nap is out." McClellan catches up about dawn, at Ashland station, where a squadron of the 2d Virginia has just broken up a flank regiment of Sheridan's, who, captured blue troopers say, is coming from the northwest. Stuart is now ahead of him.

Down in this region, all the roads lead to Richmond. The Telegraph Road heads due south after you pass Ashland, and eight miles farther down, the Old Mountain Road comes in from the west at a place called Turner's. There the two roads, coalescing, become the Brook Turnpike, and Richmond is six miles away. Half a mile south of Turner's, and east of the turnpike, is the ancient hostelry called Yellow Tavern, so named, you assume, because it was painted yellow once. In 1864 it stood empty, and out of use, and desolate. It was on a ridge that ran northwest and southwest, draining, on the north side, into the Chickahominy. The region was one of old fields, and lines and clumps of timber. Just north of where the Brook Turnpike opened the ridge, and along the Telegraph Road that passed across the high ground, Stuart proposed to form.

McClellan says he had a moment of indecision. As the land lies, he can place himself astride the Richmond Road, the Brook Turnpike, or he can take up position along the Telegraph Road, so as to lie on the flank of Sheridan's thrust toward the capitol. He has perhaps 3,200 men with him, a very light force for what he has to do. It would help if he knew whether Bragg, defending Richmond, was in condition to hold the city gates. He sends McClellan galloping, to ascertain Bragg's dispositions; but it was hours before he heard from Bragg, and he made his own decision on the ground.

Richmond, you are told, has known since yesterday that Sheridan was riding, and has suffered sharp alarm. But early on the 11th, they have this despatch from Stuart, the last he ever sent:

Headquarters Ashland
May 11 6:30 am

To Gen Bragg:

General,—The enemy reached this point just before us, but was promptly whipped out, after a sharp fight, by Fitz Lee's advance, killing and capturing quite a number. Gen. Gordon is in the rear of the enemy. I intersect the road the enemy is marching on at Yellow Tavern, the head of the turnpike, six miles from Richmond. My men and horses are tired, hungry, and jaded, but *all right*.

J E B Stuart.

The unquenchable soul of Jeb Stuart flames in the last sentence.

McClellan finds Bragg, a stolid man, serenely eating breakfast, and unperturbed. The city battalions, the old men, the boys, the pale clerks and the invalids, 3,000 or 4,000, are manning the Richmond fortifications, and Bragg has ordered up three veteran brigades from Petersburg, by the railroad. He has done all he can, says Bragg, but he thinks he can hold out. If there comes disaster, he just cannot help it. That is Bragg. McClellan starts back, runs into fighting on the Turnpike, and detours widely to the east, avoiding capture, and reporting to Stuart at about two in the afternoon.

In the forenoon, as Sheridan approached from the north-west, it seemed to Stuart that, no matter what objective the enemy had, he could not move past him as long as he stood on the flank. He formed his brigades, Wickham on his right and Lomax on his left, the left resting on the Telegraph Road, and the right extending along the high ground, facing west. A battery of the Horse Artillery was emplaced across the road, two guns in the road itself, and other batteries to either flank. Between ten and twelve noon the battle joined, Sheridan attacking in steady, ominous fashion, and the fighting running hottest along Wickham's front. Fitz Lee controlled the battle, his men dismounted, for the most part, with the ground favoring him; and he held well together. Sheridan's troops charged right up to him, broke into him in places, and, thrown out, came on again. They lapped around his flank, and gained the Brook Turnpike, but the main battle held to his front, and charge and counter-charge, he drew and kept the weight of Sheridan's strength. Toward two o'clock there was a lull: the rearmost of Sheridan's divisions were getting into line, and the tired Confederates drew breath for another effort.

Jeb Stuart, resting under a tree behind his right, was cheered by the word McClellan brought: he had, he said, whipped them on his right; and, if the gray infantry came out from the city, he thought he would be in position to inflict heavy damage on Sheridan. He spoke with feeling of Colonel Pate of the 5th Virginia, just killed, leading a charge with extraordinary gallantry. For an hour or more, the fight settled into an exchange of musketry, with some artillery firing. But over yonder, Sheridan is up in person, studying the field. Stuart's right has proved very strong: he will try now a combined attack, mounted and dismounted, on the left, and he will put in all his men.

It followed that, about four o'clock, a terrific racket broke out along the front of Lomax. The blue dismounted lines volleyed with their Spencers, and a strong mounted column, the Michigan regiments of Custer, broke from cover, took their losses, and overwhelmed the battery on the Telegraph Road. Lomax gave ground, and all of Stuart's left rolled back, 500 yards or so. At the first tumult, he was in the saddle and galloping to the point of danger, going so swiftly that McClellan cannot keep up, and outdistancing all of his staff but one or two couriers on fresh horses, who held in sight of him. There is trouble ahead; Major Howrigan, with the 1st Michigan, has sabred the gray gunners, and is breaking across the Telegraph Road. Right and left, the dismounted gray troopers are falling back, still firing, but their line is crumbling into little groups.

Jeb Stuart, gigantic in the smoke and dust on his tall horse, collects a handful of these, some eighty men, with Captain Dorsey. Howrigan's Michigan troopers thunder past them, on the road, and another regiment, the 7th Michigan, Major Granger, comes to support Howrigan. Jeb Stuart has his group shaken out into line, in time to fire into the flank of the charge as it went by to his left. A dust cloud goes with it, and at a little distance to the rear the dust cloud stops and swirls about: the 1st Virginia mounted has been flung at the Michigan troopers. There is shocking collision, men fight with pistols and sabres, and the blue squadrons stream back, broken. On their skirts run unhorsed troopers, and Jeb Stuart, his horse forced up into his firing-line, has his pistol out and shoots into the rout, calling to his men to stand steady, and give it to them!

Out in front, a sergeant in dusty blue, running back on foot, stops in his stride, points his Colt at the big officer on the horse, and fires one shot. Then he runs off into anonymity. Jeb Stuart sways in his saddle and his strong voice breaks. His hat falls from his head. Some troopers look, and cry out: "Oh, the General! the General!" Captain Dorsey comes, catches the charger's bits, and leads him back a little way. The animal is restive, with the bullets that harrow the dust and whip past him, and the firm hand he knows weakened on his reins. He plunges, and Dorsey gets the General down, sends for a quieter horse, lifts the General to the saddle again, and tries to lead him away. They go, slowly, a few yards, but Jeb Stuart cannot hold himself up, any more. Captain Dorsey eases him to the ground, and they rest him against a tree, and he orders all of them back to the line, for the blue people are coming again. This order Dorsey says he can on no account obey; he has sent for General Fitz Lee and Doctor Fountaine and an ambulance, and he will stay until they come. Fitz Lee arrives and throws himself from his gray mare, and Jeb Stuart says, "Go ahead, old fellow: I know you'll do what is right." Some of the staff collect, Garnett, Venable, Hulihen. The ambulance is driven to him, under heavy fire, and they lift him into it. All but the surgeon and young Hulihen, and a trooper, Wheatley, who holds his head on his knees, he sends away, to their duties: "You need every man!" They untie his yellow sash, and look, and find him shot through the liver. There is great pain, and shock, but as they drive the ambulance off, he sees his men disordered, some leaving the field, and he lifts himself and calls to them, with a shadow of his battle-voice: "Go back! Go back, and do your duty as I have done mine, and our country will be safe! Go back! Go back! I had rather die than be whipped! . . ."

Custer is re-formed and pressing, and the Yankees very nearly take the ambulance. But it gets away, somehow, by the roads to the east of the Turnpike, toward Richmond. The doctor turns him over, as they jolt along, for fuller examination, and when they do this, he says to Hulihen, using his nickname, for he was fond of the young man: "Honey-bun, how do I look in the face?"

"General," replies Hulihen earnestly, "you are looking right well. You will be all right."

"Well," says Jeb Stuart, "I don't know how this will turn out, but if it is God's will that I shall die, I am ready. . . ."

He suffers much, and they try to give him brandy, but he will not have it: there is the promise he made to his mother, twenty years ago. . . . Late in the afternoon, they bring him to Doctor Brewer's house, the home of his sister-in-law, on East Grace Street in Richmond. The house is not there now, but they remember that it was a pleasant place, behind a low wall of red brick where yellow roses bloomed.

Up at Beaver Dam station, little more than twenty-five miles away, Flora Stuart will have a message, and make frantic haste. Sheridan has the direct roads; and the railroad, partly in his hands and partly free, runs no trains. She comes some distance by hand-car, some distance by wagon, with long detours to avoid the Yankees, making slow, frantic progress like a nightmare. Stuart knows that she is sent for, and you imagine him calculating distances and time and transportation as he lies. . . .

There is no question of his getting well; next day the surgeon tells him. Outside in the street, in the night of the 11th of May, and through the hot hours of the 12th, a crowd gathers, sobbing women, and men with stricken faces, and in the ears of all of them rolls the sound of battle, Fitz Lee now, and Sheridan, fighting, to the north. I know an old man, who, as a boy of eleven years, stood in that crowd, outside the house where General Jeb Stuart lay dying. He remembers men and women weeping, and he remembers the roses, and once, he says, they made way for a tall, thin gentleman who went into the house, and presently came out, and they said, "That's the President! . . ."

Jefferson Davis took his hand, in there, and asked him how he felt. Easy, he said, but willing to die if God and his country felt that he had fulfilled his destiny and done his duty. Some of his staff get in from the battle: he talks to them kindly, between wracking paroxysms of pain: they hurt, those belly-wounds. He divides his horses among them, and gives directions, sends his gold spurs to Mrs. Lilie Lee of Shepherdstown, his sword to his son, all his other things to his wife. Then he orders them back to the fight, for the gun-fire on the Chickahominy rattles the windows: "Good-by now, Major. Fitz Lee will be needing you." Von Borcke, still an invalid, kneels by his bed, sobbing as frankly as a child. Jeb Stuart would like a song, and around him they sing

"Rock of Ages, Cleft for Me . . ."

he joining, in a weak voice. Toward evening, with the shutters drawn against the slanting sun, Doctor Brewer tells him that he will die very soon. He nods his head. "I am resigned, if it be God's will; but I would like to see my wife. . . . But God's will be done. . . ." He talks to little Flora, gone before him. The room darkens. He speaks once more; very low: "I am going fast now. . . . God's will be done. . . ."

When Flora Stuart came, after dark, they led her in to him. He was dead.

So, in the thirty-second year of his life, and in the fourth year of his country's independence, as he would say it, passed Jeb Stuart. All his life he was fortunate. It was given to him to toil greatly, and to enjoy greatly, to taste no little fame from the works of his hands, and to drink the best of the cup of living. He died while there was still a thread of hope for victory. He was spared the grinding agony of the nine months' siege, the bleak months that brought culminating disasters, and the laying down of the swords, at Appomattox. He took his death-wound in the front of battle, as he wanted it, and he was granted some brief hours to press the hands of men who loved him, and to arrange himself in order, to report before the God of Battles, Whom he served.

THE END.

INDEX